Looking for an Argument

Looking for an Argument

Critical Encounters with the New Approaches to the
Criticism of Shakespeare and His Contemporaries

Richard Levin

Madison • Teaneck
Fairleigh Dickinson University Press
London: Associated University Presses

© 2003 by Rosemont Publishing & Printing Corp.

All rights reserved. Authorization to photocopy items for internal or personal use, or the internal or personal use of specific clients, is granted by the copyright owner, provided that a base fee of $10.00, plus eight cents per page, per copy is paid directly to the Copyright Clearance Center, 222 Rosewood Dr., Danvers, Massachusetts 01923. [0-8386-3964-X/03 $10.00 + 8¢ pp, pc.]

Associated University Presses
2010 Eastpark Boulevard
Cranbury, NJ 08512

Associated University Presses
16 Barter Street
London WC1A 2AH, England

Associated University Presses
P.O. Box 338, Port Credit
Mississauga, Ontario
Canada L5G 4L8

The paper used in this publication meets the requirements of the American National Standard for Permanence of Paper for Printed Library Materials Z39.48-1984.

Library of Congress Cataloging-in-Publication Data

Levin, Richard Louis, 1922–
  Looking for an argument : critical encounters with the new approaches to the criticism of Shakespeare and his contemporaries / Richard Levin.
    p. cm.
Includes bibliographical references (p.) and index.
  ISBN 0-8386-3964-X (alk. paper)
1. Shakespeare, William, 1564–1616—Criticism and interpretation—History—20th century. 2. English drama—Early modern and Elizabethan, 1500–1600—History and criticism—Theory, etc. I. Title.
PR2970.L48 2003
822.3'3—dc21
                                                             2002153188

PRINTED IN THE UNITED STATES OF AMERICA

For Muriel, Once Again

Contents

Introduction	9
Concerning the Text	25
1. Feminist Thematics and Shakespearean Tragedy	29
• with a response from Janet Adelman et al.	49
2. The Poetics and Politics of Bardicide	55
• with responses from Daniel Boyarin	73
and Margot FitzGerald	77
3. Unthinkable Thoughts in the New Historicizing of English Renaissance Drama	82
• with a response from Jonathan Goldberg	94
4. (Re)Thinking Unthinkable Thoughts	104
5. Bashing the Bourgeois Subject	114
• with It's a Panic	122
6. Son of Bashing the Bourgeois Subject	124
7. Negative Evidence	131
8. The New Interdisciplinarity in Literary Criticism	152
9. The New and the Old Historicizing of Shakespeare	177
10. The Cultural Materialist Attack on Artistic Unity	195
11. Silence Is Consent, or Curse Ye Meroz!	210
12. The Politicized Language of Literary Criticism	227
13. The Current Polarization of Literary Studies	244

Notes	259
Texts (Formerly Works) Cited	281
Index of Plays	300
General Index	302

Introduction

THIS BOOK COLLECTS A NUMBER OF MY ESSAYS PUBLISHED IN THE LATE 1980S AND 1990s that set out to examine significant aspects of what are usually called the new approaches to the criticism of Shakespeare and his contemporaries that came into prominence in the British and American academy around 1980—principally the New Historicism, feminism, and several revised versions of Marxism and Freudianism. It may seem somewhat strange to refer to these approaches as "new," since they have now been with us for over twenty years (earlier versions of Marxism and Freudianism, of course, go back much farther), and have achieved a kind of hegemony and even orthodoxy in our most prestigious literature departments. I cannot think of another neutral term, however, that includes all of them and registers the universal recognition that when they emerged upon the scene they constituted a radical departure, even a revolution, replacing the formalist approach (then known as "the New Criticism") that had dominated the field since the 1940s, as I explain in "Historicizing."

I should make it clear at the outset that my attitude toward many aspects of these new approaches is highly skeptical and, in the words of Iago, "nothing if not critical." That in itself is certainly not unique. During this same period a number of people have criticized some of these approaches, including M. H. Abrams, David Aers, James Battersby, Harold Bloom, Lynda Boose, Graham Bradshaw, William Cain, Frank Cioffi, Frederick Crews, Natalie Zemon Davis, Morris Dickstein, Denis Donoghue, Nancy Easterlin, Teresa Ebert, John Ellis, Diana Fuss, Gerald Graff, Wendell Harris, Leonard Jackson, Lisa Jardine, Laurence Lerner, Tom McAlindon, Kathleen McLuskie, Toril Moi, Barbara Mowat, Martin Mueller, Martha Nussbaum, Edward Pechter, Raymond Tallis, Brian Vickers, Naomi Weisstein, and René Wellek, among others. In fact, I cite many of them in these essays in support of my own views. But I could not possibly agree with all of them, because they come from a number of different positions,

9

including some from within the new approaches themselves, contrary to the charges we sometimes hear that criticism of these new approaches is a right-wing monopoly.

What differentiates my essays from the work of many of these other critics and also provides, I hope, a kind of unity to this collection is the basic set of attitudes I bring with me as a result of my personal history, which I can feel free to discuss here because the confessional mode is now in fashion in academic criticism. As I wrote these essays I was sometimes reminded of the advice of Nick Carraway's father in *The Great Gatsby:* "Whenever you feel like criticizing any one . . . just remember that all the people in this world haven't had the advantages that you've had." He was speaking of social advantages, but I had in mind the intellectual advantages of my undergraduate and graduate education at the University of Chicago in the 1940s and 1950s under the tutelage of Richard McKeon, Ronald Crane, Norman Maclean, Elder Olson, and Rea Keast. Most people think of this group as "neo-Aristotelians" who practiced a particular kind of formalist criticism derived from the *Poetics*, but I also learned more general and more important lessons from them. One of the most important was a "strong" pluralism—a recognition that there are a number of fundamentally different philosophical or intellectual perspectives that generate quite different approaches to a literary work, and that these approaches should be respected as equally valid, since each of them can give us insights into valuable aspects of the work that are obscured or ignored by the other approaches (see Booth 1979 and my "Artistic Unity"). Along with this went a respect and admiration for the power and complexity of the great works of literature that have these valuable aspects, and a recognition that literary criticism is dependent upon and subordinate to these works that it seeks to comprehend and elucidate.

Even more important, for the purposes of this book, was an understanding of and a respect for the kind of rational argument that was necessary to demonstrate interpretations of literary works. For we learned that every interpretation (including our own) must be treated as a tentative hypothesis that must be supported by arguments, and that each of these arguments must be tested rigorously to see if it holds up—if it is logically coherent and consistent, and proceeds a posteriori from the facts, and takes into account all the relevant ones, especially those that might seem to conflict with it or to support a different interpretation. We also learned that the interpretations produced by other critical approaches should be held to the same high standard and therefore should be subjected to the same kind of test, because our commitment to pluralism did not mean that we abandoned our responsibility to judge interpretations and the cases made for them, and simply believed that anything goes or, in the new terminology, "whatever." This, in brief, is the kind of argument that I learned to appreciate and that I was looking for in the new approaches, which explains the title given to this collection.

The essays in this collection show that my attempts to apply these lessons to the critics operating within the new approaches have been very disappointing on all three counts. Some of them explicitly reject the very idea of pluralism, and even those who are not so explicit rarely practice it. There have been bitter quarrels among the proponents of some of these approaches on the question of which approach is really correct, and almost all of them join forces in attacking formalism, which is treated, not as another valid way of viewing literature, but as mistaken, worthless, biased, and, according to some of these critics, "complicit" with the oppression of people because of their race-gender-class. Nor do these critics seem to place much value on the literary works they are discussing, a point I will return to later. Indeed, many of them clearly believe that their critical studies of these works (and the studies produced by their colleagues) are more interesting and more valuable than the works themselves, and so subordinate the works to the criticism, instead of the criticism to the works.

Even more striking is the weakness of their arguments, for while these critics usually take pride in their theoretical "sophistication" and "rigor" (see the *PMLA* Forum letters reprinted in chapters 1 and 2), they commit many serious logical errors. They rely upon non sequiturs; they confuse a necessary condition with a sufficient cause; they contradict themselves, sometimes within the same paragraph; they invoke simplistic "either/or" binaries, as in the Morton and Zavarzadeh title (1994); they hypostatize some of their crucial concepts, usually those they are setting up to attack (such as "idealism," "humanism," the "bourgeois subject," and "patriarchy"), and can change the meanings of these concepts in midstream; they privilege their own discourse by exempting it from the negative critiques (the hermeneutics of suspicion, demystification, etc.) that they deploy to discredit the discourses of their opponents, and even use the same kinds of reasoning that they object to in these opponents (see, for example, Graff 1989 on "anti-essentialist essentialism"); they assume what they think they are proving, and sometimes assume what they think they are disproving; and they ignore or avoid obvious evidence against their theories, as I demonstrate at some length in "Interdisciplinarity" and "Negative Evidence," although this is also apparent in most of my other essays. Many of these critics begin, moreover, not by surveying the relevant empirical facts but by adopting some theory, and they seem to show a preference for a priori, totalizing theories that cannot be tested or confirmed by the facts. Clearly, in the language of Nick's father, these critics have not had the advantages that I had as a result of my training.

Since I am now in the confessional mode, I can add that my personal history may have given me another advantage in dealing with two of these new approaches, because in my youth I went through both a Marxist phase (involving membership in a purist splinter group called the Socialist Labor Party) and a Freudian phase (involving an orthodox and interminable psychoanalysis). I think of this as a possible advantage that enables me to sympathize with the new Marxists and Freudians, since I can still remember the feelings I had then, including feelings of absolute certainty and of scorn for the benighted nonbelievers. But it may also be a disadvantage, because I cannot help thinking that if I, without possessing any special powers, was able to see through these two pseudosciences so many years ago, then they should also be able to do this now when they are much older and wiser than I was then.

The confessional mode now also requires authors to reveal their own political position. It never occurred to me to do this when I published *New Readings vs. Old Plays* in 1979, since I assumed, along with almost everyone else in the field (except the Marxists, of course, who were then a small, marginalized group), that there was no necessary connection between politics and criticism, and I also knew that the great majority of academics were liberals like me, including most of the critics I was arguing against in that book. (In fact, I regarded this as evidence of the lack of connection between politics and criticism.) But all that changed with the revolution of the 1980s. Many proponents of the new approaches insist that "everything is political"—which includes literary works, criticism of those works, and criticism of that criticism (see "Historicizing"). And a number of them regard liberals (or "liberal humanists," as they are usually labeled) as enemies, who are responsible not only for bad (i.e., formalist) criticism but also for the bad (i.e., oppressive) politics that they want to connect to it, as I just noted, whereas their own criticism (which they call "activist," "committed," "emancipatory," "interventional," and "transformative") is helping to end this oppression.

I had better confess right now, therefore, that I am still a liberal (or "liberal humanist") and have been one for a great many years, ever since I saw through Marxism in my youth. As a liberal, I am just as committed to ending oppression as these critics are, but I never flattered myself with the belief that I was accomplishing this through my criticism, which, as far as I can tell, has no discernible political effect outside the academy (and I would have to say the same about their criticism). I do not claim to be politically active, unlike many of these self-professed "activist" critics (although their political activism is often confined to writing "activist" criticism), but for a long time I have been a card-carrying member of the ACLU, NOW, Amnesty International, Planned Parenthood, the New Israel Fund, and the Southern Poverty Law Center, which are all liberal organizations that are actually doing things to combat oppression and to work for a better world, instead of waiting for some complete (but undefined) "transformation of society" that many of the "activist" critics require (see "Politicized Language"). I must also confess, however, that except for my opposition to the Marxists (who had an unpleasant habit, whenever they came to power, of sending liberals to "reeducation" or slave-labor camps), I still cannot see any necessary connection between my liberalism and my criticism of the other new approaches, unless we are to assume (which I do not) that liberalism has some special affinity to logical argument.

It is also necessary to explain here that the title of this book has a double meaning (which seems to be a requirement for titles these days), because my essays are looking not only for an argument *in* the critical approaches they are examining, but also for an argument *with* the practitioners of these approaches. I am sorry to say, however, that the results of this second search have been just as disappointing as the results of the first one. The great majority of the people I criticize in my essays simply ignore them, which is their right, of course, since they are under no obligation to respond.[1] But of those who do respond, I can count on the fingers of one hand the number who actually try to argue with me by seriously addressing the issues raised in my essays. All the others find ways to evade a real argument, as can be seen in the four examples reprinted here in chapters 1, 2, and 3, which are, I am afraid, all too typical.[2] (The two in chapter 2, in fact, give us a revealing sequence, since FitzGerald's Forum letter is responding to my answer to Boyarin's Forum letter.)

Their favorite tactic of evasion is name-calling. In just these four examples I am accused, among other things, of being a "reactionary," a "red-baiter," and a "'critic'" in scare quotes, who is "dangerously anti-intellectual" or "profoundly unrigorous," "disingenuous in the extreme," "simplistic," "cynical," "insidious," "tired, muddled, unsophisticated," "paternal," and "deliberately insulting," and who engages in "crude Aristotelianism," "idealizing fictions," "demagoguery," "sophistry," "wanton misrepresentation," "sneering and nastiness" and "inept tirades," and—most unkindest cut of all—belongs to an "ilk." Their second most common tactic, found in two of these responses and in many others, is to claim that I feel "anxious" or "threatened" by them, as I explain in "It's a Panic," which is my answer to a response to "Bashing," and is appended to chapter 5. And the next most common is to construct, and attribute to me, absurd exaggerations of my views. This tactic is used in all four of the responses: in the first, my critique of a particular (and carefully specified) feminist approach to Shakespearean tragedy is transformed into an attack on "feminist criticism of Shakespeare in general" and "the approach as a whole" and, at the end, on "all varieties of contemporary criticism"; in the second, my objections to some practitioners of the new approaches are transformed into the accusation that they are "cultural commissars"; in the third, my opposition to Marxist critics is transformed into approval of "the HUAC" and a desire to make some criticism "ineligible for disciplinary scrutiny"; and in the fourth, my attempt to refute the claim that five particular (and, again, carefully specified) modern ideas were unthinkable in the Renaissance is transformed into the belief that "people have always had the same ideas," and "the mind never changes," and, ultimately, that "nothing ever changes."[3] (The practitioners of the new approaches certainly do not limit this tactic to responses to my essays; they also frequently use it in their own work, as I show in "Bashing" and "Son of Bashing," to discredit the alleged views of their enemies, especially the "bourgeois subject" and his—also alleged—philosophy of "liberal humanism.")

It is no coincidence, I think, that the two most common tactics are both forms of personal attack, because this is a rejection of the very possibility of an argument—at least of the kind of argument that I was looking for in these responses and hoping to find there. I must confess that I enjoy a good argument (arguably another Chicago legacy), even when I lose, but only if it deals with the ideas involved rather than with the people who hold them. In my own critiques of other critics I have never engaged in personal attacks on them (or in the deliberate exaggeration of their views). In fact, in *New Readings vs. Old Plays* (1979), and in my essays leading up to it, I did not even identify them, since I wanted to focus on their ideas and not on their personalities.[4] In the later essays collected here I name the critics that I oppose, but I do not oppose them as individuals or bear them any personal animus—indeed, I number some of them among my friends. (For as far back as I can remember, my personal feelings about people have not been determined by my judgment of their beliefs, which I suppose makes me a poor partisan.) I regard the fact that so many of these critics resort so often to such tactics as yet another indication of their lack of understanding of—or respect for—logical argument, not only in their application of the new approaches, as I pointed out earlier, but also in their responses to the people who challenge them, which is the main reason that I decided to reprint these exchanges. I am well aware that I have an unfair advantage in each exchange because I am always given the last word, but that does not affect the kind of tactics that the authors rely on in their responses in order to avoid any real argument.

Of course, the arguments that I am looking at (or looking for) in the books and essays and responses that I deal with in this collection are not about the nature of argument itself. They are about a subject, and that subject, ostensibly at least, is literature. Virtually all their authors are professional academic critics who, like me, earned their advanced degrees in literary studies (usually specializing in Shakespeare and his contemporaries), and are employed by our colleges and universities to "profess" or teach this subject to undergraduate and graduate students. It seems appropriate, therefore, to explain here, if only briefly, my own views about the reading, interpretation, and teaching of literary works, focusing on Shakespeare's, especially since these views are not made very explicit in my essays, which are devoted primarily to the criticism of the views of other people.

I should warn readers, however, that almost one-third of my essays in this book are not directly concerned with literature and have relatively little to say about it. But I did not choose their subject matter; it was chosen by the critics I discuss in these essays, who seem to be less interested in literature than in some other things. It is possible to traverse long expanses of recent academic "Shakespeare criticism" without encountering anything more than brief references to his work, which are embedded in much more substantial discussions of these other subjects, the most prominent being modern political and psychological theory (mainly neo-Marxist and neo-Freudian) and, especially, Renaissance history, including the politics and psychology of this period. In short, these critics are, and proudly proclaim themselves to be, "interdisciplinary," and these other disciplines are often regarded as more exciting and more important than the discipline of literary studies that is supposed to be interdisiplinated with them.[5]

Since Renaissance history is by far the most common subject matter that is employed in this interdisciplinary criticism of Shakespeare, being the principal resource of all New Historicists and almost all Marxists and a great many feminists, I want to concentrate upon it here, although many of my comments will also apply to the other types of interdisiplinarity. The first thing to say is that, as a pluralist, I recognize that historical criticism is, and always will be, a valid approach to literature, because it attempts to relate a literary work to the world in which it was produced, and that it can therefore illuminate aspects of the work that are not seen (or not seen as clearly) with the application of other approaches, including my own. Indeed, this approach has a very long and venerable history, going back to the beginnings of the academic study and teaching of literature, and although it may move in and out of fashion at various times, it is not going to disappear.[6]

Having made this acknowledgment, however, it is necessary to add that my judgment of much of the recent historical criticism of Shakespeare and of Renaissance literature in general is mainly negative, as will appear in the essays collected here that examine it. One of my major objections is that a number of the critics who practice it rely upon (or rather, invent) some very bad history of the Renaissance. My essays "Bashing," "Unthinkable Thoughts," and "(Re)Thinking" are largely devoted to refuting some of the more absurd claims announced by these critics about what people in this period thought or, more often, what they could not think— for instance, that they had no conception of individual identity persisting through time, or of the biological determination of human gender, or of homosexuality, or of literature as a special category of valued written works, or of an author, or of illusionist drama, or of dramatic structure. These claims were very easy to refute because the critics who presented them to us did not seem to have any idea of what would be required to prove them. They did not understand that a historical assertion of this kind is subject to the same rules as a literary interpretation, which, as I pointed out earlier, must be treated as a tentative hypothesis that must be supported by logical arguments that take into account all the relevant facts, especially those that might conflict with it. I had no trouble in showing, therefore, that the historical critics who made each of these assertions simply ignored some very obvious and very substantial historical evidence demonstrating that it was wrong.

My second objection is that the historical connections that these critics seek to establish between some aspect of a literary work and some aspect of contemporary society are often extremely weak. The reason, again, is that they do not treat these connections as hypotheses that must be validated by arguments that confront all the relevant evidence. More specifically, they fail to apply the first two "canons of induction" of John Stuart Mill (1884) that are designed to test the claim that C is the cause of E— "the method of agreement" (whenever C is present, E is also present) and "the method of difference" (whenever C is absent, E is also absent).[7] To take a simple example, one critic asserts that the dramatic situations in Shakespeare's romantic comedies where a man wins and marries a woman of higher social or financial status is related to the historical situation of Elizabethan courtiers who hoped to advance their careers by a marriage of this kind. But this ignores the inconvenient facts that stories in which men marry "up" can be found in many very different societies, and that some of the men in Shakespeare's comedies marry their equals or even marry "down."

Another major error, really a subspecies of the preceding one, is the failure of many of these historical critics to distinguish a necessary condition (whenever C is absent, E is also absent) from a sufficient cause (whenever C is present, E is also present). This can be seen very clearly in the attempts by some feminist critics to blame the tragic mistakes of Othello and King Lear on Renaissance "patriarchy." It is certainly true that a patriarchal society is a necessary condition for their mistakes, which could not have occurred in a more egalitarian world, but it is just as true that such a society cannot be a sufficient cause for them, because most of the other men in these tragedies, who of course live in the same society, do not make these mistakes and are even horrified by them. (It is also true that the patriarchal arrangements portrayed in *Othello* and in *King Lear* are very different, but that is another story.)

My final objection to much of the recent historical criticism of Renaissance literature has already been indicated: it often treats the history as more important than the literature. We must be very careful, however, not to overstate or oversimplify this issue. I know that some people would like to separate studies that use the history of this period to illuminate its literature from those that use the literature of this period to illuminate the history, but I am afraid that this distinction will not hold up under scrutiny, because many studies do both. It makes more sense, I believe, to place them on a continuum ranging from the most literary to the most historical. It is also very important to recognize that there is nothing wrong with the studies at the far end of this continuum that subordinate the literature to the history. Indeed, academic historians who specialize in the Renaissance sometimes treat Shakespeare's plays as evidence of certain aspects of contemporary society, and I do not see any reason why academic literary critics who specialize in Shakespeare should not also do this at times, for I am not going to try to enforce a disciplinary boundary line that people are prohibited from crossing.

The problem arises, however, when some of these critics assert that this particular kind of historical criticism is the best approach to Shakespeare (some even assert that it is the only valid approach, since, as I noted earlier, they tend to reject pluralism). One obvious objection is that, if the primary (or only) purpose of these critics is to learn about Renaissance society, it would be much more efficient to consult some good sociological histories of the period, which have the advantage of including many other kinds of evidence and of examining the society directly. And if they are going to use plays for this purpose, it would be much more efficient to examine Ben Jonson's and Thomas Middleton's city comedies, which are located in contemporary London and actually depict the social phenomena that many of these critics are interested in (mainly class and gender conflicts), whereas all Shakespeare's plays (except *The Merry Wives of Windsor*) are set in other times and places and so must be "translated" in order to derive this knowledge from them. It is also difficult to understand why these critics, once they have done this and learned their historical lesson from his plays, would have any reason to read or see them again. That, in fact, is my most basic quarrel with this kind of historical criticism: it reduces the plays to conveyors of historical information that are therefore discardable once they have served this purpose, because they possess no lasting value in their own right.

This brings me, finally, to my own critical approach to literature and, specifically, to Shakespeare's plays, because it does attempt to show that these plays possess a lasting value or appeal in their own right and why they do. It is necessary, however, to begin with two important qualifications.[8] When I say that their value or appeal is lasting, this does not mean that it is universal and that the plays can be appreciated by all people in all cultures, which is obviously false. In our world there is no such thing as a universal literary work. But it does mean that their value or appeal has outlasted their own particular historical moment, since we can still appreciate them, and also that it outlasts our first contact with them, since we can still appreciate them after we have seen or read them many times. And when I say that they possess this value or appeal in their own right, this does not mean that we respond to each play "in itself," which, again, is obviously false. In our world there is no such thing as a play (or anything else) "in itself." The play always comes to us within a context, and we cannot respond to it or even understand it without this context, which includes the meanings of the words, the specific theatrical conventions that Shakespeare worked under, and the much broader conventions that establish the very possibility of mimesis or representation and of communication. But given this context, I believe that my approach shows us that—and also how—we can appreciate these plays in their own right, because it treats them as works of art possessing an aesthetic quality that inheres in them (or, more precisely, in our response to them) rather than as bodies of information to be used for some nonartistic purpose.

My approach, as I already noted, is a type of formalism derived from

Aristotle's *Poetics*, which means that it is intentionalist, since it begins with the conception that literary works are constructed by their authors to be unified wholes that will produce some effect in their audiences, and therefore seeks to determine the authorial intention of each work and to explain how this intention is actualized in every part or aspect of that work. This in turn means that, in dealing with Shakespeare's plays, my approach is mimetic, since it treats them as representations of the actions of individuals that are designed to evoke a moving and pleasurable reaction in the spectators and readers. We have a great deal of evidence that this was what he and most of his fellow dramatists intended in their plays and how their original audiences regarded them.[9] We have much more direct evidence that this is also how they are regarded in our own day by most nonacademics who read them or see them on the stage or in a movie house or on television. Although very few of these people are concerned with critical theory, the great majority are mimeticists, who assume that the plays are representations of the actions of recognizable human beings, and also intentionalists, who assume that the purpose of this representation is to produce a pleasurable response. Indeed, they commonly say that they are reading or seeing a play "for pleasure," and if they approve of the play or the performance, they commonly praise it for being so "moving" or so "enjoyable."

This pleasure, of course, is not a single or uniform response. Comic pleasure, for example, is clearly not the same as tragic pleasure. Moreover, the pleasure can be evoked by different parts of the play—by its action, or some of its major characters, or the thoughts or emotions that they express, or the poetry in which they express them—or by any combination of these parts,[10] and their relative importance will vary in different spectators or readers and also in different plays. (Those seeing a performance can also enjoy the acting, but this usually means that they find it is a convincing and moving realization of the characters and their feelings.) My contention here is simply that these people see or read the plays in order to experience some kind of pleasure and that they admire and value them for producing it, because that points to one of the most important differences between the formalist approach and most of the newer approaches to Shakespeare. I said earlier that it is possible to traverse long expanses of recent academic "Shakespeare criticism" without encountering anything more than brief references to his plays, and I would have to add that it is possible to traverse much longer expanses of this criticism without encountering a trace of admiration for these plays or of any pleasure derived from them. A surprising number of these critics, in fact, adopt an attitude of downright hostility toward Shakespeare, insisting that the praise or even the mere enjoyment of his plays makes one "complicit" with race-gender-class oppression (see

"Silence Is Consent"), or treating them as a kind of enemy that must be resolutely resisted and defeated (see "Bardicide"), or searching through the historical archive in order to discover—and to savor—any occasions when they were employed to promote colonialism, cultural imperialism, chauvinism, Eurocentrism, phallocentrism, anthropocentrism, heterosexism, aestheticism, elitism, war, religion, chivalry, and other nefarious projects. Because formalism focuses upon and attempts to explain the pleasure that most people take in these plays and in other literary works, and that presumably brings them to literature in the first place, I believe that it is, and always will be, a valid critical approach. Like the historical approach, it may become unfashionable in the academy during certain periods, but it is not going to disappear.

My formalist approach to Shakespeare's plays has other advantages that follow from its conception of these plays as unified wholes intentionally constructed by him to evoke a pleasurable response. For one thing, it enables us to test our interpretation of each play—that is, of his intended meaning or effect—by seeing if it can account satisfactorily for everything in the play, so that, if it does not, we can hypothesize another interpretation and test it in the same way. (It also, of course, requires us to remain open to the possibility that he may not have been completely successful in realizing this intention, or even that he may have made some mistakes that work against it.) Another advantage, closely related to this testing, is that the approach gives us the crucial concept of dramatic or artistic function, which makes it possible to examine and to explain every component of the play, even down to the level of the individual speeches,[11] in terms of a means-end or cause-effect analysis, which in turn depends upon some hypothesis concerning the author's intended purpose. For function, of course, is an intentionalist concept and would be meaningless without an authorial intention. A third major advantage of this approach is that it leads us to an artistic judgment of each play. This used to be considered one of the responsibilities of a literary critic, but it has been abdicated by almost all the practitioners of the new approaches, who do not show any interest in artistic judgments and do not have any method for arriving at them. The formalist approach provides such a method, since with it we can determine the relative success of the various components of the play and of the play as a whole in realizing the intended meaning or effect, so that we can formulate and also defend the judgment that one play or one playwright is better than another, and therefore can recognize and appreciate the greatness of Shakespeare.

One does not have to be a formalist critic, of course, in order to appreciate Shakespeare, because there is plenty of evidence of his increasing popularity with the general public. More people are studying his plays in our schools and in adult education courses and private reading groups, more movies are being made of them, and more performances are being staged in our theaters, especially in the growing number of summer Shakespeare festivals,[12] so that the size of his audience is now much larger than it was in his own day, or at any other time, and is continually expanding. There are, to be sure, some nonartistic reasons for this remarkable expansion—people are receiving more formal education, and are retiring earlier and living longer, and have more leisure time and more money to spend enjoying it. There are also some nonartistic reasons for attending the production of a Shakespeare play, including the excitement of going out (and often dining out) for a social evening, and the rewards of engaging in a prestigious activity that yields considerable "cultural capital." But I do not think that most people would go to see these plays (or read them) if they did not derive from them the kinds of artistic pleasure that I discussed earlier, which surely is the main reason that Shakespeare has become so popular and has attained the status of what is now called an "icon." I am quite certain that very few of these people go to his plays in order to learn about the economic and social conflicts of Renaissance England that absorb so much of the attention of recent Shakespeare critics, including those mentioned above who are openly hostile to him. (I suppose it is one of the ironies of the history of the academic criticism of Shakespeare that this hostility is flourishing at the time of his greatest success in the extramural world.) But in fact these critics, even the hostile ones, actually depend upon his popularity and his iconic status to justify their own work, and their work, in turn, actually serves to confirm this popularity and to enhance this status.

The formalist approach has another important advantage that is really a consequence of the three just discussed: it is very well suited to the teaching of literature to our undergraduate students. My many years of teaching Shakespeare courses at this level have convinced me that most of these students, like the nonacademic audiences I described earlier, come to their classes (and hence to his plays) as mimeticists and intentionalists, which means that they want to understand the characters and actions of each play and the functions that they serve in terms of the purpose of the play as a whole. Above all, they want to understand the value of the play that accounts for the admiration it has elicited. The formalist approach, therefore, fits their assumptions and expectations,[13] and I have even heard a few of the practitioners of the new approaches admit that they rely on it in their undergraduate classes and save their new approaches and new critical theories for graduate seminars.

Of course, many recent critics who are more politically "committed" refuse to use the formalist approach in their teaching at any level, because they insist that it is "complicit" with the oppression I mentioned earlier. And others argue that formalist interpretations of Shakespeare are much less interesting than those generated by the new approaches.[14] Clearly the formalist interpretations are now less interesting to *them*, which is inarguable, and it is easy to understand how they might become bored with applying this approach to the same plays in class after class over the years. When I said that formalist criticism could explain why the appeal of these plays outlasts our first encounter with them and why we can still appreciate and enjoy them after seeing or reading them many times, I was not suggesting that this process could be extended indefinitely. Perhaps no one was meant to teach the same plays in the same way for an entire academic career, and surely the plays themselves were not meant to undergo such an ordeal. But our undergraduate students, who have not experienced this repetition, do not seem to be bored by a formalist interpretation of Shakespeare (assuming, of course, that it is presented effectively) and seem to derive considerable pleasure from the insights that it gives them into the meaning and the value of his plays.

There is no reason, however, why teachers should not use other approaches to Shakespeare in their undergraduate (or graduate) courses if they prefer them. In fact, I would strongly defend their right to do so, both as a liberal, who believes in academic freedom, and as a critical pluralist, who believes that these other approaches can illuminate aspects of the plays that are ignored or obscured by formalism. Nor is there any reason why teachers should not use several different approaches to the same play in the same class. Even though I am a committed formalist, I have done this many times, because I think it is a very instructive experience for my students; it shows them the power of these other approaches and also helps them to reach an understanding of what a critical approach is, which requires some kind of comparison and therefore cannot be attained if they are limited to a single approach. Indeed, I regard this as one of the responsibilities of my commitment to pluralism, which is more fundamental than my commitment to formalism.

☙

I would like to make some final points. Although my essays are very critical of many aspects of many of the new approaches to Shakespeare and to literature in general, I hope that they have not suggested any feeling of what I call geriatric rage, which afflicts a number of academics of my age group. There is often a personal reason for this rage because, if the revolution of the 1980s had not taken place, they could now expect to be reaping the rewards of their long years of labor (including visiting professorships, invitations to lecture or to serve as consultants and referees, perhaps a Festschrift, and—probably most important—the respect of their former students and other young people in the field), but instead they find, like Macbeth, that "that which should accompany old age, / As honor, love, obedience, troops of friends, / I must not look to have." I am not concerned here, however, with this personal factor but with the two principal manifestations of this rage that I have tried my best to avoid—an unqualified condemnation of all the new approaches, which are frequently homogenized as a monolithic, wrongheaded, or even evil entity, and an unqualified nostalgia for the good old days (before the advent of these new approaches), which are also frequently homogenized as an era of idyllic harmony. I am keenly aware of the many differences among the new approaches, and therefore I have always been careful to indicate which particular approach, or which particular aspect of several approaches, I am dealing with in each essay (which has not protected me, as I noted earlier, from charges that I am attacking all recent criticism). Nor do I believe that they are all entirely wrong—indeed, I have positive things to say about some of them, for example, in the introduction to "Unthinkable Thoughts," the section on women characters in "Feminist Thematics," and the discussions of the canon and the subject in "Polarization."[15] And I am just as keenly aware that you can never return to the status quo ante—or, in the vernacular of Thomas Wolfe, that "you can't go home again."

Even if it were possible to bring back the good old days, moreover, anyone familiar with my *New Readings vs. Old Plays* knows that I do not think they were so good. The thematic and ironic "new readings" produced by the old New Criticism that dominated this earlier period exhibited some of the same kinds of logical errors as the approaches that I examine here (as I demonstrate in "Negative Evidence"), and many people were coming to realize that they had reached a dead end. In fact, by the time that *New Readings* was published, the New Criticism was on its way out (although I do not think that I had anything to do with this), and we were moving into the critical revolution of the 1980s. Similar bad timing marked my essay "Feminist Thematics," since this approach, which attempted to combine the new feminism with the old thematism, was being abandoned when the essay appeared (again, I claim no credit for this). And it may well be that the newer approaches discussed in my other essays are about to suffer a similar fate, as Jeffrey Williams suggests.

As I write this introduction it is still too early to tell, although it is clear that the need for periodic revolutions is more or less built into our academic system of professional advancement and professional publication. I do not think that this will affect most of the older Marxist and Freudian critics, who have no reason to reconsider their doctrines, since they do not subject them to any reality test, and so we can expect to see a few more years of the curious afterlife of these two archaic theories in the humanities departments of the American and British academy, long after they have been discredited and discarded just about everywhere else in the world, including our academic departments of economics and psychology that are supposed to be their disciplinary home bases.[16] But we can probably assume that the new generation of critics, eager to distinguish themselves (in both senses), will make some kind of break with the no-longer-so-new approaches of their predecessors and teachers.

Having turned in my crystal ball many years ago when I graduated from Marxism, I am not going to try to predict what the result will be—perhaps a revisionist version of one of these approaches, or an amalgamation of some of them with some of the older ones, or something quite novel. Whatever it is, however, I believe that we should greet it with the same set of attitudes that I learned as a student and have tried to apply here: a pluralistic openness to the possibility that it can bring us new and valuable insights into literature, coupled with a rigorous—even skeptical—interrogation of the nature of its reasoning and its use of evidence, which in time could lead to the correction of its errors and therefore to some kind of progress in our profession. For I still hold to the faith, expressed at the end of my reply to the Forum letter in chapter 1, that rational argument will eventually prevail. That is the principal reason that I wrote these essays and collected them in this book.

Concerning the Text

EACH OF THESE ESSAYS WAS PUBLISHED SEPARATELY IN THE JOURNAL OR BOOK NAMED in the source notes, and, except for "(Re)Thinking Unthinkable Thoughts," they are independent and can be read in any order. They are reproduced here as they first appeared, except for the following changes. In many of them the mode of citation of the works that I discuss is altered for the sake of consistency, and I sometimes substitute later (and hence more available) editions or reprints of these works, but I try to include the original date in my list of texts cited. I tinker with the style occasionally, and in some essays I make minor substantive changes to clarify my views or, more frequently, to avoid repeating material that appears in another essay, using endnotes to refer readers to the other essay where the same idea is developed. I should explain, however, that while I tried to reduce this repetition, it was not possible to eliminate it entirely, because I had to retain essential points so that each essay would present a complete argument that stood by itself. I also added a few afterthoughts, indicated by asterisks, as footnotes. But I made no substantive changes in the three essays ("Feminist Thematics," "Bardicide," and "Unthinkable Thoughts") that elicited the responses reprinted here, since I did not think this would be fair to the responders.

Looking for an Argument

1
Feminist Thematics and Shakespearean Tragedy

Feminist criticism of Shakespeare appeared on the scene as an identifiable "movement" a little over ten years ago, with the publication of Juliet Dusinberre's *Shakespeare and the Nature of Women* in 1975 and the first Modern Language Association special session on the subject in 1976. In this brief period it has enlisted a number of intelligent and dedicated critics and has produced a substantial body of publications. Its remarkable growth can be measured, moreover, not only in these statistics but also in the steady enlargement of its range from the first tentative efforts, aimed primarily at rectifying sexist misinterpretations of Shakespeare's female characters, to much more confident and ambitious studies of many other aspects of the canon.[1] Today it may surely be said to have come of age and to have taken its place as one of the established branches of Shakespearean research.

It seems to me, then, that this is an appropriate time to examine the nature of this criticism, for while some of the individual studies have been subjected to scrutiny over the years (including some searching scrutiny from the feminists themselves),[2] there has not yet been any systematic investigation of the methodology and consequences of the enterprise itself. Its very success has made such an undertaking difficult, since the quantity and diversity of the interpretations it has generated cannot be encompassed within a single article. I have therefore narrowed the scope of this inquiry to one major trend of the movement in this country, which defined itself in our only anthologies of feminist criticism of Shakespeare—*The Woman's Part* (Lenz, Greene, and Neely 1980) and two special issues of *Women's Studies* (Greene and Swift 1981/2). Most of the contributors to those anthologies (many of whom went on to write other essays and books) shared an interpretive approach, which a number of other critics have also employed and which I focus on in this investigation. This focus means that I have had to exclude those feminist critics who adopt other approaches, even though some of them have given us significant studies that may be riding the wave of the future.[3] It should be understood, therefore, that the following inquiry is meant to refer only to the particular body of work produced by this one approach within the larger enterprise of feminist criticism of Shakespeare, and to the critics actually named here, although I think much of the discussion will also apply to similar kinds of feminist criticism in other fields. Because of space limitations I have further narrowed my focus to the tragedies, which are generally regarded as Shakespeare's greatest achievement and so should provide the clearest test of this approach.

Probably the best way to begin the investigation is to ask what these critics think the tragedies are—or what they are about, which amounts to the same thing—since that should lead directly to a definition of their approach. On this crucial question there seems to be virtual unanimity, as some representative quotations demonstrate. Coppélia Kahn finds in *Romeo and Juliet* "a critique of the patriarchal attitudes expressed through the feud" (1981, 86). According to David Leverenz, *Hamlet* is concerned with "the opposition between male and female"—between "the world of the fathers," dominated by reason, public roles, and duty, and the feminine world of emotion and the true self (1980, 125–26). Irene Dash says that *Othello* is a "stud[y] of the complexity of marriage and of the pressure of conventional patterns" or "stereotyped ideals" of marital roles (1981, 129–30), and Gayle Greene says it is a "radical critique of some of society's most cherished notions [concerning] accepted ideals of manly and womanly behavior" (1995, 61). Edward Snow tells us that this play "treats jealousy . . . [as] an object of inquiry, and pursues it beyond superficial explanations to the grounds of human tragedy" in the "pathological male animus toward sexuality" (1980, 387–88). Harry Berger claims that *Macbeth* portrays "the dialectic of gender conflict" (1982, 73), and Robert Kimbrough finds that it "contains a fierce war between gender concepts of manhood and womanhood played out on the plain of humanity" (1983, 176). Madelon Gohlke says all the tragedies "may be viewed as a vast commentary on the absurdity and destructiveness of th[e] defensive posture" of "the masculine consciousness" in relationships with women (1980, 162–63). For Marilyn French, the entire canon is examining the "division of experience" into a "masculine principle" and a "feminine principle" that are often "at war" (1981, 49, 67, 145, 201, 286). Peter Erickson finds "a pervasive motif in Shakespeare's drama" in its "sustained critical exploration" of "the basic conflict" between "male-female relations" and "male bonding," which he sometimes simplifies to "the male/female dialectic" (1985a, 1, 122). And

Marianne Novy believes all the plays deal with "the conflict between mutuality and patriarchy and the conflict between emotion and control. Both conflicts involve the politics of gender: the first, in power relations between the sexes; the second, in the relative value of qualities symbolically associated with each gender" (1984, 3–4).

More quotations of this sort could be produced, but these should be enough to make the point, which is, quite simply, that this body of criticism is thematic. These critics agree that the plays are not really about the particular characters who appear there but about some general idea and, consequently, that they are not primarily dramatizations of actions but explorations of or commentaries on or inquiries into or critiques of that idea, which the characters and actions subserve. Some of the critics are explicit about this conception of drama—Gohlke, for example, says the tragic plots "may be regarded as expanded metaphors" for that masculine defensive posture (1980, 152), and Novy asserts that the plays are "symbolic transformations" of attitudes toward gender and that Shakespeare "used the potential of the theater to personify" these attitudes (1984, 3, 202). But even those who do not make such statements usually assume that character and action exist for the sake of the thematic idea. It is true that there are few appearances of the term "central theme," which seems to be going out of fashion, and very few of the "My Theme Can Lick Your Theme" arguments that used to serve as the standard opening gambit of thematic readings;[4] in fact, some of these critics (as may be seen in the phrasing of the two quotations from Gohlke) state or imply that they are only presenting one possible way of viewing the plays. But whether they claim to have found the only correct theme or not, it is clear that they all interpret the tragedies in terms of a theme.

It is also clear that the themes employed in their interpretations are basically the same. Although the terminology may vary, these critics all find that the plays are about the role of gender in the individual and in society. Moreover, their formulations of this theme usually turn on a polar opposition between two abstractions that are supposed to encompass and divide the world of the play and all human experience. This kind of formula was very common in the older thematic criticism of Shakespeare, which regularly discovered that his plays portrayed the conflict of appearance and reality or reason and passion or the like, so we might expect these new gender thematists to adopt the same strategy, especially since it is implicit in the very concept of gender, which comes in two varieties. Thus their thematic dichotomies usually turn out to be some version of the eternal struggle of yang and yin. Even the readings that make "patriarchy" the theme are really not an exception, since they always define it in terms of this gender opposition. And that opposition, we must remember, is not between the female and male characters (although there may be some relation to them) but between two abstract entities that can "conflict" inside one character or outside any character, somewhere in the thematic ether, just like "appearance versus reality."

This last point is especially important when we are dealing with tragedies, which all end in disaster, because any reading will have to account for this disaster, and any thematic reading will have to account for it in terms of the critic's formulation of the theme. We will not be surprised to learn, therefore, that in these studies the cause of the tragedy is located not in the particular characters but in one of those two abstractions whose opposition constitutes the theme, nor will we be surprised to learn which one always turns out to be the guilty party. According to Kahn, "the primary tragic force" in *Romeo and Juliet* is "the feud as an extreme and peculiar expression of patriarchal society, which Shakespeare shows to be tragically self-destructive" (1981, 84). Leverenz says that "Hamlet's tragedy is the forced triumph of filial duty over sensitivity to his own heart," wherein resides "the woman in Hamlet [that] is the source of his most acute perceptions about the diseased, disordered patriarchal society" that destroys him (1980, 111, 113). For Snow, "the principle of evil and malice" in *Othello* is "the outraged voice . . . of the patriarchal social order," which kills Desdemona to "undo the breach her sexuality has created in the stable male order of things" (1980, 410–11). Berger finds that not only Macbeth but all the thanes are guilty of a "pathologically protective *machismo*," supported by their "mystified male-dominated cosmology," which is responsible for every crime in the play (1982, 68, 74); and for Kimbrough, Macbeth's downfall is caused by "a definition of masculinity which comes from dominant societal norms that equate machismo with manhood" and thus teaches us the "destructiveness of polarized masculinity and femininity" (1983, 177, 183). Novy concludes that the sufferings of Lear and Cordelia are "created by [sex-role] behavior patterns" and show the "vulnerabilities of men and women in a patriarchal society" (1984, 162).[5] "What Shakespeare's tragedies portray," according to Gohlke, "is the anguish and destruction attendant on a . . . culturally supported set of fictions regarding heterosexual encounter," embodied in that "defensive posture" of "the masculine consciousness" (1980, 161–63). French asserts that the tragedies of Othello, Lear, Macbeth, Timon, and Coriolanus turn "on 'masculine' values," since their worlds "place supreme value on the qualities of the masculine principle" and show a "blindness to or rejection of 'feminine' values" (1981, 202). And Erickson finds that a number of tragic catastrophes are brought about by the inability of heterosexual relations to overcome "male bonds that have behind them the force of patriarchal social norms" (1985a, 1). Of course, the characters themselves are unaware of the real cause of their misfortunes (as many of the critics acknowledge), which seems a pity, for if they only knew they might have given us some great last words. When the dying Desdemona is asked by Emilia, "Who hath done this deed?" she could have answered, "Nobodie, twas the male order of thinges, farewell." And the dying Laertes could have ended his confession to Hamlet by exclaiming,

> I can no more; the Patriarchie, the Patriarchie's to blame!

I think we can conclude, then, that one defining characteristic of this approach to Shakespearean tragedy is its location of the cause of the tragic outcome in "masculinity" or "patriarchy," operating through individuals and the society as a whole. (Even studies like Dash 1981, Greene 1995, and Novy 1984 that put part of the blame on a stereotype of "femininity" agree that this stereotype is imposed by the patriarchal ethos, so the result is the same.) There is some truth in this view. Except for *Antony and Cleopatra* (which many of these critics treat separately), the tragic actions all take place in societies dominated by males and male attitudes and could not have taken place in a society that was matriarchal or androgynous or egalitarian, because gender relations are an essential aspect of the "world" of each play, and this "world" is built into the author's dramatic conception so that it is inseparable from the characters and actions, as they are from it. But this intimate connection between the characters and their society means that we really cannot say that Lear would not have come to grief if he had not lived in a patriarchy, for if he had not lived in a patriarchy he would not have been Lear. Moreover, it is equally true that none of these tragic actions could occur in a capitalist or socialist economy or in *any* "world" significantly different from the one presented in that play (which would even include other forms of patriarchy: Lear, for example, could not exist in Othello's Venice). And since gender relations are only one of the components of each "world," we have no reason to single them out as the basic cause of events. Actually, these components cannot be called causes in the usual sense: they are necessary *conditions* of the action but are not in themselves sufficient to *cause* it. Many of these critics seem to have confused these two different kinds of agency.

The distinction may become clearer if we look at some of the crucial actions that these readings blame on patriarchy. Novy, for instance, devotes some time to arguing that Lear's rejection of Cordelia in the opening scene is based on patriarchal assumptions concerning the father-daughter relationship (1984, 151–55). But the witnesses to this rejection—Kent, Gloucester, Burgundy, France, even Goneril and Regan—all of whom presumably share these patriarchal assumptions, regard his behavior as a shocking abnormality, which must mean that, while the assumptions made his behavior *possible* (by giving him absolute power over Cordelia), they cannot have *caused* it, for then it would appear normal. Similarly, Greene (1995) argues that Othello's killing of Desdemona is the consequence of the gender roles imposed on the pair by their patriarchal society; but, again, we note that the characters who comment on it (including Othello himself after he learns the truth) do not view it as one of your everyday patriarchal events; instead, they consider it a horrifying violation of the norms of their world. The same must be said of the tragic deeds in the other plays: they are all made possible by the kind of society in which they occur (otherwise they would not seem convincing), but they are all regarded by that society as extraordinary calamities (otherwise they would not seem tragic). It is hard to see, then, how these plays could be blaming the patriarchal society for the tragic outcome. It is even hard to see how they could be conducting an inquiry into patriarchy, when the actions they focus on are clearly meant to be atypical.

This attempt to blame the catastrophes on patriarchy is illogical in another sense as well, for while it is true that they would not have occurred in a nonpatriarchal society, it is also true that they would not have occurred in a society that was even *more* patriarchal than the one we are shown—a society, for instance, where Juliet and Desdemona could not be married, or Ophelia be courted, without the consent of their fathers, or where Goneril and Lady Macbeth were completely subservient to their husbands (which is just another way of saying that each tragedy could only take place in the specific "world" depicted in the play). Moreover, if patriarchy is held responsible for the unhappy endings of the tragedies, then it must be equally responsible for the happy endings of the comedies and romances, which are also brought about in patriarchal worlds. Some of the critics try to account for the happy endings by claiming that women have more active roles in these other genres, which is true (with a few notable exceptions), but that does not alter the nature of the society. In fact, in their final scenes all these "strong" heroines reinsert themselves into the patriarchal structure, which presides over the marriages and reconciliations.[6] It seems evident, then, that patriarchy cannot have any necessary causal connection to misery, when it is just as capable of producing happiness. Nor can this conclusion be averted by distinguishing, as Erickson does, between a "harsh" form of patriarchy that creates problems and a "benign" form that resolves them (1985a, 12, 32, 148), although this is a step in the right direction, since "patriarchy" is obviously not a single entity, or even two, but a general class covering a wide range of attitudes and practices found in very different societies (and in very different individuals). It is only the logic of this critical approach that has reified it as a sort of Platonic Idea that is supposed to serve both as the subject of these tragedies and as the cause of their catastrophes.

The preceding difficulties are peculiar to this feminist branch of thematism (i.e., to the kind of central theme it employs), but there is another, more general difficulty that it shares with all other thematic criticism of Shakespeare—namely, that it does not work. In the older thematic readings that I have examined, the concrete facts of the play never really fit the abstract theme of the critic, and I am afraid that the same must be said of these new feminist thematic readings of the tragedies. Thus, in the first example cited above, the actual presentation of the feud in *Romeo and Juliet* does not support Kahn's attempt to subsume it under her theme of "patriarchy." The chief patriarch of the play's world, Prince Escalus, is vehemently opposed to the feud, and although the patriarchs of the Montague and Capulet clans are drawn into the brawling of the first scene (where both seem ridiculous), they are then pledged to keep the peace (1.2.1–3). After that we never see them fighting or encouraging anyone else to fight; in fact, Shakespeare shows Capulet exercising his patriarchal authority at the ball to prevent Tybalt from challenging Romeo.[7] The feud is carried on by the young men, who are not acting "on behalf of their fathers," as Kahn claims (1981, 83, 86, 93): Tybalt does not pursue Romeo on behalf of Capulet (who is not his father), Mercutio is not even a Montague, and when Romeo finally attacks Tybalt, his motive is not to uphold "the honor of his father's house" (1981, 93) but to avenge Mercutio. Kahn is surely right in pointing out that some of the youths treat the feud as a test of manhood, but it is, if anything, an *anti*patriarchal test in defiance of the older generation and its laws. Moreover, the reconciliation of Montague and Capulet that ends the feud (and that Kahn never mentions) does not weaken the patriarchy but strengthens it, by joining their power with the prince's. I do not see, then, how Shakespeare can be presenting the feud as an expression of patriarchal attitudes.

Kahn's essay struck me as one of the most perceptive of these readings, especially in its treatment of Juliet's growth and the lovers' deaths; yet even it is undermined by this basic weakness of thematism, which can be found in all the others. Since I cannot discuss each of them in the same detail, I must limit myself to some representative examples of the principal ways by which these critics accommodate Shakespeare's facts to their themes. By far the most common of these strategies is selectivity—the critic just cites those facts that support the theme and ignores those that do not. (This need not imply conscious deception, for the thematic idea can function as a kind of lens in the mind's eye that brings only the "right" facts into focus and filters out all the rest, so that the critic may not even notice them.) Often the selectivity simply involves passing over the material that is not relevant to the critic's formulation of the theme. Thus Greene's essay on *Othello* (1995) never refers to the cashiering of Cassio or the loss of the handkerchief, which do not seem to figure in the play's "critique" of gender roles, and many more examples could be cited, since none of the themes espoused by these critics (or by nonfeminist thematists) accounts for all the significant characters and actions in the play.

The selectivity becomes much more disturbing when the facts omitted are not merely irrelevant to the critic's theme but actually contradict it. A striking example is provided by Berger in his handling of the episode in *Macbeth* in which Macduff learns that his family has been killed: Berger quotes Malcolm's line urging Macduff to "Dispute it like a man" (4.3.220), which fits his theme of an all-pervasive "*machismo*" (1982, 70), but he passes over Macduff's answer, "I shall do so; / But I must also feel it as a man," which asserts a very different sense of manhood.[8] And Neely gives us several examples in her attempt to prove that the thematic "central conflict [in *Othello*] is between the men and the women" (1985, 108), which leads her into a series of contrasts placing all the men on one side (always the wrong one) and all the women on the other. In one part of this demonstration, she accuses the men of "persistently placing blame for their actions outside themselves" and compares this attitude to that of Desdemona, whose last words exonerating Othello and assuming responsibility for her own death "provide the sharpest possible contrast to the men's excuses" and to "Othello's evasions" (1985, 124–25). But Neely fails to mention Othello's response, "She's like a liar gone to burning hell: / 'Twas I that kill'd her" (5.2.129–30), which rather blunts that sharpest possible contrast. (Nor does she mention here Desdemona's crucial evasion of responsibility about the handkerchief in 3.4.80–87.) And in an earlier section showing that the play "sharply contrasts the genuine intimacy of the women with the hypocritical friendship of the men," she asserts that "romantic love is destroyed by the semblance of male friendship" (1985, 121–23), ignoring the fact that Cassio's friendship with Othello, which was not hypocritical, fostered the romantic love, as we are told in 3.3.70–73. But there is no need to go on, since it should be obvious that any demonstration that all the men in the play have the identical vices (in addition to their evasion of responsibility and incapacity for friendship, they are all supposed to be competitive, cowardly, foolish, jealous, passive, vain, swaggering, and murderous) would have to omit a number of uncooperative facts. The same can be said of Berger's essay on *Macbeth* (1982) and Leverenz's on *Hamlet* (1980), which also discover a thematic similarity in every male.[9] This kind of reading, however, is not limited to feminist thematists. In one common form of the older "theme and structure" studies, the critic set out to prove that all the characters in a play are basically alike as exemplars of the central theme—that each of them takes appearance for reality, or subordinates reason to passion, and so on. The difference is that this process of homogenizing was applied to the entire cast, while these feminist thematists limit it to the men, but the effect on its victims is the same, for the homogenization is always down to the lowest common denominator encompassing that group of characters. Thus every male in *Othello* descends to the level of Iago, the thanes are all as bad as Macbeth, and all the men in *Hamlet* become "mini-Claudiuses." And this result can only be achieved by filtering out any facts that differentiate the characters and so contradict the critic's theme.

This selectivity in the use of evidence is even more obvious in those essays that place all the tragedies under a single theme (which is really another form of homogenization, applied now to the tragic heroes rather than to the men in one play). Gohlke, it will be recalled, views the tragedies as one "vast commentary on the . . . destructiveness of th[e] defensive posture" of "the masculine consciousness" (1980, 162–63). That posture, she says, involves "shared fictions on the part of the heroes about femininity [which they see as a weakness in themselves] and about their own vulnerability in relation to women" and leads to "a violence of response on the part of the hero against individual women, but more important, against the hero's ultimately damaging perception of himself as womanish" (1980, 152, 159). But she only tries to demonstrate this pattern in five tragedies—*Hamlet, Othello, King Lear, Macbeth,* and *Antony and Cleopatra*—and even with them she has problems. While she shows that Hamlet, Lear, and Antony exhibit aspects of "the masculine consciousness" at times, she fails to establish any causal connection between that consciousness and their catastrophes, although such a connection is supposed to be essential to her pattern: "What Shakespeare's tragedies portray is the anguish and destruction attendant on . . . [this] set of fictions" (1980, 161). Lear shows no sign of these feelings until his confrontation with Goneril and Regan some time after he made the fatal mistakes that bring about the tragedy, and it could be argued that Antony comes to grief because he does *not* act against Cleopatra as the pattern says he should. Moreover, except on the verbal level, none of these three heroes engages in any "violence against women," which is also supposed to be part of the pattern (1980, 156, 159, 161).

(Gohlke says that Hamlet kills Ophelia [154], which is not true.) It seems, then, that only Othello and Macbeth fit "Shakespeare's tragic paradigms," as she calls them, and even Macbeth requires some stretching,[10] which suggests that they are really Gohlke's paradigms rather than Shakespeare's.

This kind of criticism may be unfair to Gohlke, who states that she is treating the plays as "metaphors" (1980, 150–53), and so is apparently not concerned with the actual causal sequence of the plots or the distinction between verbal and physical "violence"; but Judith Wilt's argument that a single theme informs *Julius Caesar, Hamlet, Othello, King Lear,* and *Macbeth* seems to make a more literal claim. The theme is "the male world's banishment of the female" (1981/2, 93), which, she asserts, precipitates these tragic actions, and her case rests on specific events in each play: Brutus's ordering Portia to bed before he joins the conspirators (2.1) and Caesar's denial of Calphurnia's plea that he stay home (2.2); Hamlet's attack on Ophelia in 3.1; Othello's sending Desdemona away in 4.2; Lear's renunciation of Cordelia in 1.1; and Lady Macbeth's calling on the spirits to unsex her (1.5). But, once more, we can see a process of selection that passes over crucial facts contradicting the critic's theme. There is no reason to believe that Brutus would have abandoned the conspiracy if he had confided in Portia in 2.1, for we learn in 2.4 that he has told her his plans and she has not dissuaded him; and while Caesar could have averted the assassination if he had listened to Calphurnia in 2.2, the same result would have ensued if he had heeded the male Soothsayer in 1.2 or read the letter of the male Artemidorus in 3.1. Hamlet's "banishment" of Ophelia in 3.1 has no discernible effect on his later actions, and we find in 3.2 that he has apparently unbanished her again. In 1.1 Lear does not banish "the female"— he banishes one female and embraces two other females, who proceed to destroy him. And the application of the theme to *Macbeth* is only figurative; if we applied it literally, we would have to say that Macbeth's banishing "the female"—Lady Macbeth and the witches—would have saved him (and the same could be said of Antony and Coriolanus, who fall outside Wilt's purview). So we are left again with *Othello,* the only tragedy that actually bears out this thematic lesson of what happens to men when they do not listen to women.[11]

These critics also have another means at their disposal for accommodating Shakespeare's facts to their themes: instead of selecting the facts to fit the theme, they can manipulate the theme to fit the facts (again, without necessarily meaning to deceive). This too is a standard strategy of the older thematists that reappears in their feminist successors. Undoubtedly, the worst offender is French (1981), whose masculine and feminine "principles" undergo some strange metamorphoses. As Greene notes in her review of

French's book, "'masculine' and 'feminine' are defined so loosely and arbitrarily that their meanings slip about in response to the exigencies of the argument" (1983, 481). But French has to do more manipulating than the others because she is applying her theme to many more plays than they are. Examples of theme stretching can also be found in their readings, especially when the theme involves "patriarchy." In Kahn's study of *Romeo and Juliet* (1981), we saw, the term applies primarily to rule by the father (or head of the clan) but also includes manifestations of machismo by the young men, even when those actions are opposed by their patriarch; and in Novy's book (1984) it seems to cover almost anything that interferes with "mutuality" between the sexes. Moreover, the critics can always make their thematic concepts of gender fit the facts of the play, because the facts are defined by the theme, rather than the reverse. Erickson provides a revealing example of this process in his chapter on *The Winter's Tale,* where he asserts that Leontes' "spontaneous outburst of jealousy" is "intrinsic to the male psyche" (1985a, 148). But no other man in the play ever shows a trace of jealousy, and all the men who comment on Leontes' accusation of Hermione take *her* side, which is not what one would expect if his feelings also resided in their own psyches.[12] Why then does not Erickson infer that the play presents their faith in Hermione as the intrinsically male attitude and Leontes' jealousy as an aberration (as they themselves regard it)? Obviously, because he is not deriving his idea of what is "intrinsic to the male psyche" from the play but is imposing it on the play. That is what the older thematic critics did with their themes (which is why they always found that the plays were "saying" something that echoed their own beliefs), and the practice of these feminist thematists seems no less arbitrary. Indeed, it is virtually forced on them by their approach: since they are dealing with tragic outcomes (Erickson is concerned with the near-tragic movement in the first part of *The Winter's Tale*), and since, as we saw, they must explain this tragic outcome in terms of their gender themes, then whatever causes the outcome (i.e., Leontes' jealousy) has to be defined as "masculine," which requires a lot of thematic flexibility.

Although there are other, less important features of their methodology that might also be discussed, I would like to turn now to the results of this approach to Shakespeare's tragedies, focusing on four areas of major concern: the characters, the final effect, the conception of tragedy, and the role of Shakespeare himself. Here I must emphasize that I can only speak of general tendencies, since in most of these areas we find a range of individual practice and some exceptions. There are no significant exceptions, I think, in the treatment of the female characters in these plays, where the results have been entirely positive. This group of critics has not only cleared up long-standing sexist misinterpretations of these characters (which was the main thrust of the early studies) but has given us many valuable insights, from a new perspective, into their personalities and especially their situations as women in male-dominated worlds. This is a very impressive achievement, and I do not dwell on it, only because it seems so obvious.

Unfortunately, however, the same cannot be said of their treatment of the male characters, particularly the tragic heroes. Although Romeo and Antony are often exempted from the general curse and there are a few appreciative comments on the others, in most of these studies most of the tragic heroes emerge as a sorry lot indeed, having lost virtually all their admirable qualities and even their individuality. This result is by no means unique to their approach. For some years now a number of critics of various persuasions have been busy attacking these characters (along with Henry V, Duke Vincentio, Prospero, and others), often claiming that an apparently sympathetic portrayal of them is undercut by a pervasive irony that renders them antipathetic. But these feminists have made their own contribution to this campaign against the protagonists, a contribution that seems to follow from their methodology. We saw that the thematic approach adopted by them treats the characters as exemplars of a general theme (which means it will pass over their more particular traits) and that it tends to homogenize them down to the lowest moral level, so the protagonist, who is usually the most individualized and most admirable character, will suffer the greatest diminution on both counts. Moreover, this general thematic pressure on the protagonist is increased considerably by the specific themes they use. Since most of those themes involve some form of gender opposition, their positive treatment of the female characters seems to require a negative treatment of the males. And since, as we noted, the masculine half of this thematic opposition must be responsible for the tragic catastrophe, it is usually loaded with deplorable traits, which are of necessity embodied in the hero. (The obvious exceptions are studies like Dash 1981, Novy 1984, and Kimbrough 1983 that blame the gender roles imposed on both men and women by "patriarchy," which allows them to be more generous to the heroes.) All too often, the result is what can only be called a sexist stereotyping of the protagonist.[13] Indeed, the stereotyping in real-life prejudices may be seen as a kind of thematism, with the stereotype acting like the critic's theme as a lens that selects, or focuses on, any facts that confirm it and filters out any that do not. It would almost appear, then, that the general evolution of this body of criticism—again, with notable exceptions—has been from freeing Shakespeare's women of negative stereotypes to imposing such stereotypes on his men. That is very unfortunate, because there really is no necessary connection between these operations.

If we do not view the tragedies as thematic "conflicts" of the two sexes, we find that our appreciation of one sex never depends on the depreciation of the other. On the contrary, it seems easy for us to respond positively to both—to sympathize with Ophelia *and* Hamlet, Othello *and* Desdemona, Cordelia *and* Lear.

This denigration of the tragic hero will of course influence the treatment of the tragic effect, to which I now turn, although I should first note that some of these critics virtually ignore it. This too may be seen as a result of thematism, which tends to minimize emotional involvement with the characters in its concentration on an intellectual grasp of the thematic lesson.[14] But other critics do discuss the effect of the tragedies, and most of them do not find it very tragic. In their response to the ending there is usually little sense of compassion for the hero, which is not surprising when we consider their view of him. And there is even less sense of any resolution or catharsis. Here, for example, is French on *Macbeth:*

> The play ends as it began, in a totally masculine world. . . . Although some balance is restored to the kingdom, there is no change in its value structure. What is restored is the sacred inner circle, in which men are expected to refrain from applying the standards of the outer [i.e., feminine] one; what is reasserted is moral schizophrenia. (1981, 249–50)

And Leverenz on *Hamlet:*

> The play ends in a mindless sequence of ritual male duties, roles without meaning. . . . [Fortinbras], who inherits an irrevocably corrupted world, is the arrogant, stupid, blundering finale to the theme of filial duty. . . . The hawkish voices of blood, honor, and ambition inherit the world of the fathers, with its false roles and false proprieties. (1980, 123–25)

And Neely on *Othello:*

> The restoration of military order provides little satisfaction here. . . . The conflict between the men and the women has not been eliminated or resolved. . . . The "tragic lodging of this bed" . . . signifies destruction without catharsis, release without resolution. The pain and division of the ending are unmitigated. (1985, 135)

And Snow on the same scene:

> The directions for Iago's torture reconstitute society in terms of the same impotent dialectic of violence and repression that caused its rupture. . . .

> We are left with . . . [the state] blindly revealing in itself the evil it seeks to . . . punish in its victim. There is neither transcendence nor catharsis in *Othello*. (1980, 385)

It is not difficult to understand why these critics do not find any resolution in these endings, for this is a direct consequence of their approach. Since the basic issue (and cause) of the tragedy is defined in terms of the thematic problem of gender, rather than in terms of the protagonist's individual character and situation, it is not and cannot be resolved by his death. From these critics' point of view, at the conclusion of the play nothing has really ended or even changed—"patriarchy" has simply produced another disaster and will go on producing more. This also helps to explain why they do not find any catharsis here, because that depends, in part, on our "sense of an ending," our realization that the action has run its course. But catharsis in Shakespearean tragedy involves other factors as well, I believe, including some kind of restoration of order and a renewal or enhancement of our positive feelings for the hero, who usually achieves or learns something at the end and regains his earlier noble stature. Neither of these effects, however, can be recognized by this group of critics. Because their view of the hero before he enters the final scene is usually very negative, he has no noble stature to regain, and anything he achieves there (confronting his enemies, revenging his father, executing justice on himself) will not alter that view, since they regard this as another example of his "machismo" and his evasion of the real issue. Their definition of that issue, moreover, makes it impossible for them to accept any discovery on his part, for while many of the heroes learn many things, they never seem to learn what these critics insist is the thematic lesson the play—namely, that the concept of masculinity itself is to blame for the tragedy.[15] (Nor does anyone else in the play ever learn it.)

This conception of the theme also prevents these critics from accepting any restoration of order at the end, because what is being restored is always the same patriarchal order that, according to them, was responsible for all the calamities. Indeed, from their standpoint such a restoration not only fails to resolve the problem of the play but actually exacerbates it, since, as Berger says of the ending of *Macbeth,* "it will only enable, by concealing, the ongoing dialectic of gender conflict" (1982, 73). Thus in their lexicon "restoration" becomes a dirty word; the solution is part of the problem. Yet while it is easy to see why they find these endings so untragic, it is much more difficult to imagine the kind of ending that could give them a satisfactory sense of resolution and catharsis. Presumably it would require a complete change in the men's attitudes that would result in a dismantling of "patriarchy" and the establishment of a new order of gender equality and harmony. But that does not sound very tragic either.

This problem leads me to the conception of the tragic genre itself that emerges from these studies. In most of them I did not find any real sense of the genre as an important determinant of dramatic form and effect. Like many other results of their approach, this can be partially explained as a tendency of thematism in general. As we just noted, most thematists are much more interested in the intellectual theme they derive from a play than in its emotional effect, which figures so prominently in our recognition of genre. And they typically formulate this theme as some universal proposition about life that cannot be genre specific; in fact, it is seldom possible to tell from their account of a play's central theme whether they are dealing with a comedy or a tragedy. But this general tendency of thematism is strengthened, again, by the specific theme of gender relations adopted by this group of critics, since they usually regard it as the real subject of *all* the plays, and that must diminish the significance of any generic distinctions. Thus French can say that "the comedies and tragedies deal with identical material" (1981, 35), and Erickson in his review of her book can complain that she is still too concerned with differentiating them, instead of "stress[ing] the ways in which the two forms converge" (1981/2, 195). Moreover, their commitment to this one theme leads some of the critics to compose a thematic biography for Shakespeare, wherein his entire career is seen as a sustained inquiry into the problem of gender, so that the genres he employed are merely stages of this enterprise, of no major importance in themselves.[16]

For at least two of these critics, this view of the canon leads to a further diminution of the tragic genre in particular. Gohlke, who says she is "reading the development" of Shakespeare's portrayal of gender relations "from the comedies through the problem plays and the major tragedies," speaks of "the failure of [*Romeo and Juliet*] to achieve the generic status of comedy" and of "interpret[ing] the tragedies . . . as comedies gone wrong" (1980, 154, 152; 1981/2, 175). And Neely approaches *Othello* from the "context" provided by "Shakespearean comedy, to which [it] shows pervasive and profound resemblances," and concludes, in similar terms, that in it "the comic resolution . . . is aborted" (1985, 108–9, 135). But I suspect this treatment of tragedy as failed comedy depends less on the chronological place of those genres in the canon than on the thematic conception governing both. Since, according to these critics, Shakespeare is always grappling with the problem of gender, the comedies, which end in gender harmony, are often seen as his solution to the problem, the goal he is seeking, and therefore the tragedies come to represent a failure to solve this problem and achieve this goal. Moreover, the difference between the two genres is explained by the role of the women in the thematic gender conflict: when they are able to cure or at least restrain the men's masculinity, the result is a comic resolution, and when the men will not let them do this, the result is tragedy, which makes it, again, a kind of failure. The idea has obvious affinities to the view of Wilt (1981/2) and Greene (1995), and apparently Leverenz (1980), that tragedy is what occurs when the men do not listen to the women. And this tendency to reduce tragedies to comedies manqués is reinforced by the description of the tragic effect in negative terms as a lack of resolution and of cathartic release, which does not sound like something a dramatist would aim for. Most of these critics, it appears, do not see Shakespeare deliberately setting out to write a tragedy, where the nature of the genre (its conventions, expectations, and appropriate pleasure) might determine the nature of the gender relations portrayed in the play, rather than the other way around. But then it is hard to believe that they see him deliberately setting out to write a comedy gone wrong.

This uncertainty about Shakespeare's relation to the tragic genre raises the whole question of authorial intention, which I think is one of the greatest problems of this group of critics, although they seldom acknowledge it, for they all seem to assume that their interpretations correspond to his intended meaning.[17] That is not what I expected when I began this investigation, because I thought they would often find themselves in disagreement with a male author writing in such a male-dominated society. But I later realized that this situation does not arise in the tragedies, since "patriarchy" always comes to grief there, and so Shakespeare's attitude toward gender would seem in accord with their own. In some of the other genres, however, where a happy resolution is often accompanied by, or is even dependent on, the subordination of women, they run into difficulty and must either argue that the ending is ironic or else give up the intentionalist position.[18]

That position is inherent in thematism itself, because thematic critics (including these feminist thematists, as we saw) regularly claim that the play is "exploring" or "commenting on" the central theme, which implies a conscious purpose. An unintended exploration seems self-contradictory; to adapt the dictum of E. D. Hirsch (1976) on meaning, there can be no exploring without an explorer. All thematists therefore have the obligation of proving that the play really is intended to be about their theme. And this general obligation becomes even greater in these feminist readings, for they assert that each tragedy is meant to call into question some of the most basic beliefs in the fictional world it dramatizes and in the real world of its author, which ought to place a very heavy burden of proof on them. Plays of this sort have of course been written. An obvious example is *Ghosts,* and it is obvious because Ibsen takes some pains to let us know that he is criticizing the pieties of the play's society (and his own) by subjecting them to intensive discussion, during which Oswald attacks them at length; by presenting a much more desirable alternative to them in Oswald's description of the idyllic bohemian life in Paris; by establishing explicit causal connections between them and all the unhappiness depicted in the play; by showing in the resolution that the world governed by them rewards the worst people and punishes the best; and by having Mrs. Alving converted to Oswald's view of them, when she learns the lesson that her son and the play are teaching. I am not suggesting that every play that criticizes its own world must include all these factors, but we would expect to find at least some of them present. We do find them in Webster's *The Duchess of Malfi,* which is probably the best Jacobean example of this kind of play: the corrupt society depicted there is condemned at the outset by Antonio, who also gives us a possible alternative to it in his report on the reformed French court; it is made responsible for the misery of the sympathetic characters; it punishes the innocent Duchess and her family while rewarding the flagrant adulteress Julia (though she is killed at the end); and its cruelty even brings about the conversion of Bosola, who finally takes the Duchess's side against it.

Do we encounter anything like this in Shakespeare's tragedies to support the claim that they are criticizing the gender assumptions of their worlds? There is no explicit attack on those assumptions, except for a few speeches of Emilia. There is no necessary connection between them and the tragic outcome—in fact, we found that this outcome is usually regarded as an extraordinary deviation from the normal life of the play's world. There is no unjust distribution of rewards and punishments that they can be blamed for. There is no conversion leading to a rejection of them, because, as we saw earlier, nobody in these plays ever learns the lesson that these critics say is being taught there. And, except in *Antony and Cleopatra,* there is no suggestion of an alternative society with different assumptions that might serve as a basis for judging them. In view of this lack of evidence, then, it seems more reasonable to conclude that the tragedies are not criticizing their own gender assumptions but just assuming them, along with other conditions underlying the dramatized action that is their real subject. This does not mean that *we* cannot criticize those assumptions; it only means that we should separate our activity from Shakespeare's.

There are signs that some of these critics are in fact moving in this direction, although they may not always be clear about it, for we can sometimes discern a nonintentionalist subtext within their intentionalist readings. It is apparent, as we noted, in their view of tragedy as failed comedy and in their account of the tragic effect, which can hardly have been what Shakespeare intended. It is more obvious in Greene's statement that "feminist critics may direct their attentions to freeing female characters from the stereotypes to which they have been confined by the critical tradition or from the biases and prejudices of authors themselves" (1981/2, 30). The first operation, presumably, seeks to recover the author's intended meaning by correcting previous misinterpretations of it, but the second implies a very different conception of the relation between critic and author. So does Wheeler's statement that "it has taken the energies of feminist criticism to dislodge [Desdemona, Emilia, and Bianca] from the play's powerful rhetoric of both idealization and degradation" (1985, 209), for if we remember who is responsible for that rhetoric, then this operation too involves rescuing characters from their own creator.[19] And that is apparently what Leininger is doing when she asserts that "Caliban is made to concur in the accusation" that he assaulted Miranda (1980, 289), as if the accusation were not true (although she later hedges by referring to "his real or imputed lust" [292]).

These critics seem to be treating the plays as biased accounts of real people that they must correct, which seems absurd; but I think the impulse behind their undertaking is sound, since they are trying to articulate their own views of the gender assumptions of the plays. They are treating those assumptions, that is, as assumptions, and so can distinguish their attitudes toward them from Shakespeare's (which is also what Erickson recommends). I would say that they are moving here in the right direction, toward a promising line of inquiry for feminist critics into the actual nature of the gender assumptions in these plays.[20] It would mean holding in abeyance (temporarily, of course) their own attitudes toward gender, as well as their claim to be interpreting Shakespeare's intention, which required a transformation of the assumptions into the thematic subject he was exploring (to arrive at conclusions happily coinciding with their own), since in such an inquiry their attitudes and his intention would be irrelevant. Above all, it would mean abandoning their preconceptions of what those assumptions will be. They might begin with one tragedy and try to determine what its gender assumptions really are by deriving them inductively from the play itself, and then proceed, again inductively, to see if they can derive valid generalizations about the assumptions of the tragedies as a genre. It is an inquiry for which they are uniquely suited, because their feminist perspective gives them the "distance" needed to recognize the assumptions. And it is one that would put the rest of us greatly in their debt.

As my final point I would like to pursue the question of preconceptions just referred to, by looking at the psychoanalytic theory that apparently underlies a number of these essays. It is not the theory of Freud, of course, but the revised feminist versions of Dorothy Dinnerstein (1976), Adrienne Rich (1976), Nancy Chodorow (1978), and others, which retain the Freudian faith that some basic childhood trauma is responsible for all our problems but locate that trauma in the child's relation to the mother during the "pre-Oedipal stage" of development. I am less concerned here with their account of that stage, however, than with the picture of the adult male psyche that has filtered down, perhaps in distorted form, to affect this body of criticism. The general idea seems to be that men, because of difficulties in their infantile experience with mothering (which is supposed to be very different from the experience of female infants), grow up with an unconscious but overpowering fear and hatred of femininity, both in women and in themselves, which they try to repress by certain defense mechanisms, including an obsessive need to idealize or degrade women and to control them. They are all, in short, unconscious misogynists. This is the conception of masculinity that presumably stands behind Gohlke's assertion that the tragic heroes share a "defensive posture" resulting from feelings about "their own vulnerability in relation to women," which leads to "violence against women" (1980, 152, 161, 163); and Berger's that all the Scots thanes suffer from a "pathologically protective *machismo*" based on "the male fear of feminine contamination" and "fear of impotency and vulnerability to women" (1982, 58, 71, 76); and Erickson's that the "spontaneous outburst of jealousy" in Leontes is "intrinsic to the male psyche" (1985a, 148); and Snow's that Othello kills Desdemona because of the "pathological male animus toward sexuality" and "underlying male fear" of "thralldom to the demands of an unsatisfiable sexual appetite in woman" (1980, 388, 407), which are triggered in him by the consummation of his marriage.

We can presume that such assertions come from this "feminist" conception of masculinity that these critics bring to the plays, since they cannot come from the plays themselves. For this conception does not fit any of the tragic heroes (or any of the thanes). It is true that four of them —Hamlet, Othello, Lear, and Antony—express some of these misogynist feelings at certain times, but always in situations of crisis and always in response to what they view as a very serious provocation by a woman. Not one of them, in his usual or characteristic state of mind, could be termed a misogynist; in fact, Shakespeare shows us that in this state each is (or was) capable of forming a loving relationship with a woman, and this applies to the other tragic heroes as well.[21] The imposition of this conception, therefore, radically distorts their characters. It also eliminates their individuality, since they all turn out to have the same stereotypical male sickness. And it debases them to a level beyond the reach of tragic sympathy. We saw that this is a tendency more or less inherent in the approach of these critics, but this conception of masculinity further contributes to it.

This conception also affects their treatment of female characters, for one of its corollaries seems to be that, while men grow up sick, women grow up healthy—that is, without unconscious fears or hatreds. (I am speaking not of the theory itself but only of its deployment by these critics.) Sometimes this results in what can only be called an idealization of the female, which may seem strange since feminists are so opposed to it, but apparently it is acceptable if couched in the language of modern psychology. Berger, for example, regards Lady Macduff as the sole representative of "saneness" and "authentic humanity" (1982, 71) in a sea of male pathology (Lady Macbeth is disqualified because of her "mimetic desire to join the manly ranks," and the witches are "scapegoats of the masculine imagination" [72, 74]). And Snow almost grows lyrical in his praise of Desdemona for her "erotic vitality," freedom from "Oedipal guilt," and similar virtues (1980, 406–7). She seems flawless, and he gets very angry at her mistreatment by Robert Dickes, an orthodox Freudian, who finds in her a "castrative" need to "dominate Othello in terms of phallic rivalry" (1970, 287, 293).[22] Snow insists that "the reality of [her] behavior" does not support this diagnosis (1980, 405), which is true; but it is equally true that the reality of Othello's behavior does not support Snow's own account of a "pathological male animus" and "underlying male fear" (388, 407). Snow, in other words, condemns Dickes for doing to Desdemona what he himself does to Othello, since they are both imposing on the character an unconscious (and of course unsavory) motivation that is dictated by their own preconceptions. But apparently Desdemona (and Lady Macduff) cannot have an unconscious like the men, which may be a new form of sexual discrimination.

I think we would also have to say, finally, that this "feminist" conception of masculinity is just as much a distortion of real life as it is of the tragedies. In both areas it contains an element of truth, for some men, like some tragic heroes, do have those misogynist feelings at some times (some men, of course, have them all the time). While it is very important to recognize this phenomenon, to elevate it into a universal definition of the gender is absurd, as may be seen if we try to apply the statements quoted above. If Erickson's statement were true, then most men would walk around suffering spontaneous outbursts of jealousy. If Snow's were true, most wedding nights would terminate in uxoricide. Indeed, if any of them were true, half the human race would be pathological. Why then do some of these critics accept this conception of masculinity and employ it? They cannot be convinced by the evidence offered for it, since there is none. The explanation must be that they want to believe it. And they want to believe it, apparently, because it neatly turns the tables on the Freudian theory of "penis envy" by making female development the norm and male development abnormal. One can easily understand their dislike of Freud's theory, for in it, as Gohlke says, "femininity itself is defined as the condition of lack" (1980, 162). She is right, but the theory she sponsors does the same thing to masculinity, by defining it as a malady. Surely the only sensible course is to abandon both these theories, along with the fruitless search for a single basic cause of gender difference and all its problems, and give our support to a scientific study of the complex factors in human development, which would investigate the similarities as well as the differences between men and women, based on evidence that compelled the assent of all rational people, regardless of their gender or ideology.

A Letter to the *PMLA* Forum

Richard Levin's "Feminist Thematics and Shakespearean Tragedy" embodies precisely those flaws it falsely accuses feminist critics of: arbitrary selectivity, reductive thematizing, misplaced causality, unexamined and untenable assumptions about intentionality, irresponsible slippage from particulars to abstractions. His readings of feminist criticism of Shakespearean tragedy ignore its explicit premises, methods, and goals and fail to acknowledge the assumptions and anxieties that underlie his critique.

While Levin's target is clearly feminist criticism of Shakespeare in general, his selected focus is on early work on tragedy by American feminist critics. He treats this one strand of feminist criticism as if it represents the approach as a whole and ignores, mislabels, or marginalizes other strands, represented, for example, by the work of Janet Adelman, Linda Bamber, Catherine Belsey, Lynda Boose, Lisa Jardine, Kathleen McLuskie, and Linda Woodbridge. He fails to understand the serious concerns about inequality and injustice that have engendered feminist analyses of literature, and he constructs a pseudohistory of feminist criticism of Shakespeare that does not account for the complex development or great diversity of the approach. He privileges his favored genre, tragedy, without acknowledging that feminist critics have resisted this traditional hierarchization of genres.

Levin thematizes his selections along lines familiar from his 1979 book, *New Readings vs. Old Plays*, presenting snippets of decontextualized quotations to support conclusions presented as self-evident. But the charges fail to stick. Feminist critics do not often concern themselves with theme, and never in isolation from characters or structure or culture. We do not claim that our interpretations account for everything in the play (as Levin notes in some puzzlement in the midst of accusing us of doing so [31]). We do not argue that the plays are "about the role of gender" or that gender or patriarchy is the sole "cause" of tragedy. It is Levin who is obsessed with *cause,* confusing it with *conditions* (33), and who imputes this claim to us. It is Levin who valorizes Shakespeare's intentions, concluding that "the tragedies are not criticizing their own gender assumptions but just assuming them" (45). It is Levin who construes "gender" and "patriarchy" as Platonic idea(l)s. We argue that gender difference is a historically specific cultural construction with diverse forms and representations and damaging consequences for characters in the plays, subjects in the Renaissance, and for us—and Levin—today.

Accusing us of his own flaws, Levin paternally tries to preempt our strengths by recommending our project to us as if it were his idea. We have, of course, been analyzing "the actual nature of gender assumptions in these plays" (46) for over fifteen years; we examine the interactions between gender and dramatic genres and question conventional generic assumptions (43); we forthrightly acknowledge the partiality of our own interpretations; we "separate our activity from Shakespeare's," "criticize (his) assumptions" (45), and debate the question of his intentions in instances when we accept the concept of a unified author with discernible intentions. Levin applauds us for providing "many valuable new insights, from a new perspective, into [female characters'] personalities and especially their situations as women in male-dominated worlds" (40). But, absurdly, he wants us to provide these insights without revealing the strategies, structures, psychologies, and oppressiveness of the domination that particular male characters enact.

Levin does not recognize the profound challenges that feminist criticism poses to the crude Aristotelianism he has advocated since his introduction to his 1960 textbook, *Tragedy: Plays, Theory, and Criticism:* "There can be no dispute over the fact that the tragic form has, over long periods of history, seemed to authors, audiences, and critics alike well suited to the most exalted, significant, and beautiful of man's artistic creations" (iii). Tragedy, Levin assumes everyone assumes, is the highest genre, has a formal cause, a hero deserving sympathy, an experience of catharsis, a resolution that allows the hero self-knowledge and restores order. Our criticism has argued against each of these generalizations with detailed analyses of the specific actions of particular heroes (always a Levin desideratum). We can only reiterate here that the tragic heroes represent the values and contradictions of their societies, that abnormal behavior in crisis is always an intensification of tendencies present in "normal" behavior, that the tragedies repeatedly and poignantly ask what it is to "be a man," that the heroes often fantasize "a very serious provocation by a woman" (47) when there is none, that self-knowledge, catharsis, and the restoration of order are vexed in many of Shakespeare's tragedies.

Levin's last sentence calls on feminist critics to support "a scientific study of the complex factors in human development, which would investigate the similarities as well as the differences between women and men, based on evidence that compelled the assent of all rational people, regardless of their gender or ideology." Levin seems unaware that what passes for "rationality" in a particular historical moment is likely to look irrational from the perspective of another, that affirmations of shared attributes often mask oppression based on unexplored assumptions of hierarchical difference, that many dreadful thoughts and brutal deeds have compelled the assent of people fully convinced of their own rationality and the irrationality of a cultural other. The view that "science" and "rationality" can comprehend "complex factors in human development" without the messy intrusion of "gender and ideology" is an Enlightenment dream, long since turned to nightmare.

We are puzzled and disturbed that Richard Levin has made a successful academic career by using the reductive techniques of this essay to bring the same predictable charges indiscriminately against all varieties of contemporary criticism. We wish to know why, in view of the energetic, cogent, sophisticated theoretical debate that is currently taking place within and among schools of Renaissance criticism, *PMLA* has chosen to print a tired, muddled, unsophisticated essay that is blind at once to the assumptions of feminist criticism of Shakespeare and to its own.

> Janet Adelman, Margaret J. Arnold, Linda Bamber, Catherine Belsey, Harry Berger, Lynda Boose, Peter Erickson, Shirley Nelson Garner, Gayle Greene, Dianne M. Hunter, Lisa Jardine, Coppélia Kahn, Carol Leventen, Kathleen McLuskie, Carol Thomas Neely, Marianne Novy, Rebecca Smith, Edward A. Snow, Madelon (Gohlke) Sprengnether, Carolyn Ruth Swift (Lenz), Ann Thompson, Valerie Wayne, Richard P. Wheeler, Linda Woodbridge

My Reply

This letter must set a Forum record for the number of signers and the number of charges levied against one article. Although these signers seem to take a dim view of "intentionality," they begin by constructing an intention for me—and one I explicitly disavow. They charge that my "target is clearly feminist criticism of Shakespeare in general" and that I treat one strand "as if it represents the approach as a whole"; yet my second paragraph clearly states that I am dealing not with this entire approach but with only one strand. I say it in so many ways that the copy editor objected to my redundancy, but I retained the wording to ensure that no one would make the mistake they have made. Moreover, in notes 3, 14, and 20 I name feminist Shakespeareans who are not in this strand, so I cannot be claiming it "represents the approach as a whole." Four of those named there are in the list of seven whom, according to the next charge, my article "ignores, mislabels, or marginalizes." Thus they are not ignored; nor are they marginalized—I say they "have given us significant studies that may be riding the wave of the future." And the only labels I apply to them are "not thematic" and, for one group, "cultural materialist" (note 20). If that is mislabeling, the letter should explain why. I also do not understand the charge that I construct a "pseudohistory" of feminist Shakespeare criticism, since my few remarks about this history are based on an essay (cited in note 1) by a signer of the letter.

I am then charged with "presenting snippets of decontextualized quotations to support conclusions presented as self-evident." I do rely on such "snippets" since I know of no better method of discussing many essays, and I see the letter uses "snippets" from my article. There is nothing wrong with this practice unless the passages are excerpted in a way that distorts them, which I presume is implied by "decontextualized." But every "snippet" I quote is identified, so it should be easy to detect distortions of the author's meaning, especially for the ten signers who are authors of essays I "snippet" from. Yet they do not cite any instances of it, which suggests that this charge too is without substance. And I cannot be presenting my conclusions "as self-evident" if I present "quotations to support" them, so the charge contradicts itself.

The signers' tactics then shift from these unsubstantiated charges to a series of general pronouncements about what "we" do or do not do that are supposed to refute my article. But I try to show that each essay I discuss (with two exceptions cited in note 17) does what they claim "we" do not do, and does not do what they claim "we" do; and if I am wrong, they should be able to name at least one essay that does not argue that the play is about gender, or does not valorize Shakespeare's intentions, or does criticize his assumptions, and so on. They never attempt it, because they are talking not about these essays (which are not even mentioned) but about an abstraction called "feminist criticism" that "we" practice and that seems to have no faults. Thus, this tactic allows them to dispose of all my criticisms of these essays without confronting any of them. And it places those signers who wrote the essays in the position of making assertions about "we" that do not apply to their own work.

The charges in the fifth paragraph are easily answered: I do not "assume" any of the generalizations about "tragedy" listed there, although a few are conclusions I have reached about Shakespeare's tragedies; and I cannot assume that "everyone assumes" them, since I quote critics who do not. That 1960 textbook, by the way, presents five other theories of tragedy in addition to Aristotle's, without "advocating" any of them. But I wonder why those signers who do not "accept the concept of a unified author" would want to unify me with the person who wrote that book thirty years ago.*

The letter's last two paragraphs introduce more general issues. My appeal to evidence acceptable to all rational people is rejected because brutal deeds have been committed by people "convinced of their own rationality." (Of course brutal deeds have also been committed by people convinced they were promoting equality and justice, yet that does not prevent the signers from invoking those values.) But if we cannot appeal to such evidence, on what basis are we to prefer one theory of human development over another? If we judge them by their conformity to the right ideology, we are on the road to Lysenkoism, and while the cultural materialists among the signers might welcome this, I do not think the rest would.

I will not descend to answer their charge about how I "made a successful academic career," which is unworthy of them, and I leave it to anyone familiar with that career to judge the accuracy of the charge. But their objection to the publication of my article raises a more important question. In my reply in the last Forum, written before I saw this letter, I reported that many of my correspondents felt *PMLA* is now controlled by the feminist and other new approaches. This letter's signers apparently would like to strengthen that impression: the fact that it is publishing a steady stream of feminist articles is not enough, in their view; they also want it to deny publication to any criticism of them that they disapprove of. But if *PMLA* is to remain an open journal, it cannot be subject to the veto of any group, and all of us must be prepared to find articles in it we oppose.

I am under no illusion that my reply will convince the signers or others who share their feelings. For them, critiques of feminist criticism are permissible from within the fold (in note 2 I name six signers who engage in

---

*I also wonder how many of the signers have actually looked at this 1960 textbook that they are attacking (and misrepresenting) here. All those I have asked about it admit that they have never seen it. I might add, throwing modesty to the winds, that the book is still in print and has sold over 225,000 copies.

it, which further vexes their use of "we"), but not from "a cultural other." Then objections to one strand of this criticism become an attack on "the approach as a whole," and that becomes an attack on feminism itself, which is implied in the charge that I fail "to understand the serious concerns about inequality and injustice that have engendered feminist analyses of literature"—something they could not possibly know from my article. I think I understand those concerns as well as a man can, and I strongly support efforts to rectify the inequality and injustice, which is why I joined NOW; but that does not affect my view of the essays, since a just cause cannot justify interpretive faults. And my criticism of these faults cannot be explained by charging me with "anxiety," the way Freudians treat objections as "resistance." I have faith, however, that rational argument will eventually prevail, or I would not have written the article or this reply, and I even hope that one day some of the signers and I can enter into a real discussion of the issues I tried to raise.

2
The Poetics and Politics of Bardicide

Anyone who has tried to keep up with the ensemble of new critical discourses currently circulating around and recirculating Shakespeare's dramatic texts must have noticed that a curious thing has happened to Shakespeare himself. Any trace of his responsibility for what goes on in these texts is being systematically occluded, and even his name, if it appears at all, is often placed under erasure by quotation marks, so that uninitiated readers might think they have inadvertently transgressed onto some anti-Stratfordian discursive space.[1] This situation is, of course, the result of The Death of the Author, which was celebrated twenty years ago in France under the auspices of "Roland Barthes" and "Michel Foucault," although the obituaries took some time to cross the Channel and the Atlantic. Since their arrival, Peter Erickson points out, "it has become conventional to use whatever cumbersome locutions and passive constructions are required to avoid sentences that make Shakespeare the active subject of a proposition about the plays" (1986, 254). My concern here, however, is not with the stylistic blemishes of this latest convention but with its significance, which is seldom discussed because the discursive practices that rapidly evolved to replenish the void hollowed out in The Author Function are now ossifying into logistic formulas that can be ventriloquized almost automatically without requiring the critics and their readers to confront either the assumptions enabling these formulas or the attendant problems. I would therefore like to examine those assumptions and problems, first in the poetic realm and then in the political, and for this purpose I focus on a group of readings that provide the clearest illustration of these practices in their most highly developed form, although I also consider some "weak" intentionalist readings that still retain the concept of authorial agency but have been contaminated, or at least inflected, by this new mode of discourse. The examples were not selected on the basis of their approaches, but most of the first type that I found come from the Marxist cultural materialists and the feminists associated with them, and most of the second from critics employing a feminist revision of Freud that I call neo-Freudian.[2] Although almost all my examples are recent studies of Shakespeare, I believe that the conclusions should apply to other terrains where these practices are appearing, for he is not the only "author" to suffer this fate.

Before beginning this examination, however, we should note that the interment of the author is part of a much larger campaign waged by these new critical discourses against what they call "formalism" (mainly the old New Criticism) and the philosophy of "liberal humanism" that is supposed to underlie it. They define themselves largely in terms of their opposition to this criticism and philosophy, and their essays often attack a number of fallacies attributed to formalism/humanism, among which the belief that literary texts are created by "autonomous individuals"—that is, authors—ranks very high. A second such fallacy is the belief that we can attain objective knowledge of a text's real meaning, which usually depends on authorial intention and therefore disappears with the author's death. These critics maintain, on the contrary, that there is no "unmediated" access to the text "in itself" and that all interpretations of it are "appropriations" determined by the interpreter's political position, based primarily on class or gender. This will help to explain some of the practices that I am about to examine; it also explains why these critics would regard my attempt in the preceding paragraph to separate the poetic and political realms as another formalist/humanist fallacy—indeed, their conceptualization of those fallacies assumes a necessary connection between formalist poetics and the politics of liberal humanism. Moreover, their polarizing of right and wrong interpretive approaches has its counterpart in the political polarities of the two discursive systems that most of them deploy, which also posit a fundamental conflict between right and wrong—between oppressed and ruling classes in the Marxist system and between oppressed and ruling genders in the neo-Freudian—so that these critics are able to conflate this conflict with the opposition of the two modes of interpretation, associating formalism (and so humanism) with the upper class or patriarchy and their own approach with the victims. The consequences of this double polarization become evident as soon as we turn to the practices that have followed in the wake of The Death of the Author.

There is no difficulty in ascertaining what takes over The Author Function in the practice of these critics: it is the play itself or, as they usually prefer to call it, the text. As a result of its new status as authorial surrogate, the text acquires a repertoire of new activities that, because of the polarization just noted, can be divided into Bad Moves and Good Moves. We will begin with the former, since they appear to be—and are supposed to be—much more obvious, at least on the surface.

The text has a project. This is the equivalent of the rejected concept of authorial intention, now introjected into the text. Presumably the word *project* is favored because it avoids the awkwardness of attributing a human will to the text, while still enabling a functional analysis in terms of means and end. One does not ask how or why the text gave itself, or was given, this project—that is treated as a donnée. The project is always bad, since it involves the reproduction or reaffirmation of some aspect of the oppressive and deceptive ideology (in the Marxist sense of "false consciousness") that dominated the Renaissance world and that is represented by what I will call the hegemonic characters who constitute the dominant class in the world of the play. According to Jonathan Dollimore and Alan Sinfield, the project of *Henry V* is the "establishing [of the] ideological unity" of the state and its class system and the "containment" of threats to it (1985, 225); Jean Howard finds that in *Much Ado about Nothing* the "project . . . [is the] legitimation of aristocratic, male theatricality" and power, which is "the play's ideological function" (1987b, 182, 174); Paul Brown says that *The Tempest* "serve[s] the colonialist project" (1994, 68); Francis Barker and Peter Hulme also find that this play "functions within the projects of colonialist discourse" and "colonialist ideology" (1985, 201, 204); and so on. The neo-Freudian version of the project is usually a *fantasy* that is said to be "enacted" or "embodied" by the text or its hegemonic characters and that is also always bad because it is masculinist and misogynist.[3] (This position is of course quite different from that of many earlier Marxists and feminists who were "strong" intentionalists and who often claimed that the play—i.e., Shakespeare—set out to challenge the dominant ideology or the patriarchy.)[4]

The text has strategies. These are the means employed by the text to attain its end, to win our assent to its project, and since the project is bad, so are the strategies. Yet they succeed in deceiving the formalist/humanists, who are not even aware of them *as* strategies because those critics are supposed to believe that textual meaning is transparent or self-evident and so to accept it at face value (which is another one of their fallacies) and because their own ideology, as was noted earlier, is supposed to coincide with the ideological project of the text. The recognition of these strategies is connected to The Death of the Author by Kathleen McLuskie, who says she will be "refusing to construct an author behind the plays and paying attention instead to the . . . strategies which construct the plays' meanings" (1994, 92). Dollimore and Sinfield speak of the "strategies of containment" in *Henry V* (1985, 225), Brown of the "strategy of colonialist discourse" in *The Tempest* (1994, 62), and Howard of *Much Ado*'s "strategy for holding in place certain inequalities of power" (1987b, 183). James Kavanagh discusses "the discursive and rhetorical strategies" that accomplish the "ideological work" of *A Midsummer Night's Dream* and *King Lear* (1985, 152), and Dollimore, in his reading of *Measure for Measure*, refers to "the strategies of power" adopted in the "ideological process whereby authority . . . relegitimat[es] itself" (1994b, 84). The remaining textual activities examined in this section cover the most significant of these strategies.

The text displaces. Frequently it displaces the issue at stake in the action, which always turns out to be some basic conflict in Renaissance society. According to Dollimore, the real concern of *Measure for Measure* is not "the supposed subversiveness of sexual license," as the rulers of Vienna claim, but the "social tensions" of Shakespeare's world, which are "displaced from authority *to* desire and by implication from the rulers to the ruled," so that the anxiety about sexual morality is "an ideological displacement" of "much deeper fears . . . corresponding to more fundamental social problems" (1994b, 76, 73, 80). Peter Stallybrass asserts that in *Othello* class tensions of the time are "displaced onto the enchanted ground of romance, where considerations of status are transformed into considerations of sexual success" (1986, 134). In her study of *Much Ado*, Howard takes a somewhat different tack by attributing this strategy, not to the text, but to the formalist/humanists, whom she accuses of "the displacement of political questions" by a "moral criticism" that focuses on the ethical instead of the social distinction between Don John and Don Pedro and so fails to recognize that these characters are engaged in a kind of class struggle (1987b, 165, 174). Yet she admits that the play itself "produce[s] moral differences" between the two men "in ways that obscure the social differences . . . held in place by moral categories" (176), so the displacement is perpetrated by the text after all, and the critics are only guilty of accepting it at face value.[5] In these Marxist readings, the displacement proceeds from the social to the sexual, but the neo-Freudian version works in the opposite direction: David Sundelson claims that, in *The Merchant of Venice*, Shylock's Jewish "strangeness distracts Venetians . . . from the more mysterious and perhaps more frightening strangeness of women," and therefore "anti-Semitism . . . serves as a screen for misogyny" (1983, 88), and Harry Berger finds that on "the surface level" of *Macbeth* "the masculine/feminine conflict is displaced . . . under the disguise of the battle between Good and Evil" (1982, 73). Both groups of critics know that professions of morality are displacements of much more basic and much less noble motives, although they disagree on what those motives are; the belief that people can really do things for moral reasons is another formalist/humanist fallacy.

The text conceals. The most important things it conceals are the contradictions in its own ideological project. In "many of Shakespeare's comedies," says Howard, "the ending ... attempts to smooth over, or erase, the contradictions or fissures which have opened in the course of the play" (1987b, 180); Catherine Belsey states that "the strategies of the classic realist text divert the reader from what is contradictory within it" (1980, 128); and Dollimore agrees with "Brecht's claim that bourgeois theatre aims at 'smoothing over contradictions'" (1993, 67–68). Sometimes it is said that the formalist/humanists conceal any contradiction because of their belief in "organic unity," which is another one of their fallacies: Dollimore adds that Brecht's account of the aims of bourgeois theater "applies equally to them" (68), and Howard and Belsey blame these critics as well as the text for this concealment.[6] The neo-Freudian version of concealment is typically *repression* or *suppression,* which is now attributed not to individual characters (or to the author) but to the text itself; and what it represses is typically a feminine or maternal "subtext" that conflicts with, and often exposes the true nature of, the dominant patriarchy (and so is homologous to the Marxists' contradictions within the dominant ideology). Coppélia Kahn refers to "the repressed mother" in "the patriarchal world" of *King Lear* (1986, 40), and Louis Montrose, in his essay on *A Midsummer Night's Dream*, says that "the play would suppress" any "traces" of "the seductive and destructive powers of women" (1988, 45). But the terms seem to be interchangeable, for Dollimore and Sinfield can speak of ideological conflict that "is suppressed in *Henry V*" and that "the play represses" (1985, 217) and Timothy Murray of "a concealed but radical woman's vision of things" in *Othello* (1985, 75).[7]

The text is silent. This is the ultimate concealment, and it is usually directed at the same kind of target—elements of the situation in the play or in the Renaissance world (which, we saw, is the real subject of these plays) that would expose contradictions in the dominant ideology. Belsey refers to "the omissions which [the text] displays" and "its absences" (1980, 109) and Malcolm Evans to "what it endeavours to keep silent" (1986, 48); Howard says she "will focus precisely on the silences," as well as the "contradictions," in *Much Ado about Nothing* (1987b, 164); and Dollimore discusses "the history which [*Measure for Measure*] contains yet does not represent" (1994b, 73).[8] The neo-Freudian equivalent of silence is usually the *exclusion*—often said to be *conspicuous*—of characters, who are always women: Janet Adelman sees a "radical exclusion of the female" at the end of *Macbeth* and a "strikingly motherless world" in *The Tempest* (1987, 109, 91); Kahn refers to the "conspicuous omission" of Lear's wife (1986, 35); "Prospero's wife," according to Stephen Orgel, "is a figure conspicuous by her absence" (1988, 217);[9] and Montrose finds that "the relationship between mother and daughter" is "conspicuously excluded" from *A Midsummer Night's Dream*, while "the mother's part is wholly excluded" (1988, 40). Of course, the conspicuousness of these exclusions depends entirely on the critic's prior knowledge of what should be included in the play, but the same can be said of the audibility of the Marxists' silences.

The text makes offers we should refuse. The most general of these is the offer of a *subject position* for viewing and judging the action. As Belsey puts it, the "text proffers a specific subject-position from which it is most readily intelligible" (1985b, 6). This may seem to be merely a new way of stating the belief of the formalist/humanists that a skillful dramatist shapes the audience's response by establishing within the play the perspective from which it should be interpreted. They assumed, however, that this was a good thing for the dramatist to do and that it was a good thing for them to ascertain and adopt this perspective in order to get at the real meaning of the play, which was the meaning the author meant. But in the new discourse, which has eliminated the author and authorial meaning, this offer of a subject position is bad, for it now becomes a strategy to *implicate* us in, or make us *complicit* with, the text's ideological project. Edward Snow warns that *Othello* "invites our complicity" in the "false consciousness that shapes . . . the world of the play" (1980, 387); according to Belsey, formalist/humanist criticism "becomes the accomplice of [the] ideology" of the play (1980, 109); Howard says this criticism "has been complicit" in the "ideological effects" of *Much Ado* (1987b, 176); and Barker and Hulme claim that it has "often been complicit" with the "colonialist ideology" of *The Tempest* (1985, 104). That is why McLuskie wants us to "resist the position which the text offers" (1994, 92). The text also makes more specific offers at various points, the most important of which occur at or near the conclusion.

The text offers scapegoats. This is actually another form of displacement, involving the onus of guilt rather than the issue at stake in the action. The two are often related, however, as in the passage quoted earlier from Dollimore, which states that the cause of the problems in *Measure for Measure* is displaced not only from the social to the sexual arena but also "from the rulers to the ruled"; he later explains that responsibility for the "disorder generated by misrule . . . is ideologically displaced on to the ruled," whose sexual behavior is "demonised" by "the scapegoat mentality" of the rulers (1994b, 73, 78). Sundelson claims that the displacement of misogyny onto anti-Semitism in *The Merchant of Venice* makes Shylock "an excellent scapegoat" (1983, 88). Berger says we are "invited to contribute to the scapegoating" of the witches in *Macbeth*, who "appear as scapegoats of the masculine imagination," for through them the "dialectic of gender conflict" is "concealed" and "displaced," as noted earlier, "under the disguise of the battle between Good and Evil" (1982, 73–74). In Adelman's view, since "ferocious maleness is the creation of the male community, not of Lady Macbeth or the witches, the women are scapegoats who exist partly to obscure the failures of male community" (1987, 119). Howard says that *Much Ado* "polices" its ideological project "by creating [the] villainous" Don John, since "in the ideological economy of the play it is useful" for him to serve as "a scapegoat figure" (1987b, 182, 175). Carol Cook finds in this play a "strategy" wherein "Claudio's guilt is displaced on to Borachio and ultimately on to Don John," who "function as scapegoats, deflecting attention from the unresolved" problems at the end (1995, 97, 76–77). Snow claims that *Othello* gives us Iago to "serve as a scapegoat," for the character "is really only the name and local habitation of an invisible spirit within Othello and the texture of his world," and Iago's punishment "reveals the complicity of the forms of justice . . . [in his] own villainy" (1980, 385–87). And Stallybrass says the threat of "subversion" of "the social order" is

> localized and demonized in the figure of Iago. Thus the play allows those who laughed at the misogynistic jokes [of 2.1] to misrecognize in Desdemona's dead body the workings of "a devil." . . . The discursive contradictions that generate the text are displaced from the center to the periphery. For Iago is the projection of a social hierarchy's unease in the hypostatized form of envy. And the complicities of the dominant culture in [Desdemona's death] are reinterpreted as the marginal operations of an individual. (1986, 140)[10]

I did not note any difference between the Marxist and the neo-Freudian treatments of this strategy. In both, the scapegoating always proceeds in the same direction, from the hegemonic characters or their society to a nonhegemonic individual. And both adopt the same rationale: the critics do not claim that the scapegoat is innocent (they scarcely could) but insist that the scapegoaters are also guilty of or "complicit" in the scapegoat's crimes; indeed, they, or rather their class ideology or misogyny, should be seen as the real source of evil in the play and in the Renaissance world (and in our world as well). The play's offer of a scapegoat to absorb all the blame is designed to prevent us from seeing this, which is why it should be refused.

The text offers an imaginary resolution. These texts work very hard to reach resolutions—Barker and Hulme speak of "the lengths to which the play has to go" in its "drive to closure" (1985, 204), Cook of its "drive towards comic closure" (1995, 100), and Dollimore and Sinfield of its "drive for ideological coherence" (1985, 222)—but they never succeed, because they can only offer bogus ones. Snow asserts that "there is neither transcendence nor catharsis in *Othello*, although false appearances of both abound" (1980, 385). Stallybrass says that "Othello's final speech permits an imaginary resolution in which [Venice] is reenclosed" against "the demonized Other" (1986, 140). According to Dollimore and Sinfield, *Henry V* "offers a displaced imaginary resolution of one of the state's most intractable problems" (1985, 225). Howard finds that the ending of *Much Ado* is based on "a kind of wish fulfillment or magical thinking" and adds that "Shakespeare's romantic comedies often provide such utopian resolutions to the strains and contradictions of the period" (1987b, 179, 182). "In so far as it avoids what is crucial to its conflicts," says Cook, "the explicitly offered comic resolution [of *Much Ado*] is something of an artful dodge" (1995, 76). In Kavanagh's reading, *King Lear* presents "an imaginary resolution of irreconcilable class projects" (1985, 157). The ending of *The Taming of the Shrew*, Karen Newman claims, is a "sexual/political fantasy . . . that the play projects as an imaginary resolution of contradictions which are . . . present[ed] as seemingly reconciled"; it is "an imaginary or formal solution to unresolvable social contradictions" (1987b, 134, 144–45).[11] And Dollimore states that in *Measure for Measure* "through a process of displacement an imaginary . . . resolution of real social tension and conflict is attempted," which he calls "a fantasy resolution," a "wish-fulfilment of the status quo" (1994b, 74, 84). Again, there does not seem to be a significant difference between Marxists and neo-Freudians on this strategy. For both, the proffered ending is deceptive because it does not resolve the basic problem of class or gender that, it was noted earlier, is supposed to be the real source of evil in the play and in the Renaissance world. Thus, we are told that Iago's punishment will "reconstitute society in terms of the same impotent dialectic of [male] violence . . . that caused its rupture" (Snow 1980, 385); that "there can be no resolution" in *Macbeth* "so long as the . . . ideology of restoration prevails, for it will only enable, by concealing, the ongoing dialectic of gender conflict" (Berger 1982, 73); that the final speeches in *The Merchant of Venice* "stress the profound uneasiness that sex continues to inspire" (Sundelson 1983, 84); that the "anxieties about language and gender" have "not been dispelled" at the end of *Much Ado* and that "Messina's masculine ethos survives unchanged" (Cook 1995, 77, 100); and so on. That is why the resolution offered by the text is "imaginary" or "utopian" or a "wish fulfillment" and therefore should be refused. These critics never explain what would make an acceptable ending, but from their arguments we can infer that it would require a complete transformation of the play's social structure (for the Marxists) or of the psyches of its male characters (for the neo-Freudians) that eliminated all class or gender conflict.[12] In the peculiar logic of this new discourse, only such an ending, apparently, would *not* be an imaginary and utopian wish fulfillment.

The text offers pleasure. The contention that this is another deceptive strategy that we must reject may puzzle the uninitiated reader, who could be pardoned for thinking, along with virtually all commentators on the subject from the Greeks down to the present, that pleasure is one of the things we go to literature for. But these critics do not think so. Many of them never mention it (indeed, one might call the omission conspicuous), but those who acknowledge that pleasure is evoked by the plays do this only to warn us against it: we are told by Brown that the "pleasurable narrative" of *The Tempest* "seeks... to mystify the political conditions" of colonialism (1994, 48), by Snow that *Othello*'s "most dramatically satisfying moments of clarification and release work to dissemble the true grounds of its woe" (1980, 386), and by Cook that, "although Beatrice's outburst [*Much Ado*, 4.1.301–7] is extremely gratifying," it is "important to recognize that her fury imitates" the "brutal, irrational masculinity" that is also the true ground of all the woe in this play (1995, 91–92).[13] These warnings follow logically from the conception of the text and its strategies that we are tracing, for pleasure is seen as a kind of bait offered by the text, along with the punishment of the scapegoat and the closure at the end (both of which are themselves, of course, pleasurable), to make us complicit in its ideological project. That is why this offer, too, should be refused.

The Bad Moves that have just been surveyed are all strategies designed to serve the textual project. The Good Moves, by contrast, all work to defeat this project or to enable the right kind of critic to defeat it—they are good, that is, for us but bad for the text, just as the preceding moves are bad for us but good for the text. They are therefore not strategies at all but things that the text seems to do against its will, or would do against its will if it had a will. I will look at the most important of them.

The text gets nervous. The uninitiated reader may have assumed that inanimate objects have no nervous systems, but with The Death of the Author the text acquires human emotions, as well as purposes. These emotions are usually triggered when the text confronts its own contradictions or its feminine subtext, and they are therefore good, since they help the critics to locate these weak spots in the textual project, which can then become sites for critical "intervention." Barker and Hulme, in their reading of *The Tempest*, refer to "the text's anxiety concerning the very matters of domination and resistance," "the text's own anxiety about the threat posed to its decorum," and its "disquiet concerning its own functions within the projects of colonialist discourse" (1985, 198, 203–4); Brown says that "the play oscillates uneasily between mystification and revelation" (1994, 64); Terry Eagleton finds that at its end *A Midsummer Night's Dream* "dismiss[es] itself nervously as a dream" and that in *Antony and Cleopatra* "the play [is] both fearful and admiring" of the heroine's "feminine" qualities (1986, 26, 88); Sundelson, in his study of *The Merchant of Venice*, comments on "the play's fearfulness about women" (1983, 84); according to Evans, some of the language of *Macbeth* "sits uneasily in the text" (1986, 118); in her reading of *The Four Elements*, Belsey claims that "the text betrays its unease" about its ideology; she also speaks of "the unease of the formal disjunction between unity and discontinuity" in *Doctor Faustus* and, in discussing *Mariam*, of "the play's consistent unease about its heroine's right to speak" (1985b, 68, 45, 173). These critics never say that the text is *feeling* anxious or uneasy or fearful, which would sound even stranger, but what else could they mean?

The text reveals (discloses, exposes, etc.). *Reveals* seems to be the verb most favored by these critics to denote how the text defeats its own project or helps them do this, and one may easily see why. The verb elides (a less kind interrogator might claim that it occludes) the problem of intentionality, even in the active voice, since we can say that people reveal things advertently or inadvertently, and even inanimate objects can reveal something. But it always means that what is revealed must really be in the text prior to the revelation, a point I will return to later. The word implies, moreover, that what is revealed is not immediately evident, which is important because this revelation always turns out to be precisely what the text is trying to *conceal* or *suppress*, its ideological contradictions or feminine subtext, and thus precisely what the critics want to find there. Howard says that a passage in *Much Ado* "reveal[s] the potential contradictions" in "the patriarchal order" (1987b, 180); Brown finds that the exposition in *The Tempest* "reveals internal contradictions which strain its ostensible project" (1994, 59); Montrose tells us that "the text of *A Midsummer Night's Dream* discloses—perhaps, in a sense, despite itself—that patriarchal norms are compensatory for the vulnerability of men to the powers of women" (1988, 45); and many similar passages could be quoted. This connection between *concealing* and *revealing* is often made more explicit: in Cook's essay on *Much Ado*, "the play masks, as well as exposes, the mechanisms of masculine power," and the end "suppresses but simultaneously exposes" its sexual tensions (1995, 76, 100); Brown says that *The Tempest*'s project involves the "euphemisation" or "effacement of power—yet . . . the play also reveals precisely" the power structure that "actually underpins it" (1994, 64), and we just saw that he has the play oscillating "between mystification and revelation" (64); and Dollimore and Sinfield state that "the actual purpose of the war . . . is suppressed in *Henry V*—yet it twice surfaces obliquely" (1985, 217). Sometimes, as in this last quotation, the revelation is qualified to suggest that it is having a hard time evading the text's concealment strategy. Thus we get "obliquely revealing" (Cook 1995, 100), "hints . . . but only obliquely" (Howard 1987b, 182), "partially reveals" (Dollimore 1994b, 84), "glimpsed" (Belsey 1985a, 183, 188, 189, 190), "laid bare . . . if only for a moment" (Barker and Hulme 1985, 202), "revealing . . . if only momentarily" and "momentarily revealed" (Brown 1994, 66, 67), and so on. And a few critics reveal that the text may require some outside assistance in these revelations—McLuskie speaks of "making a text reveal" (1994, 106); Howard says that "under the pressure of a political analysis" the play "reveals" its "strategy" (1987b, 183); and Brown states that he has "attempt[ed] a repunctuation of the play so that it may reveal" its "ideological contradictions" (1994, 69). The equivalent verb for the neo-Freudians is frequently *suggests*, which is used in a similar manner to show that the text contains what the critic is looking for.[14]

The text can/may be read/seen/discerned as. This locution is also a favorite of these critics and itself can be read as another version of the *reveals* usage—in fact, the two are sometimes combined, as in "the play can be read to reveal." They are similar in that they both have the text divulging the *concealed* or *suppressed* material that undermines its project, for what the text "can be read as" is always precisely what it does *not* want to be read as, which is what the critic wants to read it as. According to Howard, one episode in *Much Ado* "can be read" as showing "the process by which the powerful determine truth," while another "can be read as an acknowledgment" of the power relations in the play (1987b, 179-80); Stallybrass tells us that "Iago can be seen as a function of the projected fears of class hierarchy" (1986, 141); and Brown says that the plot of *The Tempest* "may be discerned as displacement" and that its "colonialist discourse may be discerned as an instrument of exploitation" (1994, 66, 68).

But the usage is so common that further quotations are unnecessary. It differs from *reveals* because it seems to be making a more modest claim, by implying that the text can be read in other ways. But it also implies that there are ways in which the text *cannot* be read and hence that there must be something in the text that justifies the contention that it "can be read" the critic's way.

The text taketh, but the text giveth (itself) away. I have chosen this phraseology of an older discourse to sum up the overall pattern resulting from the oppositions that have been traced between the play's ideological project and its contradictions, the masculine fantasy and feminine subtext, the Bad Moves and Good Moves, and the concealing and revealing; but this pattern is best described in the summary statements of the critics themselves. (1) The "play speaks against itself"; its ideology "is both secured against threats to itself and also laid open to their demystifying power." (2) The play "exposes the process it trades on" and "is partly a record of its own limitations." (3) The play "implicitly criticizes its own ideology; it contains within itself the critique of its own values." (4) The play "destabilizes the reconciliation effect that [it] seeks to achieve within a given cultural ideology." (5) The play is "clinging to Elizabethan patriarchal ideology and at the same time tearing it away." (6) "At the same time that the play reaffirms essential elements of a patriarchal ideology, it also calls that reaffirmation in question" and "at once sanctions and subverts the doctrine of domestic hierarchy." (7) The play "dramatises the material conditions which lie behind assertions of power within the family, even as it expresses deep anxieties about . . . the threat to the family posed by female insubordination." (8) "Even as [the play's ideology] consolidates, it betrays inherent instability." (9) The play's "operations encode struggle and contradiction even as they . . . strive to insist on the legitimacy" of its ideology.[15] And from these statements we can derive the basic conception of the text that emerges when it takes over The Author Function. Put in the simplest terms, the text is personified, reified, mystified, hypostatized, alterized, and demonized and so is constructed as the enemy, bent on defeating us; but it is a very vulnerable enemy that can easily be defeated. Its project is to lie, yet even as it lies it reveals the truth—to the right critics.

We are now in a position to answer the question that must have troubled the uninitiated reader who was trying to follow the reasoning of these critics: why do all the plays exhibit this pattern?—or (what is really the same question), how do the critics know that all the plays exhibit this pattern? The answer cannot lie in anything peculiar to the plays themselves, for these critics find the same pattern in many other texts that seem to be quite different, and so we had better look for our explanation in the two ideologies that the critics bring with them. For both these ideologies claim to give us the fundamental cause of all human behavior, and this cause must therefore determine the nature of these plays. In the Marxist version, the economic "base" is the ultimate cause of all aspects of the "superstructure," including ideology and literature. And since in every presocialist society this base is beset by "contradictions" (the term is usually preceded by "irreconcilable" or "unresolvable"), the hegemonic ideology of such a society will also contain them, and they will therefore appear in the literary texts that are produced by and produce this ideology. It is true that many revisionist Marxists claim a more autonomous status for ideology and so must seek some rationale to account for its strange habit of exposing its own weaknesses—thus Howard reports that "much contemporary work on ideology suggests that a dominant ideology . . . always bears traces of the contestatory or subversive elements it has attempted to recuperate" (1987a, 355).[16] Yet her use of "always" suggests that those investigatory workers always already knew what they would find, since we are placed in the presence of a general law. (This may seem surprising, because these critics object to the belief in "universal truths" or "eternal verities," which they regard as another formalist/humanist fallacy; but since they clearly have some of their own, the real objection must be that their adversaries believe in the wrong ones.) This law, moreover, explains all the Bad and Good Moves of the text that we surveyed, or, rather, it explains how the critics always already know that these strategies will turn up in the text. The law tells them that, no matter what the text may seem to be about, it must really be about some contemporary economic or social conflict that is "displaced" onto another arena; that no matter how "silent" the text may be about elements of this conflict, it must really contain them; that no matter how unified the text may appear, it must really be fissured by contradictions that are "concealed"; that no matter how guilty the villains may seem, they must really be the "scapegoats" of the hegemonic society, where the principal guilt resides; that no matter how satisfactory the resolution may appear, it must really be "imaginary," because the contradictions it seems to resolve are by definition unresolvable; and finally, that no matter how hard the text tries to marshal all these strategies for the success of its project, it must really "reveal" the failure of that project, since, like the socioeconomic system in which it is implicated, it always carries within itself the seeds of its own destruction.

It should be evident by now that these critics, despite their disclaimers, not only believe in universal truths but are also guilty of another formalist/ humanist fallacy noted at the outset—the idea that we can attain objective knowledge of the real meaning of a text. They regularly reject this idea: Evans insists that "there is no such thing as the object as in itself it really is" (a reference, of course, to Matthew Arnold's definition of criticism) and that "all reading [is] an intervention . . . rather than a simple decoding" (1986, 85, 137); Howard asks us to "break with [the humanists'] fundamental assumptions about the nature of interpretation as the uncovering of 'what is already there'" (1987a, 340); according to Belsey, materialist criticism "is not a process of recognition but work to produce meaning" (1980, 138); Dollimore and Sinfield, in the foreword to *Political Shakespeare*, explain that this approach "does not, like much established literary criticism, attempt to mystify its perspective as the natural, obvious or right interpretation of an allegedly given textual fact" (1994a, viii); McLuskie speaks of the "spurious notion of objectivity" (1994, 91–92); and Barker calls any appeal to it "hubristic objectivism" (1984, 15). Yet their assertions that the text "reveals" things make sense only if those things are actually in the text, prior to any critical intervention, and even the "can be read as" locution, we saw, implies some access to given textual facts. Moreover, because of their assumption that the text is really about social conflicts in Shakespeare's time, these critics know not only what it "reveals" but also what it tries to "conceal" or "displace." Dollimore and Sinfield identify the "real historical conflict" in *Henry V* and "the actual purpose of the war" (1985, 225, 217); Brown explains what "is really at issue" in *The Tempest*, what "actually underpins" the play, and what its ending "is in fact" about (1994, 60, 64, 67); McLuskie discusses the "real socio-sexual relations in *King Lear*" (1994, 100); and, of course, all those contradictions must actually be there if they have to be "concealed" by the text (or by formalist/ humanist criticism).[17] Whenever these critics claim to know what the text "conceals" or "displaces," therefore, they are committing the sin of hubristic objectivism. And we found that they even claim to know what the text is "silent" about, which is surely as hubristically objectivist as one can get.

In the Freudian scheme of things, the basic cause of behavior lies in the individual psyche—primarily in the unconscious part, which determines many of our conscious thoughts and actions. And since in every pretherapized person the unconscious is beset by deep conflicts, they will necessarily appear in the productions of that person, including literary texts. Thus Freudian critics (both orthodox and revisionist) always already know that, no matter what the text may seem to be about, it is really about an unconscious conflict that is "displaced" onto another arena; and they always already know the nature of this conflict, for they, too, are governed by a universal law. Unlike the Marxists' law, however, theirs has undergone a remarkable change in our own day (which is why I need the *neo-* prefix). It used to tell them that this conflict must derive from the "Oedipal" rivalry of the male characters with their fathers, but because of the recent swerve in psychoanalytic theory, the conflict now always derives from their "pre-Oedipal" dependence on their mothers, which is embodied in a feminine or maternal "subtext" that, we noted earlier, subverts or exposes the dominant patriarchy of the play's world. That is why Kahn can assert that "the psychological presence of the mother in men whether or not mothers are represented in the texts they write or in which they appear as characters, can be found throughout the literary canon" (1986, 37) and then proceed to interpret *King Lear* in this light; it is also why Sundelson can be certain that, although *The Merchant of Venice* presents a "conflict about fatherly possessiveness," this conflict is not as significant as the "more fundamental" and "much more threatening" male fear of "maternal engulfment" (1983, 76, 83, 86).[18] And the basic similarity of the two causal schemes makes it easy for Marxists to adopt the Freudian concept of "displacement," since both schemes proceed "from below upwards"—from the one universal cause to its many particular effects, from base to superstructure, from unconscious to conscious, from the real displaced subject of the text to the apparent subject that displaces it. Unlike the Freudians, however, the Marxists have no psychic mechanism to explain why this displaced material always comes back to the surface, which, we saw, causes them some difficulty; but they can get around it by endowing the personified text with a Freudian psyche, as when Brown refers to the "*political* unconscious" of *The Tempest* (1994, 69; the term comes from Jameson 1981) or Belsey to an ideological "return of the repressed" (1985b, 94), although it seems possible that "the repressed" that is returning here could be the author himself, killed off and then resurrected in this disguised form.

This problem brings us, finally, to the political implications of killing the author—or, rather, of the discursive practices we have examined that result from this killing. Of course, in one sense of the term—the new, expanded sense promoted by these discourses themselves—we have been talking about politics all along, because the Marxists insist, as was noted at the outset, that every interpretation is determined by the interpreter's class bias, so that it is impossible to separate criticism from politics; and the neo-Freudians, similarly, assert that all interpretations are implicated in "sexual politics." But many Marxists also claim to be politically engaged in the narrower and older sense, for they regularly end their articles and books with calls for action to change society. The title of Belsey's final chapter is

"Changing the Present" (1985b, 222); Barker's last words urge us to "undo" the terrible thing that, he explains earlier, "was done to us in the seventeenth century" by the bourgeoisie (1984, 116, 68); Eagleton asks for "the transformation of a society divided by class and gender," and his closing sentence expresses the hope that materialist criticism "may help the lion to awaken" and overthrow the lion tamer (1983, 210, 217); and Dollimore and Sinfield conclude their foreword to *Political Shakespeare* by asserting that cultural materialism "registers its commitment to the transformation of a social order which exploits people on the grounds of race, gender and class" (1994a, viii).[19]

These calls to political action, however, are always very brief and very vague. They never explain what the goal is, though one can guess that it would be some form of socialism (totally unlike any existing forms) based on true freedom and justice; or how it can be achieved, although that presumably would require a revolution by the oppressed working-class "lion"; or how this process is promoted by writing literary criticism. As Edward Pechter observes, "If transforming an exploitative social order should be the prime directive of one's activity, then there are simply more effective ways of proceeding" (1987, 300). We may be forgiven for suspecting, then, that these concluding statements are a kind of ritual—or, one might even say, an imaginary, fantasy resolution of the critics' need for "commitment"—that cannot be taken at face value, especially since the critics themselves tell us that taking professions of moral purpose at face value is a formalist/humanist fallacy and that we should always look instead for more realistic and less noble motives.

What, then, seem to be the real "political" motives behind this mode of discourse, which has displaced and replaced the author? We can find the answer, I think, by comparing it with an older formalist/humanist approach to which it bears a striking resemblance. In that approach, deployed in the Shakespearean field by Harold Goddard (1951), Roy Battenhouse (1969), and many New Critics (and represented here by the "weak" intentionalist readings in Berger 1982 and Snow 1980), the play is divided into two opposed levels of meaning—the apparent, or surface, meaning, which seems to present the main characters and their values in a favorable light and has misled earlier critics, and the real, deep, ironic meaning discovered by the more perceptive critic, which undercuts these characters and values.[20] The Marxist readings we have examined seem to be based on the same formula with a new terminology: the apparent, surface meaning has become the text's ideological project, promoted by the Bad Moves, which, as in the old New Critical version, took in previous commentators (who are now the old

New Critics), and this level is undercut by the real, ironic meaning, now embodied in the contradictions revealed by the Good Moves, which the Marxists discover. Indeed, the Marxists often use adjectives such as *apparent*, *supposed*, *seeming*, and *ostensible* to describe the first level of meaning and *real* and *actual*, as we saw, for the second, just as the formalist/humanists did.[21]

The crucial difference between these two formulas, of course, is that the older critics claimed that they were interpreting the intention of the author, who deliberately created the deceptive, apparent meaning and deliberately subverted it in order to convey the real, ironic meaning, whereas the Marxists, having eliminated the concept of authorial intention—or, rather, transferred it to the textual project—assert that the real, ironic meaning is revealed inadvertently by the text, as if against its will. But since the formulas are otherwise so similar, we should be able to answer our question about the Marxists' motives by determining what they have gained by this change, which seems to define the principal effect that The Death of the Author has had on their actual interpretations. One advantage is that the change avoids the difficult problem of explaining why the author made the apparent meaning so persuasive that the audience is very easily taken in by it, and conveyed the real meaning so unobtrusively (or ineffectively) that it escaped notice up to now, because in the Marxist version the text wants the audience to be taken in by the apparent meaning and does not want the real meaning to be noticed.

A second advantage of the change is that it avoids the need to attribute the critic's own beliefs to the author or the text. In both versions, of course, the real meaning always turns out to be an idea the critic endorses, for this is the inevitable result—or purpose?—of the division into real and apparent meanings. Thus the formalist/humanists, since they claimed that the real meaning was intentional, had to demonstrate that the author shared their views on life. In the field of Shakespearean studies this seldom presented any special problem, because the critics typically found that the views affirmed by the plays were some vague moral platitudes (those "eternal verities" we encountered earlier) that Shakespeare might have believed. The Marxists, however, find that the real meaning of the plays confirms their conceptions of ideology and class conflict, which, according to their own historical scenario, could not be understood until a later period (see, for example, Kavanagh 1985, 149). By killing off the author, therefore, they are able to make the plays reveal Marxist truths without making Shakespeare a premature Marxist. (The neo-Freudians solve this problem by claiming either that the truths revealed by the feminine subtext emerged, unbidden and unrecognized, from Shakespeare's own unconscious or that the playwright intuitively understood these truths without having to read about them in Nancy Chodorow.)

These two advantages of The Death of the Author are rather obvious, for they enable the Marxists to retain the most desirable feature of the ironic intentionalist readings—to prove, that is, that the play is really saying what the critic wants it to say—while avoiding the difficulties of those readings. But there may also be another, more subtle advantage that involves the altered relationship between the critic and the play. All modes of interpretation construct such relationships, which can be arranged in a sequence. Most educated lay spectators or readers see the play as a friendly object to be accepted and enjoyed on the terms it offers (this is also the view of the older critical tradition, as I noted in connection with the text's offer of pleasure). For many of the New Critics, the play is a thematic puzzle to be solved by a "close reading," which brings its own pleasure. And those who adopted the ironic approach I just discussed must regard the play as a trick to be seen through, although they maintain that the author wanted the audience (or at least some of them) to see through it. But the Marxists, at the far end of this sequence, treat the play as an enemy to be fought. We saw that the discursive practices they deploy to replace the author construct each play as the enemy, but we also saw that they construct it as a vulnerable enemy that is easily defeated or that defeats itself. Thus The Death of the Author enables these critics to wage—and to win—a kind of class war against the forces of evil, embodied in the text's hegemonic ideology, and therefore to achieve in this displaced and "imaginary" arena their avowed political goals. It is impossible to prove such a motivation, which presumably would not be recognized, and I only offer it as a hypothesis, but it might explain the solemnity with which many of these critics enter into what they call "the struggle for meaning"[22] in each reading and the sense of triumph when they reach the foregone conclusion, as if this somehow brought us closer to that "transformation of society."

A final political implication that we should look at is the rhetoric of "liberation" that has accompanied announcements of The Death of the Author ever since they first appeared. Foucault argues that the author is an "ideological product" of "bourgeois society" and functions as a "constraining figure" that "impedes the free circulation" and the "free manipulation" of fiction (1979, 159); and Barthes maintains that literature has been "tyrannically centred on the author," who is used to "impose a limit" on the text, so that removing the author will be a "truly revolutionary" act that "liberates" the reader (1977, 143, 147). This idea of freeing texts and readers has been taken up by many of the critics we are considering: Belsey says, "The

Death of the Author . . . means the liberation of the text," allowing criticism "to release possible meanings" in the text, as if they were imprisoned there (1980, 134, 144); Howard calls on critics to "break free" from the formalist/humanist assumptions that "still inhibit" them (1986a, 43); and Eagleton even claims that this move will lead to "the liberation of Shakespeare" (1983, 217). Yet we discovered that in the readings produced by this liberation the texts sound very much alike, and so do the critics, because the "possible meanings" that these readings "release" usually turn out to be the same one meaning. The explanation is simple enough and has already been indicated. The rejection of The Author Function is not just a negation, the removal of a constraint, since it creates a hermeneutic vacuum that must be filled by something else that replaces authorial intention as the determinant of meaning. And for these critics, we saw, what fills the vacuum is a universal law—the Law of Concealed-But-Revealed Ideological Contradiction (or, for the neo-Freudians, the Law of the Absent-Yet-Omnipresent Mother)—that dictates what one must look for, and must find, in every play. The Death of the Author, then, has left these critics not more but less free—certainly less free than a comparable group of formalist/humanists trying to interpret Shakespeare's intended meaning. And that, I think, is the most important lesson to be derived from the poetics and politics of Bardicide.

A Letter to the *PMLA* Forum

Richard Levin's "The Poetics and Politics of Bardicide" is, to speak generously, disingenuous in the extreme. A similar collection of favored technical terms and phrases could be produced for any theoretical school whatsoever, including New Criticism, where our exhibits would include such terms as *ambiguity*, *irony*, *organic unity*, and so on. This is such an oft-told tale by now that I find it hard to believe, much less understand, the apparent approbation of this demagoguery by the topic coordinator of the issue, who remarks that Levin's essay has forever cured him of the use of the word *projects!* Although many aspects of Levin's rhetoric can be exposed as such, given the limitations of the format I will analyze only one particularly egregious bit of his sophistry.

Levin caricatures practitioners of "new historicism" and "cultural materialism" as cultural commissars prescribing what would be a "more acceptable" way for Shakespeare to have written his texts. Levin complains of readings that insist that the text provides an imaginary resolution while it in fact leaves the text-generating conflicts in place:

> These critics never explain what would make an acceptable ending, but from their arguments we can infer that it would require a complete transformation of the play's social structure (for the Marxists) or of the psyches of its male characters (for the neo-Freudians) that eliminated all class or gender conflict. In the peculiar logic of this new discourse [I am surprised that the term *discourse* has not been anathematized like *project*—DB], only such an ending, apparently, would *not* be an imaginary and utopian wish fulfillment.

It must surely be obvious to any reader of this criticism that the critics in question do not indicate that the endings of the plays are "unacceptable" or suggest in any way that Shakespeare could have or should have written the endings differently; these critics only state that the problems of society and culture that the plays manifest remained unsolvable within the context of the Renaissance social formation. The resolution, then, that the ending claims to provide is *false*, and it only makes the intractability of the social conflicts and contradictions all the more palpable.

Further, and along the same lines, Levin produces another in his list of cartoonlike "Bad Moves" that new historicists and others write about:

> **The text offers pleasure.** The contention that this is another deceptive strategy that we must reject may puzzle the uninitiated reader, who could be pardoned for thinking, along with virtually all commentators on the subject from the Greeks down to the present, that pleasure is one of the things we go to literature for.

To expose the fallacy of this remark, all we need to do is to replace the words "text" and "reader" with "cocaine" and "user" or with "pimp" and "john." That users go to cocaine pushers for the pleasure of doing a line or johns to a pimp for the pleasure of having a prostitute does not mean that social critics ought not to condemn the strategies of panderers as deceptive ones that we must reject. Now I do not propose, of course, that the pleasures of literature are as pernicious as the pleasures of cocaine, but I believe that the analogy exposes the underlying postulate of Levin and others of his ilk—namely, that literary criticism (as opposed to all other academic disciplines) is exactly the same practice as literary consumption, except that criticism is done more skillfully. According to them, literary study in the university is comparable in function to the swimming pool rather than to the department of sports medicine, to the dining room rather than to the department of nutrition. Such departments are necessary, of course, because not all is healthy with our practice of sports or of eating. If critique of the pleasures of Shakespeare is not appropriate, it follows that all *is* right with the practice of that pleasure. In short, Levin and his ilk are just as political as the politicized critics that they attack. Levin simply wishes to affirm the values asserted on the surface of texts like *The Tempest* and *The Taming of the Shrew;* other critics disavow those values. But what shall we do, after all, with *The Merchant of Venice*—simply take our pleasures there as well?

New historicists, cultural materialists, and feminists have at least one great virtue that Levin seems to consider unnecessary, the virtue of candor. They make clear what interests they choose to serve in producing their critical studies of literature. "Critics" like Levin, on the contrary, pretend that they are serving no interests but only protecting literature from the Sam the Eagletons of the ivory tower who want to take away the readers' fun. In fact—and though this should be by now commonplace, the publication of such an inept tirade shows that it isn't—they serve only the continued dominance of a particular gender, class, and culture. The appeal to common sense and common language and the caricaturing of the "jargon" of other critics should be exposed for what they are: a cynical attempt to enlist "the uninitiated" as unwitting (and perhaps unwilling) allies in the reactionary protection of the privilege of that very gender, class, and culture.

Daniel Boyarin

My Reply

Daniel Boyarin attributes arguments to me that are not mine. Although I have some fun with the locutions of the critics I discuss, I never accuse them of using "jargon," and I am well aware that every approach has its technical terms. I object to their term *project*, not because it is jargon, but because they deploy it to evade the problem of agency. And I never make an "appeal to common sense" or suggest that they are "cultural commissars" or that I am "protecting literature" from them. These are all his inventions. And some of his own arguments are simply name-calling: I am said to be "disingenuous" and "cynical" and to engage in a "tirade" featuring "caricature," "demagoguery," and "sophistry," and people like me are critics in scare quotes who belong to an "ilk." I do not descend to that tactic in my article and will not start now, even when attacked by this tirade from a "critic" of his ilk.

When this diversionary matter is cleared away, he is left with two substantive points, both of which bear out what I say about the new Marxists' practice (he wants to add the New Historicists, whom I do not focus on, but most of his remarks do not apply to them). On the question of resolutions he confirms my "caricature" of their argument that every literary text is generated by unresolvable contradictions in its society (except, presumably, texts produced in communist societies) and so its resolution must be false, imaginary, utopian, and so forth. He never tries to justify the claim that texts are always generated by these contradictions or that these contradictions are always unresolvable, nor does he confront my conclusion that, according to this reasoning, the only resolution that would not be false or utopian (I should not have used the word "acceptable") would have to present a utopia where all characters are converted to the true ideology and all social conflicts are eliminated. One of my correspondents has reminded me that this was in fact the kind of ending formerly mandated by Soviet cultural commissars in the name of "socialist realism."

In his second point he confirms another "caricature" of mine, my summary of the Marxists' argument that the text's offer of pleasure is a deceptive strategy to implicate us in its oppressive ideology and so should be rejected, and he goes even further by analogizing enjoyment of the text to using drugs or prostitutes (although this is later toned down to an analogy to exercising or eating incorrectly). Now, the moral effect of literature is a serious and complex problem that has recently been discussed by several critics, such as Wayne Booth and Martha Nussbaum, but this discussion is not advanced by Boyarin's simplistic assumption that whenever we enjoy a literary work we necessarily "affirm" all its values and act on them. That assumption is obviously false, but if it were true then perhaps we too should have cultural commissars to ensure that people do not read works with any wrong values (which would presumably include almost all works of the past) or at least do not enjoy them.

Underlying this attack on pleasure is the political polarization of criticism that I "caricature" early in my article and that he also confirms—the attempt to connect the older wrong (i.e., formalist/humanist) critical approaches to what he calls the "reactionary protection" of the "dominance of a particular gender, class, and culture" (the third term is usually *race*) and to link the newer right approaches to the liberation of the victims of that dominance. This claim has been repeated so often in recent years that some people think its truth is established (thus Boyarin expresses surprise that it is not "by now commonplace"); but it too is obviously false, for there is no necessary connection between critical approaches and political positions—we have Marxist and feminist formalists, while practitioners of the new approaches cover a wide political spectrum. And there is no connection at all between these approaches and political action. He praises the

Marxists for their "candor" in "mak[ing] clear what interests they choose to serve" (this could hardly apply to the New Historicists) but ignores the section of my article where I point out that, while these critics regularly and candidly call for a "transformation of society" in the interests of the oppressed, they are never candid about explaining what sort of transformation they have in mind or how it can be achieved or how they are promoting it by writing literary criticism, and where I quote Edward Pechter's observation that, if this actually is their goal, "then there are simply more effective ways of proceeding." Probably the most effective way today would be to proceed to Eastern Europe and try to convince people there—especially workers, women, and minorities—that they are making a terrible mistake by moving toward political pluralism and market economies, since they were much happier under their former Marxist regimes, even though they did not realize it (perhaps because they were deceived by the pleasures offered by literature with the wrong values). For the political polarities of these critics assume that oppression based on gender, class, culture, race, or anything else is caused by capitalism, bourgeois democracy, and liberal humanism (which we saw is really "reactionary") and will only be cured by communism. But this is an illusion that has been abandoned just about everywhere in the world except in the humanities departments of some universities sponsored by capitalist bourgeois democracies, and if Boyarin is still affirming it now, I think that is funnier than any of the views I caricature in my disingenuous, demagogic, cynical, sophistical tirade.

Another Letter to the *PMLA* Forum

I did not initially respond to Richard Levin's "The Poetics and Politics of Bardicide," although I was angered by the article's sneering tone and by its seemingly wanton misrepresentation of literary-critical history. In Levin's confused account of his own discipline's history, the concept of the author as a culturally produced function appears ridiculously late, as an invention of Foucault, when it has been with literary criticism from the discipline's methodological inception in the work of the Russian formalists and Prague-school structuralists. Levin's reply [to Daniel Boyarin] in the March Forum, however, asserting that the term *project* begs the question of agency and suggesting that those who criticize so-called "political pluralism and market economies" should go to Eastern Europe, continues along dangerously anti-intellectual (or at least profoundly unrigorous) and deliberately insulting lines and so compels my response.

The term *project* takes an explicit position on the subject of agency.

The word deliberately foregrounds public (here, scholarly) writing's function as a social act with concrete material consequences. I use it in my own work to acknowledge my responsibility for the observable fact that scholarly writing contributes to, endorses, or gives rise to various material outcomes. Dismissing the term as evading the issue of agency (an issue that it in fact specifically raises) does not, however, get around this condition of writing. Just because the English gained an enormous advantage from *not* applying *project* to their dissemination of the English literary tradition throughout their colonies and to their simultaneous suppression of indigenous literatures and tongues surely does not mean that these actions had no material consequences. Critical essays inspiring, lauding, or rationalizing England's promotion of its literature as superior to that produced by the cultures it dominated or retroactively endorsing this promotion are, similarly, social projects in miniature with specific material effects.

All Levin's sneering and nastiness do nothing to rid scholarship of its documentable role in advancing certain values and points of view and discouraging others. The routine and inevitable scholarly promotion and demotion—or even mischaracterization and evasion of texts, models, and values that Levin and others want to make ineligible for disciplinary scrutiny—clearly have specific and ascertainable real-world effects. Levin's own work intersects in myriad ways with communities and bodies around the world, as does everyone's. His attempts to ridicule and (hence) efface these intersections suggest that Levin would prefer not to think about what his own project might be or about what effect it might have on the social realm it inhabits.

Finally, Levin's suggestion that Marxists or those with stances critical to one or another form of capitalism should go to Eastern Europe and defend totalitarianism turns on the nasty assumption (time-honored among red-baiters and especially promoted by the HUAC) that all who criticize capitalism or specific forms of capitalism are communists and that all communists are totalitarian. By implication the remark also suggests that Levin and all capitalist boosters are ultrademocratic. None of these assumptions are correct, and I challenge Levin to come up with a less simplistic and ill-conceived account of the theoretical debates within our discipline and to better inform himself concerning the wide variety of noncapitalist economies that have existed and that now exist in our world. I also invite him to say why, since he holds Marxists responsible for explaining away the misfortunes of the Soviet Union's one-time bloc, Marxists should not expect him to tour Panama, Grenada, Nicaragua, Chile, the Philippines, Guatemala, the Occupied Territories, South Africa, Northern Ireland, Brazil, Mexico, Argentina, Kenya, India, the bombed-out ruins of Baghdad, and the ghettos of the United States and other industrialized capitalist countries and explain to the (nonelite) people he finds there that they simply don't know how very happy they really are *now*, under capitalism.

Margot FitzGerald

My Reply

Margot FitzGerald is right and I was wrong about the origins of The Death of the Author, although I would still argue that the current popularity of this concept stems directly from the essays of Barthes and Foucault, as Peter Erickson states in the sentence I quote. Her criticism of my remarks on the term *project*, however, is based on a misunderstanding. I never say that the term itself evades the issue of agency; my objection, explained in my article and in my Forum reply to Daniel Boyarin, is to the way certain critics deploy this term to evade the issue of agency in literary texts. The term *project*, that is, does not itself have a project but is used by these critics for their project. Of course, *people*, including critics, can have projects, but I want to know how a *text* can acquire an ideological project without the help of any human agency. Boyarin fails to address this question, and so does FitzGerald.

Her principal target clearly is the suggestion in my reply to Boyarin that Marxist critics attempt an intervention in Eastern Europe, which is a response to his praise of the "candor" of these critics in proclaiming their political project, namely, the replacement of capitalism by socialism. It seems obvious that the greatest threat to this project today is the collapse of socialism in that part of the world and the movement there toward political pluralism and market economies—a movement that, if successful, will probably set back the socialist cause for a very long time—and I therefore suggest that the most effective way for these critics to further their project would be to try to arrest this movement instead of writing literary criticism. FitzGerald never confronts this argument head-on but makes several indirect and often cryptic attacks on it that I would like to consider.

1. She inserts "so-called" before "political pluralism and market economies." It is a kind of potshot that allows her to cast doubt on the movement in Eastern Europe, and thus on my argument, without having to give us any reasons. She never does explain it.

2. She implies that these events in Eastern Europe are irrelevant to the Marxists' project, because the countries involved were "totalitarian." This is now a standard Marxist move designed to set up a game where any problem

in any capitalist country can be blamed on capitalism (which is apparently the point of her long list at the end), while no problem in avowedly socialist countries can be blamed on socialism, because what those countries have, despite their socialization of the land and the means of production and elimination of the profit motive, is not real socialism but an aberration—totalitarianism, Stalinism, state capitalism, or whatever—and so does not count. It is a game the Marxists must always win, but who do they think they're kidding?

3. She calls my argument "anti-intellectual." The only sense I can make of this is that she regards the Marxism of these critics as a purely intellectual exercise with no bearing on events outside the academy (this may be implied in her reference to "the theoretical debates within our discipline"), so that bringing up those events in an argument with them is like Johnson's attempt to refute Berkeley by kicking a stone. But Berkeleianism did not claim to be a program for action in the external world. If these critics will stipulate that their Marxism makes no such claim, I will be happy to withdraw my suggestion about that trip to Eastern Europe.

4. She says my argument assumes "that all who criticize capitalism . . . are communists and that all communists are totalitarian." This assumption that she attributes to me is itself an example of the polarized thinking that characterizes Marxism and that I oppose. Of course there are many people (including myself) who are critical of aspects of capitalism and are not Marxists, but I think that all the critics I call Marxists have identified themselves as such—if I am wrong I would like to know which ones I mislabel. And I am well aware that there are many kinds of Marxists, but I believe they all share the project of replacing capitalism with socialism, which is the only thing I assume about these critics in this argument.

5. She says my argument also implies that "Levin and all capitalist boosters are ultrademocratic," which is another example of Marxist polarizing. Criticism of Marxism need not imply uncritical boosting of capitalism, just as criticism of capitalism need not imply boosting of Marxism. Obviously, there have been tyrannical capitalist regimes, and I rejoice as much at their overthrow as I do at the overthrow of the Marxist tyrannies, since what I really am a booster of is "so-called" political pluralism.

6. She uses my argument to link me to "red-baiters" and "the HUAC." This is yet another example of the polarized logic of Marxists, here lumping all their opponents together, and it is all too typical of what anyone who criticizes them can now expect. If I were to retaliate (which I would not dream of doing) by linking her to the KGB or the Stasi, I am sure she would be indignant, because this kind of abuse is only supposed to proceed in one direction.

7. She tries to impugn my motives by saying I "would prefer not to think about what [my] own project might be." She never reveals what it is (perhaps to spare my feelings), but it must be pretty bad. It may be related to her contention that I want to make some critical activities "ineligible for disciplinary scrutiny." I do not know where she got this idea, for I believe that all the activities should be open to scrutiny, including my own and those of Marxist critics.

8. She asserts that my use of this argument in the reply to Boyarin is "nasty," "sneering," and "deliberately insulting," apparently because I do not take the Marxism of these critics as seriously as he (or she) does. I wonder if she thinks my reply is more insulting than his letter, which calls me, among other things, a sophist and a demagogue and an ilkist. Or does she think the people she agrees with should not be held to the same standards of civility as those she disagrees with?

3

Unthinkable Thoughts in the New Historicizing of English Renaissance Drama

THE PAST DECADE HAS SEEN A REMARKABLE RESURGENCE OF HISTORICAL STUDIES OF English Renaissance drama, most of them emanating from two groups that have come to be known as the New Historicists and the cultural materialists (or new Marxists), and from a number of feminists. These critics in fact often define themselves in terms of their opposition to what they regard as the antihistorical bias of the New Criticism, which they usually refer to as "formalism." But they also take some pains to distinguish their approach from that of the older historical critics, such as Lily Bess Campbell (1930) and E. M. W. Tillyard (1943), who preceded the New Criticism (which in turn defined itself through its opposition to them).[1] Many of these older historical critics practiced what I call the ideas-of-the-time approach, which proceeded by first discovering "the Elizabethan attitude" on some subject, usually through an extensive search of moral and religious treatises, sermons, courtesy books, and similar "authorities," and then applying it to the plays, since according to their basic argument this attitude necessarily determined the feelings of the playwright and the audience on that subject. In their critique of this approach, the new historical critics have shown that it homogenized the thought, and hence the literature, of what was really a very heterogeneous society, for the kind of evidence it relied on only presents the dominant ideology of the period, which was being contested by other ideologies or discourses in circulation then, so that we cannot assume it was simply recapitulated or rehearsed by dramatists in their plays or by audiences in their responses. They have also shown that the critics who used this evidence were really producing an Elizabethan climate of opinion that mirrored the critics' own ideology (which is now called "humanism" and is supposed to underlie "formalism" as well). Of course, others pointed these things out before them in different language,[2] but their influence seems to have been decisive in putting the ideas-of-the-time approach to rest. Thanks largely to them, we should no longer be hearing that Shakespeare and his audience must have condemned Lear for violating the Great Chain of Being, or Desdemona for disobeying her father, or Hamlet for revenging his, or Juliet for committing suicide, and so on. And for that we are clearly in their debt.

Unfortunately, however, the new historical critics do not always apply these valuable insights in their own "historicizing" of the plays, which sometimes depends upon other discoveries made by them about Elizabethan thought that seem at least as dubious as those of the old ideas-of-the-time critics. Often their new discoveries are formulated in negative rather than positive terms: instead of stating what Elizabethans must have been thinking, they state what people then did not and could not think, because the idea in question was first conceived in a later period (usually under the hegemony of "humanism" and its partner "bourgeois individualism"), so that this might appropriately be called the nonideas-of-the-time approach. And the evidence to support them is not derived from the "authoritative" homiletic literature relied upon in the older historical criticism,[3] although it is commonly announced with the same categorical certainty. Since these recent discoveries and the general tendency that they reflect have never been seriously challenged, as far as I can tell, I thought it might be useful to examine some of them here, along with the kind of evidence on which they are based. The first example I have selected may be idiosyncratic, but the others seem more or less typical, and the last is well on its way to becoming an article of faith in the newer historical approaches.

Discovery No. 1: Jonathan Goldberg has found that the use of characters as "foils" was "surely not part of Elizabethan dramaturgy" but was "timebound" to the nineteenth century (1983b, 346, 348). He offers no supporting evidence.

Discovery No. 2: A number of these critics claim that Elizabethan audiences, unlike those of later times, did not enter into the illusion of a theatrical performance and therefore did not become emotionally involved in it. Graham Holderness explains that "the Elizabethan theatre was [not] a theatre of illusion," which he associates with "nineteenth-century theatre," but "a theatre of alienation," where "the audience would always sustain an awareness of the constructed artifice of the proceedings, would never be seduced into the oblivion of empathetic illusion" (1985, 202, 212). Derek Longhurst implies the same thing when he says that a modern production of Shakespeare's plays "misconceives" them, since the "naturalism" of "the bourgeois theatre ... directs an audience towards an empathetic response to individual characters" (1982, 158). According to Malcolm Evans, "Jacobean audiences [were] familiar with plays that called for a 'double' vision, incorporating a response to the action *and* a continuing recognition of theatricality," and so were in the same position as "later theatre-goers who, under the influence of Brecht or Artaud, are unable to wholly forget themselves ... by submitting to the discreet charm of the bourgeois realism many critics and consumers would like Shakespeare's work to be" (1986, 140). Francis Barker contrasts "bourgeois naturalism" to the "anti-naturalist" Jacobean theater, where "the audience was never captivated by the illusion because the spectacle never produced itself as other than it was" (1984, 18, 20). And Simon Shepherd finds this "is endemic to Elizabethan theatrical practice, where the very theatricality of presentation" creates in the audience a "distancing awareness" that counteracts the dramatic "illusion" (1986, 109). The evidence for these claims centers on what are held to be antimimetic or anti-illusionist aspects of the Elizabethan theater (the absence of scenery, the use of boy actors for female parts, doubling, asides, and so on) and of the play-texts themselves, including inconsistencies in characterization, conflicting perspectives or moral standards, and shifts in rhetorical or poetic style.

Discovery No. 3: According to several of these critics, our conception of "literature" as a special category of written works of lasting value was unknown in this period. James Kavanagh says, "Shakespeare did not understand ... the terms of the literary," which "would be incomprehensible" to an Elizabethan, since "literature was invented ... in the late eighteenth and early nineteenth century"; and he adds that the modern distinction between the literary and the political "would have been unimaginable" then, as would "the kinds of distinctions we make among the political, the religious, the sexual, the scientific and the aesthetic," because "all these elements [were seen] as immediately and inextricably united" (1985, 147–49, 151, 160). Terry Eagleton also insists that "literature itself is a recent historical invention," which he dates "around the turn of the eighteenth century" (1983, 18, 204). Derek Longhurst tells us that Shakespeare and his contemporaries "would not have understood ... the category of 'Literature' itself" in the modern sense, since "'Literature' in the seventeenth century meant *all* forms of writing" (1982, 151–52). And Louis Montrose is a little more cautious: "During the sixteenth and seventeenth centuries, the separation of 'Literature' and 'Art' from explicitly didactic and political discourses or from such disciplines as history or moral and natural philosophy was as yet incipient.... This modern, essentialist orientation to 'Literature' ... had barely begun to emerge at the turn of the seventeenth century" (1986b, 12).⁴ The only evidence given by these critics is that the language of the time "lacks the word" for this concept (as Kavanagh puts it), since the *OED* records the first use of *literature* in this sense as 1812.

Discovery No. 4: Jonathan Goldberg asserts that people of Shakespeare's day did not believe "the notion that biological difference is an *a priori* fact" in defining gender. The only evidence presented (which he says "critics forget") is that "boys and girls in the Renaissance wear female clothes in their early years; femininity is there the undifferentiated sex from which maleness comes" (1985, 118). Jonathan Crewe also claims that they did not connect gender with biology; his evidence is that "the cultural construction of gender—as distinct from sex—is implied in *The Taming of the Shrew* [4.5], in which Petruchio can whimsically make Kate turn an old man into a young virgin and back again," which shows the "unrestricted convertibility of male and female figures" (1987, 75). In a closely related discovery, Stephen Greenblatt states that "sexual pleasure was not conceived as inherently gendered" in the Renaissance, because it was thought that "the law of nature . . . bound sexual pleasure to procreation, and all sexual practices that did not further this end were sinful and hence prohibited," which meant that there was no conception of homosexuality itself (1986b, 6).⁵ His only other evidence is the fact that, at the trial of an Italian nun in 1619, the investigators were chiefly interested in the possibility of demonic possession, rather than in her sexual relations with another nun.

Discovery No. 5: Many of these critics maintain that the modern conception of the self or individual did not yet exist in the Renaissance, or was only coming into existence then. Jonathan Goldberg tells us, without offering any evidence, that to comprehend Shakespeare we must "give up . . . notions of character as self-same, owned, capable of autonomy and change," because the worldview of his day "excludes" these "conceptual categories" (1985, 118). Stephen Greenblatt bases his claim primarily on the Martin Guerre case, the trial of an impostor in France in 1559–60, which is supposed to show that the "conclusions" comprising our sense of identity—that it is an "inalienable possession," that it is "primal," "irreducible," and "continuous," that it is "permanently anchored" in our "biological individuality"—were not "drawn either explicitly or implicitly by anyone in the sixteenth century. They are irrelevant to the point of being unthinkable." And he finds further evidence in Renaissance plays that turn on impersonation or mistaken identity, since this involves an "exploration of the issues at stake in the trial" (1986a, 214–15, 219).

The various cultural materialist versions of this discovery all connect our concept of the individual (or "the subject," as they prefer to call it) to the rise of capitalism, although they disagree on other points. Jonathan

Dollimore marks out three distinct stages: the medieval ideology of "Christian essentialism presented the soul as metaphysically derivative" and "identity as hierarchical location" in society; this changes in the Renaissance to a "sense of the self as flexible, problematic, elusive, . . . contradictory"; and the modern "idea of the autonomous, unified, self-generating subject" depends on "the humanist ideology of individual man" (or "essentialist humanism"), which "only really emerges with the Enlightenment" (1993, 155–56, 179). Catherine Belsey claims that the medieval individual was seen as "disunited, discontinuous," with "no single subjectivity," and so was "not a subject" in our sense, and that the concept of "the unified subject of liberal humanism," who is "autonomous" and has an "inalienable identity" and a "continuous and inviolable interiority," is "a product of the second half of the seventeenth century" and "becomes an orthodoxy at the moment when the bourgeoisie is installed" in power (1985b, 18, 33, 40). According to Francis Barker, however, the prebourgeois individual, free of "subjectivity," possessed a happy "coherence" through "incorporation" into an organic society in which "alterity of placement" was "unthinkable," whereas the bourgeois subject with his "deadly subjectivity" (which is "imaginary") is disunited as a result of "deleterious separations" of mind from body, individual from society, and subject from object that reduce it to "wretched pathos" (1984, 24-25, 31-32, 56, 66).[6] Most of the evidence for their accounts of the Renaissance idea (or nonidea) of selfhood comes from plays of the period that are said to reveal, primarily by an "absence of character 'consistency,'" the "impossibility" of portraying an "autonomous individual" because the concept "does not yet fully exist" or is "as yet . . . unspeakable" (Dollimore 1993, 176; Belsey 1985b, 42, 74, 77; Barker 1984, 38–39).

Even before we go on to examine these discoveries, it should be evident that they all make the same kind of error that their authors rightly condemned in the ideas-of-the-time approach: they homogenize Renaissance thought, for their claims that no one then could have held some idea are just as universal as the old claims that everyone must have held some idea. (Indeed, the two often amount same thing, when the assertion that no one held an idea means that everyone held another idea that opposed it, as may be seen in a number of the quotations.) Moreover, these negative claims stand on even shakier grounds than the positive ones of the older historical critics, whose citations of the "authorities" did prove that at least some people believed (or believed they should believe) the idea-of-the-time in question. The contention that nobody believed one of these nonideas-of-the-time is much harder to prove and much easier to disprove, as we are about to see.

Discovery No. 1: Since no evidence was presented to show that the use of foils was "not part of Elizabethan dramaturgy," the disproof need only cite some references to this practice in the drama itself. Shakespeare's Prince Hal says, in *1 Henry IV*, that "My reformation, glitt'ring o'er my fault, / Shall show more goodly and attract more eyes / Than that which hath no foil to set it off" (1.2.213–15); and Hamlet, just before their duel, says, "I'll be your foil, Laertes; in mine ignorance / Your skill shall like a star i' th' darkest night / Stick fiery off indeed" (5.2.255–57). In *The Masque of Queens* Ben Jonson explains that his antimasque will "have the place of a foil," because its characters are "the opposites to" the main character (ll. 13–19); and in *Epicoene* Dauphine calls the lesser Ladies Collegiates "mere foils" to Madame Haughty (5.2.15). And although he does not use the term, Simon clearly states the idea in Thomas Middleton's *Hengist, King of Kent*: "there's nothing in a play to a Clown's part, if he / Have the grace to hit on't, that's the thing indeed: / The King shows well, but he sets off the King" (5.1.135–37). It seems, then, that at least three major dramatists of the time were aware of this particular nonidea-of-the-time.

Discovery No. 2: Almost all the evidence brought forward to prove that Renaissance drama was nonillusionist and hence nonempathetic falls into two classes, neither of which can withstand scrutiny. One class is made up of inconsistencies and other unresolved problems in the plays themselves. But it does not seem to occur to the critics that these can be attributed to the inadequacies of the dramatist (or of the state of the art, for the earlier plays). In their failure to entertain this possibility, they bear a striking resemblance to some of the older New Critics, who argued that what appear to be defects in Shakespeare's and Jonson's plays when these are taken at face value are really intentional (and usually brilliant) ironies,[7] although they never thought of extending this justification to plays like *Locrine* and *Selimus*. The new historical critics can apply it to any play, no matter how crude it may appear (this is especially true of Shepherd 1986), and while they seldom invoke the author's intention, which most of them regard as a "humanist" myth, the result is the same: what seemed to be defects when viewed from the illusionist perspective turn out to be antiillusionist virtues. But that is to assume that all plays are flawless and also—although these critics certainly would not like this—that all playwrights are infallible. The second class of evidence, the allegedly "antinaturalist" conventions of the Renaissance stage, is even less convincing, for while those conventions seem "unnatural" to us, there is no reason to think that they seemed so to audiences at the time and hence kept them aware of the "theatricality of presentation," as the critics maintain. Indeed, the effect of a well-established stage convention is that it does *not* call attention to itself. So it would appear that here the new historical critics are guilty of a serious anachronism.[8]

If we turn from these theoretical considerations to the actual responses of the people of the Renaissance to their drama—which these critics never mention—we find no evidence of anything resembling the "distancing" or "alienation" that was supposed to be so pervasive. On the contrary, these responses all indicate that the plays of the period were expected to create the illusion of "real" human actions and thus to secure the emotional involvement of the audience, and that they (and their authors) were praised when they succeeded in doing this.[9] Shakespeare's Prologue to *Henry VIII* asks us to think that we see the characters "as they were living" and to "let fall a tear" for them. Thomas Nashe asserts that the death of Talbot in *1 Henry VI* has evoked "the tears of ten thousand spectators at least (at several times), who in the tragedian that represents his person, imagine they behold him fresh bleeding." In the introductory material in the Second Folio, an anonymous poem tells the reader to observe "a tragic strain, / Then weep"; and the poem by "I. M. S." states that Shakespeare "works upon" us "To steer th' affections" so that we are "stolen from ourselves." A couplet on the title page of Beaumont and Fletcher's *A King and No King* predicts that readers of the play will "weep, as if 'twere done indeed." James Shirley's introductory epistle in the Beaumont-Fletcher Folio says that passions in the plays are "so powerfully wrought" that "you shall not choose but . . . go along with them," since they "shall persuade thy eyes to weep." T. Palmer's commendatory poem in this volume recalls that in the theater these plays would "call tribute from our eyes" and "make us feel" the action was so "true" that, "Frozen with grief, we could not stir away / Until the epilogue told us 'twas a play"; and in other poems in the same collection by Jasper Mayne, George Lisle, and Richard Lovelace, we are told that the plays present "feeling objects to draw tears from eyes," that they "strik[e] our sense so deep," and that audiences "have wept to see" them. According to Shackerly Marmion, in the theater Jonson "fram'd all minds, and did all passions stir"; and Thomas Dekker says he wants to be a playwright who

> Can give an actor sorrow, rage, joy, passion,
> Whilst he again, by self-same agitation,
> Commands the hearers, sometimes drawing out tears,
> Then smiles, and fills them both with hopes and fears.

Actors of this period were similarly praised for creating the illusion of reality and thereby engaging the spectators' emotions. The Overburian Character of "An Excellent Actor" says that "what we see him personate, we think truly done before us." Thomas Heywood explains how audiences react "as if the personater were the man personated, so bewitching a thing is lively and well spirited action." Thomas May has a character report seeing "a player personate Hieronimo" in "such a lively color" that

> he has drawn true tears
> From the spectators' eyes. Ladies in the boxes
> Kept time with sighs and tears to his sad accents
> As had he truly been the man he seem'd.[10]

An anonymous elegy on the death of Richard Burbage says that Hieronimo, Lear, Othello, and other characters "lived in him," and that he acted the part of Hamlet "so lively" that spectators, "whilst he but seem'd to bleed, / Amazed, thought even then he died in deed." Richard Flecknoe also praises him for "so wholly transforming himself into his part." Thomas Randolph says, in his poem on Thomas Riley, "When thou dost act, men think it not a play, / But all they see is real." The same thing applies to the boy actors playing women's parts, despite the claims of these critics that this was one of those "antinaturalist" conventions that produced a "distancing effect." Henry Jackson records a performance of *Othello* in which Desdemona "always acted her whole part supremely well, yet when she was killed she was even more moving, for when she fell back upon the bed she implored the pity of the spectators by her very face." Thomas Middleton asks if there is anyone who saw Webster's Duchess of Malfi "live and die, / That could get off under a bleeding eye." In his poem prefixed to the Beaumont-Fletcher Folio, Thomas Stanley says that the fates of Bellario/Euphrasia, Aspatia, and Lucina (in *Philaster*, *The Maid's Tragedy*, and *Valentinian*, respectively) evoked tears from the audience. An anonymous elegy on the death of Walter Clun states that his performances in female roles "made us weep, at seeming sorrow swell, / To hear and see like truth a fiction fell." And John Downes asserts that when Edward Kynaston was very young he acted women's parts "so well, especially . . . parts greatly moving compassion and pity, that it has since been disputable . . . whether any woman that succeeded him so sensibly touch'd the audience as he." I think we could sum up all this evidence by saying that it proves precisely what the new historical critics denied—that viewers and readers of the Renaissance drama were "captivated by the illusion" and could "wholly forget themselves" by "submitting" to it and were "seduced into the oblivion of empathetic illusion," and therefore that this could not have been a nonidea-of-the-time.

Discovery No. 3: The fact that Elizabethans "lacked the word" for literature in the modern sense does not mean that they lacked the concept. The Greeks also had no word for it, as Aristotle points out in the *Poetics;* but he must have had the concept, otherwise he could not have pointed this out.[11] If ideas cannot precede the words for them, no new words would ever be coined. It seems very clear that the Elizabethans did conceive of a special category of written works that were of lasting value. This is what Sidney is defending in *A Defence of Poetry*, and what Jonson is discussing in *Timber*. And in his classification of the fields of knowledge in book 2 of *The Advancement of Learning* (1915, 82), Bacon creates a separate division for "Poesy," which includes prose as well as verse, although he limits it, like Aristotle, to what is now called "imaginative literature." (His scheme also places under separate divisions each of the other areas—political, religious, sexual, and scientific—which Kavanagh insists were then so "inextricably unified" that the modern distinctions among them were "unimaginable.") Of course, the criteria for entry into this category have undergone changes over the years. Shakespeare apparently did not think that plays belonged to it, since he took no interest in publishing his, but his dedications to *Venus and Adonis* and *The Rape of Lucrece* show that he regarded them as literature in our sense (despite Kavanagh's claim that he "did not understand" the category). Many of his contemporaries shared this view of the drama. That is why there were some adverse reactions when Jonson published his First Folio under the title *The Works of Benjamin Jonson*, but those reactions make sense only if the term *works* was then reserved for the valued category that we call literature.[12] And in his commendatory poem prefixed to the Shakespeare First Folio, Jonson also places Shakespeare's plays in this category (along with those of Aeschylus, Sophocles, Euripides, Seneca, Plautus, and Terence), because they were "not of an age, but for all time." It would seem that he, as well as his detractors, did not know that this category was a nonidea-of-their-time.

Discovery No. 4: Goldberg's evidence that people then did not think gender was biologically determined would give a fascinating new meaning to the adage that "Clothes make the man,"[13] but it is based on anachronistic reasoning, for while the apparel worn by Elizabethan children may look like "female clothes" to *us*, to the Elizabethans it was simply children's clothing and did not define the gender of those who wore it. (The gender of clothes, unlike that of people, really is culturally defined—witness the kilt.) Their baptismal gowns were also unisex, but it could hardly be a coincidence that all babies with vaginas were given girls' names and all babies without them were given boys' names. Obviously they ascertained the sex of a child at birth,[14] just as we do, and assumed, like us, that it determined the child's gender throughout life. In fact, Crewe's evidence from *The Taming of the Shrew* (4.5) confirms this, since the whole point of the humor here is that Kate, Petruchio, and the audience know that Vincentio really is a man and will remain one, no matter how he is addressed (or dressed). (The humor also involves his age, since he is "old, wrinkled, faded, withered" and is greeted by Kate as a "young budding virgin, fair, and fresh"; but I do not think Crewe would maintain that this implies "the cultural construction" of age, or shows the "unrestricted convertibility" of old and young figures.) Attitudes toward gender have certainly changed from the Elizabethan period to the present, but its connection to biology was an idea of their time as well as of our own. And the same is true of homosexuality. The law of nature may not have distinguished it from other nonprocreative (and hence "sinful") sexual practices, as Greenblatt claims, but the law of the land did. Men were hanged in the Renaissance for homosexual activity, but there is no record of anyone being penalized for the "sins" of masturbating or engaging in coitus interruptus or deriving excessive pleasure from marital intercourse. Even adultery, which was a crime, was differentiated from homosexuality, because people then, like people today, did conceive of sexual enjoyment as gendered.[15] And the trial of the Italian nun cited by Greenblatt merely proves that demonic possession was considered more serious than homosexuality, not that the latter was a nonidea-of-the-time.

Discovery No. 5: Much of the evidence derived from the drama to support the claim that Elizabethans had a radically different concept of the self rests on the same kind of error we found in the case of the second discovery—the belief that inconsistency in characterization cannot be explained by the inadequacies of the playwright or of the state of the art at that time. But a more fundamental error is involved here as well, because the arguments of many of these critics assume that there must be a simple equation between the way characters were represented and the way members of the audience thought of themselves. This is clearly not true. People watching a morality play did not think they were abstractions or personifications; nor did people watching an early movie think that they spoke to each other by first mouthing their words silently and then flashing them on large screens. There obviously have been major changes in the representation of character in the drama and in other literary forms from the Middle Ages to the present (and some of these critics have acute observations to make about this), but we have no reason to believe that these corresponded to any changes in the basic conception of selfhood.[16]

I think we would also have to say that the Renaissance conception of selfhood discovered by these critics simply does not make sense (I would have invoked common sense, but most of them regard it as another "humanist" myth). It is a good example of the kind of historicist error that E. D. Hirsch terms the "fallacy of the inscrutable past," since it "infer[s] from the past a state of mind so different from our own that . . . [it] seems to be populated by beings who might have come from Mars" (1976, 39).[17] For if they are to be believed, then a Renaissance woman waking up in the morning would not realize she was the same person who went to sleep the night before, would not recognize the members of her own family, and could not make any plans for the day, since that assumed her "continuous" identity as well as the "interiority" that would have enabled her to think that she could think about "herself." Such an idea, moreover, contradicts not only our common experience (or common sense), but also the findings of investigators who have studied the actual process by which we acquire our idea of selfhood. These findings, which are never mentioned by this group of critics, show how every normal child gradually develops the sense of an identity that it is—to use Goldberg's own words—"self-same, owned, capable of autonomy and change"; and while this process would not occur outside a human culture, there is no evidence I know of to suggest that it occurs differently in other cultures or produces significantly different results. For any child who did not emerge with such a sense of identity could not survive in the world, which also applies to the hypothetical Renaissance woman described above. The fact that people in the Renaissance did survive, therefore, would prove that their basic concept of selfhood was much like our own.

If anyone still requires specific historical evidence to support this conclusion, we can point to the history books themselves, along with the biographies or "Lives," that were written during the Renaissance, since these all necessarily assume that their human "subjects" possessed selves that were autonomous and unified and persisted through time and change. Without those assumptions there could be no history. These same assumptions also underlie the French trial of 1559–60 that Greenblatt cites in order to prove that they were "unthinkable" in this period,[18] for if people then did not believe that identity is an "inalienable possession" that is "continuous" and "permanently anchored" in one's "biological individuality," they would not have held a trial to determine whether the accused really was the man he claimed to be or an impostor; in fact, there would be no such thing as an impostor. The same point applies to the plays involving impersonation or mistaken identity that Greenblatt also presents as evidence for his discovery, because it seems clear that they do not explore the question of identity, as he maintains, but assume it. Again, unless identity is assumed to be fixed and continuous, there can be no impersonation and certainly no "mistaken identity," and so these plays actually provide additional evidence that this conception of identity could not have been a nonidea-of-the-time.

It turns out, therefore, that all five of these historical discoveries are false to history, because the ideas that they insist could not be thought in the Renaissance were in fact thought by at least some people then, and most of them by a great many people. There clearly is a tendency to produce these claims of "unthinkability" with very little thinking, and it seems to be increasing as the critics uncritically accept the claims of their colleagues and use them to produce more of their own. Surely the time has come to challenge it by asking those who define themselves as historical critics to show more respect for the demands of historical evidence and historical reasoning. But this tendency has not been limited to studies of the past. We can see an example of its extension into the current scene in Belsey's assertion that the conventional "humanist" conception of a text is now "literally unthinkable" (1980, 3).* Her statement is untrue, since many critics still accept this concept of a text; but it is also self-contradictory, since she herself must have thought of the concept or she could not say it was unthinkable. It is "literally unthinkable" to think of an unthinkable thought. Of course, this does not mean that we cannot think of ideas that were unthinkable to people of the Renaissance, but we ought to be extremely cautious in making such claims. There is, however, one idea that I suspect really was unthinkable to them—that anyone in the future would

---

*In her reply, Belsey objected to my paraphrase, because what she "said there [in her 1980 book] was that *in the context of* post-Saussurean theory," which "has no terms for the author-as-origin" or "meaning as single," this conception of the text "was unthinkable" (1990, 455). I see now that I misread her statement and I apologize for that, but it is still untrue, because even if one accepts this context it is possible to think of these concepts, as the post-Saussurean theorists (she named Barthes, Lacan, Althusser, and Derrida) must have done when they argued against them. You cannot oppose or reject something without thinking about what you are opposing or rejecting. Moreover, if *she* accepts this context (as she apparently does), then she forfeits the right to object to my misreading of her statement, because her intention would no longer be the "origin" of its meaning, which would no longer be "single," and so my reading of it would be just as valid as hers and there would be no such thing as a misreading. De Grazia and Stallybrass fell into the same pit as a result of their essay in which they asserted, among other things, that the concept of authorial meaning was an "illusion" (1993, 276–80), because when Pechter (1997) criticized the conclusion of their essay, they replied that this was not what they really meant and appealed to their intended authorial meaning: "we did not . . . mean to suggest," "we certainly were not trying to replace," and so on (1997, 71, 73). See also the discussion of this typical post-Saussurean inconsistency in my "Interdisciplinarity" and in Abrams 1995, 34–37.

seriously maintain that they were unable to think of the relationship of gender to biology, or of a unified and continuous self, or of any of the other alleged nonideas-of-the-time presented in these discoveries.

Jonathan Goldberg: Making Sense

For some time now, Richard Levin has been the self-appointed protector of old plays from new readings, and the present essay, along with a recent one in *PMLA* ("Feminist Thematics"), continues the assault. Homogenizing various new historical practitioners and their practices, Levin charges them with a failure to "make sense." "I would have invoked common sense," he continues, "but most of them regard it as another 'humanist' myth." The *OED*, however, hardly a repository of Marxist materialism, records the historic specificity of the concept Levin would invoke—for, despite his assertions, it is not the case that people have always had the same ideas, with their vocabularies simply lagging behind. And even words that appear lexically identical change their meanings. For example, "common sense," in Aristotle, and in Elizabethan physiology and psychology, is literally located in a particular part of the mind; the *OED* cites Burton's *Anatomy of Melancholy* as an example: "Inner senses are three in number, so called because they be within the brainpan, as common sense, phantasy, memory." A more general notion of common sense based on this psychobiology survived it, and the term came to have philosophic force in the eighteenth century; it now underlies the ordinary use of the term to mean "good sound practical sense," a usage which is hardly univocal or unproblematic, as might be inferred from Empson's brilliant discussions of "sense" in *The Structure of Complex Words* (1951), or the argument of Stanley Fish's "Normal Circumstances, Literal Language, Direct Speech Acts, the Ordinary, the Everyday, the Obvious, What Goes without Saying, and Other Special Cases" (1980, 268–92).

Levin's "sense" cannot be separated from the tail end of an empiricist psycho-philosophy that is idealistic, too, in its assumption that the mind never changes. His attempt to prove the unthinkable thinkable founders in the thoughtlessness (the common sense) that thinking has always thought the same. Implicitly, in his argument, there could be no history of philosophy; equally implicit is an equation of the mind with consciousness, of the self with the ego. The thinking denied by such assumptions depends upon "common sense," and thus no sooner has Levin denied himself the term than it insists upon itself: "Our common experience" is glossed with a parenthetical definition "(or common sense)." The term remains unexamined and necessarily so (it is the very term for that which does not *need* to be thought). Experience is treated as a transparency, as something "we" all have, and all have the same. "Without those assumptions there could be no history." These assumptions—however "commonsensical"—need to be queried. For while they seem founded in an egalitarian belief (humanist?) that all humans are the same, they, in fact, depend upon massive exclusions. Their homogenizing same rules out spheres of difference that the various new historicisms seek to disclose, differences that rupture history or that divide the subject. If those are unrecognizable to Levin and make no sense it is because they threaten the grounds upon which he attempts to stand. But the history that he invokes is a history of the same, and no history at all. In Levin's commonsense history, common sense is a shared possession, something "we" all have and always have had. It is community property.

Levin depends upon the evidence of the senses, "the actual responses of the people of the Renaissance," and these are gathered in one accepted mode of making sense: citation of evidence. Evidence, so understood, is simply that which is evident, self-evident, clear proof (in this case, that Renaissance plays produced emotional effects). "Actual responses," however, are written responses, and they must be read, not merely received as sensory data. "Shakespeare's Prologue to *Henry VIII* asks us to think that we see the characters 'as they were living' and to 'let fall a tear' for them," Levin writes and cites. We are to weep—a bodily response is assumed, or induced; the body is being made to produce tears (Burton's body has an *organ* of common sense). And how is this response secured? By taking the actor for the character, an assumption governed by an "as"—"as they were living." "As" opens a distance in the identification between the actor and the character; tears are wept for a "life" that is also seen as *not* alive. More evidence: "A couplet on the title-page of Beaumont and Fletcher's *A King and No King* predicts that readers of the play will 'weep, as if 'twere done indeed.'" *As if.* Such locutions appear in almost every cited instance. They reveal emotions produced *not* on the basis of identification (*not* on the basis of sameness), but within a simulative economy—one recognized in the similes.

Not that these writing-effects are necessarily real effects; they are not "actual responses," but written, and those aimed at a reading public have already chosen as their audience the literate portion of the populace. Whether they describe or prescribe remains in question. In short, not only are they not "actual responses," it is by no means easy to decide whether they describe a response assumed to be common, or solicit one. If they induce or desire common responses, a *sensus communis* is then *produced*, as an effect.

These representations put themselves in question, admitting the violence of their imputations and their imaginary force, registered in similitudes whose effect is being denied. It is the work of the historicist to attempt to read the margins of difference in these citations, the ideological space opened up by an "as if." As even these few comments might suggest then, Levin's evidence supports the arguments he would deny. The audience made (up) in these citations is produced through difference; it is an audience divided by the simulative representations that "'strik[e] our sense so deep.'" The descriptions register their violence; and as they strike and divide "our sense" they also arise from the visible division between the actor and the part impersonated. "As if the personater were the man personated," Heywood writes. On stage or off, all persons then are personated.

Is "our sense" (their "sense") "our" sense? "If these critics are to be believed, then a Renaissance woman upon waking up in the morning would not realize that she was the same person who went to sleep the night before." This is an example of Levin's other mode of argument. No self-evident (and unread) evidence, simply the evidence of "our" experience. No one is cited here (though the invocation of "the findings of investigators" presumably would not include psychoanalysts since their "findings" are not empirical facts; clearly, Levin has no use for the unconscious, no notion either of its existence as a historically differentiated phenomenon). This evidence is so evident "we" need nothing more than the citation of our ordinary experience (but why a woman?), the assurance that only some inept play (for example, one not by Shakespeare) could ever lead us to such aberrant thoughts (but whose thoughts *are* these?), thoughts no doubt caused by taking literature too seriously (plays are only plays, Levin implies, let's be sensible and not confuse them with the real evidence of our senses, let's not assume that representations have any part in the constitution of reality).

Demetrius.	These things seem small and undistinguishable, Like far-off mountains turned into clouds.
Hermia.	Methinks I see these things with parted eye, When everything seems double.
Helena.	So methinks; And I have found Demetrius like a jewel, Mine own, and not mine own.
Demetrius.	Are you sure That we are awake? It seems to me That yet we sleep, we dream. Do not you think The Duke was here, and bid us follow him?

Hermia.	Yea, and my father.
Helena..	And Hippolyta.
Lysander.	And he did bid us follow to the temple.
Demetrius.	Why, then, we are awake: let's follow him, And by the way let us recount our dreams.

(*A Midsummer Night's Dream* 4.1.186–98)

A scene of awakening in a play structured around sleeping and waking, a play in which it is a sign of sheer opacity to wake up and believe that one awakens into the same or as the same (witness Lysander's impassioned declarations to Helena, Demetrius's to Hermia, Hermia's serpent dream and its living realization, Titania's monstrous embrace). Ordinary experience in this scene: mountains metamorphosed into clouds, seeing double, having and not having at once; common sense is constructed before our eyes—on the authority of the Duke and Duchess and the father. What is "by the way" in this scene can never be separated from the common path these characters follow.

What is to be seen here? What John Downes saw in Edward Kynaston's acting of women's parts "'so well, especially . . . parts moving compassion and pity, that it has since been disputable . . . whether any woman that succeeded him so sensibly touch'd the audience as he'"? Levin sees to it that the woman is the same, morning and night; by the end of the paragraph in which she appears, she is the child secure in its identity. Downes sees a boy beneath the woman's costume, sees that he is "sensibly touch'd" in a gendered relationship of male identification. He can weep best with the woman if the woman is really a man; Kynaston succeeded only by denying the very character he played. The collusive, communal fiction that binds the lovers and secures their identity for themselves in Shakespeare's play denies the dreams (the play) that continue to structure and to fracture their identities; the communal construction of gendered identity cannot be read apart from this structuration.

Cited above are the last lines Hermia and Helena speak in the play, the one to acknowledge her father, the other to name Hippolyta. They have arrived at the end of "their" desires. At the end of the play, the only woman who will speak will be Hippolyta; if she has a "life" after marriage, it is because class privilege can overcome gender difference (in Hippolyta's case, from the start, it is suggested that as an Amazon a *different* sexuality may also be figured, one that would not be made to disappear in marriage, much as Oberon recelebrates his marriage once he has possession of the Indian boy). "Mine own, and not mine own" names a shared condition in the play, but one everywhere inflected differently, riven and recemented through class and gender hierarchies; this multiple condition is transferred to the audience in Puck's final lines, to be ratified by "our" applause.

It is an idealizing fiction to suppose therefore that there is such a univocal thing as "a Renaissance woman." For Levin, "a Renaissance woman" is a wife who had better wake up the same as she went to bed, ready to attend to her family and make "plans for the day" (shopping, perhaps?). For Downes, the best woman is a boy. And for Shakespeare? The answers multiply: because the boy actors provide one way of putting pressure on the construction of sexuality; because patriarchal fantasies are exposed and reproduced on his stage; because gender difference is also class difference (a further route of understanding between the position of boy-actors and women); because commonsense distinctions are community constructions which are seen through (in the double sense of the phrase).

But this is not common sense, and will not "make sense" to Levin, so it's time to stop. Better to close with the insidious, elementary definitions of common sense that circulate in his writing. Their bedrock is gender.

Common sense: "babies with vaginas" are girls, are women, are woman. "Obviously they ascertained the sex of a child at birth, just as we do, and assumed like us, that it determined the child's gender throughout life."

Common sense: "people then, like people today, did conceive of sexual enjoyment as gendered"—that is to say, as heterosexual.

They killed homosexuals, just like we would, and thought of women as vaginas, just like we do.

Stop "making sense."

"The first example that I have selected may be idiosyncratic." (But what else would a commonsensical reader expect from someone who writes about sodomy?) Marshal the evidence: they had the word, they had the concept. What concept? The word without a context (don't read the examples, just count them; readings don't count as evidence). Foils are foils are foils. Nothing ever changes. But is Brian Gibbons's hypostasization of characters as dramatic foils really coincident with the cited usages? Do any of them imagine an inherent, unchanging character whose sole function is to serve as a contrast to the equally stable, unchanging character of some other character? This skirmish over foils brings us back not only to Levin's inability to historicize the subject (as "they prefer to call it"); no doubt the review offended him from its very first sentence: "If the function of a standard edition is to present usual assumptions, widely shared information, and conventional interpretations, then Brian Gibbons's New Arden *Romeo and Juliet* admirably fulfills the demands" (1983b, 343). It offers, in other words, common sense. It upholds literature (another one of those timeless phenomena for Levin, who is incapable of recognizing that what counts as being "for all time" depends upon the historicity of canon formation; changes in authorial functions and powers; the place of critics and criticism; of editors; of pedagogic sites: all these affect the institutionalization of literature, and they are by no means in the same place in the Renaissance as they are now). For Gibbons, *Romeo and Juliet* stands as "the artifice of eternity" (74). Who could object? Just the "idiosyncratic," the Marxists, the women, the theorists—all those people who have no place in the profession, that Levin protects, of those who profess common sense.

From them old plays must be protected. So—no new readings of old plays; no readings at all. There's nothing to read, after all, it's all the same, always has been. Obvious, isn't it? Don't give it a thought.

My Reply

Jonathan Goldberg undertakes to defend all five discoveries, and he does this by lumping together my arguments against them as stemming from a single general position that he tries to impugn with two transparently sophistical tactics.[19] One is the attempt to reduce this entire position to a naive notion of "common sense," which begins in his opening paragraph and continues throughout his response in references to "Levin's commonsense history," "a commonsensical reader," "those who profess common sense," and so on. The fact is that none of my arguments was based on an appeal to common sense, as I explained in the sentence he quotes from my essay; but that does not deter him from using it against me. It is just a new form of name-calling, like labeling someone an "idealist" (which he also does to me), that is designed to dispose of adverse arguments without having to confront them.

The second tactic he uses throughout his response is to construct absurd exaggerations or distortions of my position that are supposed to represent it and thus discredit it. Most of them make me deny all change and difference. I argued against the claims that five specific ideas were unthinkable in the Renaissance, but he has me believing that "people have always had the same ideas," that "thinking has always thought the same," that "the mind never changes," that "nothing ever changes," that we "all have the same" experience, that "all humans are the same," that "it's all the same, always has been." And along the way he also saddles me with some other inanities—that there is "an equation of the mind with consciousness," that representations do not "have any part in the constitution of reality," and even that Marxists, women, and theorists "have no place in the profession." Nothing in my essay would justify imputing such ideas to me.[20] I do not believe any of them, and I am sure that Goldberg, at least in his more rational moments, knows I do not. What he does not seem to know is that by descending to such a tactic he only exposes the weakness of his own case against my essay.

This weakness becomes apparent as soon as we turn to the actual arguments he presents—after the irrelevant discussion of common sense—to refute my criticisms of the five discoveries. (Since he jumps about a great deal, I have reassembled these arguments under each head.) On **Discovery No. 1**, he tries to get around my evidence that Elizabethan had a conception of dramatic foils by adding three qualifications to it: foil characters must be "unchanging," their "sole function" must be this role, and the characters they are foils to must also be "unchanging." But these additions are his own invention; they are not assumed in the ordinary use of the term or in Brian Gibbons's introduction, and they certainly do not apply to the foils in the later drama, where Goldberg acknowledges their presence. It is hard to think of any dramatic character that could qualify as a foil under his new rules, since he has virtually defined the category out of existence. And if the passages I quoted from Shakespeare, Jonson, and Middleton do not refer to foils in his sense, he should explain what they do refer to.[21]

Goldberg is correct in noting that the quotations I presented as evidence against **Discovery No. 2** are not actual responses to the plays but records of such responses, or in some cases requests for or predictions of responses. He is also correct in noting that, like any other form of evidence, they must be interpreted or "read." My interpretation of them was that they all pointed to the conception of an illusionist/empathetic theater. He tries to refute this by showing that they assume a "simulative economy" where the audience responds to a play "as if" it were real, and so reveal a "distance" or "difference," rather than an "identification," between the play and reality and between the actor and his role. He is right again, but this is precisely what is meant by illusionist drama. No one supposes that it actually makes audiences forget they are watching a play rather than real life. Indeed the very idea of "illusion" depends on this distinction. (The idea of "empathy" depends on a similar distinction: when we empathize with people we react "as if" what happens to them is happening to us, but we know it is not.) I do not see, therefore, how my interpretation of the evidence is affected in any way by all his talk of "distance" or "difference" or "division" or even "violence" (his term for evoking emotion), or by the question he raises about whether the passages "describe or prescribe" a response, since in either case they assume that the drama is supposed to be illusionist and empathetic. Nor is it affected by his special "reading" of the passage where Downes praises Kynaston's acting of female roles, which Goldberg explains as "male identification": "he can weep best with the woman if the woman is really a man."[22] But Downes does not say *he* was moved by Kynaston; he says "the audience" was, and this audience included many women, who could not have felt much "male identification" and have been erased by Goldberg in one of those "massive exclusions" that he accuses me of.

In responding to my arguments against **Discovery No. 3**, which holds that Elizabethans had no concept of "literature," he relies on his second sophistical tactic described earlier, claiming that I believe that literature is "timeless" and that the functions of authors, critics, and editors "are in the same place in the Renaissance as they are now." But I never suggested anything of the sort; in fact I said, "Of course, the criteria for entry into this category [of literature] have undergone changes over the years." I was only arguing that Elizabethans had such a category, and I assembled a body of evidence to show this, which Goldberg never confronts.

He has the least to say about my criticism of **Discovery No. 4**, and that seems strange, because it is the only one explicitly concerned with gender, which he claims at one point (with no explanation) is the "bedrock" of my errors. As evidence that Elizabethans thought gender is biologically determined, I noted that "all babies with vaginas were given girls' names and all babies without them were given boys' names." (I could just as easily have used the presence or absence of a penis as the determinant, but I was striking a blow against phallocentrism.) His reply is first to dismiss this as "common sense," and then to transform it so that Elizabethans "thought of women as vaginas, just like we do," where "we" presumably includes me but not him. That of course is not what I said at all: there is a big difference, although Goldberg seems unable to recognize it, between thinking women *have* vaginas and thinking of them *as* vaginas; but if it were true it would be even stronger evidence that Elizabethans believed gender is biologically determined, so here he is arguing against his own discovery. On the related question of whether they had a conception of what he calls "homosexuality per se," where I produced as evidence the fact that they hanged homosexuals, his reply seems to be (it is not easy to follow his train of thought here) that I favor this practice: "just like we would," with "we" again presumably including me but not him. If that is what he means, let me state for the record that I do not want to hang homosexuals. We (again excluding him) should note that none of these replies makes any contact with my case against **Discovery No. 4**, yet they are all he has to say in its defense. We might also note that nothing more is heard of those "female clothes" that little boys were supposed to wear then.

In dealing with **Discovery No. 5**, I presented three separate arguments against the claim that the Renaissance had no conception of a self continuing through time. The first was a kind of reductio ad absurdum where I tried to imagine what the consequences would be if this claim were true, using as my example the plight of a Renaissance woman facing the day. Goldberg tries to avoid the issue here by a series of digressions. First he objects that I did not cite any evidence, but that is irrelevant in hypothetical examples of this sort. Then he asks, "Why a woman?"—to which the obvious answer is, why not? His question implies that the choice of a male example would be natural and would require no explanation. Then he accuses me of "idealizing" her because she "is a wife" who is "ready to attend to her family" and may go "shopping." But none of these details can be found in my example, where the only assumptions made about her are that she slept at night, woke in the morning, and was in a family (which would all be just as applicable to a Renaissance man), and so they must come from Goldberg's own "idealizing." (He keeps trying to rush to the defense of women when none is called for, and in the process keeps tripping himself up.) All this has nothing to do with the issue raised by my example—namely, does he believe that Renaissance people (either gender) actually were in the plight I described? If he does not, he will have to undiscover his discovery that they had no notion of "character as self-same, owned, capable of autonomy and change"; if he does, he better discover some evidence for it.

My second argument (which he conflates with the first) drew on recent empirical investigations of how children develop a sense of identity.* I, of course, have no expertise in this area and can only report what I have learned of their findings, subject to correction. I think they are very important here, because Goldberg and those who share his views seem to regard the human brain as a tabula rasa upon which society can "inscribe" anything at all.[23] But while society has an enormous influence on our mental life, its power is not unlimited, for these findings show that the brain, as the result of evolution, is now already "wired" at birth in certain species-specific ways that had an obvious survival value, including those that map out the development of a sense of identity that is self-same, owned, and capable of autonomy and

---

*Easterlin 2000 cites and provides a useful summary of several of these studies, which all draw upon cross-cultural research. Not so incidentally, their findings directly contradict the "agonistic" theories of the orthodox Freudians, Lacanians, and feminist neo-Freudians. See also my criticism of the clinical evidence of psychoanalysts in "Interdisciplinarity."

change. And since our brain could not have undergone a major evolutionary development in a mere four centuries, it follows that the "Renaissance subject" constructed by Goldberg and Greenblatt is a biological and historical impossibility. Goldberg's only response to this argument is that I left out the psychoanalysts. He does not reveal which ones he has in mind, but if he knows of any who have disproved these findings or proved that the Renaissance sense of identity was radically different from ours, he should name them. (Greenblatt, in the essay [1986a] I quoted from, criticizes the psychoanalysts because they do *not* differentiate the Renaissance sense of identity from the modern one.)

My third argument pointed to the histories and biographies written during this period, which assume that their human subjects possessed selves that, I said, "persisted through time and change." (I could have added many other specific examples of this kind, since every time Elizabethans engaged in any activity involving the past or the future—and that covers a lot of activities—they demonstrated their belief that they and those they were dealing with possessed such selves.) Goldberg's only reply is the assertion that "the history that [Levin] invokes is a history of the same, and no history at all," which is another example of his second sophistical tactic. Now, a history clearly depends on difference and change, which his tactic would have me deny; but it also depends on sameness and continuity, for it must be a history of something (not necessarily of individuals, of course) and that entity must in some sense persist during the course of the history, which otherwise would be a series of unrelated events. Any history requires both, as I affirmed in the statement (which he quotes out of context) that "without those assumptions there could be no history," where "those assumptions" refers to the selves that "*persisted* through time and *change*" (italics added). If he denies persistence, then, it is his history and not mine that would be "no history at all."

I think we must conclude, therefore, that Goldberg has not succeeded in refuting any of my evidence or arguments against any of the discoveries, or in producing any convincing evidence or arguments for any of them. But I would not want to end without commenting on his opening charge that I am "self-appointed," which is supposed to score another point against me. I was under the impression that all of us in our critical activities are self-appointed and do not require any authorization or imprimatur. If I am wrong, however, perhaps he will tell us who appointed him to do what he does.

4
Re(Thinking) Unthinkable Thoughts

SEVEN YEARS AGO I PUBLISHED AN ESSAY THAT INTERROGATED THE RECENT discoveries made by a number of New Historicist, feminist, and cultural materialist critics that people in Renaissance (now early modern) England were unable to think of five ideas widely held today—that dramatic characters could serve as foils, that the drama could be illusionist and empathetic, that there was a category of valued writing that we now call "literature," that there was a biological basis for gender division, and that humans possessed a self or identity persisting through time and change. I presented evidence to show that each of these "unthinkable" ideas was in fact thought during this period, and I am happy to report that soon after the essay appeared some of my arguments were endorsed by Lee Patterson (1990, 97–98) and David Aers (1992), and I also learned that two years earlier one of them had been anticipated by Natalie Zemon Davis (1988, 602). I cannot report, however, that the objections of Patterson, Aers, Davis, and myself have had any discernible effect on the unthinkability enterprise: none of the critics we criticized, as far as I know, has modified his or her views, and more discoveries of this kind keep cropping up. I want to move on, then, from a description of the enterprise, which is all I attempted in my earlier essay, to propose some explanations for it, but before doing this I will list a few of the additional discoveries that have been announced, or have come to my attention, since I wrote the essay, and to demonstrate that they are not limited to the Renaissance, I include two from other periods.

Discovery No. 6: Linda Charnes claims that "in early modern England, Love with a capital L" (which she defines as the idea of a love that "transcends" any "specific material, political, and social conditions") "would not have been thinkable"; but she goes on to say that *Antony and Cleopatra* "examines the implications" of transcendent love and "subversively insists on" questioning it (1992, 4–5, 13), so Shakespeare and his audience had to think of this unthinkable idea.

Discovery No. 7: Margreta de Grazia and Peter Stallybrass claim that "neither heterosexuality nor homosexuality existed as categories in early modern Europe," because "the latter-day incontrovertible male/female binary . . . was not yet in place" (1993, 272). But both the laws against sodomy and the well-known passage in Leviticus, "If a man also lie with mankind, as he lieth with a woman, both of them have committed an abomination" (Lev. 20:13; King James Version), prove that the categories of heterosexuality and homosexuality were very thinkable and that they were based on an incontrovertible male/female binary that was very firmly in place.

Discovery No. 8: James Kavanagh claims that our idea of "dramatic structure" was "unutterable" and "unimaginable" in the Renaissance, because it is "invested . . . with two hundred years of a discourse on the literary and the aesthetic whose most basic terms could not be uttered until two hundred years after Shakespeare wrote" (1985, 164–65). But Ben Jonson discusses this unimaginable dramatic structure in the final section of *Timber, or Discoveries*, and so does Aristotle in the *Poetics*, written more than two thousand years before the term could be uttered.

Discovery No. 9: Karen Newman claims that "by the time of Rymer's attack on *Othello* [in *A Short View of Tragedy*, 1693], Shakespeare's heroic and tragic representation of a black man seemed unthinkable" (1987a, 154–55); but on the preceding page she quotes from Aphra Behn's novel *Oroonoko*, which was written a few years before Rymer's book and presents a heroic and tragic black man, as does Thomas Southerne's popular tragedy with the same title, produced in 1695. We also know that *Othello* was frequently performed in London at this time (in versions close to Shakespeare's text),[1] and so can infer that many people in the audiences were able not only to think of this unthinkable thought but also to approve of it.

Discovery No. 10: Terry Eagleton claims that the modern failure "to see eye to eye on all the most vital matters" concerning "human happiness" is "a condition which would have been mind-bendingly unimaginable to the ancients" (1994, 1). But Thucydides and Plutarch tell us that disagreements on these very matters were responsible for much of the civil strife in the Greek city-states, so the partisans in that strife must have imagined this mind-bending condition.[2]

I would have to say that these discoveries are subject to the same objections I directed at the five examined in my earlier essay. They all homogenize the mentality of a historical period, since they claim that no one then ever thought of the idea in question (which often means that everyone must have held the idea opposing it—that love cannot transcend material conditions, that black men are never heroic, and so on). Many of these claims, moreover, are just asserted without any evidence, and when evidence is presented it usually cannot withstand the briefest scrutiny. Still more important, each of them is contradicted by obvious evidence proving that the idea was thought by at least some people in the period, and often by a great many people. Since this evidence is so easy to find, I can only conclude that the discoverers failed to look for it (Charnes and Newman even cite evidence that contradicts their claims without recognizing this). That failure is certainly not unique to these critics or to this critical enterprise; it is very common because of the tendency of our minds (not, of course, of human nature) to overlook evidence against a theory we espouse.[3] But while this tendency can explain why these critics do not notice the evidence against their discoveries of unthinkable thoughts, it cannot explain why they make these discoveries in the first place. I believe several causes are involved, since the enterprise is, in the current patois, overdetermined.

One such cause, probably the least important, is the intersection of two very different discourses—the elitist discourse of Cutting-Edge High Theory in the academy and the lowly colloquial discourse of the street. This intersection has become a site of confusion (not of contestation, which is what such sites are currently supposed to be), because in colloquial language the terms "unthinkable," "unimaginable," and "inconceivable" have undergone an inflation or slippage that linguists call the normalization of hyperbole, and now usually mean "impossible" or just "highly improbable." An obvious example is Henry Kamm's comment on Dariusz Jarosz's plans to write a social history of Poland under Marxism: "That he . . . can even conceive of such a project . . . would have been unimaginable before Communism began to crumble" (1995, A1)—that is, it could not have been imagined as possible that he could conceive of it as possible. The terms "incredible" and "unbelievable" have suffered a similar fate: when a store advertises "incredible savings" it wants us to give credence to their prices and realize they are very low, and when I say, "I don't believe this is happening," I do believe it is and regard it as unlikely or absurd. But my favorite example of this inflation comes from Joe McCarthy, who once snorted, in response to an objection, "That's the most unheard-of thing I ever heard of."

We should not be surprised to learn that this street usage has infected, or at least inflected, the language of some poststructuralist academic critics. Valerie Traub states, "I find it inconceivable that within . . . early modern culture, 'feminine' bodies did not meet, touch, and pleasure one another" (1994, 79), but she must find it conceivable and conceives of it as impossible. Stephen Orgel suggests that King James's admonition against women's cross-dressing may have been directed at his wife and adds, "The possibility is not inconceivable" (1995, 6); yet its conceivability cannot be at issue, since he just conceived it—what he is struggling to say is simply "It is possible." When Jonathan Crewe asserts that certain propositions about criticism are "virtually unthinkable" and "practically inconceivable" (1987, 132, 145), he means "very improbable," for actual unthinkability and inconceivability, unlike improbability, do not admit of degrees (remember McCarthy's "most unheard-of"). We have all encountered other usages of this kind in recent critical practice.

I am not deploring this linguistic change or advocating a return to the Good Old Days when words kept their "right" meanings, which is "unthinkable"; but we should be aware of the slippage and of its possible influence on the recent proliferation of discoveries of unthinkable thoughts. That influence should not be large, however, because this colloquial slippage usually occurs in statements about our own thinking in the present (as in the above examples), whereas the academic discoveries we are examining all claim that some idea was unthinkable for other people in another era. Yet it is sometimes difficult to tell which discourse we are hearing. The only critic I know of who explicitly addresses the problem is Francis Barker in his comment on the form of "subjection" in the period before the bourgeoisie took over, when "alterity of placement is always-already encoded as unthinkable. Or at least no more conceivable than the absurd proposition that the arm could take the place of the spleen" (1984, 32).[4] A few of the discoveries that people in the past could not think of some idea may also be claiming only that they could not think of it as possible or probable—this apparently is what Newman means when she says that the idea of a heroic black man "seemed unthinkable" to the English in 1693, since it could not "seem" anything to them unless they thought of it.[5] But most of these critics are claiming actual unthinkability; in fact some even insist that an idea was "literally unthinkable," which shows that they are aware of the colloquial usage and want to distinguish theirs from it.[6] It seems, then, that we must find other explanations for these discoveries.

A more important cause is the doctrine, employed by many of these critics, of what has been called "the prisonhouse of language,"[7] which holds that language determines thought, since no one can think of any idea unless there is a word for it in the vocabulary of the time. They sometimes invoke the authority of Ferdinand de Saussure for this doctrine—wrongly, I believe.[8] However, I am interested here not in what he really said but in what they do with what they think he said. We have already seen the claim that people in the Renaissance could not think of "dramatic structure" because the "basic terms" for it did not yet exist (Kavanagh 1985, 164–65);

and we are also told that these people had no conception of "the individual" because "it was not perhaps until 1690 that the essentialist sense of the word emerges" (Dollimore 1993, 156); and that they could not conceive of "'literature' in [our] sense" of "that word," which would be "unimaginable" because "literature" does not acquire its present meaning until the eighteenth century and so their language "lacks the word" for it (Bennett 1979, 13; Kavanagh 1985, 147, 151);[9] and that they could have "no recognition of homosexuality *per se*" because "there were no discrete terms for homosexual behavior in the period," since "the word itself is a nineteenth-century invention" and "sodomy" and "buggery," the words in their vocabulary, "could be used with as equal ease to mean bestiality" (Bray 1988, 13–14; Shepherd 1986, 199; Goldberg 1991, 75).

An obvious objection to these arguments about Renaissance nonthinkability is that they rely on the earliest recordings of a word or meaning in the *OED*, which are notoriously unreliable; the pages of *Notes and Queries* are filled with antedatings of the *OED*, some by over a hundred years.[10] But even if the *OED* were right about the first appearance of these words, the Renaissance often had other words with similar meanings, such as "poetry" for "literature," as I noted, and "person" for "individual," and "sodomy," "buggery," "pederasty," "catamite," and "pathic" for male "homosexuality." The meanings of the earlier and later words are not identical, but Renaissance thinking was not limited by this. Although their words "sodomy" and "buggery" included bestiality as well as homosexuality,[11] they surely were able to distinguish relations between two men from relations between a man and a beast (unless we are to be told that the human/beast binary "was not yet in place"). Indeed, the first sodomy law (25 Henry VIII c.6) distinguishes them in condemning the "abhomynable vice of buggery commyttid with mankynde or beaste."[12] Goldberg insists that "there were no discrete terms for homosexual behavior" at this time, yet the law's "buggery commyttid with mankynde" and the Bible's "lie with mankind, as . . . with a woman," quoted above, were such terms, which he does not recognize because he wants a term to be a single word. But we do not think in single words.

This last point leads us to the most basic objection to these arguments: they all assume a doctrine about the dependence of thoughts upon words that is demonstrably wrong. It may be true that we cannot think without language, but we certainly can think of an idea without having a specific word for it.[13] We do this all the time—we search for "the right words" to express "what we want to say," so our idea must precede those words, and we can also decide "to put it in other words" or translate it from one language or discourse into another, none of which would be possible (or even thinkable?) if words determine thoughts. And how could new words come into existence or old words change meaning? In this "post-Saussurean theory," presumably, the words would have to possess the power to do this all by themselves, just as they have to possess the power to control our thinking. Steven Pinker, who should know, says that cognitive scientists regard the doctrine as an "absurdity" (1994, 55–67).[14] It is curious that the critics who claim to be "interdisciplinary" when they adopt this doctrine never ask how it is judged in its own discipline. It is also curious that they can attribute these mystical powers to words and yet accuse the people they oppose of "mystification" and "logocentrism."

Another major cause of these discoveries of unthinkability is a doctrine that might be called "the prisonhouse of ideology," which derives from Louis Althusser's conception of ideology, not as a consciously held set of beliefs, but as "the very condition of our experience of the world, *un*conscious precisely in that it is unquestioned, taken for granted."[15] According to this doctrine, all "subjects" in any society are "interpellated" into its ideology, which causes them to experience their form of society as natural and unalterable (and so serves the interests of those who rule that society). The doctrine clearly underlies Francis Barker's claim, quoted earlier, that within prebourgeois ideology (or "subjection") "alterity of placement is always-already encoded as unthinkable" (1984, 32); and Jonathan Dollimore universalizes this process in his statement that the ideological ratification of existing social realities "work[s] to make both potential and change literally unthinkable" (1993, 271). It is no wonder, then, that critics who adopt this doctrine will expect to find that many ideas, especially those in conflict with current social arrangements, could not be thought by people in the Renaissance or other periods.

We would have to add, however, that this doctrine, like that of the prisonhouse of language, is demonstrably wrong. There is no period of recorded history when all people held the same ideas or experienced the world in the same way, or when no one ever thought of possible alternatives to that world. This applies even to apparently homogeneous periods like the Middle Ages, as I noted in my objection to Barker's claim, and it certainly applies to the Renaissance, which was marked by bitter social, political, and religious controversies between groups with very different ideas about what the world was or what it should be, and produced books like Montaigne's *Essais* and More's *Utopia* that conceptualized other forms of society. There would be no way to account for all this if potential and change had been "literally unthinkable"—indeed, there would be no way to account for any changes in history.

A third cause of the discoveries of unthinkable thoughts, closely related to the preceding one, is the doctrine that we can call "the prisonhouse of the episteme," which comes to us from Michel Foucault. It holds that in every "epoch" there is a basic mental paradigm that determines what ways of thinking about the world are possible, which in turn means that all other ways of thinking would be impossible at this time, as we can see, for example, in Jonathan Goldberg's assertion that "the world" perceived by Elizabethans "excludes . . . the conceptual categories" of individual autonomy and growth (1985, 118). Thus it is very similar, not only to the Althusserean view of ideology, but also to the older historicists' Zeitgeist or "ideas-of-the-time" approach, which produced such studies as Lovejoy's *The Great Chain of Being* (1936) and Tillyard's *The Elizabethan World Picture* (1943). It is hard to understand why some new historical critics, who have been so scornful of the old Zeitgeist theory, are so willing to accept the doctrine of the episteme, which makes the same kind of assertion (although in more up-to-date terminology), but it is easy to understand why, having accepted this doctrine, they are prepared to find that many ideas—those not enabled by the contemporary episteme—must have been unthinkable in the Renaissance and in other "epochs."

Clearly this doctrine is open to the same objections as Althusser's theory of ideology (and Zeitgeist theory), since it homogenizes each period in history by insisting that all people then thought alike, which we know is not true. Moreover, it has even greater difficulty than these other theories in accounting for historical change, because it requires us to believe that the ideas forming the episteme in any epoch were unthinkable in the previous one, which would eliminate the possibility of a causal connection between one epoch and the next. (Its notion of a "rupture" between successive epistemes acknowledges the failure to provide such a connection.) These obvious problems have recently led some of the newer historical critics to question the doctrine; Alan Sinfield, for instance, notes that it is "vulnerable to any scrap of empirical evidence showing ideas or behaviors occurring at the 'wrong' time" (1994a, 14). But I have been able to present much more than scraps of evidence to show that each idea I was discussing occurred to quite a few people at the "wrong" time—at a time, that is, when it was supposed to be "unthinkable" because of the prisonhouse of the episteme or of language or of ideology.

There is a more fundamental objection to all three of these prisonhouse doctrines: they all sell short the human mind by insisting that it is always limited to a kind of tunnel vision as a result of blinders imposed upon it by some aspect of the surrounding society, from which it cannot escape, like the people in the Myth of the Cave in book 7 of Plato's *Republic*, who are chained down and can only look in one direction, which prevents them from seeing that "reality" is not confined to the shadows of the puppet show they have to watch. But this too is demonstrably wrong because, unlike Plato's cave, none of these alleged prisonhouses is static or hermeneutically sealed off. They all continually undergo internal changes in response to external influences, so they must be permeable—indeed, they often overlap or interact, as we saw in the case of academic and street language. Moreover, we can move (or be moved) from one language or ideology or episteme to another and adapt to it, which is a common experience of immigrants and converts. We can even become aware of, and thus escape from, the constraints of our own language/ideology/episteme, because, as James Battersby points out, "we can always talk *about* what we talk *with*, we can always go 'meta-' on any discourse" (1996, 24), and if this takes us into another prison, we have the same ability to escape from that one. The use of this ability may vary in different cultures and situations and individuals, but since I have it I assume that others have it too, now and in the Renaissance, unless we are to believe that the human brain went through a further major evolution in a mere four hundred years.

My knowledge of this ability of the mind to escape from these prisonhouses is not limited to introspection, however, because I also have irrefutable evidence supplied by the very critics who assert that we cannot escape. For it is obvious that *they* must have left their prisonhouse, or else they could not recognize it *as* a prisonhouse and explain it to us, although they do not explain how they are able to accomplish this. (Plato has someone dragged out of the cave into the "real" world against his will by an unidentified agency, but that is a myth.) Apparently they believe, unlike me, that their minds have some special power denied to the rest of us, similar to psychoanalysts who claim they can bring to consciousness the material trapped in the unconscious, which is the Freudian prisonhouse (remember that Althusserean ideology, which these critics are conscious of, is supposed to be "*un*conscious").[16] I am afraid that I cannot discern any extraordinary mental qualities in them, except for the hypertrophied chutzpah (now hubris) responsible for this belief that they possess extraordinary mental qualities enabling them to escape from the prisonhouses of language or ideology or episteme that everyone else must languish in. But the fact that they can escape, for whatever reason, proves that these entities are not really prisonhouses after all, and therefore, while they undoubtedly influence our thinking in many ways, they do not control it and cannot make any thoughts unthinkable.

I suspect, however, that the most important cause of the discoveries of unthinkable thoughts in the Renaissance is to be found not in these prisonhouse doctrines but in the motivation of the discoverers, and this suspicion is confirmed by several of them, who tell us that a history of the past is never objective but is always "fabricated" or "fictioned" to serve as a "history-for" some interest in the present.[17] If we apply their own law by asking what interests are served by these historical claims about unthinkability, the obvious answer is that they serve the professional interests of the people making them. For their discoveries are often announced in the course of refuting earlier critics and are often presented as the most telling point in that refutation, since they supposedly prove that those critics were ahistorical in attributing ideas to Renaissance literature that were unthinkable then, and at the same time prove the need for, and the superiority of, the kind of criticism practiced by the discoverer that can supply such crucial historical information. Sometimes this weapon is able in one move (formerly stroke) to demolish a whole army of rivals, as when de Grazia and Stallybrass assert that the recent discovery that the Renaissance had "no notion of human character" has "done nothing less than overthrow almost three centuries of 'character study'" of Shakespeare's plays (1993, 273).[18] That is a pretty heady prospect, and it helps to explain the professional interests at stake in the discoveries that Renaissance thinking (or nonthinking) was so different from our own.[19]

These discoveries also serve the political agenda of some of the critics (mainly Marxists) who make them, and who can be quite open about this—Catherine Belsey, for example, says that the claim of the kind of history of the Renaissance she advocates "is not that such a history . . . is more accurate, but only that it is more radical" (1992, 44); and Terence Hawkes says that its aim is "not simply to describe the past 'as it was.' It is, rather, polemically to reread, renarrate, and so reclaim the past in the name of the construction of a more acceptable present" (1995, 66). It is no coincidence, therefore, that almost all the modern ideas that they insist were unthinkable in the Renaissance, discussed in my earlier essay and here, are ones that they themselves oppose. Nor can it be a coincidence that they almost always insist that these ideas became thinkable only with the advent of bourgeois hegemony, which they also oppose. Thus their historical discoveries serve a double political purpose—to prove that these evil ideas are not natural, inevitable, unchanging, God-given, and so forth, which their opponents are supposed to believe (although I have never met anyone who does), and to blame these ideas on the evil bourgeoisie, who supposedly foisted them on us as part of their oppressive ideology. In the light of this purpose, then, the evidence I assembled against these discoveries, showing that each unthinkable idea was thought in the Renaissance, would be irrelevant, since they want them to be judged not in terms of their accuracy (describing the past "as it was") but in terms of their "radical" effect in constructing a "more acceptable present" or, as they usually put it, in helping to bring about a "transformation of society."[20]

It is by no means clear, however, that these discoveries really have the radical political effect claimed for them, even within the confines of our discipline, where some of them might work in the opposite direction. For example, the discovery that the "incontrovertible male/female binary . . . was not yet in place" in the Renaissance, cited above, would do nothing less than overthrow all the recent feminist studies of Shakespearean "patriarchy," which depend on this binary being in place. And it is even less clear that they have any radical political effect in the extramural world, unless we are to assume that the oppressed masses will arise and throw off their chains upon learning (if they ever read these critics) that the ideas of individual autonomy, dramatic structure, and so on, were unthinkable in the Renaissance and were imposed by the bourgeoisie three centuries ago. (Indeed, if they are persuaded that their sense of themselves as autonomous individuals is a bourgeois imposition, they will no longer believe that they possess the agency required to arise.) The Marxist critics themselves never explain how their discoveries will "transform" society; they do not even explain what kind of "transformation" they desire. For the truth is that they have no program of action in the arena of politics, and what I called their "political agenda" looks more like an apolitical, academic game they are playing, in which they score points against an imaginary opponent by announcing these discoveries of unthinkable thoughts.

5
Bashing the Bourgeois Subject

ANYONE WHO HAS TRIED TO KEEP UP WITH THE CURRENT STATE OF CRITICAL discourse does not need to be told that the Bourgeois or Humanist Subject (hereafter abbreviated as BHS) is in very serious trouble. Something like a major industry has developed, primarily among the cultural materialists, New Historicists, and some feminist critics, that is devoted to BHS-bashing. And since no one else has risen to the BHS's defense, I have reluctantly agreed to take on this thankless task. I had better confess at the outset, however, that I am a card-carrying BHS myself, as are the members of my nuclear, affective family and most of my friends, because some people might object that this firsthand acquaintance with the subject (in both senses) is "empiricist" and therefore disqualifies me from discoursing about it. They may be right, for it seems that the principal qualification of those who are doing all the discoursing—i.e., the bashing—is that they have never seen a real, live BHS. But I must leave that for the reader to judge.

The basic claim of all the bashers is that the BHS was created (or "constructed") in the late seventeenth century, by the bourgeoisie of course, in order to consolidate their hegemony over the oppressed masses, and that before this period people had a radically different sense of selfhood (or "subjectivity"). Indeed, calling it radically different turns out to be an understatement, when we look at the absurd (and sometimes contradictory) accounts of the pre-BHS given to us in Barker 1984, Belsey 1985b, Dollimore 1993, Goldberg 1985, and Greenblatt 1986a. But since I examine (and refute) these accounts of the pre-BHS elsewhere,[1] I want to turn now to their descriptions of the BHS, focusing on the BHS's view of himself that emerges from this body of criticism. Most of these descriptions consist of a list of qualities that, according to the bashers, are attributed to the BHS by himself or by his alleged ideology of "humanism" (usually preceded by "essentialist" or "bourgeois" or "liberal"). Jonathan Dollimore, for example, refers to "the autonomous, unified self-generating subject postulated by essentialist humanism" that "emerges only in the latter part of the seventeenth century and the eighteenth century" (1993, 155–56), and Louis Montrose to "the freely self-creating and world-creating subject of bourgeois humanism" (1986a, 306); and Catherine Belsey says that "liberal humanism proposes that the subject is the free, unconstrained author of meaning and action, the origin of history," and that this conception of the "subject of liberal humanism is a product of the second half of the seventeenth century" (1985b, 8, 33). In Antony Easthope's account,

> at the centre of bourgeois ideology is the idealist conception of the self-conscious individual (typically male) as an unconditioned source of decision and action—owing nothing to anyone, depending on nothing but himself, choosing freely and autonomously . . . as if (in the words of Coriolanus) "a man were author of himself / And knew no other kin." (1982, 142)

And a feminist version is presented by Toril Moi, who is summarizing and endorsing the views of Luce Irigaray and Hélène Cixous:

> This integrated self [of the BHS] is in fact a phallic self, constructed on the model of the self-contained, powerful phallus. Gloriously autonomous, it banishes from itself all conflict, contradiction and ambiguity. In this humanist ideology the self is the *sole author* of history and of the literary text: the humanist creator is potent, phallic and male—God in relation to his world. (1985, 8)

It was descriptions of this sort that led me to suggest at the outset that these critics have never seen a real, live BHS, even though according to their own historical analysis they should be surrounded by innumerable instantiations of this creature. Have they ever known anyone, outside a mental institution, who believed that he generated himself or the world, or that he was completely free to choose and act without any conditions or constraints, or that he had no internal or external conflicts, and was entirely independent of all other persons and things, or that he could make words mean whatever he wanted, and created history all by himself, and was attached (loosely speaking, of course) to a self-contained, autonomous phallus? Clearly this conception of the BHS is just as absurd as their conception of the pre-BHS, and so the historical claim of these critics that the BHS did not exist in the Renaissance turns out to be true after all, in a sense they certainly did not intend, because the kind of BHS they describe has never existed, except in their imaginations. It was not produced by the bourgeois Ideological State Apparatus in the second half of the seventeenth century, as they maintain, but by academic bourgeois-bashers in our own day.

The explanation is simple enough, for when these critics discourse on the BHS they are not talking about actual individuals they have known or even individuals unknown to them; they are talking about an abstraction—an abstraction that they have (to adopt their own terminology) reified, personified, mystified, stereotyped, caricatured, scapegoated, hypostatized, fetishized, alterized, ventriloquized, and, above all, demonized. This process of demonization can be seen very clearly in two accounts of how the BHS will precipitate a nuclear apocalypse through its own internal dynamics. According to Belsey, the BHS longs for suicide, which puts

> an end to the endless desire . . . to be precisely autonomous, to be not just free, but also the origin and guarantee of its own identity, the source of being, meaning and action. Suicide re-establishes the sovereign subject . . . [and is] the crowning affirmation of the supremacy of the self.

And nuclear war is "communal suicide, an absolute act of universal sovereignty," which, since it "clos[es] off in the moment of fulfillment the desire to be absolute, is [the BHS's] diamond of unnamable desire" (1985b, 5). Barker says that "the death drive" is the BHS's "unknown objective":

> A nuclear denouement . . . would secure the [conclusion] . . . which bourgeois discourse is committed to seeking. . . . The desire . . . for a finality, a plenitude of arrival—which must shape itself as the most complete absence possible—is [its] secret aspiration. . . . Its aim [is] to find in a general catastrophe . . . the end of all desire . . . [where] the hollowing would finally be filled, the absence supplied . . . by a last erasure of the doubled architecture of presence and absence that describes . . . bourgeois subjectivity. (1984, 110–11)

We should note that in both these fantasies (for that is surely what they are) the BHS produces the ultimate disaster all by itself with no help from the outside material world—no changes in the mode of production or social formation, no conflicts between or within classes, no competition for raw materials or markets, no clash of rival ideologies, no enemy, real or imagined, and no external goal, not even the need "to busy giddy minds with foreign quarrels."[2] Belsey and Barker presumably regard themselves as materialists, but here they sound much more like theologians trying to explain how Satan's self-generated "pride" caused him to revolt and bring evil into the universe.*

Now that we have seen how these critics describe the BHS, we should be in a position to determine why they have made their historical claims that it only appeared toward the end of the seventeenth century and that before then people had a completely different conception of the self. On this question, fortunately, we can learn something from the critics themselves, for a number of them have been telling us that historical statements are never objective or impartial, because every history of the past is actually "fabricated" or "fictioned" to serve as a "history-for" some interest in the present.[3] We should therefore apply their own law by asking whose interests are served by this history of the subject that they have discovered. The obvious answer is that it serves the interests of these critics and their projects, but there seems to be a significant difference here between the New Historicists and the cultural materialists. The historical discoveries of the former group are made—or at least announced—in the course of refuting someone else, and are meant to be the most telling point in that refutation. Thus Goldberg's assertion that the BHS did not exist in the Renaissance is directed against what he calls "the ahistorical tendencies in feminist criticism" of Shakespeare, which "lacks historical support" and "historical specificity" (1985, 117, 137); and Greenblatt's is aimed at previous "psychoanalytic interpretation" of Renaissance texts, which, he says, "is causally belated," since the concept of selfhood it assumes had not yet emerged, so

---

*Neither Belsey nor Barker tells us why the BHSes did not start a nuclear war, despite the many opportunities, and neither of them compares the actual suicide rates in BHS and non-BHS societies, which presumably would be "empirical" and therefore bourgeois. Eagleton also criticizes the BHS (he calls it the "bourgeois individualist") for its "endless expansion of the self" and "unslakable thirst for some ultimate mastery which will never come" (1986, 4), although he does not make it suicidal; but in a later essay he dismisses the Marxists' attacks on the BHS as a "tiresomely dogmatic" and "shoddy caricature" that "vulgarly reduced" the "magnificent emancipatory heritage" of "the great liberal tradition" to "the bugbear of the 'autonomous subject'" (1994, 6, 9), so the tide may be turning. The *New York Times* reports that at a recent meeting of the Shakespeare Association of America Linda Charnes criticized "our institutionalized solidarity in bashing the 'bourgeois subject'" and said that "the time to make a career beating that horse has passed" (Rosenbaum 2000, 13).

that it "can redeem its belatedness only when it historicizes its own procedures" (1986a, 221).[4] The chief value of their discovery of the history of the subject, apparently, is to put down other critics, whose ignorance of it demonstrates their ahistoricality, and therefore to establish the superiority of the discoverer who can supply this crucial historical perspective. It is in their own interest, then, to find that the Renaissance pre-BHS is radically different from the modern BHS, because that provides them with the weapon to defeat their opponents, and at the same time proves the need for, and the validity of, their kind of "historicizing"; but as far as I can see they have no stake in the specific nature of the pre-BHS or the BHS.[5]

The cultural materialists also deploy their historical discovery at times to refute the readings of the critics they oppose (usually the "formalists" or "humanists"), but they seem much more concerned with the pre-BHS itself, because they want it to be not merely different from the BHS but also superior (which the New Historicists never claim). For their primary interest is in attacking, not other critics, but the evil bourgeois world of modern capitalism, and since they are operating within the standard Marxist two-term dialectic—or, a less kind observer might say, under the standard Marxist difficulty of counting beyond two—the prebourgeois conceptions of the Renaissance must be antibourgeois and therefore good, or at least better than the later bourgeois conceptions. That is why they have discovered (or, to adopt their own term, "fictioned") a history of the subject wherein the Renaissance pre-BHS contains qualities that they approve of and hence want to find there, which turn out to be the opposite of the BHS's individualism, essentialism, autonomy, and so on, that they disapprove of. Thus, while they regularly accuse older historical critics like Lovejoy (1936) and Tillyard (1943) of producing a Renaissance that reproduces their own ideology (which is true enough), that is just what they themselves have done here, although the ideology itself is of course very different.

There is also, I would argue, another interest served by the production of this history, which I call Edenism. It is the belief—or the need to believe—in some idyllic period of the past from which we have fallen away, and, in most versions, to which we should return. The Garden of Eden performs this function for many Jews and Christians, as did the Golden Age for pagan Greeks and Romans. German and Italian fascism relied heavily upon Edenic accounts of ancient national glories. Americans have several Edens—the days of the Founding Fathers, the frontier, the simple life of the small town—that are now exploited by conservatives. In fact, we usually think of this as a right-wing phenomenon and call the wish to return to such an Eden "reactionary," but it also flourishes at or near the other end of the political spectrum. The early Protestant attacks on the papacy appealed to a second Eden in the practices of the primitive church, and there was an old radical tradition in England that evoked the original Eden, where Adam delved and Eve span and there were no gentlemen. Much more recently, we have seen some black activists Edenizing the condition of the race in precolonial Africa and some Hispanics Edenizing the civilization of pre-Columbian America; and there are some feminists who believe in a prehistoric era of gender equality—or, more often, matriarchy—that has now been described in several books. One of them, for instance, claims that women were worshipped by men as supernatural beings, and that they invented agriculture, cattle breeding, and architecture, among other things, before the men seized power.[6] Even feminists who do not explicitly invoke such ideas will sometimes employ the rhetoric of "reclaiming" or "recovering" what "we lost" or what "was taken from us," which is a form of Edenism.

The Marxists possess an Eden of their very own in the myth of "primitive communism," which has now been revived and "theorized" in Fredric Jameson's *The Political Unconscious* (1981). And it seems that some of them have constructed a second Eden in the feudal world. Indeed, in doing this they are simply following the lead of their founding fathers, who began *The Communist Manifesto* with an indictment of the bourgeoisie for pitilessly tearing asunder all earlier human ties and leaving no other nexus between people than naked self-interest, drowning chivalrous sentiment in the icy water of egotistical calculation, resolving personal worth into exchange value, and reducing the family to a mere money relation (Marx and Engels 1959, 9–10), in passages that resemble Thomas Carlyle's *Past and Present* and Edmund Burke's complaint, in *Reflections on the French Revolution*, that the age of chivalry is gone and all the decent drapery of life is rudely torn off, even though their attack comes from the political Right. A few of the critics we are considering here warn against this tendency to idealize the Middle Ages and Renaissance,[7] but they all indulge in it to some extent.

The most indulgent by far is Francis Barker, who yearns for the lost organic "coherence" of feudalism and berates the BHS for its "deadly subjectivity" (which is nonetheless "imaginary") and for its "deleterious separations" of mind from body and individual from society, which he characterizes as "what was done to us in the seventeenth century" by the bourgeoisie, and which his final words urge us to "undo" (1984, 24–25, 31, 68, 116).[8] At times he sounds like T. S. Eliot lamenting the "dissociation of sensibility" in this same period (1932, 247), which is another example of how Edenism can make strange political bedfellows. And his moving account of the "wretched pathos of the subject" (i.e., the BHS) created by those separations (1984, 66) would lead one to conclude that people living after the seventeenth century were never happy, although he might claim that the bourgeois Ideological State Apparatus tricks them into thinking that they are happy, just as it tricks them into thinking that they are thinking, which is why their subjectivity is "imaginary."

Dollimore's Edenism is somewhat different, since it is limited to the Renaissance, which he views as a kind of breathing space (and a window of opportunity for his project) of relative flexibility for the subject that opened up between the "Christian essentialism" of the Middle Ages and the "essentialist humanism" of the Enlightenment (1993, 155). We get further variations when the critics attempt to combine Marxism and feminism. Catherine Belsey, for instance, argues that the wife in a bourgeois companionate marriage, even though it is "founded on consent" and allows for divorce, is "in reality" less free than her feudal predecessor in an arranged and indissoluble marriage, because the "overt" external control of the ecclesiastical courts has been replaced by "a new mode of control" that is "internalized and invisible" and therefore "more insidious" (1985b, 145–47); and Gayle Greene asserts that the effect of capitalism is to "reduce" women "to objects of appetite and trade" who must sell themselves (1981/2, 39). She never explains what they have been reduced *from*, but it can only be from their status under feudalism, when they were sold by their father. Selling oneself might seem a step up from being sold by someone else, but Greene regards it as a descent because she has idealized feudal social relations in order to score a point against capitalism. Thus, in both her account and Belsey's, Marxist Edenism has won out over feminist concern for the situation of real women in the real world.

Edenism may appear to be nothing more than a harmless exercise in nostalgia and wishful thinking, but it is often accompanied by other ideas that are far from harmless if people act upon them. The most dangerous of these is the belief in a villain who is responsible for the loss of Eden and hence for our present fallen state. In the biblical Eden it was Satan, and in most of the other versions it is some group or institution that is usually hypostatized and endowed with satanic powers—the papal Antichrist for early Protestants, International Jewry for the Nazis, Secular Humanism for American fundamentalists, and so on. The Marxists have two Edens and therefore two villains, since "primitive communism" was destroyed by private property and the class system, and Renaissance wholeness or flexibility by the BHS and its alleged sponsor, Liberal Humanism. (Not so incidentally, Liberal Humanism bears an eerie resemblance to Secular Humanism: the latter is a nonexistent religion recently invented by the far Right to serve as the evil enemy, and the former is a nonexistent ideology recently invented by the far Left for the same purpose.) This conception in turn usually leads to a rejection of any reforms as deceptive "Band-Aids" or "window dressing," and an insistence upon a radical "final solution" that will transform society, extirpate the satanic villain, and so restore the lost Eden in a utopia of idyllic harmony. We now call this a "totalizing" view of the world, because it posits a single cause for all our problems and a single cure, and within it the processes of Edenizing and demonizing feed upon and reinforce each other in an ascending spiral of fantasy. The belief in a demonic causation enhances the need to Edenize the world that it destroyed, and the belief in that Edenic world enhances the need to demonize the cause of its destruction, which, I am suggesting, helps to explain the incredible portrayals of the BHS that we looked at earlier.

There is, finally, one more reason that the cultural materialists have produced this history of the change from the pre-BHS to the BHS, which can be found in another interest of theirs that it serves. For they themselves want to change the BHS and therefore, in addition to bashing away at it through these portrayals, they must argue that it was itself the result of a radical change in the recent past and so is susceptible to another radical change in the near future. This history, then, justifies their hopes of "producing a new kind of human subject altogether," as Terry Eagleton puts it (1983, 191),[9] which brings back memories of the reports we used to get from Moscow about the "human engineering" that was creating a "New Soviet Man" (with his female counterpart presumably trailing along behind), who would be sober, chaste, and cultured, strong but gentle, industrious but not competitive, independent but obedient to the Party, free of all internal and external problems, and, above all, selflessly dedicated to the common good—in short, a kind of socialist super Boy Scout. (We have not heard much about him lately, perhaps because the Soviet press has been too busy complaining about drunkenness and absenteeism in the workplace, black-marketeering, and general "hooliganism.") At the end of her essay, Belsey states the idea in more general terms as the purpose of this kind of history, which is "to demonstrate that since change has occurred in those areas which seem most intimate and most inevitable, change in those areas is possible for us" (1992, 44).[10] But this too is a fantasy. I do not think many workers will be induced to mount the barricades upon being informed that the conception of the "subject" underwent a change in the seventeenth century, especially when they are also informed—for surely these critics will be honest about it—that "the claim is not that such a history . . . is more accurate" than other histories that deny this change, "but only that it is more radical" (1992, 44), and that it has been deliberately "fictioned" as a "history-for" in order to induce them to mount the barricades. Moreover, since they presumably are BHSes themselves, they will believe that *they* are "the sole authors of history," and so on, and will resent all the unkind things these critics have been saying about BHSdom. In the immortal words of P. T. Barnum, you can't expect to bash them and bamboozle them at the same time.

It's a Panic

Not so very long ago, within the memory of people yet living (including myself), large segments of the Western intelligentsia, as they were then called, were under the spell of the two great pseudosciences of Freudianism and Marxism. Looking back on that period now, it is easy to understand their tremendous appeal, since they both claimed to explain the one fundamental cause (and the cure) of all our major problems, and so offered to true believers a sense of absolute intellectual power and superiority over the rest of us. They offered absolute certainty as well, because their causal scheme could also explain—and hence explain away—all criticism of them. The Freudians asserted that anyone objecting to their doctrines was driven by unconscious "anxiety" at the threatened exposure of his or her "repressed" desires, and so was "resisting" the truth.[11] The Marxists in those days eschewed the Freudian concept of the unconscious, which they regarded as "subjectivist," "escapist," and "reactionary" (the epithets were more or less interchangeable),[12] but asserted instead that anyone objecting to their doctrines was driven by "anxiety" at the threatened loss of his or her class privileges in the coming revolution. In either case, then, the very objections to the doctrines were interpreted by those doctrines to be evidence for them, and there was no way out for the poor objectors, since they could not prove their nonanxiety, and the more they protested that they were not anxious, the more anxious they sounded. Thus the two schemes were closed and always already self-confirming. This is one reason that they were pseudosciences, since, unlike the real sciences, they never risked the possibility of refutation (Cioffi 1970).

We do not hear these assertions very often today, at least in their pure form, for obvious reasons. A Freudian would look pretty silly telling women that they questioned the theory of penis envy because they were unconsciously "resisting," and Marxists can scarcely say that professional historians who question the theory of economic determinism want to avert the imminent revolution. Yet the basic tactics still crop up, usually in a diluted mixture, as can be seen in Catherine Belsey's reply to my "Bashing the Bourgeois Subject," where she claims that my critique of the latest Marxist accounts of the BHS is generated by "anxiety," "fear," and "panic," and is even "slightly hysterical," because I found those accounts so "unnerving," "disturbing," and "threatening" (1989, 87, 88, 89, 90). She does not explicitly invoke either my unconscious or my class status, nor does she explain just what in those accounts is supposed to be so frightening to me, but the tactic has the same advantages as the earlier versions. It means that she does not have to confront my arguments, and presumably gives her a pleasant illusion of power when she imagines that she and her colleagues have me quaking in my liberal humanist jackboots. She must know that I cannot possibly disprove this, but what she does not seem to know is that I could just as easily turn the tactic against her. I could claim that she clearly has a substantial emotional and intellectual investment in her fantasy of a satanic and suicidal BHS, and so when it was threatened by me she panicked and projected her feelings by accusing me of panicking. And as evidence I could even point to her compulsive repetition of the charge seven times on one page (89), since she herself informs us, on the same page, that "the compulsion to repeat is always an indication of anxiety." I would not do this for two reasons. I do not believe it is true, because I have met her and she impressed me as being relatively unpanickable (apparently I did not make the same impression on her). But much more important, even if it were true, it would be completely irrelevant to the question of judging her arguments or mine.

The validity of an argument is not determined by the arguer's emotional state, any more than it is by his gender, race, ethnicity, nationality, class, age, sexual orientation, religion, or politics. All these factors, of course, can affect a person's argument, but they cannot tell us how to judge it. Even the most panicky, sexist, racist, agist, ethnocentric, homophobic, Freudian Marxist can produce a valid argument, and even the coolest liberal humanist (like me) can produce an invalid one. The only way to tell is by looking at the argument and not the arguer. On this crucial point we might learn something from the natural sciences, since Belsey seems to believe that her critical approach is more "scientific" than the approaches she opposes (1980, 128, 138). Scientists are only human and can get very attached to a theory, yet when someone challenges it they do not accuse her of anxiety or hysteria or anything else, but instead deal with her evidence and her reasoning. I think we should do the same, and stop trying to close off adverse criticism by dragging in these *ad personam* (formerly *ad hominem*) red herrings. And this means that, like the scientists, we must be open to the possibility of being refuted.

6
Son of Bashing the Bourgeois Subject

THE APPEARANCE OF "BASHING THE BOURGEOIS SUBJECT" HAS PRODUCED SUCH A widespread popular demand for a sequel that I have finally bowed to this pressure and agreed, again with considerable reluctance, to take on the task.[1] Since that essay dealt only with the bashers' account of how the bourgeois or humanist subject (abbreviated here as the BHS) views itself, I have focused here on the view of the world, especially of our socioeconomic system, that they attribute to the BHS or to its supposed ideology of "liberal humanism." Since the New Historicists have very little to say on this topic, I had to limit my cast of characters to the cultural materialists (or new Marxists) and some feminist critics, but I tried whenever possible to use the same ones who starred in the first version, which I assume is what the fans crying out for a sequel would want.

It will be useful to begin here, as in my "Bashing" essay, with some representative quotations from the bashers themselves that define the alleged beliefs of the BHS in this area. One of them comes, appropriately, from Catherine Belsey's response to that essay, where she asserts that "the first imperative of bourgeois ideology is to proclaim itself natural and universal" (1989, 88). A similar account of bourgeois "ideological formations" is given by Francis Barker and Peter Hulme, who state that "capitalist societies have always presupposed the naturalness and universality of their own structures" (1985, 194). In one of the "fundamental mystifications of bourgeois ideology," Alan Sinfield explains, "the power relations which are peculiar to market society are seen as how things have always been," as "universal [and] unchangeable" (1994b, 162, 165).[2] Malcolm Evans finds that this ideology "assumes unchanging essences" and "propose[s] a world . . . of the apparently universal and perfectly natural" (1986, 35). Our "social formation or power structure," Jonathan Dollimore says, "is itself represented by that ideology as *eternally or naturally given*—i.e. as inevitable, immutable" (1993, 9). Margot Heinemann objects to bourgeois theatrical productions because they represent "our present social arrangements and behaviour as fixed and inevitable" (1994, 239). According to James Kavanagh, bourgeois "literary ideology" assumes "an eternal, natural *and* transcendent, cultural reality" (1985, 164). And Tony Bennett refers to "the bourgeois myths" of "a frozen world of idealist and essentialist categories," which are "myths of . . . eternality and universality" (1979, 169–70).

Although more quotations of this sort could be produced, I think these are enough to make my point, which is that the bashers all insist that the BHS believes the socioeconomic arrangements of its own world are natural, universal, and unchanging, since they are based on essential aspects of human nature. This alleged view of the external world, therefore, is of a very different order from the BHS's alleged view of itself that was scrutinized in my "Bashing" essay. I argued there that the beliefs about itself attributed by these bashers to the BHS (that it is self-created, completely free to choose and to act without any internal or external constraints, completely independent of all other persons, and so on) were never held by anyone outside a mental institution; but this belief about the world has been held by a great many sane people. The trouble is that they are not BHSes. It is an extreme form of ethnocentrism, of our tendency to assume that everyone in the world must be like us, which is corrected when we learn about people and cultures that are different. That is why it is such a common trait in very young children, and why among adults it is usually limited to those who live in very isolated and static societies. We would therefore expect to find it in the caves of a Mesolithic tribe or in the serfs' hovels on a medieval manor, but not in the modern cities inhabited by the BHS. Indeed, many of the major projects of the bourgeoisie, such as exploration, commerce, colonialism, secularization, urbanization, the spread of literacy and education, the development of mass media of communication, and research in anthropology and other social sciences (often in the service of commerce and colonialism), have worked against this ethnocentrism. Far from being part of bourgeois ideology, it seems to be the antithesis of BHSdom, which is responsible for the virtual elimination of this worldview, which must have been widespread in earlier eras.

It is this kind of obvious discrepancy between their descriptions and the actual facts that led me to suggest in my earlier essay that these bashers have never seen a real, live BHS. Have they ever met a person who believes that capitalism is natural or universal or unchanging? Surely anyone with the slightest knowledge of history would be aware that it is a relatively recent development and so cannot be natural; and anyone who watches the television news would know that many societies have other economic systems, so it cannot be universal; and only a little more sophistication is required to realize that capitalism operates today in a very different way than it did two hundred or even fifty years ago, which means that it cannot be unchanging. The idea itself is absurd, and it is just as absurd to claim that any significant number of people today believe in it. (I should add that the belief that the gender arrangements of one's own world are natural, universal, and unchanging, which the bashers also attribute to the BHS, is still held by many people, indicating that, contrary to orthodox Marxist teaching, the attitudes in this area are separate from and more deeply embedded than those integral to the ideology of capitalism. But this belief too has no necessary connection to BHSdom, since it is much more pervasive and powerful in pre-BHS societies.)

The bashers' description of the BHS's ideology, moreover, contradicts not only these obvious facts but also the account given to us by the founders of their own ideology. In my "Bashing" essay I paraphrased a section near the beginning of *The Communist Manifesto* that characterizes the bourgeoisie as the destroyers of any faith in a natural, universal, and unchanging social order—as pitilessly tearing asunder all earlier human ties, drowning chivalrous sentiment in the icy water of egotistical calculation, reducing the family to a mere money relation, and so on. This is followed by an even more dramatic passage where their continual disruptions within the superstructure are emphasized and connected to changes in the material base:

> The bourgeoisie cannot exist without constantly revolutionizing the instruments of production, and thereby the relations of production, and with them the whole relations of society. . . . Constant revolutionizing of production, uninterrupted disturbance of all social conditions, everlasting uncertainty and agitation distinguish the bourgeois epoch from all earlier ones. All fixed, fast-frozen relations, with their train of ancient and venerable prejudices and opinions, are swept away, all new-formed ones become antiquated before they can ossify. (Marx and Engels 1959, 10)

How can we explain the startling difference—indeed, the direct contradiction—between this description and the one presented by the new Marxists, which even extends to the opposite use of the same metaphor in Bennett's statement, where the bourgeoisie do the freezing, and in the *Manifesto*, where they are the defrosters? One possibility is that the BHS (along with its ideology) has changed—that, like a person, it started out full of energy and daring but then grew old and stodgy. This analogy is implicit in many of the older Marxist histories, which find that the bourgeoisie was once a "progressive" force and later became "reactionary"; but the new Marxists think differently. Belsey assures us that, even though it has undergone some "development," the ideology of "liberal humanism, laying claim to be both natural and universal," is essentially the same today as when it "was produced . . . in the second half of the seventeenth century" (1985b, 7), so even in its most "progressive" stage the BHS supposedly believed this "reactionary" doctrine; and none of the other accounts of the BHS's view of the world quoted earlier suggests that it altered over the years. Furthermore, the bourgeois "agitation" recorded by Marx and Engels has not slowed down but has accelerated continually to affect more aspects of life in more radical ways at a more rapid pace. Anyone in America or Britain who is over forty has seen during his or her lifetime profound changes in industry, finance, politics, the family, education, technology, science, the arts, and literary criticism, for the new critical approaches, including those practiced by the BHS-bashers, are part of this "constant revolutionizing" generated and sustained by the BHS. It is therefore hard to see how the BHS could be a less dynamic agent of change now than it was in Marx's day, or how it could have frozen itself into this belief in a frozen, unchanging world.

If the striking difference between these two descriptions of the bourgeoisie cannot be accounted for by changes in bourgeois behavior or ideology, then it seems reasonable to look for an explanation, as I did in my earlier essay, in the lesson taught to us by the new Marxists themselves, who insist that descriptions of this sort are never objective or impartial but are always "fabricated" or "fictioned" to serve someone's "interest."[3] The interests served here are obviously those of the authors of these descriptions, the original Marxists and the new ones, and they seem to be basically the same interest—to bash the bourgeoisie. But this bashing takes place in very different situations that call for very different rhetorics. It is easy to understand why Marx and Engels were more impressed by the "revolutionizing" effects of the bourgcoisie than we are today, since they were closer to the old world that was being revolutionized and were less accustomed to the kind of rapid change that we now take for granted. They could also assume that the public they wrote for shared this impression of bourgeois activity and its threat to traditional values, and they emphasized the aspects of the bourgeoisie that would seem most pernicious to this public. That does not mean that they were insincere; I am sure they believed their description, which is much nearer to the truth than the one presented by the new Marxists, and they may even have felt a nostalgic admiration for the dying old order.[4] The new Marxists, however, are writing in a world that has grown used to change, and writing for a small group of academics who, like themselves, have already been poststructuralized. Neither they nor their readers would be disturbed by a threat to traditional values, which they have already rejected, and so these new bashers accuse the BHS of the opposite crime, of asserting that our social arrangements are natural, universal, and unchanging, and therefore of promoting what they and their readers regard as the most pernicious of all heresies—essentialism. This again does not mean that they do not believe their description or do not share the attitudes they appeal to. Like Marx and Engels, they "see" the bourgeoisie in what to them and their audience is the worst possible light. Thus the difference between these two descriptions can be explained by their authors' common "interest" in demonizing this enemy. The enemy has not changed that much, but the definition of the demonic has undergone a major transformation.

Further evidence that the new bashers are demonizing the BHS can be found in some of the other beliefs about the world that they attribute to it and to "liberal humanism"—beliefs that are always bad but are often contradictory, which demonstrates again what I referred to in my earlier essay as the Marxists' inability to count past two. This means that all beliefs that are not on their side—i.e., all the wrong ones—are lumped together on the enemy's side, even though they may seem to the rest of us to be very different. I cited there as an example Catherine Belsey's claim that the view of history as a decline from a lost Eden and the view of it as an ascent toward a better world, while they appear to be opposites, are really "counterpart[s]" and are both "characteristic of liberal humanism" (1985b, 223). A more common example is the claim that liberal humanism is both "idealist" and "empiricist," a highly unlikely combination, one would think, but since Marxists are against each of them, the BHS is charged with both.[5] This same operation where contradictory ideas are yoked by violence together has been carried over to their attack on critical approaches that they want to associate with the BHS. John Drakakis argues that the older historical criticism and the ahistorical New Criticism, though "ostensibly opposed," are both forms of bourgeois "essentialism" (1985, 18); James Kavanagh, that the approach to Shakespeare's plays as poetry and the "ostensibly alternative" approach to them as stagecraft both belong to bourgeois "ideological discourse" (1985, 147); and Alan Sinfield, that E. M. W. Tillyard's reading of Shakespeare and Jan Kott's reading, which is "apparently . . . the opposite," are "really two sides of the same conservative coin" (1994d, 155). (Note that in his statement liberal humanism has become "conservative," which is yet another example of the Marxists' inability to count past two; some of them even conflate liberals and "reactionaries,"[6] since in their polarized dialectic all non-Marxist positions, whatever their ostensible or apparent differences, turn out to be the same enemy.) This also confirms the conclusion I reached in my earlier essay that the BHS was produced, not by the bourgeoisie in the late seventeenth century, as the bashers maintain, but by the bashers themselves in our own day to serve as a target for their bashing.

Of course, this "interest" in bashing the bourgeoisie is itself supposed to serve a further "interest" also shared by the old and new Marxists, which is, in Alan Sinfield's words, to "bring down capitalism" (1994b, 178).[7] But there is again an important difference. The old Marxists went about this by trying to organize the workers to overthrow the capitalist power structure; but the new Marxists instead try to *refute* capitalism in their literary criticism, which they call an "intervention" (as Sinfield does in 1994b, 178). Therefore, just as they created an imaginary BHS that is very easy to bash, so they have created an imaginary case for capitalism that they attribute to this BHS and that is very easy to refute—the claim that it is natural, universal, and unchanging. They seem to think that by accusing the BHS of this claim, and then proving it is fallacious, they are hastening the demise of capitalism. (They also seem to think that they are hastening its demise by referring to it as "late-capitalism," which in their discourse has become a single word like "unresolvable-contradictions.")[8] Unfortunately for them, however, the most convincing case for capitalism rests, not on this alleged belief of the BHS or on liberal humanist ideology or any theoretical argument, but on the observable fact that it has so far proved to be much more efficient that any other economic system, including socialism, in the production and distribution of goods and services, which can readily be demonstrated by comparing the per capita incomes of East and West Germany, or North and South Korea, or the USSR and any "late-capitalist" country.[9] It was the observation of this fact that led large numbers of people, many of them workers, to flee from the socialist to the capitalist world, which can hardly be explained by their clandestine interpellation into the ideology of BHSdom before they fled. (This in fact would have been virtually impossible, since every Ideological State Apparatus in their homeland was under the complete control of the hegemonic Marxist regime.) They did not believe that capitalism was natural, universal, and unchanging; they just saw that it was much better than what they had. This same observation is now leading many socialist countries to abandon the system completely and others to begin dismantling it by introducing elements of a market economy. To adapt an old American advertising slogan, among the people who know socialism best, it's capitalism ten to one. But the new Marxist critics in the humanities departments of American and British universities cannot hear the voices of these people, because they are too busy listening to and echoing each other, convincing themselves of the imminent collapse of "late-capitalism" as a result of its "unresolvable-contradictions" and of their own "intervention" through the project I have named Bashing the Bourgeois Subject.

7
Negative Evidence

> The human understanding, once it has adopted an opinion, collects any instances that confirm it, and though the contrary instances may be more numerous and more weighty, it either does not notice them or else rejects them, in order that this opinion will remain unshaken. Thus he responded well, who, when he was shown the votive tablets people had hung in a temple to thank the gods for answering their prayers to be saved from the perils of the sea, and was asked if this did not prove the divine power, asked in his turn, "Where are the tablets of those who said the same prayers but then drowned?"
> —Francis Bacon, *Novum Organon*[1]

> Whenever a published fact, a new observation or thought came across me, which was opposed to my general results, [I made] a memorandum of it without fail and at once: for I had found by experience that such facts and thoughts were far more apt to escape from the memory than favourable ones.
> —Charles Darwin, *Autobiography*

BACON AND DARWIN ARE MAKING THE SAME TWO POINTS, WHICH WILL BE TWO OF the three basic points of this essay. The first point is that we cannot hope to prove any proposition unless we look for negative evidence that might contradict it, and the second point is that many of us ignore the first point, because of the tendency of our minds to look only for positive evidence that confirms the proposition we want to prove. This tendency explains the remarkable tenacity of superstitions (as Bacon states immediately after the passage I quoted) and of prejudices: people who believe that breaking a mirror brings bad luck will mentally register every occasion when this happens and fail to register all the occasions when it does not, and people who believe that gift-bearing Greeks are devious notice and remember any devious ones they meet, but either do not notice or forget the nondevious ones. In both cases the beliefs can be maintained only because those holding them never consider the negative evidence that Bacon refers to as "contrary instances" and that we now call counterexamples.

This seems obvious enough; however, my concern here is not with mental phenomena of this sort but with discursive arguments. Let me begin with the imaginary case of Professor X, who, for personal reasons we need not go into, sat down one day and theorized that people born under the sign of Libra are especially prone to divorce. He applied for seed money to investigate this and received a grant from the Olin Foundation (they misread his application and thought he was investigating Liberals rather than Libras), which enabled him to buy a computer and set up a database in which he entered the names of every divorced person he knew who was a Libra, and to hire some graduate students and send them out into the field to locate and record more Libra divorcees. He began to publish his findings and as a result of the feedback was able to refine his techniques. To answer the charge that his research design was too simplistic, he set up new databases for multi-Libra divorces (where both parties were Libras) and for multidivorced Libras, thereby strengthening his case; and to answer the charges of racism and classism, he went multicultural and won grants from liberal foundations to send his research teams into working-class and minority neighborhoods and to send himself to more exotic places, from which he wrote articles with titles like "Divorced Libras among the Quechuan-Speaking Tribes of the Upper Amazon Basin." He seemed to be set for life, with a project that was guaranteed never to run out of new evidence to confirm it and never to encounter any evidence that might challenge it. But that is the trouble, for it is clear that he cannot prove anything by looking for positive evidence, the divorced Libras, unless he also looks for negative evidence, which here would be divorced non-Libras. If he did this he would probably discover that the divorce rate is fairly constant along the whole zodiac.

I think most of my readers will agree with me so far, since they are not committed to astrology, but I may lose some with my next example, which is not imaginary and is not divorced from their commitments. In the course of an argument for censoring pornography because of the harm it does to women, Susan Cole reports that she has "undertaken a research project in conjunction with shelters for assaulted women" in which she asked them whether their spouses used pornography and found that "a full 30 percent in our survey answered yes" (1990, 192). She then moves on to other matters, confident that she has scored a point, but she has not, because she avoids the negative evidence, which would consist of nonviolent pornography users. If she wanted to prove that pornography causes domestic violence, she would have to go outside the shelters and ask a comparable group of women who had never been assaulted whether their spouses used pornography. If she did, she might find that the percentage is just as large, indicating that pornography does not increase domestic violence, or that it is even larger, which would support the opposing theory that pornography decreases this violence by allowing men to indulge their sadistic fantasies without acting them out. I am not arguing for that theory or trying to minimize the horror of this violence, but we should not allow our feelings about it to obscure the fact that Cole's research project fails because it only looks for positive evidence. Counting pornography-using wife-beaters cannot prove a connection between using pornography and wife beating, just as counting Libra divorcees cannot prove a connection between Libra-ness and divorce. Like Professor X (and our mirror-breaker and Hellenophobe), Cole ignores the negative evidence of counterexamples and so is guilty of the fallacy that Bacon calls "simple enumeration" (1878, 1.105).

I now want to examine the role of this fallacy in literary studies, drawing my examples from studies of the drama of Renaissance England. I am not suggesting that these studies can or should be "scientific," but since they usually present arguments for some thesis, they can and should be judged in terms of this same general fallacy of neglecting negative evidence, although the nature of that evidence will vary with different critical approaches. Fortunately, it turns out to be a nonpartisan fallacy, since it figures significantly in many of the approaches, old and new, so I should not be accused of picking on any particular one (although I do not think that will protect me, for reasons I explain at the end). It is found in several branches of the old historicism that dominated the field before the New Criticism. Attribution studies, for instance, often focused on the accumulation of "parallel passages" in the known works of an author and in the anonymous work that the critic wanted to attribute to him, but they failed to look for negative evidence. In this approach, however, such evidence would not be the presence of nonparallel passages (passages found in the author's known works but not in the anonymous work, and vice versa), because authors do not always repeat themselves, but the presence of these same parallel passages in the works of other authors of the time. This will be obvious if I resort to another absurd example: the appearance of the phrase "I thank you, sir" in a play by Robert Wilson and in an anonymous play does not establish a connection between them, since many other dramatists used it, and a hundred similar parallels would not establish a connection.

The positive evidence of parallel passages will only count if the passages are unique to the author in question, and the only way to determine this is by seeking the negative evidence that they are not unique. Unless that is done, they cannot prove anything because they can prove anything—that any author wrote any work. This in fact is what happened, for critics using this method attributed the same work to many different authors and many different works to the same author. An approach that simply enumerates these items of positive evidence is thus fatally flawed, no matter how many items it enumerates.[2]

This fallacy is also frequently encountered in a more prominent branch of the old historicism known as topicalism, which tries to show that a literary work is designed to allude to actual people or events of the time that are not presented in it. We can examine this approach in the books of Lilian Winstanley (1921, 1922, 1924) that demonstrate, as their extended titles indicate, that Shakespeare's four major tragedies are really detailed allegories about recent events in England, Scotland, France, and Italy, and a long essay by Edith Rickert (1923) in which Bottom in *A Midsummer Night's Dream* is shown to be a parody of James VI of Scotland, before he became James I of England. The method used by both critics is again the simple enumeration of positive evidence, the similarities between the fictional characters and their alleged real-life prototypes that function in the same way as the attributionists' parallel passages. By this method Rickert sets up connections not only of Bottom to James, but also of Oberon to Henry VIII, Titania to Elizabeth, and Titania's dead votaress to Lady Katherine Grey. Winstanley's procedure is more complex, because she claims that *Hamlet* alludes simultaneously to the succession of James VI in Scotland and the Essex conspiracy in England, so its main characters have dual roles (Hamlet is James in the Scottish story and Essex in the English one, Claudius is Bothwell and Cecil, etc.), and that both *Macbeth* and *King Lear* allude to the Darnley murder in Scotland and the Massacre of St. Bartholomew in France, requiring both Duncan and Lear to double as Darnley and Admiral Coligney, Lady Macbeth and Goneril to double as Mary Stuart and Catherine de Medici, and so on. These are of course extreme examples, which is why I chose them, since my points about their methodology will be clearer, but the same points also apply to many less spectacular topical readings of this type.

Winstanley and Rickert easily prove their cases, as do other similar topical readings, for no failure has ever been recorded.[3] The reason is clear: they only look for positive evidence that confirms the connection they want to make between the dramatic character and the historical prototype and ignore all the negative evidence, which now comes in two varieties—the differences between the two figures, and the presence of the same traits that are supposed to connect them in other characters and other historical personages. The differences between the character and the alleged prototype usually turn out to be, as Bacon puts it, "more numerous and more weighty" than their similarities. It is hard to think of two men more unlike than Bottom and King James or King Duncan and Darnley—unless one is only looking for the likenesses. Both these critics, however, present an argument that is supposed to justify their ignoring this first kind of negative evidence and to explain it away: Winstanley tells us that Renaissance dramatists were forced to "evad[e] the censorship by representing their politics or history in some convenient disguise" (1922, 4), and Rickert that "topical matter" in the plays would have to be "sufficiently disguised to have got by the censor" (1923, 60). The censorship is also invoked by some other topical readings and is clearly very useful, since it mandates that the allusions must be in a kind of code and so gives the critic a mandate for resorting to a deciphering operation (which is what these readings amount to), with success guaranteed in advance. But even if we put aside the question (which topicalists never ask) of how a playwright could count on these allusions being at the same time "sufficiently disguised to have got by the censor" and sufficiently clear to be grasped by the audience, we can still see that something is seriously wrong with this argument, because it eliminates the possibility of the first kind of negative evidence—in fact, it converts any such negative evidence into positive evidence of the author's need for concealment.[4]

This brings me to my third basic point, in addition to the two stated in the epigraphs. We must recognize, not only that we cannot hope to prove any proposition unless we look for negative evidence that might contradict it and that we have a tendency to look only for positive evidence, but also that we cannot hope to prove any proposition unless this negative evidence could exist. The principle is well known to scientists and philosophers of science, who call it disconfirmability. They insist that if a proposition does not invite disconfirmation, if there is no conceivable evidence the existence of which would contradict it, then it cannot be tested and so cannot be taken seriously. If it is not disprovable, it is not provable. Many of the other approaches we will examine also ignore this principle, but the results may not be as obvious as they are in the topicalists' use of the censor to explain away any differences between the work and the events it supposedly alludes to. For this makes it impossible to challenge any of Winstanley's or Rickert's claims about the allusions they find in these plays, but makes it equally impossible to challenge any of the claims of other critics who find different allusions in the same plays. Therefore, by invoking the censor to avoid this first kind of negative evidence a topicalist may score a short-term gain, but at the expense of a devastating long-term loss.

The second kind of negative evidence relevant to these topical readings is the presence of the same traits that supposedly connect the dramatic character to a particular historical prototype in other characters or other historical personages, which is similar to the kind we applied to attribution studies. For the positive evidence of similarities between the character and the prototype, like the positive evidence of the attributionists' parallel passages, depends on their uniqueness and so is canceled out when they turn up elsewhere. We can see this in Glynne Wickham's argument that the heroes of Shakespeare's romances (Pericles, Cymbeline, Leontes, and Prospero) allude to King James because, like him, each of them is "a father figure wracked by adversity, brought near to death and disaster, but steadfast in his faith, constant in his purpose and protected by providence to bring his policies to a successful and joyous conclusion" (1973, 46). This may seem more plausible than the intricate topicalities of Winstanley and Rickert, until we realize that the same thing can be said of other Shakespearean father figures (such as Aegeon, Leonato, and Duke Senior) created during the reign of Elizabeth, some years before James VI became James I (thereby bringing his policies to a joyous conclusion), and can also be said of other real-life rulers, including Elizabeth herself. This second kind of negative evidence, therefore, unlinks the connection Wickham is trying to establish by the simple enumeration of similarities that I just quoted. It is easy to see, then, why topicalists who pass over these two kinds of negative evidence always make their case, like the attributionists. And this leads to the same situation we noted in attribution studies: their readings find many different historical prototypes for the same character (in fact we saw that Winstanley does this in a single reading),[5] and the same prototype for many different characters—thus King James is discovered by Winstanley in Hamlet and by Rickert in Bottom and by Wickham in Pericles, Cymbeline, and so on. Their method, too, can prove anything and so proves nothing.

I will conclude this section by looking at two other branches of the old historicism, source studies and occasionalist readings, that are conveniently combined in Josephine Bennett's attempt (1966) to connect *Measure for Measure* and King James's *Basilikon Doron*. It is a source study, because it argues that Shakespeare's portrayal of Duke Vincentio took material from the king's book, and, like many such studies, it proceeds by enumerating positive evidence, the similarities between the duke's ideas and James's.

Here, however, the two kinds of negative evidence we discussed do not apply. There are differences between the ideas of these two men; and the ideas that they share, which are commonplaces of Renaissance political thought, appear in many other plays and treatises. But neither of these facts proves that Shakespeare did not draw on the king's book, for he would have had no reason to avoid using other ideas different from those in the book, or to use only those ideas in the book that are unique to it (if he could find any). This is true of most source studies; they cannot be contradicted by any negative evidence, since there is no way to disprove that authors were influenced by any work available to them, which is why discoveries of "possible sources" fill the pages of *Notes and Queries*.[6]

The situation changes, however, when a source study serves an occasionalist reading—a reading that claims a play was designed, not for paying customers in the public or private theaters, but for a special group of people assembled at a special occasion (usually a court festivity or noble wedding). Such readings were common in the old historicism, even though, as Alfred Harbage notes (1962, 19–20), we have no positive evidence that any regular play performed by any regular theatrical company was originally written for a special occasion during Shakespeare's lifetime, and all the evidence we do have indicates that the plays these companies presented at such occasions were taken from their public repertoire. Most occasionalists ignored this and went about enumerating their own positive evidence, aspects of the play that were supposed to connect it to the specific occasion they had in mind. But here our two kinds of negative evidence must apply (although these critics also ignored them): the presence in the play of aspects that were inappropriate to this occasion, and the presence of those aspects that supposedly connected it to the occasion in other plays that were not occasional. They also apply to Bennett's argument, for she is claiming, not merely that *Measure for Measure* borrows from the king's book, but that it was written for the court and uses this borrowing "to please and flatter the King" (1966, 81, 109). Thus the negative evidence that I said did not contradict a simple source study now becomes crucial, since if this was Shakespeare's purpose, he would not give his duke ideas that were different from James's, or that were limited to commonplaces that had no special relation to James. Instead of confronting this evidence, Bennett explains it away, not by the censorship, which she could hardly invoke in a play designed to flatter the king, but by Shakespeare's fear of offending the king if the duke was too much like him (1966, 105). She does not reveal why this would offend James, but it is a convenient excuse because, like the censor, it allows her to dispose of the inconvenient negative evidence of differences between the duke and the king by converting it into positive evidence of their connection, so there is again no possibility of any negative evidence that could disconfirm the argument.

༄

Although the old historicism included other approaches, some of which did not rely on simple enumeration, I will now turn to the New Criticism that superseded it, and here my choice of approaches is easy, because there is one that dominated the New Critical enterprise. This is the thematic approach, which finds that the work being interpreted is about some abstract idea, usually called the "central theme," that is subserved by the characters and actions presented there.[7] One might have thought that critics using this approach would feel an initial obligation to show that the work is actually about an abstract idea, but they did not; instead of first asking *whether* it is about a central theme, they typically began by asking *which* central theme it is about, under the assumption that when they answered the second question this would settle the first. It does not, however, and by beginning in this way they avoided an important kind of negative evidence, as we will see.

To prove that the work is about the particular central theme they favored, the thematists usually proceeded, like the attributionists and topicalists and occasionalists, by simply enumerating the positive evidence, the components of the work that are supposed to subserve this theme. And, as in the old historicist approaches, they always succeeded, which soon led to the same kind of situation we saw earlier: many different central themes were found in the same work and the same central theme was found in many different works. Our examination of the older approaches showed that this is a symptom of a serious methodological flaw and also showed what that flaw will be—the failure to consider any negative evidence, since this failure makes it possible for critics to use the method to prove whatever they want to prove. It is not easy, however, to determine what the negative evidence would be in this approach. We might expect to find it in components of the work that did not subserve the central theme espoused by the critic, and this in fact is what rival thematists often seized on when they began their own thematic readings by asserting that previous candidates for the central theme of the work in question could not account for certain parts of it and that their candidate would rectify this, which I call the "My Theme Can Lick Your Theme" gambit. But there are two reasons that this kind of negative evidence is not relevant here. First, the themes employed by these critics were usually on such a high plane of generality—cosmic oppositions like appearance versus reality, order versus disorder, and so on, or cosmic problems such as the nature of man (in those days the [usually male] critics did not have to tell us if this referred to half or all of humanity)—that they could encompass any part of any work, and this was even more true of the reflexive metathemes that later came into fashion, like the nature of communication or of drama. Try to imagine an episode that would *not* be about appearance versus reality or the nature of communication.

The second reason that we cannot rely on this kind of negative evidence is that most thematists had a pretty relaxed notion of the relation of the theme to the parts of the work. According to the definition given us by Norman Rabkin, one of the leading thematizers of Shakespeare, a theme is "a simple and generalized statement about the world which may be abstracted from a literary work, to which the larger part of the work contributes, and with which the rest is generally consistent" (1967, 76). This obviously makes a thematist's task much easier but makes ours much harder, for while it is difficult enough to imagine an episode that would not be about appearance versus reality, it is virtually impossible to imagine one that would not be "generally consistent" with this theme, or with any of the other themes favored by these critics. In view, then, of the very generalized nature of the central themes that they applied to the work and their very loose rules for applying them, it seems fairer to say of most thematists, not that they ignored this kind of negative evidence, but that they eliminated any possibility of it, which means, we saw, that their claims to have found the central theme of a work are not disconfirmable, and that there is no way to prove that a work is about any particular theme rather than any of the other candidates. This explains the endless proliferation of different thematic readings of the same works that finally helped to bring about the collapse of the New Criticism from its own success.

I mentioned earlier, however, that there is another area of negative evidence applicable to this approach that is raised by the question of whether the work is about *any* central theme, rather than about some particular one. The thematists typically passed over this question, I said, because they assumed that when they proved the work is about the particular theme they championed, they would have proved that it must be about a theme. But we saw that this is not true; since it is so easy to prove that any work is about any particular theme, that cannot settle the prior question of whether it is about a theme. The only way to prove that it is about a theme is by looking for the negative evidence that it is not, which would be evidence that it can be fully understood and appreciated on the level of its characters and actions viewed in their own right rather than as subserving an abstraction. If the New Critical thematists had looked for such evidence, their enterprise might never have left the ground.

☙

My choice of examples among the newer approaches that followed (and speeded the demise of) the New Criticism is much more difficult because there are so many, and I must therefore limit myself to a few broad categories. Most of these approaches are emphatically historical, which marks their decisive break from the ahistorical New Critics. But they also claim to be making a decisive break from the old historicism by rejecting its conception of an unproblematic, factual historical context that is prior to and determines the meaning of the problematic literary work, and adopting instead a poststructuralist theory of history and literature as equally problematic texts that construct each other. While the new historicizers regularly assert this theory, however, they regularly violate it in their own practice, as Edward Pechter shows (1987, 293–94), since their readings usually begin with some privileged and prioritized historical "facts" that are then applied to explain the meaning of the literary text (no longer a work), just like the old historicizers. This contradiction between profession and practice can even be found within the same study.[8]

We will not be surprised to learn, then, that some of the old historical approaches reappear in the new historicism, along with the fallacy of simple enumeration that so often accompanies them. It has produced more occasionalist readings of Shakespeare. Paul Brown claims that *The Tempest* had its "initial production at the ... Jacobean court in 1611 and 1612–13" before "the assembled aristocrats ... in the original courtly audiences" (1994, 48, 53); James Kavanagh, that *A Midsummer Night's Dream* was probably "designed to be performed on a private stage in celebration of the marriage of an aristocratic couple" (1985, 234); Jonathan Crewe, that "the historical *circumstance* of a courtly setting and audience" for this play "would now go without saying," and "there can hardly be any question" that it "was conceived specifically for a performance in front of the queen" (1987, 139–40—he adds that *The Comedy of Errors* may have been written for one of the Inns of Court); John Turner, that Shakespeare wrote *King Lear* "no doubt with a court performance in mind" and wrote *Macbeth* "perhaps with a court performance in mind" (1988, 93, 121); Dianne Hunter, that *Macbeth* "was written to celebrate the coming of the Stuart dynasty to the English throne, and to please and flatter Shakespeare's new royal master,

King James" (1988, 134); Peter Stallybrass, that this play "was probably first produced in 1605 or 1606 under royal patronage" (1983, 100); and Jonathan Goldberg, that *A Midsummer Night's Dream* was "performed before Queen Elizabeth" (1985, 134), that *Measure for Measure* "seem[s] to include King James in its designs" (1985, 126), and that "the text of *Macbeth* that we have derives from a court performance" and "alludes to the presence of King James . . . in the audience" (1987, 251).[9] These readings, like those of the old occasionalists, only cite positive evidence connecting the play to the claimed occasion and neglect the two kinds of negative evidence that we saw were relevant to this claim, as well as the contrary positive evidence that the plays presented at these occasions were regularly taken from the theatrical company's public repertoire.

The topical approach is much more prominent than occasionalism in the new historical criticism, as it was in the old, but here we find a significant difference. The allegories of the new topicalists usually do not operate at the level of specificity seen in Winstanley, Rickert, and Wickham, where dramatic characters are equated to particular people, although a few come pretty close: Jonathan Crewe's essay on *A Midsummer Night's Dream*, for example, objects to the kind of "immobilizing identification" practiced by Rickert, but then proceeds to argue for an "allusiveness" coming "dangerously close to effecting a quasi-identification" that connects the quarrel between Titania and Oberon to Elizabeth's relations with Raleigh and Spenser (1987, 140-46); and Annabel Patterson finds that the depiction of Lear "comes perilously close to presenting a fictional portrait" of King James (1989, 106).[10] But most of their readings locate the topical allusion in a looser analogy to some more general historical situation. We are told by Jonathan Dollimore and Alan Sinfield that "the attempt to conquer France" in *Henry V* is "a re-presentation of the attempt to conquer Ireland" in Shakespeare's day, which is the "real historical conflict" behind the play (1985, 225); by Margot Heinemann that "Goneril, Regan, and Edmund were likely to be identified" with "contemporary flatterers, cadgers, and upstarts at the Jacobean court" (1991, 77–78); by Simon Shepherd that the mutilation of Lavinia is an "imaging of the brutal censorship" and "may be taken to typify the activities" of the government "backlash of the late 1580s" (1986, 83–84); by Leah Marcus that the cross-dressed heroines of Shakespeare's comedies "mirror" Queen Elizabeth's "androgynous" self-presentation (1986, 137); and by Marilyn Williamson that these comedies, because they show men making upscale marriages, are causally related to the plight of aspiring male spectators in the 1590s who "faced a dwindling relative number of places at court" and elsewhere (1986, 37).

These new topical readings, like the old ones, only notice the similarities between the text and its alleged historical context and ignore the two relevant kinds of negative evidence: the differences between the text and this context, and the nonuniqueness of the similarities—their presence in other texts and in other contexts. In Williamson's case, for example, the first kind of negative evidence is the fact that most of the men in these comedies marry their equals and some even marry down;[11] and the second is the fact that upscale marriages figure in many texts produced in very different societies, including all those folktales where the hero wins the king's daughter. And in Shepherd's case, the first kind is the fact that Lavinia's mutilation is not a governmental activity or a punishment for anything she did or said, and the second is the fact that similar episodes appear in literary texts written long before the 1580s (such as Ovid's account of the rape of Philomela) and in later periods. Indeed, Leonard Tennenhouse, another new topicalist, asserts that the "mutilation of the female body" is specific to Jacobean rather than Elizabethan "political iconography" and so must explain away Lavinia's fate, which now becomes negative evidence against his own topical thesis, as an exception (1986, 107, 115–16, 122).

Many of these new topicalists, moreover, make the same kind of initial leap that we noted in the thematists, since they typically begin by asking, not *whether* the play alludes to some contemporary person or event, but *which* one it alludes to. Thus both Crewe and Marcus assume that the characters they are concerned with must have real-life prototypes, so that the only problem is to identify them: Crewe arrives at the allusion to Spenser by asking, "Who else could have counted as the Oberon/*obermensch* of the Elizabethan poetic world *ca.* 1594?" (1987, 146), and Marcus states several times that the "closest" or "only genuine historical analogue" to the cross-dressed heroines is Elizabeth (1986, 137, 138, 146, 147).[12] Many of them also assume, like the thematists, that if they can produce an answer to the *which* question, it will settle the *whether* question, but we found that this does not follow. It is very easy, as my examples suggest, to construct a connection between characters or actions in a play and many different contemporary persons or events—that is, if one only looks for the positive evidence of their similarities and ignores all the negative evidence of their dissimilarities (and of the nonuniqueness of their similarities)—but this in itself cannot prove that the play is actually alluding to any of them. It only proves that if you ask any play the topical question ("What contemporary person or event is it about?"), the play will always give you a topical answer, just as asking any play the thematic question ("What abstract idea is it about?") will always give you a central theme. It is still necessary to argue the prior proposition that we should ask this play this kind of question, but the topicalists, like the thematists, fail to do this, and consequently never have to deal with the negative evidence against the assumptions underlying the topical question, as well as the negative evidence against the particular topical answers to it that their readings present.

∽

Rather than multiply these examples, I now want to focus on two major approaches that have become very important in the current critical scene, Marxism and Freudianism (which is of course nonhistoricist). They were both with us as marginal operations during the hegemony of the old historicism and the New Criticism, but now these two schools, or revisionist versions of them, have entered—some would say taken over—the critical mainstream. They are especially relevant to my argument, since both of them depend on eliminating the possibility of negative evidence in order to avoid disconfirmation, which is why Frank Cioffi calls them pseudosciences (1970, 509). This is both a cause and an effect of their peculiar histories. Freud and Marx thought they were constructing empirical sciences (and many of their followers, including literary critics, still claim to be "scientific"), but they proceeded in isolation from and in opposition to the other sciences, including those they were supposed to be representing (or supplanting). The result was that Freudianism and Marxism developed along different lines from those sciences, which they viewed as enemies, and became closed, self-confirming, a priori systems that in many respects resemble religions more than sciences. They are named for their founders, like some religions, and have revered canonical texts provided by the founders,[13] and excommunications for heresy. (Marxists also had Internationals and Party Congresses that functioned like church councils and synods to define the true faith and anathematize heresies, and in Marxist lands heretics were often executed, although not by burning at the stake.) And they have separate associations, conferences, and journals that preach only to the faithful.

This isolation has a crucial effect on their relation to negative evidence, because of the tendency noted by Bacon and Darwin. Since scientists, like the rest of us, often overlook negative evidence against their own theory, they depend—or rather their science depends—on colleagues, usually those who doubt the theory, to find this evidence (if it exists) that will force them to amend or abandon it. That is why the sciences are self-correcting and can progress. But Freudianism and Marxism never had to confront the negative evidence presented by nonbelievers, who are the only ones likely to look for it; that is why they are self-confirming rather than self-correcting and therefore do not progress but just keep splitting into more rival sects and heresies.[14] Moreover, they both have an all-purpose answer to those who object to their theory—they attack the motivation of the objectors. Freudians say that such people are "resisting" the painful truth about their "repressions," and Marxists that they fear the loss of their class privileges in the coming revolution. Thus, any objections that cite negative evidence against their theory become, as Freud tells us, "actual evidence in favour of the correctness of its assertions" (1975, 13.180).[15]

Both schools also have more specific techniques for eliminating the possibility of negative evidence that are related to the kind of claims they make. Freudians claim to have found the one fundamental cause of all adult behavior in unconscious conflicts deriving from the experiences of childhood, centering on the oedipal situation. Their basic problem, then, is to prove the causal laws connecting childhood experiences to adult behavior, and their basic method for proving this is "clinical evidence." But clinical evidence, as several commentators have shown,[16] cannot prove any theory, because it is predetermined by the theory. Analysts interpreting a patient's words are in a position similar to that of thematic critics interpreting a literary text, since they only collect the positive evidence, the words that confirm (or can be made to confirm) what they are looking for. Indeed, their procedure is even less controlled than the thematists', because the text itself is not affected by the thematic critics, whereas patients clearly are affected by their analysts' expectations and tend to speak the words that they think their analysts want to hear, and also because the patients' words, unlike literary texts, are not available to others and so the analysts' interpretations cannot be checked.

Freudians, moreover, have an explanation of the fact that their patients' words rarely establish the causal connection to childhood experiences that they want to find: it seems that the unconscious conflicts involved in these experiences are "repressed" because they are too threatening to emerge into consciousness, and so can only appear in disguised form. Thus this "repression" serves the same useful purpose for psychoanalysts that censorship did for the topicalist critic (in fact they sometimes call the psychic process or entity that is supposed to produce it "the censor"), since it mandates that the real meaning they seek must be concealed in a code that they must decipher. (We just saw that they also use it to explain away objections to Freudianism.) They posit a number of mechanisms—condensation, decomposition, displacement, etc.—that operate in the patient's coding and enable them to decipher its real meaning, but this allows them to prove that anything the patient says confirms their theory, since their application of these mechanisms converts any conceivable negative evidence against the theory into positive evidence for it, so there is no possibility of negative evidence. We even have positive evidence of the impossibility of negative evidence, since analysts of the heretical schools that split off from Freudianism all report clinical evidence from their patients that proves their own theory and disproves Freud's.[17] This reliance upon clinical evidence is a major cause of the Freudians' separation from empirical scientists, who have little respect for evidence that cannot be observed or replicated by others and is not submitted to objective tests that can be administered by nonbelievers and can yield negative results.

We would expect to meet these same methodological flaws in Freudian readings of literature, since they treat literary characters or texts (or their authors) as patients to be analyzed, and find the real meaning of textual events in unconscious conflicts that only emerge in disguised form and that they demonstrate by enumerating pieces of evidence that are supposed to "suggest" them. The most famous example of this approach is Ernest Jones's book on *Hamlet* (1954), which has a lot going for it (that is why it is famous), because Hamlet's situation comes close to Freud's oedipal paradigm. But Freudians, like Marxists, are totalizers, so Jones must force other characters into this paradigm and thus manages to snatch defeat from the jaws of victory, as we can see in his treatment of Laertes (158–61). He says that Laertes is "identified" with Polonius and so "represents the tyrant father" of Hamlet, who must fulfill his oedipal duty by killing them both. But there is also a "'decomposition' of Laertes's father" into Hamlet and Polonius, with Laertes as the oedipal son who must kill Hamlet (but not, apparently, Polonius), which makes Laertes and Claudius psychological "equivalents," each "representing . . . both the son and father aspects of Hamlet's mentality." Finally, we have a "brother-sister complex" (a "derivative" of the big one), in which Laertes and Hamlet are "doubled" as brothers of Ophelia. Thus Laertes is equated to Polonius, Claudius, and Hamlet, and becomes Hamlet's father, son, and brother, and there is nothing he could do that would constitute negative evidence against any of these transformations.

The Freudianism that is now most prominent in Shakespeare criticism, however, is a feminist revision, associated primarily with Nancy Chodorow (1978), that also claims to find the one fundamental cause of all adult behavior in unconscious conflicts deriving from childhood experiences, but locates these experiences in the child's relations with the mother during the preoedipal stage, rather than in oedipal relations with the father. Yet it retains Freud's basic methodology with all its flaws. The crucial conflicts are, again, "repressed" and only emerge in a code that the experts must decipher to find the concealed real meaning that they know in advance must be there, and the whole theoretical edifice rests, again, on what

Chodorow refers to as "the clinical situation that ultimately provides psychoanalysis its truths" (1989, 12), even though the truths provided by her clinical situation are so different from the truths provided by the clinical situations of orthodox Freudians, Adlerians, and the rest. The application of this theory to Shakespeare has focused on showing that the real cause of the male hero's problems lies in his unconscious conflicts with his mother, which requires that the text supply him with a concealed surrogate mother figure that is "repressed" by him or the text or the author, so that, as Coppélia Kahn explains, "the absence of a mother in the play serves to highlight her psychological presence" in the hero (1982, 37), and thus negative evidence against the theory becomes positive evidence for it. In her essay introducing this theory to critics, Kahn applied it to *King Lear*, arguing that he unconsciously views his daughters as mothers, which was a good choice (like Jones's choice of *Hamlet*), because there is evidence for this in some of his speeches. But since then she and her colleagues have provided many of Shakespeare's other male heroes with much less likely concealed preoedipal mother figures, who are now as plentiful as concealed oedipal father figures were in orthodox Freudian criticism.[18] According to their readings, these mother figures now include Cleopatra, Cressida, Desdemona, Helena, Hermione, Imogen, Lady Macbeth, Miranda, Portia, and Rosalind. But they do not have to be women, because mother-figurehood has also been conferred upon Shylock and Falstaff;[19] and even upon nonhumans such as a lioness, Fortune, and the sea. There is no end in sight, for the sheer variety of this list shows that almost anyone or anything can become a mother figure, since the method does not admit the possibility of any negative evidence that could prove that she/he/it is not one.

This crucial flaw in their method can be seen, for example, in the readings of Peter Erickson (1985a, 93–94, 190), Marianne Novy (1984, 132–33, 140, 146–47), and Edward Snow (1980, 404–5) that claim that Othello treats Desdemona as a mother figure. Although their interpretations of *Othello* differ in many ways, on this point they produce the same basic argument. All three cite the speech where Othello refers to her as "The fountain from the which my current runs / Or else dries up" (4.2.59–60), which, they say, "bodies forth the nurturant maternal breast" (Erickson), "brings to mind the dependence of the infant at the mother's breast" (Novy), and reveals "primitive fantasies of a more ancient maternal betrayal" (Snow); and two also cite her words about entreating Othello to "wear your gloves, / Or feed on nourishing dishes" (3.3.77–78) to show that she is adopting "the maternal role" (Snow) and "sees herself as taking care of him as a nurturing mother does a child" (Novy). That is all the specific positive evidence they muster, and it collapses under scrutiny. Othello's speech constructs an analogy between Desdemona and a fountain of water, which these critics have simply replaced with a very different analogy that he does not use but that fits their thesis; and Desdemona's speech may tell us how she sees herself, but not how Othello sees her (after it he calls her "Excellent wretch," which does not sound very maternal). Moreover, it is easy to find negative evidence against this thesis, such as the facts that Othello fears he is too old for her (3.3.265–66), that he seems to assent to Iago's depiction of her as a clever child (3.3.209–10), and (if her sense of her role is relevant) that she at one point thinks of herself as his "young babe" (4.2.111). The most important negative evidence, of course, is that Othello never expresses this attitude toward her that these critics attribute to him (and that we noted in some of Lear's speeches about his daughters). None of this matters to them, however, for their thesis is derived not from evidence in the text but from the theory they bring to the text—the theory that a man's reactions to women are based on his preoedipal reactions to his mother. It is only because their minds are always already programmed by this theory that Othello's fountain metaphor "brings to mind" the maternal breast; but they do not really need the fountain, since even without it, or any other specific positive evidence, the theory would still tell them how he must view Desdemona. And this theory itself, like their application of it to *Othello*, does not depend on evidence. It is supposed to be a universal law, but there is no way to subject it to empirical verification. Like all other universal laws of the Freudian tradition, it functions not as a testable scientific hypothesis but as an article of faith, safe in an a priori realm where it does not require any positive evidence to confirm it and is not vulnerable to any negative evidence that might disconfirm it.

Marxists, like Freudians, claim to have found the one fundamental cause of all human behavior, which they locate not in psychic conflicts within the individual but in class conflicts rooted in the material socioeconomic "base" that ultimately shapes all activity in the "superstructure." Their main problem then is to prove these causal connections between events in the base and in the superstructure that constitute their laws of economic determinism. Unfortunately for them, however, they have nothing equivalent to the Freudian's clinical evidence to appeal to in this demonstration. Marxists deal with large-scale phenomena that occur, not in the privacy of the analyst's office, but on the public stage of history where we can all see the two kinds of negative evidence that contradict their laws: cases where the basal cause is not accompanied by the designated superstructural event, or where this event is not accompanied by the designated situation in the base. It is even more unfortunate for them that their laws, again unlike the Freudians', involve large-scale predictions whose results are highly visible.[20] Marx and his followers said that capitalist regimes would continually lower the working-class standard of living and would soon collapse (with some help) from their own "unresolvable contradictions," but this did not happen. They also said that socialist regimes would end all injustice and create a paragonic "new man" before they benignly withered away, but this did not happen either, and many of these regimes recently collapsed from the "unresolvable contradictions" they were not supposed to have. To explain away the failure of capitalism to live down to their predictions and expire on schedule (its imminent demise was proclaimed regularly from the time of *The Communist Manifesto* to our own day), they have various excuses, which I have discussed elsewhere.[21] And to explain away the failure of socialism to live up to their predictions they have one standard excuse—that the avowed socialist regimes, even though they met the Marxist specifications (public ownership of the land and means of production, abolition of profits, etc.) were not really socialist and so do not count.[22] (They never explain why it is that whenever Marxists gain power they always establish un-Marxist societies.) The best excuse of all, however, comes from Fredric Jameson, who announced that "the Marxist 'science of society'" is not "a matter of prediction or making claims about historical inevitability" (1983, 290), which eliminates in one move (formerly stroke) any possible negative evidence, so that Marxism cannot be disconfirmed, although he does not tell us why it should then be considered a science.

Marxist critical readings do not depend on such predictions (though they often end by calling for a "transformation of society"), but they do depend on the base-superstructure scheme of causation. Many recent readings claim to be influenced by a revision of Marxism associated with Louis Althusser, but it is much less drastic than the feminist revision of Freud, because it does not relocate the base (which is in effect what Chodorow does to Freud) but only loosens its causal connection to the superstructure, which is thus granted a limited "autonomy." Despite this claim, however, all the recent Marxist readings that I have seen continue to find the real cause of textual events in the socioeconomic base. The major new influence that distinguishes them from the older Marxist readings seems to be Freudianism. While they are unhappy with Freud, they are happy to adopt his mechanisms, especially displacement, which is very useful for making connections between events in the text and the underlying basal cause that can be demonstrated by enumerating pieces of evidence that supposedly provide "glimpses" or "traces" of this cause.[23] In Freud it is a mechanism of the psyche to disguise repressed material, whereas Marxists have no agency or motive to explain it, but that does not stop them.

The role of this mechanism in their method can be shown, for example, in Jonathan Dollimore's reading of *Measure for Measure* (1994b), which argues that the actual concern of the play is not sexuality, as all the characters (and previous critics) believe, since this is a "displacement" of "more fundamental social problems" of class "tension and conflict"; and in Peter Stallybrass's reading of *Othello* (1986), which argues that the actual concern of the play is "class aspiration" and the threat of "subversion" of "the social order," which are "displaced" onto the issues of love, race, and jealousy that apparently occupy the characters.[24] Neither critic asks who or what does the displacing or why, but their reason for using this concept is clear, since it allows them to prove that, whatever the play seems to be about, it is really about what they want it to be about (trouble in the "base"), and also eliminates any possibility of negative evidence, for there is no conceivable element in a play that could not be explained away as a displacement. But Marxist critics do not even need this concept, as we can see in the reading of *King Lear* by Kevin Ryan (1995), since he never invokes displacement and yet manages to reach the same conclusion—namely, that the "causes" or "main-springs" of the action are "housed beyond" the problems of the individual characters and lie much "deeper" in the injustices of a "class-divided" society. He does not confront the obvious negative evidence that all the tragic actions in both plots involve relations between members of the same ruling class and so cannot be caused by class divisions. This is irrelevant, because he already knows from his Marxist theory that the real cause of the action must be in the material base. No evidence from the text could disprove his application of this theory to it, and no evidence from anywhere could disprove the theory. It is an a priori universal law that, like the laws of Freud and Chodorow, precludes any negative evidence and so is undisconfirmable.

There is an important difference, however, between Freudian and Marxist criticism and the approaches examined earlier. I said that attributionists, topicalists, and thematists, by passing over or eliminating negative evidence, were able to connect the same author or current event or central theme to many different works and, conversely, to connect the same work to many different authors or events or themes. (It is true that some obsessed critics always found their favorite author/event/theme in every work they encountered,[25] but that was a personal idiosyncrasy and not a function of the method itself.) Freudian criticism and Marxist criticism are not symmetrical in this way: they can prove that the same kind of unconscious conflict or class conflict underlies many different texts, but they cannot prove the converse, for they assume that this conflict underlies every text. This is not an idiosyncrasy but a function of the method, or rather of the theory behind the method, which, we saw, claims to have located the one fundamental cause of all human behavior, including literature. Therefore, the elimination of negative evidence makes it possible for Freudian and Marxist critics to find this cause underlying any literary text, but makes it impossible for them to find any other underlying cause in any text, and also makes it possible for them to avoid questioning the theory itself. That is why they are still able to keep the faith.[26]

An examination of the role of negative evidence in literary studies cannot ignore the fact that the very concept of evidence, negative or positive, is now under attack in parts of the academy (mainly our part) on two related fronts, epistemological and political. The attack on the first front is led by poststructuralists who argue that evidence is not something lying out there waiting to be discovered, but is "constructed," like everything else that we (think we) know, by our minds, so that we make evidence in the same way that we "make knowledge"; and anyone who thinks otherwise is accused of the heinous sins of empiricism, objectivism, and positivism, often preceded by "naive," although the accusers do not seem to recognize any other kind.[27] Like many other poststructuralist doctrines, this has a valid point that is carried too far. The evidentiariness of any evidence is created by a specific project, but the project does not create the evidence itself. Jones's Freudian approach to *Hamlet* made the death of Shakespeare's father in 1601, which was irrelevant to earlier interpretations of the play, a significant piece of interpretive evidence (1954, 128), but it did not make Shakespeare's father die in 1601, for this was known to non-Freudians as well on the basis of other evidence, independent of any critical approach. I have never seen an argument that did not cite some independent evidence of this kind—even the poststructuralists appeal to such evidence in their attack on evidence. Therefore, in judging arguments, including those in literary criticism, we should try to determine whether their evidence is good or bad and whether, as I am insisting, they take account of negative as well as positive evidence.

The political attack on evidence stems in part from attempts by some poststructuralists on the Left to connect empiricist-objectivist-positivist epistemology to right-wing ideology. Thus Toril Moi asserts that empiricism is "inherently reactionary" (1983, 10). But this ignores, again, the two kinds of negative evidence that are relevant—the many radicals, including Marx himself, who regarded themselves as empiricists (and pretty naive ones by today's standards), and some real reactionaries who are just as scornful of empiricism as Moi is. The appeal to empirical evidence has no inherent politics, and the same is true of the opposition to it. It seems to me, however, that the main reason for the rejection of evidence can be found, not in this (naive) equation of epistemology and politics, but in the current critical war (which has of course influenced the equaters). When combatants in this war encounter an argument, they do not ask about the evidence for or against it; they just ask if the argument is for or against their side, since they believe, like Michael Sprinker, that "the only real question . . . is: Which side are you on?" (1991, 116). This is related to another human tendency that is a corollary of the second point made by Bacon and Darwin in my epigraphs: we not only tend to overlook or forget negative evidence that contradicts our beliefs, but when others point such evidence out to us, instead of thanking them for this chance to correct our beliefs, we tend to get angry with them, and this anger increases in direct proportion to our commitment to these beliefs. Clearly the critical war has exacerbated this tendency, especially for those who have convinced themselves (on no evidence at all) that the readings on their side are helping to bring about a "transformation of society" that will eliminate the injustice of racism, sexism, and classism,[28] for this means that anyone who presents negative evidence against these readings must be on the enemy side and so is supporting this injustice or is at least "complicit" with it. I expect, therefore, that some of these partisans will claim that my objection to Susan Cole's research project implicates me in pornography and wife-beating,[29] and that this entire essay proves I am not only a naive empiricist-objectivist-positivist but also an evil racist-sexist-classist McCarthyite who is threatened and scared by them.

8
The New Interdisciplinarity in Literary Criticism

It seems clear that one of the best things a literary critic can do today is to become interdisciplinary. Anyone who doubts this has only to look at the publishers' advertisements, which regularly urge us to buy some critical book or anthology because it "succeeds in crossing traditional disciplinary boundaries" or words to that effect. The impression they are designed to create is that this is a courageous, difficult, and cutting-edge undertaking that is valuable in itself, implying that critics who remain within their own discipline are timid (or at least lazy), narrow-minded, and hopelessly out-of-date. And in recent debates in the field the failure to be interdisciplinary is usually viewed as a serious fault, almost as serious as the failure to theorize. Indeed, the two failings are often linked as the products of formalism, and we will see that there is an obvious connection between interdisciplinarity and theorizing, as the terms are now used.

Despite the current excitement about it, interdisciplinarity is not new in criticism; it appears in the oldest critical texts we possess. For Plato all true knowledge must be interdisciplinary, since any inquiry within the confines of a single science has not reached the highest level of the divided line where the separate sciences are integrated dialectically. Thus, in his dialogues art is never treated as independent but is always subsumed under more general considerations. Aristotle's system is based on a separation of the sciences, one of which is poetics; but his book on that science begins with the concept of "imitation" derived from metaphysics, its analysis of "character" in chapter 2 depends on ethics, and the discussion of "thought" in chapter 19 refers us to the *Rhetoric*. These two interdisciplinary traditions continued into the Renaissance, when most critics adapted some Aristotelian concepts to a Platonic scheme. Sidney's *Apology for Poetry,* for instance, judges poetry in terms of ethics and in competition with history and philosophy.

The early study of English literature in the university also drew on other disciplines such as philology, and the dominant mode of interpretation in the period preceding the New Criticism was historical, which often involved other fields as well. Lily Bess Campbell's *Shakespeare's Tragic Heroes* (1930), to take a notable example, is based on a survey of Elizabethan moral philosophy and humor psychology, but she did not think she was crossing traditional disciplinary boundaries; she was being traditional. Even formalists could go to science. I. A. Richards, often seen as an ancestor of the New Critics, introduces us to the physiology of sensation, complete with a diagram (1926, 116), and Norman Rabkin, one of the last of the breed, to the physicist's principle of complementarity (1967, 22—no diagram).[1] And frequently in the New Criticism we find borrowings from other disciplines that are unacknowledged and perhaps unrecognized; in *The Well Wrought Urn* Cleanth Brooks reports that "a river is the most 'natural' thing that we can imagine," a fact presumably learned from geology, and he later relies on knowledge of obstetrics, the Irish school system, and so on (1947, 6, 44, 166). It would be impossible to interpret a literary text without recourse to some interdisciplinary knowledge in this sense.

Virtually all English departments of the forties, when I had my training, professed a number of different disciplines: literary history, criticism, linguistics, the history of the language, textual bibliography, rhetoric, and composition. Yet no one thought it was interdisciplinary, since the departmental organization defined all these as "English." There was, however, some activity in this period that was regarded as interdisciplinary (though the word was not used),[2] such as the committees formed at the University of Chicago to bring together members of several departments. One was the Committee on Social Thought, to which we owe Allan Bloom's closing of the American mind (1987), and I can remember that even in my student days it was known as a hotbed of conservatism. I mention it because crossing traditional disciplinary boundaries is now usually seen as a radical project; but in order to understand this it will be necessary to investigate the nature of the new interdisciplinarity. My investigation, of course, makes no claim to cover all contemporary interdisciplinary criticism, which would be impossible. I have instead focused on what seem to be the basic problems of some of the dominant trends in this body of criticism, produced by some of the more prominent critical approaches. And while most of my examples come from recent studies of Shakespeare, I believe these trends dominate other fields as well.

Selecting a Theory

> I am using Joseph Zinker's views [on Gestalt psychology] because, first, they meet these conditions. Second, I am comfortable with the language in which he talks about therapy because it is frequently the language of literary criticism.
> —Jean Kennard, "Ourself behind Ourself: A Theory for Lesbian Readers"

A good way to start would be to ask how most critics today go about becoming interdisciplinary. They usually do not proceed by first selecting another *discipline* and then trying to master it, which would take a lot of time and would be unnecessary, as we will see. My impression is that most of them do not even try to acquire an overall sense of the other discipline, of the sort that could be derived from a few good introductory courses. Instead they typically begin by selecting from the discipline a particular *theory* that they want to use. This is the obvious connection between the new interdisciplinarity and theorizing noted earlier, for in the current critical scene to theorize usually means to adopt a theory from another discipline.[3] But since this procedure in effect bypasses the other discipline itself as an organized body of knowledge and mode of investigation, critics do not select a theory on the basis of its standing in its own discipline, and so we must ask on what basis they do select it. Here it will help to look at some examples, which I have limited to the selection of theories taken from psychology.

A revealing example is provided by Coppélia Kahn's 1982 essay in which she introduces and recommends the neo-Freudian theory of Nancy Chodorow, Dorothy Dinnerstein, and Adrienne Rich to American feminist critics.[4] Early in the essay she admits that Freud's concept of penis envy "has justifiably angered many feminists and regrettably alienated them from psychoanalysis" (34). One can see why this concept alienated feminists (and nonfeminists) and led them to question the assumptions and methodology of a system that features it, but for Kahn their reaction is regrettable, since she wants to detach and change this concept (and others that seem masculinist) without giving up Freudianism. And the theory she is recommending does this: it retains the Freudian assumption that a single basic cause in the child's "family drama" accounts for all our problems, but simply relocates it in the "pre-Oedipal" instead of the "Oedipal" stage and so foregrounds the mother rather than the father. It also retains the methodology required to support this assumption—the reliance on a fixed and universal scheme of developmental stages, the hypostatizing of mental entities like "the unconscious," and the multiplication of mechanisms (displacement, condensation, splitting, etc.) that can force all possible data to fit the prescribed thesis, which now turns out to be that young boys' experience with mothering is responsible for misogyny and all the gender conflicts in society.

Our concern, however, is not with the theory itself but with the basis of Kahn's recommendation. It cannot be the evidence, for she makes only one passing reference to "clinical evidence" in favor of the theory (34), without noting that it was the clinical evidence of orthodox Freudians that confirmed penis envy (a point we will return to); nor can it be the standing of the theory in its own discipline, which she never mentions. Instead she gives another kind of reason for adopting it, or rather two related reasons: that it can serve the feminist cause in opposing the "oppression of women" in "patriarchal society" (33), and that it can serve feminist criticism in uncovering a "maternal subtext" in "patriarchal texts" (36). She selects the theory, in other words, on the basis of its utility rather than of its truth. Now, most scientists, who are skeptical about absolute truths, could agree with this. They would also judge a theory by its utility, that is, by whether it proves more useful than competing theories in accounting for all the relevant data, in making predictions, and in generating productive research to test, refine, and expand it. That would determine its standing in the discipline and would be what they mean by its "truth"; it will also be what I mean by the term here. But that it not how Kahn views the utility of this theory, which for her is its usefulness, not to its own discipline, but to her political agenda. The question of whether it is true, in this sense, seems to be irrelevant.

A similar project underlies Toril Moi's essay of 1983 that introduces and recommends some French "feminist theoreticians," primarily Julia Kristeva, to a group of British critics, most of them Marxists. She begins by attacking Anglo-American feminist criticism because its "empiricist and humanist" concept of the subject and the text is in "fundamental complicity" with "bourgeois ideology" and is "inherently reactionary" (4, 10), and contrasts it to Kristeva's theory of human development. Again we can pass over the details of the theory (which takes the child from the "semiotic *chora*" of the mother to the "symbolic order" of the father, roughly analogous to Chodorow's "pre-Oedipal" and "Oedipal" stages), since we are only interested in the reasons Moi gives for recommending it. And again we find they are not based on any evidence for it (that apparently would be "empiricist" and hence "reactionary") or on the evaluation of it in its own discipline. It is recommended because it provides a theoretical ground for "disrupt[ing] the strict symbolic order" and the "identity" of the subject, and so can "be a valuable dimension of any Marxist analysis of the conditions for revolutionary activity" and can also give us "a revolutionary form of criticism" (9–10).

The choice between these two ways of judging a theory is even more explicit in Catherine Belsey's essay of 1981 on Freudianism, also aimed at a predominately Marxist audience, which starts out by asking what the present status of this theory is: "The question is not, to my mind, as it once was, an epistemological one ('is it true?', 'how do we know?'). Post-Saussurean linguistic theory . . . closes off questions about how accurately language represents the world. . . . In asking 'what is the status of psychoanalysis?', I want to pose a political question: 'what challenge to the existing order is inscribed in [it]?'; 'what is its radical potential?'" (1986, 57). Thus, she goes further than Kahn or Moi by deliberately rejecting the criterion of truth and arguing that the theory should be judged only by the criterion of utility, which is defined again by a political agenda—challenging "the existing order." And she finds it is useful in this sense for much the same reason that Moi found Kristeva's theory useful: because it "radically undermines" the "unitary subject of bourgeois ideology" that is "the central justification of liberal humanism" and of "bourgeois criticism" (58, 75). Presumably, if it could be shown that the Elizabethan humor psychology surveyed by Campbell (1930) had even more "radical potential," Belsey would prefer it to psychoanalysis.

Although all three critics choose a theory primarily for its political utility, they all claim that it is also useful for criticism; but this is not an independent factor, since the kind of criticism they favor is determined by their politics. There are others, however, who focus on critical utility. David Leverenz explains that he is selecting Sullivan's "interpersonal theory" rather than other psychoanalytic theories because "it is more useful for literary criticism" (1980, 126); but its usefulness in criticism, like its usefulness in politics, cannot tell us if it is true, or even if it is closer to the truth than other theories that are less useful here. Moreover, many other critics claim that Freudian theory is the most useful for criticism, so this too depends on the kind of criticism that each critic prefers. That preference need not be based on the critic's politics, but it functions in the same way as the political agendas of Kahn, Moi, and Belsey in determining the choice of a theory.

My last example is the passage by Jean Kennard used as the epigraph to this section, where she states that she is adopting Zinker's psychological theory because she is "comfortable" with it (1986, 67). (The other "conditions" that it meets, we will not be surprised to learn, have nothing to do with the evidence for it or the evaluation of it by psychologists.) She does not seem to realize that the test of a scientific theory is not whether it makes people comfortable, or that some of the most important scientific theories of modern times made many people very uncomfortable.[5] But then all these critics could be said to choose a theory because it makes them comfortable, which means that it serves their needs, although different things serve those needs and so give them comfort.

While this section has focused on the way interdisciplinary critics select a psychological theory, the same procedure is adopted in many of their borrowings from history, sociology, economics, and the other "soft" social sciences. It seems fair to conclude, then, that the world of the new interdisciplinarity is viewed by these critics as a kind of cafeteria presenting a tempting array of theories that have been produced by other disciplines but are now detached from them, where they are free to choose whatever suits their taste, which turns out to be whatever is useful for their political or critical projects. And there is a clear connection between these two aspects of the scene, for if the theories are detached from their discipline, then a critic cannot select one in terms of the criteria of that discipline, and so the only criterion that remains is the critic's own "comfort."

Improving the Theory

> My use of Freudian terms does not mean that I endorse its ahistorical, Europocentric and sexist models of psychical development. However, a materialist criticism deprived of such concepts as displacement and condensation would be seriously impoverished.
> —Paul Brown, "'This Thing of Darkness I Acknowledge Mine'"

Although it is not a necessary step in the process of becoming interdisciplinary, it is not uncommon for critics, after selecting a theory, to set about changing it. One might have thought that they would hesitate to do this, since they usually know so little about the discipline that generated theory and provides its context, but the opposite is true. It is because they do not know the other discipline, and because the theory has been validated, as it were, by their own choice rather than by the discipline, that they feel free to improve it. And since its validity depends entirely on its usefulness to them, they can improve it by making it more useful. The neo-Freudian theory sponsored by Kahn can be seen in this way as an improvement on Freud, though we do not owe it primarily to literary critics.[6] Kahn herself derives from it another account of penis envy to replace Freud's (which, we saw, she wants to separate from his system): the little girl now desires a penis because "she wants to detach herself from her mother and become an autonomous person, not because she feels castrated without one" (1982, 34). No evidence is given for this change, but it clearly makes the theory more useful for Kahn's agenda.[7] Belsey, from a Marxist position, objects to the "universal, transhistorical and transcultural" nature of Freudian theory (1986, 57), yet she thinks she can amputate that and still keep enough of the theory alive to retain its "challenge to the existing order." And the epigraph to this section shows that Brown, another Marxist, also believes he can improve Freudian theory by dropping the parts he dislikes and keeping those (the concepts of "displacement and condensation") that he finds politically useful (1994, 71). Nor is he troubled by the fact that in Freud displacement and condensation occur within the human psyche, while he wants to relocate them in the text or "colonialist ideology" where there is no psychic mechanism to explain them. And Moi, after endorsing Kristeva's theory on political grounds, adds that its conclusions are "politically unsatisfactory" but reassures the audience that this "should not prevent us from drawing others" (1983, 9)—that is, from improving the politics of those conclusions.

Critics can also enhance the utility of the theory they select by making it a universal law. Freud's theories were supposed to be universal since they derived from a single basic cause of all human behavior, as we saw, and critics employing the new improvement of Freud often make similar claims. Edward Snow says that Othello's gynophobic reaction to the consummation of his marriage is felt in "every civilized white man," which he later extends to "every sexual relationship" (1980, 400, 402). He does not explain how this law (in either version) was derived, but it is obviously useful for establishing Othello's gynophobic reaction, which escaped the notice of virtually all viewers and readers of the play and all the characters in it. And Kahn's revised theory of penis envy is presented as a universal law, as was Freud's original account. One might think it would first be helpful to find out whether it is true that all little girls in all family configurations in all societies actually want a penis before arguing about why they want one, but neither the orthodox Freudians nor the neo-Freudians have shown any interest in such an investigation.

Unlike the Freudians, Marxist critics profess to reject universal laws (we saw Belsey attacking the "universal" claims of Freudian theory), but they have some of their own, since their theory also posits a single basic cause of human behavior. When Frank Lentricchia refers to "the ultimate problem of linking repressed and master voices as the agon of history, their abiding relation of class conflict" (1983, 131), the terms "ultimate" and "abiding" tell us that this is supposed to be a universal law determining all historical events and thus all literary events. But probably the most useful universal law for these critics (derived from this law of class conflict) is found in Jean Howard's assertion that "a dominant ideology . . . always bears traces of the contestatory or subversive elements it has attempted to recuperate" (1987a, 355), for this guarantees that every text will contain "traces" of ideological conflicts or contradictions. (And they will always be unresolvable, which is another universal law derived from the "abiding" nature of class conflict.) There is, however, a difference between the universal laws of the Marxists and neo-Freudians and those of orthodox Freudians, since the first two groups insist that their laws depend on social arrangements and will be repealed in the future when we have a society without classes or without a gender division of labor that assigns mothering to women. This is very important to them, since both groups, unlike the Freudians, believe the situation their laws describe can be ended by political action;[8] but it seems clear that until this day arrives their laws are supposed to be just as universal as the Freudians'. It also seems clear that the critics in all three groups have no notion of the evidence that would be required to establish this kind of universal law in the discipline involved.

Seeing If (Proving That) the Theory Works

> The imprint of mothering on the male psyche, the psychological presence of the mother in men whether or not mothers are represented in the texts they write or in which they appear as characters, can be found throughout the literary canon.
> —Coppélia Kahn, "The Absent Mother in *King Lear*"

After selecting (and perhaps improving) a theory from another discipline, the critic must then apply it to the interpretation of a literary text. This is the last step in the process of becoming interdisciplinary, and it is regarded as the payoff, a kind of test to see if the theory really works in criticism. The trouble is that all theories always pass this test; no failure has ever been recorded. We can get an idea of why this happens by looking at the neo-Freudians' application of their theory to Shakespeare, which requires that all his male heroes must have problems with mothering, which in turn requires that all his works must have a mother. There are many mothers in Shakespeare, but except for Volumnia in *Coriolanus* they have usually been ignored by these critics, because their relationship to the hero does not fit the theory and because the theory is based on unconscious motivation and therefore seems to call for a surrogate mother figure concealed in a "maternal subtext" that is repressed by the hero or the text or Shakespeare (the critics are often uncertain about this). Consequently, as Kahn explains, "the absence of a mother in the play serves to highlight her psychological presence," though she later adds that in *Coriolanus* "the mother's psychological presence within the hero is no less strong for being represented" (1982, 37, 39). Heads I win, tails you lose.

As a result of the application of this theory, Shakespearean mother figures have been proliferating at a remarkable rate and are now as plentiful as his Christ figures were under the older dispensation. In her essay introducing the theory, Kahn applied it to Lear and argued that he unconsciously views his daughters as mothers, which was a good choice, since there really is evidence of this in the play. But much less likely mother figures have been found for many other heroes in the canon: Portia is supposed to be a mother figure for Bassanio (Wheeler 1981), Desdemona for Othello (Erickson 1985a; Novy 1984; Snow 1980), Lady Macbeth for Macbeth (Adelman 1987; Kahn 1981; Wheeler 1981), Cleopatra for Antony (Erickson 1985a; Stockholder 1987), Rosalind for Orlando (Wheeler 1981), Cressida for Troilus (Adelman 1985b), Helena for Bertram (Adelman 1989; Stockholder 1987), Hermione for Leontes (Adelman 1985a; Erickson 1985a; Kahn 1981; Nevo 1988; Wheeler 1981; Stockholder 1987), Imogen for Posthumus (Nevo 1988), Miranda for Prospero (Novy 1989), and Venus for Adonis (Kahn 1981).[9] But they do not have to be female, since mother figurehood has been conferred on Shylock (Sundelson 1983) and Falstaff (Traub 1989). They do not even have to be human; the hero's mother figure has turned up in the witches in *Macbeth* (Stockholder 1987; Wheeler 1981), the lioness in *As You Like It* (Erickson 1985a; Montrose 1995), mother England in *Richard II* (Kahn 1981) and *Henry IV* (Wheeler 1981), and the sea in *The Comedy of Errors* (Adelman 1985a; MacCary 1985; Nevo 1988), *Twelfth Night* (MacCary 1985; Wheeler 1981), *Pericles* (Nevo 1988), *Timon of Athens* (Kahn 1987), and *The Tempest* (Nevo 1988).

The sheer variety here helps to explain why we now have as many mother figures in Shakespeare as we had Christ figures, since the searches for both have been conducted under the same golden rule: seek and ye shall find. I once showed how easy it was to find a Christ figure, because of the many aspects of Jesus that could be drawn on to make connections to a character (Levin 1979, 212–24); and it is even easier to find a mother figure, since the theory splits her into a benign and a malevolent persona, either of which can be used by the critics, and also mandates that she must appear in every play, no matter how concealed she may be. Indeed, the concealment is part of the theory, which enables Kahn to argue that "the absence of the mother [in a play] points to her hidden presence" (1986, 36), something the Christ figure seekers could not claim. (Alert readers will have noticed that some plays already have two mother figures, and if the trend continues we can anticipate more competition, with readings that begin by asserting that "My Mother Figure Can Lick Your Mother Figure.") Therefore, the fact that the theory can be shown to work in Shakespeare tells us nothing about its validity. This is just what we would expect, and we must remember that orthodox Freudians and Jungians were able to show that their theories worked in the same way in the same plays, as did Campbell (1930) with Elizabethan humor psychology, Leverenz (1980) with interpersonal psychiatry, and Kennard (1986) with Zinker's Gestalt theory.

The Marxists also have no trouble proving that their theory works in every Shakespeare play, for it tells them that whatever the play seems to be about, it must really be about Lentricchia's "ultimate problem" of "abiding" class conflict. It also tells them, like the neo-Freudian's theory, that this real subject is usually concealed by the play and thus must be "deconcealed" (Jameson's term) by the critic. The operation is now so widespread that a listing would be pointless, so I will limit myself to one example, Peter Stallybrass's reading of *Othello*, which is a kind of test case (although I do not know if he intended this), since the play does not seem to have anything to do with class conflict: the conflicts in it, insofar as they can be treated abstractly, involve the first two terms of the race-gender-class triad. But he saves the play for Marxism by using the Freudian concept of displacement to subsume gender and race under class.[10] "Class aspiration," he finds, is "displaced onto the enchanted ground of romance," and Othello's race is "the displaced condition" of his status as "class aspirant," and even Iago's villainy is a displacement, since the ruling class's fear of "subversion is localized" in him, so he becomes "the projection of a social hierarchy's unease in the hypostatized form of envy" (1986, 134–35, 140).[11] Thus *Othello* passes the test and proves that the theory works. The problem is that this reading is a test case in another sense that certainly was not intended by Stallybrass, for if the theory works in this play, then it will work in any play, which means it has not been and cannot be proved. In order for a theory to be provable it must be disprovable—that is, we must be able to conceive of a situation where it would *not* work. And this also applies to the neo-Freudian theory. The readings produced by either theory would be convincing only if there could be a play that did not involve a maternal subtext or a class conflict. But the claimed universality of the two theories and the methodology used in applying them preclude such a possibility. They have no negative test.

Aprioritizing Theory

> A rigorous knowledge must beware of all forms of empiricism, for the objects of any rational investigation have no prior existence but are thought into being.
> —Pierre Macherey, *A Theory of Literary Production*

Having examined the current procedure for becoming interdisciplinary, we can now try to explain why it developed in this way. One of the main causes is what I call "aprioritizing theory," which includes two related phenomena implied in the two meanings of the phrase: the tendency of interdisciplinary critics to aprioritize theory—that is, to treat "theorizing" as an a priori mode of thought—and their tendency to borrow theories that are themselves aprioritizing in the sense that they depend on a priori thinking.

It is no accident that most of these borrowings, and therefore most of my examples, come from Marxism or Freudianism (including various revisionist versions), since they are already interdisciplinary. Although each has a home discipline, as it were—one in economics and the other in psychology—we saw that they both claim to have discovered the fundamental cause of all human behavior studied in other disciplines as well, which makes it so easy to apply them to literature. Of course, both Marxism and Freudianism were presented from the outset (and still are) as empirical sciences, but they evolved in isolation from and in opposition to their home disciplines, which were viewed as enemies, and became closed, a priori systems that never had to confront the objections (usually based on empirical evidence) that were raised against them within those disciplines. This isolation has affected interdisciplinary criticism, since many Marxist and Freudian critics know a great deal about the theories of the founding fathers and their descendants but virtually nothing about what is now going on in the relevant discipline. They do not have to, and if they are even aware of the low standing of these theories in that discipline, this is just further proof that it is the enemy.

Any charge that Freudianism is not empirical must confront the claims of Freud himself and the schools derived from him, including the revisionists, that their theories are generated and confirmed by "clinical evidence." Chodorow, for instance, invokes "the clinical situation that ultimately provides psychoanalysis its truths" (1989, 12). The clinical situation can provide analysts with promising hypotheses (which can come from anywhere, even an overflowing bathtub or falling apple), but it can never prove they are true because, as I have argued elsewhere,[12] it is always contaminated by the analysts' a priori theory. Analysts are not trying to deceive us (or themselves), but out of all the evidence coming from the patient they only hear things that fit their theory, which is why each school of psychoanalysis is able to validate its own theories from the clinical evidence of its own practitioners. It is similar to the situation described earlier in which critics showed that very different psychological theories "worked" in the same play, since they were in effect treating the play (or playwright) as a patient providing data that they read in the light of their favorite theory. But the clinical situation is even more contaminated than these readings, because patients are affected by their analysts' expectations and therefore say the things that they think their analysts want to hear, as acknowledged by Judd Marmor (himself an analyst): "Patients of each school seem to bring up precisely the kind of... data which confirm the theories... of their analysts!" (1962, 289).[13] Feminist neo-Freudians should be especially sensitive to this, since the clinical evidence of orthodox Freudians was supposed to prove theories like penis envy. Yet they have shown no more interest than the orthodox Freudians in submitting their evidence to empirical verification, which would require objective tests that could be administered by nonbelievers and could yield negative results. When the theory of two female orgasms, another Freudian truth proved by clinical evidence, was put to such a test it flunked badly. It seems clear that clinical evidence is not empirical but is deduced from a priori theories.

Marxists have nothing equivalent to clinical evidence, although their analyses of society, both diachronic and synchronic, seem just as aprioritized as the interpretations of Freudian therapists and critics. Their theory in its latest versions, however, is even more obviously a priori than the Freudians', since it is not merely nonempirical but antiempirical, as shown in the epigraph to this section and in the earlier quotation from Moi asserting that empiricism is "inherently reactionary" (1983, 10). This would have surprised Marx, who spent many hours collecting data for those tables in *Das Kapital;* but there are several reasons for this antiempiricist swerve of the new Marxism. Surely the most important is that the empirical facts have not been kind to Marx's theory or to the predictions based on it.[14] That in turn has contributed to the tendency of the new Marxists to distance their theorizing from the real world of political action, despite their claim to be "activists." This is related to their wholesale condemnation of all modes of thought that they associate with the bourgeoisie and the Enlightenment, including empiricism, objectivism, and positivism, which have all become bad words in their vocabulary. They have also been influenced by the general thrust of poststructuralism, which questions the possibility of access to an external reality and hence of empirical knowledge. As a result, the new Marxists not only deduce their facts from their theory (as did the old Marxists) but now insist that this is the proper way for cutting-edge state-of-the-art revolutionaries to proceed. Nor has this poststructuralist influence been limited to them, for many interdisciplinary critics of other schools have joined the attack on empirical evidence and thus have contributed to the aprioritizing of theory.[15]

Politicizing Theory

> [Our] claim is not that such a history . . . is more accurate, but only that it is more radical.
> —Catherine Belsey, "Literature, History, Politics"

The interdisciplinary critics' lack of concern for the empirical verification of the theories they borrow is closely connected to their lack of concern for the evaluation of these theories by the disciplines involved (which is based on empirical verification), and therefore to their belief that they are free to borrow any theory and make any improvement on it that suits their purposes. And since these purposes are often political, as we saw, aprioritizing theory is also closely connected to politicizing theory, which I use again in two related senses: the tendency of these critics to treat all "theorizing" as a political activity and their tendency to borrow theories that are themselves politicizing in that they are directed to the transformation of society. This is one reason that interdisciplinarity is now seen as a radical project.

Many of these critics justify this politicization with the argument that all critical approaches are political, and specifically that the formalist approach, although it may seem politically neutral, really supports "liberal humanism," which is supposed to be the ideology of the bourgeoisie that legitimates the oppression of workers and women.[16] Therefore they link formalism and liberal humanism to the other bad isms on the hit list compiled above (empiricism, positivism, etc.), which are opposed to the good isms that are linked to class and gender liberation. Politicization thus leads these critics to polarization, with all truth and virtue on "our" side and all error and vice on "their" side. And not far beneath the surface of this polarized view of the world are glimpses of a vast conspiracy that is imposing the bad isms upon us, including pluralism, which is seen as a devious strategy to maintain the status quo (like the "repressive tolerance" we heard about in the sixties).[17] Even the boundaries separating the disciplines become part of this conspiracy, because they prevent us from learning about our oppression, which is another reason that interdisciplinarity is now held to be radical and liberating.

Like other conspiracy theories, this sounds neat and simple, but it simply is not true. There is no necessary connection between critical approaches and political beliefs. Many of the early New Critics were conservatives, yet during its heyday this formalist approach attracted people of all political persuasions, including Marxists and feminists. There was also a thriving group of Marxist formalists in the USSR before they were liquidated by Marxist realists, who are now opposed by the new Marxists because realism is bourgeois. Historical criticism is practiced by conservatives, liberals, and radicals, and so is psychological criticism. The alleged connection between critical approaches and political actions (rather than beliefs) is even more dubious, as Stanley Fish (1989, 220) and Gerald Graff (1983, 150–52) point out. Formalists can even work for radical causes, and many new Marxists, we saw, distance themselves from political activity. This disjunction is noted in the essay by Moi cited earlier, in which she attacks Anglo-American feminists for adopting a "humanist" approach that is "reactionary" and praises French "feminist theoreticians" for their "revolutionary form of criticism," but then praises the Anglo-American feminists for being "politically committed" to "challenging the social and political strategies of the literary institution," while the French feminists have shown "a scandalous lack of interest in the social and political aspects of women's oppression" (1983, 6, 11). Yet she insists that the French approach is politically superior.

It also seems clear that there is no necessary connection between political beliefs or actions and the theories these critics choose to borrow from other disciplines, even though we found that their choices are often based on political grounds. Moi and Belsey urged the (partial) adoption of the theories of Kristeva and Freud, since they disrupt the unitary subject of liberal humanism and so pave the way for communism. But disrupting the subject need not promote Marxist goals; it was also on the fascist agenda, which was just as hostile to liberal humanism as Marxism is. This lack of connection is also demonstrated in the endless debates among these critics on whether some theory is really on "our" side or can serve "their" side by appropriation, co-option, and so on.[18] The debates are endless, because the theories they argue about are not bound to specific political positions. This also applies to the passage from Belsey used as the epigraph here: she endorses one version of history since it is more "radical" than others, but we have no way of determining which history is more radical. The same historical interpretations are used by different political factions, and so are the larger historical theories—there are leftist and rightist Hegelians, for instance, and the concept of history as a fall from a lost Eden figures in reactionary and radical rhetoric.[19]

There is a more basic objection to these politicizers, however, for even if we could establish a necessary connection between some theories taken from another discipline and specific political positions, it would still be wrong to judge *any* theory by political criteria instead of the criterion of truth. That is easy to see when we disagree with the political criteria; I do not think many of my readers support the assault on the theory of evolution by the religious right, yet this is the most prominent recent example of the politicization of theory advocated by these critics when their own political beliefs are the criteria. The theory of evolution seems to be true (and is used by political conservatives and radicals), but the criteria are just as objectionable when the theory is false. Freudian theory has been attacked by Marxists and some feminists because it legitimates class or gender oppression, but that cannot make it false.[20] It is false, not because it may have bad political consequences, but because it does not meet the criteria of empirical verification established in the discipline of psychology. And the revision of Freud recommended by Kahn is false for the same reason, even though it may have good political consequences in promoting the feminist cause.

The judging of theories on the basis of their alleged political consequences has itself dire political consequences, for it leads to the politicizing of the disciplines and hence to their destruction as independent modes of inquiry. This is the lesson of Lysenkoism—not of the genetic theory itself (which no one believes anymore), but of the way it was adopted on political grounds as "revolutionary," while opposing theories were outlawed as "reactionary." This was atypical, since Marxist regimes usually kept their hands off the "hard" sciences, which yield useful results when left alone;[21] but they resolutely politicized the rest of the curriculum. Thus a major demand of students after the liberation of Eastern Europe was for the *de*politicization of the university, by which they meant the elimination, not only of compulsory indoctrination courses in Marxist ideology, but also of ideological criteria in the study of other disciplines, which they wanted to be governed by the criteria of truth defined in those disciplines. Our politicizing critics should listen to those students, who have already been where these critics want to take us.

Welcoming Theory

"At sociology meetings I've wandered from session to session where people were giving papers on how absurd my work is," she recalled. "I find I'm taken more seriously by literary critics."
—Nancy Chodorow, interview by Daniel Goleman

We should not place all the blame for the present state of interdisciplinarity upon these critics, since a share belongs to the rest of us, or rather to the discipline of literary criticism. It can hardly be a coincidence that our discipline is so hospitable to discredited theories from other disciplines and is able to prove that they "work" in interpreting literature. This must be related to our interpretive procedures, which seem to operate without any rules. Martin Mueller observes that "from the perspective of other disciplines, literary scholars engage in exegetical activities that are peculiarly unconstrained" and that the "hermeneutical license that has long been claimed by literary critics . . . has always been suspect" in those disciplines (1989, 27).

This can be partly explained by the nature of the phenomena we deal with. Literary texts and the responses they evoke are highly complex and multiform and hence not amenable to precise demonstrations. As a result, our discipline will always be less rigorous than even the "soft" sciences. But another important explanation lies in the approach that dominated the New Criticism and is still influential, which I call "thematism." Thematic critics usually begin with the assumption that the real subject of the text they are interpreting cannot be what it seems to be—the particular actions of particular characters—but must be an abstract idea or "central theme" reflected in them, and then look for evidence to prove it, which they always find. And they never find any evidence that might disprove it, because they are not looking for this evidence (that is, they only "see" the data they have already thematized) and because the approach does not define what such evidence would be, for there is nothing the text could contain that cannot be accommodated to the theme. They have no negative test, which is why we have no unsuccessful thematic readings.

This should recall our earlier account of how interdisciplinary critics see if the theory they took from another discipline works in interpreting a text, since this operation is also always successful for the same reasons: they only look for evidence in the text that will prove the theory works, and there is no evidence that could disprove it. This also applies to the two favorite theories of these critics. Freudian and neo-Freudian analysts perform a kind of thematic reading of clinical evidence, for their theory tells them in advance that what the patient seems to be talking about is only a reflection of the real problem, and it also tells them in advance what the real problem must be. And Marxists produce thematic readings of history and of society; thanks to their theory, they know in advance that what seems to be happening is only a reflection of what is really happening, and that what is really happening is an aspect of class conflict. We also saw that neither Freudian nor Marxist theory is subject to a negative test, since it cannot be refuted by any conceivable evidence, which is why we concluded that they are both aprioritized.

I suggest that it is partly because of the legacy of thematism that so few critics today appreciate the importance of negative tests, which in turn would explain the fact, noted by Mueller, that our mode of interpretation seems so unconstrained to people in other disciplines. Scientists have long realized that if a theory cannot be disproved, then it cannot be proved. Ideally, any scientist proposing a new theory should try all possible means to disprove it,[22] which may be asking too much; but we do not have to rely on this, because the theory must be formulated in such a way that others can do the job—that is, it must "invite falsification" by objective tests that can produce negative results. A theory that is not "falsifiable" in this sense would not be taken seriously; it would be what Frank Cioffi (1970) calls pseudoscientific. The failure of interdisciplinary critics to grasp this principle is seen in the assumption of Marxists and neo-Freudians, noted earlier, that they can prove their theory works by finding a class conflict or maternal subtext in every play, without defining a possible situation in which it would *not* work. And because these critics operate in this a priori mode with no negative tests, they see nothing wrong in adopting theories that operate in the same way, which helps to account for the strange situation described by Chodorow in the epigraph to this section.

This may explain why these critics do not reject a priori theories, but there are also positive reasons that they accept Marxism and Freudianism (especially the revised version). The most important is the politicization of theory discussed above: those who see criticism as the continuation of political struggle by other means are drawn to a theory that seems useful for this purpose and do not care that it is discredited in its own discipline (which they view as itself politically motivated by the "enemy"). We also saw that both theories distinguish between the apparent meaning and the real meaning of the phenomena they deal with, just as many critics do, and that they both locate this real meaning in one fundamental cause of all human behavior that can easily be grasped by critics and applied to any text. And it is a very dramatic cause featuring conflicts between hypostatized entities (parts of society or of the psyche), which appeals to critics who like to find conflicts or "agons" in literary works.[23] These seem to be the main reasons that Marxism and Freudianism are thriving in literature departments when they are in full retreat everywhere else in the world.

The fact remains, however, that these theories could not become popular in interdisciplinary criticism if critics recognized the importance of negative tests, both for the theories they borrow and for the application of those theories in interpreting literature, so I now want to turn to such tests. Their role in interpretation is too complicated to discuss here,[24] but there are two simple and obvious tests for the theories themselves—tests that are easy to use and require no special expertise. I am under no illusion that they will be adopted by critics who already inhabit (or are inhabited by) Marxism or Freudianism or similar closed, a priori systems, which we saw are impervious to adverse arguments. But they might be helpful to aspiring interdisciplinarians who are not yet committed to a system of this kind and are still willing and able to judge its theories before borrowing them.

Looking at a Real Horse

> In the middle of the Middle Ages three learned doctors held a public debate at the Sorbonne on the nature of the horse's hoof. One based his case on a passage from Aristotle. The second disagreed, citing another account from Galen. The third said they were both wrong, since Pliny had a different view. They argued for hours until someone in the audience asked, "Why don't we step outside and look at a real horse?"

This is an apocryphal story that probably comes from some lost anti-Scholastic satire, like the debate over how many angels could dance on the head of a pin, but it tells us something about the nature of a priori thinking, in which the facts are deduced from the theory and so are always already "theorized" (just as the textual evidence of the New Critics was always already "thematized"). One obvious negative test of such a theory, then, is to step outside it and look at the facts—the real horse—to see if they are what the theory claims they should be. I will present just a few examples in which these theories fail this test, beginning with Snow's law, stated above, that every man or at least "every civilized white man" has an intense gynophobic reaction to the consummation of his marriage (1980, 400, 402), which is presumably derived from the neo-Freudian theory of male pathology and is supposed to explain Othello's murder of Desdemona. If the theory were true, most of our marriages would end like Othello's, but the facts are otherwise. In fact many husbands, even civilized white ones, seem to feel more loving after the wedding night (when the couple abstained until then), which is also true of Othello, as we can see from his treatment of Desdemona in 3.3.55–92.

Some feminist critics use Kristeva's theory of the child's progress from the "semiotic order" of the mother to the "symbolic order" of the father (or

Lacan's similar scheme) to maintain that language is a masculine construction from which women are "alienated" (Gohlke 1980, 166, 170). But in fact women handle the "mother tongue" at least as well as men and score higher than men in the verbal sections of many aptitude tests; some of them are even able to describe their alienation from language with real eloquence. Similar to this theory of "masculine language" is the theory of "masculine narrative," which also fails the test of fact, since however this narrative is defined, we can show that it is employed by some women. And if this evidence is explained away on the ground that they were conditioned to write like men,[25] this would show that the theory cannot be disproved by any conceivable facts, and so cannot be proved. It is simply deduced from some a priori assumption about gender difference.

Many of the Marxist theories also fail this test. It is obvious that every prediction based upon them has been contradicted by the facts. I noted that this led Jameson to deny that Marxism is predictive, which would exempt it from this test and make it, too, undisprovable and thus unprovable; but others still prophesy the collapse of "late capitalism,"[26] when in fact we are seeing the collapse of late socialism. More examples are provided by the new Marxists' campaign against the bourgeoisie, which includes the theory of Barker (1984, 110–12) and Belsey (1985b, 124–25) that bourgeois subjects possess a "death drive" impelling them to suicide. But the facts again contradict this idea, since very few bourgeois subjects commit suicide; in fact, the suicide rate varies widely in different bourgeois societies, as it does in different nonbourgeois societies, so it is not correlated to the economic system. Another Marxist theory that clearly fails this test, even though it has been endorsed by some feminists,[27] is that gender oppression is caused by class oppression and will end when capitalism is replaced by socialism. But the facts are that the subjection of women long preceded class society and survives under socialism. There are in fact striking differences in the status of women in different capitalist societies, as there are in different socialist societies, showing that this status, like suicide, is not determined by the economic system.

Many more examples of this sort could be cited, but these should be enough to make my point about the nature of a priori thinking. For I cannot believe that I possess some special ability or knowledge that enables me to find the facts that contradict these theories, since they are obvious and available to anyone who looks for them. This forces me to conclude that the interdisciplinary critics cannot have looked, because they do not want to subject the theory they are borrowing to this negative test.

Do I Contradict Myself?
Very Well Then, I Contradict Myself

> Human nature is not "natural," but is, rather, shaped by social forces and values.... In de Beauvoir's terms, "woman sees herself and makes her choices not in accordance with her nature in itself, but as man defines her."
> —Gayle Greene, "Shakespeare's Cressida: 'A Kind of Self'"

The second obvious negative test of theories borrowed from other disciplines is to see if they are contradicted, not by the facts, but by a practice or another belief of the critic who borrows them. Again I present only a few of the examples where theories clearly fail this test, most of which are related to the politicizing of theory (just as most failures of the test of fact were related to the aprioritizing of theory). In many of these cases critics adopt a theory about texts or discourse but exempt their own texts or discourse from it, so that they inconsistently "privilege" their practice. Several commentators have noted that this is standard procedure in Freudian criticism (which here includes the neo-Freudians): the critics regularly assume that every text they interpret is shaped by unconscious motives but that their interpretation of it is immune from such motives. Thus, a male critic who finds that a play is permeated by castration anxiety never has to ask himself whether that anxiety could be in him rather than in the play or playwright. If he or we did ask this, Freudian criticism would grind to a halt.[28]

Other examples of this self-privileging appear in critics employing the post-Saussurean linguistic theory invoked by Belsey, since they usually treat signifiers as freely floating in the texts they read but as firmly grounded in the texts they write; they will even complain when they are misunderstood, although this theory insists that there can be no correct understanding of a text and that its author has no control over its meaning.[29] They also contradict themselves on the referentiality of language: in the passage referred to, Belsey says this theory "closes off questions about how accurately language represents the world" but then discusses "the existing order" of the world in language that she must believe represents it accurately (1986, 57). More examples come from critics who adopt the theory that interpretation is never objective since it is always affected by the interpreter's ideology (rather than by the intrinsic volatility of language itself). Unlike many post-Saussureans, these critics often admit that the theory applies to their own discourse (as in the epigraph to the section "Politicizing Theory"), yet they can forget this very quickly when it serves their purpose. Barker says all historical interpretation is "reshaped to present needs ... and to believe otherwise would be to advance a hubristic objectivism,"[30] and two sentences later attacks critics who misinterpret the real historical basis of Shakespeare's texts (1984, 15). And the *PMLA* Forum letter reprinted in chapter 1 states that "we forthrightly acknowledge the partiality of our own interpretations," but in the next paragraph presents interpretations of Shakespeare that are meant to be independent of this partiality, since they derive from "detailed analyses of the specific actions of particular heroes." The explanation of these contradictions is political: the critics believe that the idea of interpretive objectivity belongs to the bourgeois or male enemy and so must be rejected, yet they also believe—and want readers to believe—that their own interpretations are objectively true.

There is another form of this self-contradiction in which critics espouse an interpretive theory but exempt certain texts from it, so that they are privileging, not their own practice, but the texts themselves. Most of these examples involve the "hermeneutics of suspicion"—the theory that a text is never what it seems to be, since it must contain concealed or repressed material (ideological contradictions or maternal subtexts)—which these critics adopt from the Marxist or Freudian traditions and apply selectively. Moi notes that many Anglo-American feminist critics use this "suspicious approach" on men-authored texts but not on women-authored texts, which they take straight (1983, 2–4). (Characters can also be privileged in this way: neo-Freudians typically probe the unconscious and always pathological motivation of male characters, while female characters seem free of such probing; and Snow, after giving Othello the full "suspicious" treatment, gets indignant when an orthodox Freudian does the same to Desdemona [1980, 405].) The new Marxists are just as guilty. Evans applies the "suspicion" theory (with a dash of post-Saussureanism thrown in) to Shakespeare's texts but assumes that radical texts of the Civil War period are just what they seem to be (1986, 259–62). And many Marxists who employ this theory in reading bourgeois plays abandon it when they read Brecht.[31] The explanation of these contradictions again lies in the political polarization of criticism, since the critics want the enemy's ox gored, not their own.

The last kind of self-contradiction results not from the inconsistent application of one theory adopted by these critics but from their adoption of two theories that are incompatible. Most of the examples here turn on the nature-nurture problematic, which poses problems for critics who are committed to the theory that "human nature" is created entirely by nurture—that, as Rorty puts it, "there is nothing to people except what has been socialized into them" (1989, 177)[32]—but find it politically expedient to adopt the other position. Marxists get into this contradiction because, if "the subject" is simply the product of the dominant bourgeois ideology, they have no way to explain how opposition to this ideology arises or why we should support this opposition,[33] and so must invoke values like "social justice," "equality," "liberation," or "human potential" that cannot have been inscribed in us by that ideology and seem to derive from (and assume) a concept of a basic, indestructible human nature. Thus Jameson begins *The Political Unconscious* with the command "Always historicize!" (1981, 9) and later tells us that all history is "the collective struggle to wrest a realm of Freedom from a realm of Necessity" (19), a struggle that could not be the result of historically specific conditioning but is apparently an inherent and unhistoricizable aspiration of humanity itself.

For some feminists the problem of nature versus nurture centers on the question of whether gender differences are innate or acquired, which can involve them in the same kind of self-contradiction, as seen in Greene's two sentences used as the epigraph to this section. Greene begins her essay by insisting that human nature (which for her includes woman's nature) is not natural but is "shaped by social forces" that are patriarchal, and later endorses de Beauvoir's statement that a woman acts "not in accordance with her nature in itself, but as man defines her" (Greene 1980, 133, 136). Yet there can be no opposition between woman's "nature in itself" and man's definition of her if man's definition shapes her nature, for then she would have no "nature in itself." Presumably both theories are asserted because each has political advantages: the theory that women's nature is wholly the product of conditioning (that it is all "socialized into them") is useful for arguing that it can be changed by social action, while the theory that they have an inherent nature that this conditioning violates is useful to validate and valorize such action.[34]

Although more examples could be presented, these should be enough to make my point, which is the same one I reached at the end of the preceding section. For again I must say that I did not require any special knowledge or ability to find these contradictions, since they would all be obvious to anyone who looked for them. And so we must conclude once more that these critics could not have looked, because they did not want to apply this negative test either to the theories they borrowed or to their use of them in literary criticism.

For Interdisciplinarity

> Interdisciplinary work is most difficult but also most productive when it involves the collision of strongly articulated disciplinary ethnicities.

> Work of this kind is quite rare, because it requires a hands-on experience of, and a deep respect for, the otherness of the other.
> —Martin Mueller, "Yellow Stripes and Dead Armadillos"

I want to end this investigation on a positive note, because I have been arguing not against interdisciplinarity itself but only against its abuses. I am really arguing for a genuine interdisciplinarity, or at least for something much closer to it than the studies we examined. Mueller recognizes that the kind of work he is describing, where the critic has actually practiced the other discipline, is an ideal that can rarely be achieved; but we surely can ask that critics who want to be interdisciplinary should know enough about the other discipline to use it in ways that will not seem absurd to its own practitioners. I hope it is clear that I am not calling for a rigid turfism that would discourage critics from using another discipline. Nor am I suggesting that the various disciplines as now constituted are natural, inevitable, autonomous, seamless, God-given, or any of the other inanities that we liberal humanists are supposed to believe in. The disciplines have been constructed by human beings and have evolved through time. But as a result of this evolution they have developed organized bodies of knowledge and methodologies for producing and testing new knowledge that deserve our respect, for even though they are fallible, they are still the best means we have for learning about the world. It follows, then, that a critic wishing to use a theory from another discipline should first understand what it means in that discipline and how it is judged there. To promote this goal I am presenting four proposals, in an ascending order of their importance and of the difficulty in implementing them.

The most obvious step and the easiest would be to ensure that whenever a critical article or book claiming to be interdisciplinary is submitted for publication, its referees include a representative of the other discipline.[35] This is sometimes done today, but the practice should be universal. It would not only help to screen out bad interdisciplinary work,* but would also have a positive effect on the research of interdisciplinary critics. If they

---

*The importance of this proposal was demonstrated three years later by the "Sokal hoax," in which *Social Text*, in a special issue devoted to science, published an essay by Alan Sokal (1996), a physicist, containing many obvious and absurd scientific errors, which was possible only because no scientist refereed the submissions to that issue, and which therefore exposed the vacuity of this kind of interdisciplinarity. In their reaction to the revelation of the hoax, Bruce Robbins and Andrew Ross, two editors of the journal, complained that academic work is "policed . . . at every departmental checkpoint by disciplinary passport controls" (1996, 56); but these controls must be very ineffective since, as I am arguing, this

were planning an essay that relied on Lawrence Stone's theory of the "reinforcement of patriarchy," for instance, and knew in advance that it would be refereed by a social historian, they would have a powerful incentive for finding out, before writing the essay, just how this theory is regarded in Stone's own field.[36]

Second, I would recommend changes in our requirements for literature students, both undergraduate and graduate, that would enable them to carry a double major or a strong minor in a second discipline. This, too, is sometimes done today, but it should be made much easier if we hope to encourage responsible interdisciplinary work.[37] We might also offer, as part of our general education component, an introductory course in the methodologies of the disciplines that would explain, among other things, the significance of falsifiability and negative tests and the pitfalls of enumerative inductivism. These are not very recondite concepts, yet most of the critics dealt with here have apparently never heard of them, and we saw this was also true of the older thematic critics. If our students learned about them, therefore, we would reap future benefits not only in interdisciplinary criticism but also in the kinds of criticism practiced within the confines of our own discipline.

The third proposal is to take some of the pressure off our colleagues, especially the younger ones, to engage in interdisciplinarity with its attendant theorizing. I realize this is much more easily said than done, since it involves the pressure to publish and hence to adopt the mode of criticism that is now most publishable. One has to sympathize with the plight of those who feel obliged to join this enterprise even though they are not suited for it by training, ability, or inclination, and so find themselves trafficking in undigested scraps of theory, picked up from other disciplines, that they cannot evaluate or apply properly—a practice that has led to many of the errors we examined. Clearly they would benefit, as would the rest of us, if we could convince them that they are not being timid or narrow or outdated if they stick to their own discipline and do what they know how to do. Perhaps we could even convince them that it takes more courage to buck the current fashion than to follow it.

The final proposal is the most important, since it extends well beyond

---

kind of interdisciplinarity has been flourishing for many years. Their complaint is not surprising, however, because it is now common for some of the newer critics to equate any appeal to objective disciplinary standards of validation with reactionary police oppression (compare the quotations from Tompkins, Sprinker, Crosman, Hartman, Fish, and Derrida in Graff 1983, 145–46). Nor will we be surprised to find them asserting that "professional scientists like Sokal" feel "threatened" by them (56), which bears out my point in "It's a Panic," appended to chapter 5.

the specific problems of interdisciplinarity to the general state of our discipline. I would like to see an end to the political polarization noted earlier, which locates all truth and virtue on one side and all error and evil on the other. This polarization bears most of the responsibility (much more than the lack of ability) for the problems of the new interdisciplinarity that we surveyed: for the selection and improvement of theories from other disciplines on political grounds, with the resulting arguments over whether some theory is really on "our" side or "theirs"; for the self-contradiction and the disregard of empirical evidence; for the inconsistent privileging of "our" discourse and "our" texts; and the rest. It has also created an atmosphere that is harmful to all other areas of our discipline, since it prevents us from talking to and learning from each other. Depolarization would therefore benefit not only the targets of the polarizers but also the polarizers themselves. The reason has already been suggested in the discussion of negative tests, for we tend to be lax in applying such tests to our own work or the work of critics like us. That is why we need critics with different orientations to apply the tests for us, so we will be able to refine or correct our views. I have learned more from those who disagree with me than from those who agree; but we cannot learn in this way if we dismiss adverse criticism as the machinations of the enemy.[38]

The blame for this polarizing belongs to both extremes of the political spectrum. All my examples here were on the Left, since that is where the new interdisciplinarity is coming from, but the Right is equally guilty, as can be seen in Allan Bloom's book (a product of the old interdisciplinarity), with its nostalgic idealizing of a lost Eden and wholesale condemnation of all new developments, which is just as absurd and pernicious as the opposite stance.[39] We would all benefit if we could abandon this warfare between the two sides, and even abandon the idea of two sides. There are many different political positions and many different critical positions and no necessary connection between them, as I tried to show. And in most of them we will find well-meaning, intelligent people who have useful things to tell us about our discipline and interdisciplinarity and the world we all share.

9

The New and the Old Historicizing of Shakespeare

> Always historicize!
> —Fredric Jameson, *The Political Unconscious*

According to the conventional story we tell ourselves in this part of the world, academic criticism of Shakespeare and his contemporaries (and of most other areas of literary study) went through three major stages during the twentieth century: first was the period of what is now called the old historical approach, which dominated the field until the 1940s when it was superseded by the ahistorical, formalist New Criticism, whose period of dominance came to an end around 1980 when several schools of critics—mainly feminists, New Historicists, and cultural materialists or Marxists—brought about the dramatic (re)turn to history that is proclaimed in Jameson's famous command. Like most such stories, this is considerably oversimplified, since it erases some significant work that does not fit its scheme, such as Bradley's *Shakespearean Tragedy* (1904), which was not historical and yet exercised a remarkable influence during the hegemony of the old historicism, and Freudian criticism, neither historical nor formalist, which persisted as a marginal operation during the first two periods and has now, in revisionist versions, entered the critical mainstream despite the hegemony of the new historicizers.[1] It is easy to think of other exceptions of this sort to the three-stage story of the changing fortunes of the historical criticism of Shakespeare.

The story, nevertheless, is true in its broad outlines, or at least true enough for my purpose, because I want to examine some aspects of this new historical criticism that can be highlighted by a comparison with the historical criticism of the first period. I must emphasize at the outset that my examination will be limited, since it cannot possibly encompass the vast and varied body of work that the new historicizers have produced within the space of fifteen years. It will not be an inquiry on the level of theory but will look instead at how the theorizing of these critics is enacted in their practice. And it will focus on certain aspects of this practice that I think present serious and largely unacknowledged problems. Fortunately for me, my interest in comparing these new historicizers with the old ones is shared by them, since they often define themselves in terms of such a comparison, claiming that it reveals decisive breaks on two fronts, the epistemological and the political, which I will consider in that order.

※

> The new orientation to history in Renaissance literary studies . . . may be succinctly characterized, on the one hand, by its acknowledgment of the *historicity of texts*. . . . On the other hand, this new orientation is characterized by its acknowledgment of the *textuality of history*.
> —Louis Montrose, "The Elizabethan Subject and the Spenserian Text"

We can begin with Montrose's chiasmus (which is almost as widely quoted as Jameson's command), because it succinctly sums up the theoretical opposition between the new historicizers' epistemological assumptions or tenets and those of the two main schools that preceded them. The belief in the "historicity"—or what he also calls the "cultural specificity"—of literary texts differentiates them from the nonhistorical New Critics; and the belief in the "textuality of history" differentiates them from the old historical critics, who, he explains, read problematic literary works "against a supposedly stable, coherent, and transparent 'historical' background" that is prior to these works and is used to interpret them, whereas the new historicizers realize that our knowledge of this history has "already been mediated by the surviving texts" of the period—texts that must also be interpreted, like literary works, and so are on the same problematic level (1986a, 304–5). He also adds two more oppositions between the two stages of historical criticism that function as corollary tenets of his creed: the new historicizers differ from the old ones in their "refusal of traditional distinctions between literature and history, between text and context," and they reject the old historicizers' view that literature simply reflects its culture and insist instead that it has an "impact upon the social formation" in a "reciprocal" causal interaction (304–6).[2]

There is, however, a striking contradiction between the new historicizers' theorizing and their actual practice. In 1987 Edward Pechter pointed out that, despite their claim that they are not prioritizing history, their readings regularly begin with some historical "facts" and then apply them to the literary work, just like the old historicists (293–94). He cites Stephen Greenblatt's readings of *Henry IV* and *King Lear*, but he could have added many other examples, and the new historicizing published after his essay provides still more. This contradiction between profession and practice can even be found within the same study. In Montrose's essay the theoretical introduction (from which my epigraph is taken) is followed by a long historical section, opening with the statement that "Shortly before she died in 1558, England's Catholic queen, Mary Tudor, reluctantly designated her Protestant half-sister Elizabeth as her successor" (1986a, 307), and proceeding to an account of the "dominant Elizabethan ideology" of power and gender and the problems posed for it by a woman ruler; only then, in the third section, do we get to Spenser's poetry, which is interpreted in terms of this history. Marilyn Williamson's book also begins by affirming the new historicizers' theory of the interrelation of history and literature, which, she says, rejects the older project of placing "the historical context as a background" to literature; but when she comes to "the cuckoldry theme" in Shakespeare's comedies, she first explains its significance in Elizabethan "everyday life" and then says, "We are now prepared to understand the complex code on which Shakespeare was drawing in *Merchant, As You Like It,* and *Much Ado*" (1986, 14, 45). And my most amusing example appears in an essay by Jonathan Goldberg, who attacks Greenblatt for opening his discussion of *King Lear* "with a characteristic gesture toward the unquestioned reality of dates and facts, the local event that locates the Shakespearean text within a cultural economy: 'Between the spring of 1585 and the summer of 1586, a group of English Catholic priests led by the Jesuit William Weston, alias Father Edmunds, conducted a series of spectacular exorcisms,'" but then opens his own discussion of a Latin entertainment with the same gesture: "On August 27, 1605, in the course of a visit [King] James and his family made to Oxford, they were welcomed to St. John's College by . . ." (1987, 244, 257).

My point is not the rhetorical organization of these expositions but the epistemological assumption underlying it, which is revealed in the way the new historicizers treat the history that begins their readings. Although they claim to reject the old historicists' belief in the unproblematic status of historical "facts," they seem to believe that the facts they present in the introductory section are unproblematically true; indeed, this belief is implicit in their confident reliance upon them to introduce their readings.[3] We can see that confidence in the similar opening sentences of Montrose, Greenblatt, and Goldberg quoted above, which all assume what Goldberg disparagingly calls "the unquestioned reality of dates and facts" and seek to establish what Montrose disparagingly refers to as "a supposedly stable, coherent, and transparent 'historical' background." Both this assumption and this purpose, which the old historical critics shared, flatly contradict their professed "acknowledgment of the textuality of history."

There are also striking contradictions between the new historicizers' regular practice and the other two tenets of their creed. Despite their "refusal of traditional distinctions between literature and history, between text and context," their procedure depends on both these distinctions, since it assumes that the history of the period (or the particular aspect of it they focus on) supplies the necessary context for comprehending the literary text. The context is always historical and the text is always literary, and the process they call "contextualizing" always proceeds from the former to the latter; no one presents literary works as the context necessary to understand some historical situation. Their presentation of these contexts therefore assumes that literature is a separate category, which these critics profess to deny—some even insist that the category cannot be applied to the Renaissance because it was invented later.[4] Finally, this process of contextualizing undermines their claim of a "reciprocal" interaction between history and literature, since the process involves causation as well as comprehension, and the causation, again, always proceeds from historical context to literary text. While they often claim that the literary text they are interpreting not only was shaped by but also helped to shape its society, they have no evidence to support this claim, and it has no effect on their interpretation of the text.

I am not suggesting that these contradictions between their theory and their practice are the lapses of individual new historicizers; they seem rather to indicate the impossibility of practicing their theory, because it is, as we now say, "scandalously undertheorized." Here I will focus on the most basic contradiction involving their theory of "the textuality of history." It is true that all the things we (think we) know about the English Renaissance or any other period have "already been mediated by the surviving texts" of the time, which are our only source of knowledge,[5] and that the meaning of these texts is never certain or "transparent," in the sense that it can be immediately understood by anyone without being interpreted. But the critics who endlessly ventriloquize the slogan that "Everything is textual" seem to regard this as the conclusion of an epistemology, whereas it is only the beginning, for having recognized this we must then go on to distinguish among texts in terms of their status, the kinds of interpretation they call for, and the kinds of knowledge they yield. I feel that I am belaboring the obvious, but it obviously is not obvious to the ventriloquizers.

The entry in the Stationers' Register on 26 November 1607 that records

Nathaniel Butter and John Busby's copy of "Master William Shakespeare his historye of Kinge Lear" is a text and so is the first quarto of *King Lear*, but their textual statuses are quite different. The meaning of the entry is, as I said, neither transparent nor certain; it must be interpreted by someone who knows the necessary context (the role of the Stationers' Company, etc.), and it could be an error or even a forgery. But in the absence of evidence to the contrary we take it as a "fact" about "reality" (especially when it can be corroborated by similar texts, such as records of other activities of Butter and Busby) that is much more certain, or less problematic, and much more transparent, or less mediated, than any interpretation of *King Lear*. Moreover, we take it as part of the context for any historical interpretation of *Lear*, which is prior to the interpretation and sets limits on it (precluding, for example, the equation of Kent with King Charles). Therefore, the new historicizers are right in violating their own theory by opening their readings with statements that assume the "reality of dates and facts" of this kind.

Of course, the history employed by these critics in interpreting a play is not confined to such facts; it consists mainly of inferences drawn from them in the form of various levels of generalizations about certain aspects of the period, or causal propositions, also on various levels, linking some aspects as effects of others. These inferences are much more problematic and mediated (often by the inferrer's own interests) than the facts they are drawn from and can produce even more problematic and mediated interpretations of literature, as we are about to see. It is obvious that we do not interpret *King Lear* or any other fictive work in the same way that we interpret the Stationers' Register. Even the new historicizers, despite their "refusal of traditional distinctions between literature and history," never go to this literary text for "facts" about the historical "realities" of Lear's reign or James's. Yet the interpretation of literature involves facts and levels of inferences from them that are analogous to those in the interpretation of history. Our knowledge that Edmund is the illegitimate son of Gloucester, for instance, is not absolutely certain or unmediated, yet it is a "fact" that is just as "real," within the fictional world of *Lear*, as the information derived from the Stationers' Register and much less problematic than any interpretation of the play, historical or not. Indeed, we expect any interpretation to be inferable from or at least consistent with such facts.

Let me illustrate this by asking the question, Why is Gloucester blinded in *King Lear*? Most of us would reply that this is the direct result of his attempt to help Lear—Edmund reports this to Cornwall, as we see in 3.5, and in 3.6 Cornwall and Regan punish what they regard as his "treason" by plucking out his eyes. This answer is not wholly on the factual level, because it involves a few low-level inferences, yet it is relatively unproblematic. It also involves a little historical knowledge about kings, treason, and so on, yet it is not a historical interpretation, since it does not connect the event to the Jacobean world. But some new historicizers find such a connection. According to Leonard Tennenhouse, Gloucester loses his eyes because he "disowned his legitimate son and declared the bastard legitimate," which is a "crime against patriarchy" and the purity of "the aristocratic body," two basic principles of Jacobean ideology that the play is endorsing, so his blinding is a "ritual punishment" that "purifies the aristocratic body" and permits "the reassertion of patriarchy" (1986, 138–40). Leah Marcus says he is blinded because he "passively allows the holiday violation" by Goneril and Regan when they "denied hospitality" to Lear, since the play is endorsing the hospitality celebrated on St. Stephen's Night when it was acted at court, and using this holiday custom to promote James's plan to unify England and Scotland by associating Goneril and Regan with English opponents of the union who "were hardheartedly denying the nation's obligatory hospitality to the needy Scots" (1988, 154–56).

Both of these historical interpretations contradict the "factual" account we just rehearsed, since Gloucester's purifying punishers are abetted by his polluting bastard, and he is punished not for denying hospitality to Lear but for helping him. These critics do not infer their interpretation from the dramatic facts and then relate it to the history of the period but proceed in the reverse order. They begin with their interpretation of this history, which is based on very high-level generalizations that are treated as unproblematic and unmediated, and descend from it to their historical interpretation of the play, which fits the play into this history, and from there to the dramatic facts, which are mediated (i.e., transformed) by these prior operations. This is thesis-driven historical criticism: the thesis drives the history that drives the criticism that creates the "facts" of the play.

This procedure will become clearer if we look at two other recent explanations of the blinding of Gloucester that differ from Tennenhouse's and Marcus's in that they do not even mention the event. That is unnecessary, because the critics who present them already know the explanation of all the misfortunes in *Lear*. We are told by Kiernan Ryan that the "causes" of the entire tragedy are "the iniquitous arrangements" and "injustices of a stratified society," which Shakespeare is demonstrating to induce us to "seek the implied solution" in socialism (1995, 103–4), and by Marianne Novy that the basic cause of the tragedy is "patriarchy," which Shakespeare subjects to "implicit criticism" so that we will seek the solution of gender "mutuality" (1984, 150). (This is the exact opposite of Tennenhouse's conclusion: for her the play teaches the evils of accepting patriarchy, while for him it teaches the evils of violating patriarchy.) Both Ryan's and Novy's interpretations of the play are derived from interpretations of history based on generalizations and causal propositions that are couched on a much higher level than those of Tennenhouse and Marcus, and that, again, are not supposed to be problematic or mediated. For here it is even more obvious that the critics begin with a historical thesis (the injustice of class division or patriarchy) that is prior to any literary work, and proceed from it to their interpretation of the play and then to the facts in the play, which trail so far behind that some pretty spectacular ones, such as the blinding of Gloucester, escape notice.

These two readings, unlike the preceding ones, do not contradict the facts and are even consistent with them, since Gloucester's blinding and all the other events occur in a stratified, patriarchal society and could not have occurred, at least in the same way, in a different world. The trouble is that their explanations confuse a necessary condition with a sufficient cause—patriarchy and class division are among the conditions that make these events possible, but they cannot cause the events, because other characters in the same society do not act like Regan or suffer like Gloucester. Moreover, these explanations avoid contradiction with the facts by locating the explanatory causes at such a high level of generalization that they lose the historical specificity of Tennenhouse and Marcus, for there is nothing peculiarly Jacobean in Ryan's class division or Novy's patriarchy. A final major difference is that these two readings are political; we will not be astonished to learn that Novy is a feminist and Ryan a Marxist, since they have *King Lear* teaching us a feminist or Marxist lesson. It is thesis-driven interpretation, like the two readings examined earlier, only now the thesis is politics-driven in that it is determined by the critic's political project, which is not true of the theses of Tennenhouse or Marcus, two New Historicists, who presumably have no stake in the Jacobean aristocratic body or the union of England and Scotland. But the discussion of this political aspect of the new historicizing will be reserved for the next section.

Before proceeding to that section I want to return to the readings of Marcus and Tennenhouse and to the comparison with the old historicism. I am not suggesting that they are typical of the new historicizing of Shakespeare (indeed, we can hardly speak of typical readings in such a large and varied body of criticism), but they can be used to identify the three main approaches employed by the new historicizers, which are the same approaches employed by the old ones: the occasionalist and topical approaches seen in Marcus's reading and the ideas-of-the-time approach in Tennenhouse's.[6] The least important and most historically specific is occasionalism, where the critic argues that a play was designed not for paying customers in the public or private theaters but for some aristocrats assembled at a special occasion, and so must be interpreted in relation to it, as Marcus does when she derives the meaning of *King Lear* from its performance at court on St. Stephen's Night. Although Alfred Harbage pointed out some time ago that there is no evidence that any play presented by any regular company was originally written for a special occasion during Shakespeare's lifetime (1962, 19–20), this did not prevent the old historicizers from producing occasionalist readings of many plays, such as Josephine Bennett's book-length demonstration that *Measure for Measure* was designed "to please and flatter the King" (1966, 81), and it has not prevented the new ones either.[7] I found no significant difference between old and new occasionalists—in fact they often connect the same plays with the same occasions (*A Midsummer Night's Dream* with a noble wedding, *Macbeth* with a court festivity, etc.) and sometimes use the same language to occasionalize different plays (compare Dianne Hunter's statement that *Macbeth* was written "to please and flatter Shakespeare's new royal master" [1988, 134] with Bennett's account of the purpose of *Measure for Measure*). Their basic method is also the same—a search for aspects of the literary text that can be explained by the "real" historical context (the occasion) they have decided upon.

In the topical approach, which is less historically specific and more prominent in both the old and new historicizing, the critic argues that a play was designed to allude indirectly or covertly to contemporary people or events that are not presented there, and so must be interpreted in terms of this allusion, as in Marcus's claim that *Lear* is concerned with King James's plan to unite England and Scotland (her combination of this topicalism with occasionalism is quite common). There is a difference in the way this approach is employed by old and new historical critics, at least in their general tendencies, although it is only a difference in degree. The old topicalists were more likely to find detailed political allegories in the plays, a tendency carried to an extreme in Lilian Winstanley's books (1921, 1922, 1924), which prove that Shakespeare's major tragedies are about recent events in England, Scotland, France, and Italy, and that their major characters represent one or more of the historical personages involved in these events (Hamlet is James VI of Scotland and the earl of Essex, Duncan and Lear both double as Darnley and Admiral Coligny, etc.), and in a long essay on *A Midsummer Night's Dream* by Edith Rickert (1923), who proves that Bottom stands for James VI (a much less flattering portrayal than that discovered by Winstanley), Oberon for Henry VIII, and Titania for Elizabeth. There are many similar, if less elaborate, topical readings in the old historical criticism.

The allegories of the new topicalists usually do not operate at this level of specificity, as Montrose notes (1986a, 304).[8] More commonly they disavow the specific historical equations that they suggest and relocate the allusions in a looser analogy to a more general historical situation, so they can have their topical cake and eat it too. Stephen Orgel says that "James's sense of his own place in the kingdom is that of Prospero" and that he "sounds like a gloss on Prospero," but denies that the play "is representing King James as Prospero" (1988, 225); Marion Wynne-Davies says that Tamora "may be partially identified with Elizabeth" and that the age difference between her and Saturninus "could allude to the similar discrepancy between Elizabeth and Essex," but denies any "neat identifications" (1991, 134, 145); Peter Erickson says that Hamlet's treatment of Gertrude "resonates" with "the general context of cultural tension in the 1590s" that is "exemplified by the tension in the relationship between Elizabeth and Essex," but denies "a direct topical equation of Essex with Hamlet" (1991, 74–75, 87); and Stephen Greenblatt says that Edmund's harassment of Edgar shows a "resemblance to the situation of the Jesuits in England," although this "resemblance does not necessarily resolve itself into an allegory" in which Edgar stands for Catholicism and Edmund for Protestantism, and then adds, "but the possibility . . . exists" (1988a, 121). More of these balancing acts can be found in the new topicalists; but this difference between them and the old topicalists is, as I said, only one of degree, and there are also similarities, even in their choice of topicalities—some years ago John Draper (1937) and Glynne Wickham (1973) related *King Lear* to the union of England and Scotland, and the connection of Hamlet to Essex goes back to Lilian Winstanley (1921). More important is the fact that the old and new topicalists adopt the same basic method, which is the same as the method of the old and new occasionalists, in that they all explain a literary text in terms of some "real" historical context.

There is another striking similarity between the old and new topicalists—almost all of them, as my examples show, claim that the play is concerned with the monarch or the nobility (which is also true of the old and new occasionalism, by definition, since the occasions always occur at court or a "great house"). They seem to assume that this is where topicalities must be located, as we can see in the process by which Peter Erickson arrives at his reading of *Hamlet:* he begins by stating that he is looking for "a specifically Elizabethan context" for the play and then finds it in "the tension in the relationship between Elizabeth and Essex" because of "their historical overlap" (1991, 74). Of course, *Hamlet* also "overlaps" with other Elizabethan events that might seem more closely related to it, such as the death of John Shakespeare and the vogue of revenge tragedy, but for

Erickson "a specifically Elizabethan context" has to include Queen Elizabeth herself. There are several reasons for this privileging of the privileged classes, which is, as we now say, overdetermined. One is the new topicalists' obsession with (and often hypostatization of) "power," but that does not explain the similar focus of the old topicalists. Another reason is that these are the Elizabethans we know most about, so it is much easier to find data in their lives to construct topical connections with the plays, which reminds me of the joke about the man who searches under a street light for a wallet he lost that night because the light is better there. We also like to think of a Shakespeare who traffics in the affairs of the elite—even those of us who claim to be antielitist—since it makes his plays more important and so makes us, as his interpreters, more important.[9] (That is also one appeal of occasionalism, which has him writing for elite audiences.) But this feature of the topical approach, unlike the others we examined, is not intrinsic to it.

The ideas-of-the-time approach, which is the least historically specific of the three,[10] and the most important in both the new and the old historical criticism, interprets a play in relation to some general ideas or attitudes of the age, as seen in Tennenhouse's use of the Jacobean ideology of the aristocratic body to explain *King Lear*. In this approach we find a significant difference between the two periods of historical criticism. Old historicists usually viewed Renaissance thought as a monolithic system of orthodox doctrines that everyone accepted, which is described in Tillyard's now infamous *The Elizabethan World Picture* (1943) and is what Montrose has in mind when he refers to their "supposedly stable, coherent, and transparent 'historical' background" (1986a, 304); and in their criticism they usually proceeded by determining, from contemporary religious and moral authorities, "the Elizabethan idea" on some subject and then applying it to the play. Two good examples are Lily Bess Campbell's book on Shakespeare's major tragedies (1930), which begins by establishing "the Elizabethan idea" that misfortunes are caused by the passions and then shows how this idea is used in each tragedy to demonstrate the evil effects of—and so to warn people against—succumbing to a particular passion;[11] and Eleanor Prosser's book on *Hamlet* (1971), which establishes "the Elizabethan idea" that vengeance is always evil and then applies it to show that the play condemns Hamlet's revenge. The new historicizers have routed this kind of criticism, for which we should be very grateful, by proving that there were different and even contradictory "Elizabethan ideas" on most subjects, and many have gone further by replacing Tillyard's harmonious world picture with a picture of a world torn by violent conflicts. Moreover, many new historicizers adopt a much more hostile stance toward the orthodox ideology of the period than the older ones, whose attitude toward it was usually favorable or neutral.

This difference between the old and new ideas-of-the-time critics has obvious political implications, to be discussed in the next section, but it does not affect the basic epistemological assumptions of the approach itself, which remain unchanged, because the new critics, like the old ones, see the ideas or ideology as a context that really exists apart from the literary text. Montrose's historical introduction to his essay on Spenser, we will recall, treats the problems posed for the "dominant Elizabethan ideology" by the presence of a woman ruler, but it does not treat the presence of those problems (or of the ideology) as problematic—it assumes they were actually there, and the same assumption is made by the critics who want to replace Tillyardian harmony with violent disharmony. Nor is there any significant methodological difference between new and old ideas-of-the-time critics with respect to the "reciprocal" causal interaction of text and context, which the new ones often invoke in this approach. (Indeed, it only makes sense in this approach; new topicalists never argue that *Lear* affected King James's plan to unite the two kingdoms, or that Essex's career was influenced by *Hamlet*.) They assert that their predecessors viewed the literary text as an "inert" or "merely mimetic object" that "passively reflect[s] an external reality" of "historical fact," while they treat it as an "agent" that "performs work" and "make[s] things happen by shaping the consciousness" of its audience (Montrose 1986a, 306; Howard 1986a, 24–25). But this is wrong on two counts. Firstly, many old ideas-of-the-time critics also claimed that the play "performs work" (although they used other language) by supporting the particular idea-of-the-time they focused on and teaching the audience the dangers of ignoring it (Campbell 1930; Prosser 1971), just as many old occasionalists and topicalists had the play do "work" by commenting on current issues (J. W. Bennett 1966; Draper 1937; Rickert 1923; Wickham 1973; Winstanley 1921, 1922, 1924). Of course, they usually favored very different kinds of work than the newer critics (compare the orthodox moral lesson about wrath that Campbell finds in *Lear* to the feminist and Marxist lessons found by Novy and Ryan), but that is not a difference in assumptions or method. Secondly, the new ideas-of-the-time critics never try to prove that the play they are interpreting really performed the work they claim for it (which is also true of the older critics). One can see why they assert that the play affected society, since it "means according literature real power," as Howard says (1986a, 25), and so makes them feel more important (just as occasionalists and topicalists feel more important if the play was written for or about powerful people), but it remains an unprovable and inert assertion that cannot enter their historical interpretation, which is limited to showing how society affected the play.[12]

The point of this comparison of old and new historicizers in the three main approaches of historical criticism is not to deny any differences between them, which would be absurd, but to show that in their practice of these approaches the new historicizers rely on the same basic assumptions as the old ones. They assume that the historical context actually exists, that it is prior to and independent of the literary text, and that the process of causation and explanation works from it to the text. These assumptions, which are just what their theory of "the textuality of history" rejects, are required by their theory of "the historicity of texts," since some knowable historical context must really be out there for them to historicize the text into.[13] I conclude that there is an irreconcilable contradiction between their "acknowledgment of the historicity of texts" and their "acknowledgment of the textuality of history," which is another way of phrasing my earlier contention that it is impossible to practice the epistemological theory of these critics.

> It is surely incontrovertible that Shakespeare is of his time; the question is how to describe that relation accurately.
> —Jonathan Goldberg, *James I and the Politics of Literature*

> [Our] claim is not that such a history [of the Renaissance], or such a reading of literary texts, is more accurate, but only that it is more radical.
> —Catherine Belsey, "Literature, History, Politics"

In turning to the political aspect of our comparison of old and new historicizers, we must part company with the New Historicists, since they, unlike the feminists and Marxists, have no overt political agenda that governs their historicizing. The difference is evident in my epigraphs: Goldberg, a New Historicist, seeks a nonpartisan "accuracy" and so is caught in the epistemological dilemma we just examined, for if he believes that "Shakespeare" (i.e., the plays) and "his time" (i.e., history) are only known to us through the mediation of equally problematic texts, then it is hard to see how their "relation" can be described "accurately" and even harder to see how that accuracy can be judged, which would require a judger who stood outside this textuality; while Belsey, who is both a feminist and a Marxist, claims to eliminate this problem by moving from an epistemological to a political criterion. Of course, she cannot mean this on what I called the factual level of history or literature. Even if she believed the statement that the Essex rebellion succeeded was more radical than the statement that it failed, she still would not admit this into her history of the Renaissance, and even if it seemed more radical for Jack Cade to kill Alexander Iden than for Iden to kill him, this would not enter her reading of *2 Henry VI*. She is thinking, as we will see, of high-level generalizations and causal propositions in the interpretation of history and literature, where the problems involved in "accuracy" and the possibilities of mediation by the historian's or critic's own interests (including political ones) are much more obvious. On this level, however, she has not eliminated the problem of determining accuracy but merely relocated it, for it is not easy to determine which history or critical reading is more radical, even when we accept her definition of radicalism as promoting the Marxist and/or feminist agenda. In exploring this problem of her political criterion, I will defer the question of how it applies to history and focus first on literary criticism.

We can begin by comparing Kiernan Ryan's Marxist reading of *King Lear*, discussed earlier, which concludes that the play shows us the "injustices of a stratified society" and induces us to "seek the implied solution" in socialism (1995, 104), with a Marxist reading by Paul Delany that concludes that the play endorses the "feudal-heroic values" of the sympathetic characters and reveals Shakespeare's "nostalgia" for those values and his inability "to reconcile himself with the emerging bourgeois forces" represented by the unsympathetic characters (1995, 36). Which reading is more radical? Some Marxists would opt for Ryan's because it makes the play more radical and makes Shakespeare a proto-Marxist, but others would say that Delany's is more useful for contesting Shakespeare's reactionary influence today, and there is no way to adjudicate the dispute. A similar problem arises when we compare Marianne Novy's feminist reading of the play, which claims, as we saw, that it subjects "patriarchy" to "implicit criticism," inducing us to seek the solution of gender "mutuality" (1984, 150), with the feminist reading of Kathleen McLuskie, who objects to such attempts to "co-opt" Shakespeare and says that "the tragic power of the play endorses" patriarchal ideology and that productions today should aim at "subverting" this ideology by "revealing" the "material conditions which lie behind" it (1994, 91, 100, 106).[14] Which reading is more feminist—the one that views Shakespeare as an antipatriarchal protofeminist, or the one that urges feminists to resist him by "subverting rather than co-opting the domination of the patriarchal Bard" (1994, 106)? The answer, again, is that there is no answer, for both readings could serve different feminist projects at different times. This leads me (and others) to conclude that the political valence of critical readings is not inherent in them but depends on how they are used in specific contexts,[15] which means that as a criterion for judging readings it is even more difficult to apply and even less reliable than the criterion of accuracy.

This in turn leads me to wonder if these two criteria really are as separate as Belsey assumes. She offers us a choice between accuracy and radicalism, but radicalism could involve accuracy. It seems to me that Delany's and McLuskie's readings are more accurate—with respect to the facts of the play and the facts of Shakespeare's life and times—than the readings of Ryan and Novy, and thus are more likely to persuade those who are not Marxists or feminists, so if the radicalism of these readings is determined by their promoting the Marxist or feminist agenda, and if that agenda aims at converting people to the cause (and not just preaching to the already converted), then they are more radical than the other two.[16] But if radicalism depends in this way on accuracy, then why not drop the political criterion and judge readings only by their accuracy, as the old historicizers and New Critics claimed to do?

The answer of these new historicizers is that the silence of the older critics about the politics of criticism actually endorsed a political position supporting the status quo, even though they may not have been aware of it, because "Everything is political." This endlessly ventriloquized slogan has now attained a status in critical discourse similar to the slogan that "Everything is textual": the ventriloquizers view it as the end of wisdom instead of the beginning and invoke it to justify consigning all activity to the same political level, just as the claim that "Everything is textual" is invoked to justify the consignment of all knowledge to the same problematic level. It is true that all our actions have some political dimension, but having recognized this we must then go on to distinguish the nature and relative importance of that dimension in specific activities, since it is not always the most important dimension or the cause of all the others, as these critics assume. We must also distinguish two different senses of the term "political criticism" in the study of Shakespeare (or any other author of the past). It can refer to criticism that deals with the political significance of his plays in his time, which would include all New Historicists and many old historicists like Bennett and Rickert. But the Marxist historicizers and many feminist ones do not regard that as "political criticism," because they limit the term to criticism that uses the plays to "intervene" in current politics, and to do this on the right (i.e., left) side, as we see in their references to interpretations of Renaissance literature that yield "oppositional kinds of understanding" or "create an emancipatory stance" (Sinfield 1992, 22, 106; Grady

1993, 33). Clearly the target of this oppositional and emancipatory intervention is not Renaissance society but our own. That is what they mean when they call their criticism "political" (other code words for it are "activist," "committed," and "transformative"), and that is why they condemn the silence of older critics on politics in this sense, a silence that they say abets the wrong (i.e., right) side.[17]

This raises the obvious question of how these critics can derive Marxist or feminist messages for and about our society from plays written four centuries ago for and about a very different society. Their most common strategy is to treat the aspect of Shakespeare's society that they are dealing with in his plays as if it has remained basically unchanged down to the present. That may surprise us, since these are the critics who are always pledging allegiance to the principle of the "cultural specificity" or "historicity" of texts and always scolding old historicists and New Critics for viewing the human condition as transcultural-transhistorical-essential-eternal-God-given-etc., but they are prepared to rise above their historical principle to serve their political goal. Sometimes the equation of the two societies is stated explicitly,[18] but even when it is not stated it is often assumed by these critics, because they need to make their criticism—and hence the plays—politically relevant now. This need also helps to account for other features of the new historicizing discussed in the preceding section, such as its tendency to explain dramatic events by social forces rather than individual choices (which we saw involves a confusion of condition and cause),[19] and to formulate those forces in very high-level generalizations that float free of history, since both these moves facilitate their task of discovering/producing in the plays those oppositional, emancipatory messages for our time. It would seem, then, that the political commitment of these new historicizers of Shakespeare leads to a *de*historicizing of his plays.

The politics of these critics, moreover, affects not only their interpretation of the plays but also their interpretation of history, to which I now return. It is no coincidence that the aspects of Renaissance society that they equate with our own almost always involve oppression based on class or gender. This can be explained by their desire to make the plays yield up Marxist or feminist lessons for today, because this oppression is what those lessons are oppositional to and will emancipate us from; but it is also the result of the theories many of them rely on, which tell them that this oppression is basically the same in our world and Shakespeare's because it is basically the same always and everywhere. (I pass over the question of whether their choice of these theories determined or was determined by their desire for political relevance.) Marxist theory claims to be historical, but it constructs a peculiar kind of history in which particular events are simply manifestations of a universal pattern of class struggle—a construction that Frank Lentricchia refers to as "the ultimate problem of linking repressed and master voices as the agon of history, their abiding relation of class conflict" (1983, 132). His "ultimate" and "abiding" mean that this conflict (like Jameson's command to "Always historicize!") is not itself historicizable. It will eventually disappear when we abolish the class system, but until then it is supposed to govern all human history, which is seen as a struggle against a single, transhistorical villain—oppression, exploitation, capitalism—that is essentialized and demonized as the source of all our problems. Of course, Marxists recognize that this oppression takes different forms in different historical periods, yet beneath these forms they discern the same essential demon.[20]

Some feminist critics of Shakespeare are also Marxists, since they believe that the basic cause of gender oppression (and all other evils) is class oppression,[21] so the preceding remarks apply to them as well, but many of the others regard "patriarchy," or the rule of men over women, as the basic form of oppression. As in Marxist theory, this oppression will eventually disappear when we take the right social action, but until then it is supposed to govern all human history and so is often constructed as a single, transhistorical villain that is, again, essentialized and demonized as the source of all our problems.[22] Andrea Dworkin (who is not a literary critic) is very explicit about this: "It is ancient and it is modern; it is feudal, capitalist, socialist; it is caveman and astronaut, agricultural and industrial, urban and rural" (1981, 68). Few feminists put it this starkly;[23] they usually acknowledge that patriarchy takes different forms in different periods, yet behind these different forms they often discern (as their use of the term implies) the same essential "patriarchy," the oppression of women by men, which is not defined historically. Thus, it seems that the political commitment of both the Marxist and these feminist historicizers of Shakespeare leads not only to the *de*historicizing of his plays but also to the *de*historicizing of history itself, and so doubly undermines their commitment to "the historicity of texts."

The political commitment of these critics also undermines (in fact, erases) their commitment to "the textuality of history," because they are certain that the class or gender oppression that they want to emancipate us from really exists now and really existed in the Renaissance, no matter how many texts it is mediated through. Their political agendas depend on this certainty and their political theories guarantee it, thereby reinforcing the epistemological imperative, discussed in the preceding section, to ignore "the textuality of history" in their practice, which is based on the same prepoststructuralist assumptions as the old historicism. Both of their political theories, moreover, not only assure them that they have access to Renaissance "reality" but also dictate what that "reality" is—the aforesaid oppression, which we saw is supposed to be universal. For their high-level generalizations about this oppression in the Renaissance, noted earlier, are mediated not by the "surviving texts" of the period, as in Montrose's creed (1986a, 305), but by their political theories. Thus, while they regularly accuse old historicists like Tillyard of creating a history of the Renaissance that fits their own preconceptions, which is true, they themselves do the same thing, although their preconceptions and therefore their history are very different.[24] And this history, like that of the old historicists, is *de*textualized.

The political theory of the Marxists goes even further than this, and so gives them an advantage over the old historicists, by dictating that certain aspects of Renaissance reality, those in the material base, are *more* real than those in the superstructure. This explains McLuskie's call, quoted above, for productions of *King Lear* that subvert the play's patriarchal ideology by "revealing" the "material conditions which lie behind" it (1994, 106). Her Marxist theory tells her that these "material conditions" must be more real than the ideology (she also calls them the "real socio-sexual relations in *King Lear*" [100]), and her word "revealing" tells us that they really exist in the play, and exist on a deeper level than such superstructural events as Lear's tragedy, which conceal them from non-Marxists. (We can also assume that she thinks these "material conditions" and "real sociosexual relations" exist today, since otherwise there would be no point in her calling for modern productions that reveal them.) This theory also asserts that in every society (except socialist ones) the base is torn by contradictions and conflicts that are, by definition, more basic than any appearance of harmony in the superstructure, and so justifies the replacement of Tillyard's peaceful World Picture with a picture of a strife-ridden world, which we saw in the survey of the ideas-of-the-time approach. That is why Belsey, in a passage just before the one used in my epigraph, recommends a history of the Renaissance that "reverse[s]" the older "enterprise of constructing (inventing) a lost organic world" of "uncontested order" and "uncovers a world of violence, disorder, and fragmentation" (1992, 44).[25] Her claim in the epigraph is not that such a history is "more accurate" than the older one "but only that it is more radical," yet her use of "uncovers" (like McLuskie's "revealing") indicates that she thinks it *is* more accurate, because this world of disorder could not be uncovered unless it was really there and realer than the "invented" facade of order. Dollimore universalizes this theory when he attacks "the belief in or desire for [a] profound unity" in "the social body" that is "beyond the actual strife and disunity of existence" (1990a, 422), for here unity is always just a "belief" or "desire," while disunity is always "actual." (Of course, in every viable society the unity must be more "actual" than the disunity or else the society would not be viable, but that is not "material.") The result of this base/superstructure theory, then, is to replace history with an a priori scheme that is at least as distanced from the "actual" complexity of Renaissance society as the World Picture of the old historicists, who had no such theory to tell them what they must seek—and find—in the period. It therefore contributes to the dehistoricizing of history and of literature that we already uncovered in this section on the political aspect of these new historicizers of Shakespeare, all of which forces me to conclude that there is an irreconcilable contradiction between their two projects of historicizing his plays and politicizing them.

We could go on to ask whether this political criticism really produces the political effect that is its purpose and justification. These critics do not address this question; they simply assume that their work will have the effect they claim for it (just as they assume that Shakespearean drama had the "power" to shape consciousness that they attribute to it). I suspect that it has no effect, political or otherwise, outside the academy, and that within the academy its power is pretty much limited, as I suggested earlier, to the already converted. We might also ask what this effect is supposed to be: what do these critics want their readers to do when they are persuaded by the criticism? Presumably they should enact the critics' political agenda, but here we must distinguish between the feminists and the Marxists. The feminists have such an agenda for action in the political arena, which I strongly support, but the Marxist "activists" have none, except for vague calls to "transform society" that are never explained. They are not political in the usual sense of the word, and what I have, out of politeness, called their "political agenda" is really an apolitical fantasy. But the pursuit of such questions is beyond the scope of this examination of the new historicizing of Shakespeare.

10
The Cultural Materialist Attack on Artistic Unity

Anyone who has been imbricated with or only interpellated into the current ensemble of hermeneutic theorizing and praxis must be aware that the concept of artistic unity is in very serious trouble. Since the early 1980s it has been subjected to a sustained attack by a large number of critics loosely grouped under the name "poststructuralist," with the cultural materialists (or new Marxists) in the van; and because their arguments have gone virtually unchallenged, there now seems to be a widespread impression, even among critics of other persuasions, that the concept has been invalidated and can no longer be used if one does not wish to be considered hopelessly out-of-date. It would seem, then, that the time has come to subject this attack itself to what is now called an interrogation, which will result in a qualified defense of the concept of artistic unity. This interrogation of the cultural materialists' attack on unity must begin by recognizing that it is part of a much larger attack that they, along with other poststructuralists, have mounted on what they refer to as the "formalist" approach—primarily the old New Criticism—and on the philosophy of "liberal humanism" that is supposed to underlie it. Indeed, they often define themselves in terms of their opposition to a catalog of fallacious beliefs attributed by them to this approach and its philosophy, which invariably includes the belief in unity (or "organic unity"). Later in this essay I will also present a qualified defense of the formalist approach itself, but now I want to turn to the attack on artistic unity.

Most commonly the cultural materialists assert that this unity is a fraud perpetrated by formalist criticism. According to Terry Eagleton, its "arbitrary prejudice" that "literary works form organic wholes" is imposed on the text: "[M]any suggestive frictions and collisions of meaning must be blandly 'processed' by literary criticism to induce [the texts] to . . . constitute harmonious wholes" (1983, 80–81). Francis Barker and Peter Hulme insist that it is "meaningless to talk about the unity of any given text—supposedly the intrinsic quality of all 'works of art'"—since materialist criticism "demonstrate[s] that, athwart its alleged unity, the text is in fact marked and fissured by the interplay of the discourses that constitute it"; and in their reading of *The Tempest* they find that "the play's unity is constructed only by shearing off some of its . . . complexities and explaining them away," which conceals "the text's actual diversity" (1985, 196–98). "If new criticism would see *Macbeth* as a seamless web of images," says Peter Stallybrass, "we may note that, on the contrary, it is constructed by montage. . . . Unifying the play's images, then, tends to efface the play's conflicting registers" (1983, 100–101). Malcolm Evans calls textual unity "the fetish of humanist criticism," and claims it is a "fictional unity" that must be "torn apart" to show "the discourses and social contradictions that constitute the text" (1986, 249, 254). Graham Holderness contrasts "orthodox criticism" of Shakespeare's plays, which seeks to "ratify the seamless unity of [their] ideology rather than analysing its innate incoherences," with "a materialist criticism [that] will discover, not . . . a serene harmony, but the stresses and tensions, the discords and contradictions" within them (1985, 159). Jean Howard explains that literary texts are not "organically unified wholes," since "only when their heterogeneity is suppressed by a criticism committed to the idea of organic unity do they seem to reveal a unitary ideological perspective," and so she recommends "the project of fracturing the unified surface of the text to let the multiplicity of its social voices be heard" (1986a, 30). In formalism, Catherine Belsey says, "the quest is for the unity of the work, its coherence, a way of repairing any deficiencies in consistency . . . [and] smoothing out contradiction, . . . thus effectively censoring any elements in [it] which come into collision with the dominant ideology" (1980, 109). Jonathan Dollimore asserts that the formalists' "appeal to this notion of structural coherence [in Jacobean plays] has in practice neutralised the destabilising effect of contradictory dramatic *process*" by "effacing it," and he adds that "Brecht's claim that bourgeois theatre aims at 'smoothing over contradictions, at creating false harmony' . . . surely applies equally" to these critics (1993, 60, 67–68). Other statements of this sort could be cited.

Sometimes the perpetration of this fraud of artistic unity is attributed not to formalist criticism but to the literary text itself. (Anyone who wonders why the blame should be placed on these texts rather than their authors obviously has not yet heard of The Death of the Author;[1] the belief that literature is written by "autonomous individuals" is now another major item in the catalog of formalist/humanist fallacies.) The second sentence quoted from Jonathan Dollimore shows that he subscribes to both these explanations, and so do Jean Howard and Catherine Belsey: according to Howard, in "many of Shakespeare's comedies, the ending . . . attempts to smooth over, or erase, the contradictions or fissures which have opened in the course of the play" (1987b, 180); and Belsey claims that "the strategies of the classic realist text divert the reader from what is contradictory within it," from "the play of contradictions which in reality constitutes the literary text," requiring the deployment of "a scientific criticism" (i.e., cultural materialism) that "distanc[es] itself from the imaginary coherence of the text" and "recognizes in the text . . . ideology itself in all its inconsistency" (1980, 128). Toril Moi says we can show that the text is not "what it pretends to be" by "look[ing] for underlying contradictions and conflicts as well as absences and silences in [it]" (1983, 3). And Pierre Macherey and Etienne Balibar tell us why materialist criticism rejects the "illusory semblance of *unity*" of a literary work, which they call a "mythical unity":

> The text is produced under conditions which represent it as a finished work, displaying an essential order. . . . Yet, in itself, the text is none of these; on the contrary, it is materially incomplete, disparate and incoherent, since it is the conflicted, contradictory effect of superimposing real processes which cannot be abolished in it except in an imaginary way. (1981, 49–50, 58)

Although these two explanations differ in their location of the blame, they yield the same result: a literary work that appears to be unified—whether this appearance is produced by formalist error or by the work itself—but that actually turns out to be disunified when interpreted correctly. We should notice that this conception of correct interpretation is remarkably similar to the one employed by the old New Critics, who regularly divided each text they encountered into an apparent or surface meaning that had misled previous commentators and a real or deep meaning that they themselves had just discovered. It is therefore hard to understand why the cultural materialists should include in their catalogs of formalist/humanist fallacies the idea that the meaning of literary texts is "transparent" and "self-evident," for if the New Critics believed that, they would not have undertaken those elaborate "close readings" to discover the real meaning that lurked beneath the apparent meaning. This division is in fact fundamental to the two approaches adopted (and sometimes combined) in most of the New Criticism: the thematic approach, in which the apparent subject of the work—the particular characters and actions presented there—is distinguished from the real, abstract subject embodied in the central theme; and the ironic approach, in which the apparent values, or "face value," of the work (which usually seemed to call for a sympathetic response to the main characters) are distinguished from the real, ironic values that undercut those apparent values and those apparently sympathetic characters. The cultural materialists' strategy is of course much closer to the latter approach; indeed, it seems to be based upon the same formula with only a change in terminology. The functional equivalents of the real meaning or values of the work are those "fissures" and "conflicts" and "contradictions," and they invariably undercut the apparent meaning or values, now become the "dominant ideology," which, just as in the old New Critical version, was erroneously taken at face value by earlier commentators. But there is a crucial difference between the two strategies: New Critical ironists claimed that they were interpreting the author's intention, that he deliberately subverted the apparent, "face value" meaning in order to convey the ironic meaning, which was the real meaning because he meant it (and which therefore gave us a unified work), whereas the cultural materialists, as was just noted, eliminate the author and hence his intention, so that their distinction between the apparent and real meanings must rest on other grounds.

It is not at all easy, however, to determine what those grounds are, since the cultural materialists' basic line of argument seems to be fissured by one of those internal contradictions that they like to find in other texts. For they, along with most other poststructuralists, reject the idea that a literary work has a "real" or "objective" meaning; in fact, that idea figures prominently in their catalogs of formalist/humanist fallacies. They maintain, on the contrary, that we cannot know the "real" work in itself, and that what we call its meaning must therefore be determined, not by anything intrinsic to it, but by the political beliefs of the interpreter, who is never objective or disinterested. "'Disinterestedness' is always, at best, an ideological flag of convenience," according to Evans, who asserts that "all reading [is] an intervention and a production rather than a simple decoding" of the text, since "there is no such thing as the object as in itself it really is" (1986, 85, 100, 137).[2] Holderness states that meaning is never "simply inherent in the text itself," and warns against any "reversion to an unprovable objectivity of the text" (1985, 147–48). Howard asks that we "decisively break with [the humanists'] fundamental assumptions about the nature of interpretation as the uncovering of 'what is already there'" (1987a, 340). Dollimore and Sinfield assure us that "cultural materialism does not, like much established literary criticism, attempt to mystify its perspective as the natural, obvious or right interpretation of an allegedly given textual fact" (1994a, viii). Belsey explains that "as a scientific practice [cultural materialism] is not a process of recognition but work to produce meaning" (1980, 138).[3] McLuskie rejects the "spurious notion of objectivity" (1994,

91–92), and Barker says that anyone who believes in it is guilty of "hubristic objectivism" (1984, 15). Yet in all the passages quoted earlier these critics seem to be claiming that the disunity is actually and objectively there in the work, and that the unity is not (which is, of course, one reason that I selected them). The unity of the work is always stated in terms that deny its reality: "surface," "supposedly," "pretends," "seem[s]," "alleged," "false," "fictional," "imaginary," "mythical," "illusory semblance," "arbitrary prejudice," and "fetish." It can only be created by diverting us from, repairing, smoothing over (and out), explaining away, processing, neutralizing, censoring, erasing, effacing, shearing off, suppressing, or abolishing the disunity that must therefore really be in the work prior to any critical activity (thus it is "discovered" or "recognized" by materialist criticism). This disunity is always affirmed in the language of real presence: it is "actual," "underlying," "innate," "within" the text; it is how the text "is constructed"; it characterizes "the text . . . in itself"; it "in fact mark[s]" the text; it "in reality constitutes the literary text"; and so on. Yet according to their own principles they should be saying that the disunity is no more real than the unity—if the latter is "produced" by formalist criticism (or by the text itself), then the former must be "produced" by their own approach.

If we turn from these theoretical considerations to actual critical practice, I think we can see that this alleged disunity is even more dependent upon the cultural materialist approach than the alleged unity was upon formalism. While it is certainly true that formalist critics always looked very long and hard for unity in each work they examined, and that they could adopt some very questionable expedients in order to get what they were looking for, they did not always claim to find it; in fact, they would sometimes object that a work was disunified or inadequately unified.[4] Thus, the quoted passages are simply wrong in saying that formalists assumed "literary works form organic wholes," or that they were "committed to" this idea, or that they regarded unity as "the intrinsic quality of all 'works of art'"; on the contrary, they thought of unity as an attribute of superior works but not of inferior ones. The materialists, of course, always seek disunity in the work, just as the formalists sought unity, but the difference is that they never fail to find what they are seeking, which leads one to suspect that this disunity really inheres in their approach rather than in the work itself. And this suspicion is strengthened by some of their own accounts of their methodology that we have seen, which describe it as a "project of fracturing" wherein the work is "torn apart," for then those fissures and contradictions would be created by the approach, which seems to operate on the text like a sledgehammer. And if these critics have difficulty producing fissures and contradictions in the text by this method, their approach allows them to demonstrate its disunity by finding "absences and silences" in it, as Moi explains (1983, 3).[5] Since any work must be silent about a great many things, they can always assert that there is some subject (usually a contemporary problem or conflict) that it should speak of but does not, so that this silence becomes evidence of evasion or suppression and therefore of disunity. While the formalists claimed to know what is really in the text, these materialists know, not only what is really in it (i.e., fissures and contradictions), but even what is really left out of it (i.e., absences and silences). Talk about hubristic objectivism!

❦

I think it is fair to conclude, then, that the materialists' attack on artistic unity does not stand up under interrogation. It is self-contradictory and proves nothing except that their approach can create disunity (or the appearance of it) in *any* work, so that this disunity turns out to be no more "real" than the unity they claim to be refuting. I now proceed from this negative refutation of their refutation to the positive defense of the concept of unity, but that requires an interrogation of the concept itself. The materialists never attempt this; they seem to assume that unity has a single meaning that is transparent and self-evident, so that they are attacking the same kind of unity that their opponents are affirming. But artistic unity comes in several varieties, for there are different senses in which a work may be—or may be said to be—a complete whole. Most New Critics, we noted, were concerned with thematic unity, in which all parts of a work are subordinated to and unified by an abstract "central theme." I have written some unkind words about the use of this concept of unity,[6] and I am not taking back any of them now, but it does describe one possible way that authors could integrate their works.

There is another quite different kind of artistic unity (also recognized by some New Critics)[7] that is located not in an abstract thematic idea but in the concrete structure of the plot. This is what Aristotle has in mind in his famous definition:

> [T]he plot . . . must represent a single piece of action and the whole of it; and the component incidents must be so arranged that if one of them is transposed or removed, the unity of the whole is dislocated and destroyed. For if the presence or absence of a thing makes no visible difference, then it is not an integral part of the whole. (1973, 8.1451ª32–35)

Like the New Critics, he clearly does not regard this unity as an attribute of all literary works, since in the same chapter he objects to some works that lack it (8.1451ª20–23). Coleridge has another conception of what he calls "organic unity," which influenced the New Criticism, and there are still others. I am not going to survey them all here; I only point out that there are a number of different ways of viewing the unity of a literary work—many more than are dreamt of in the cultural materialist attack. For the purposes of this argument, however, I am grouping them all under the formalist label because, despite their important differences, they resemble the New Critical conception in two crucial respects: they regard unity as something that is intended by the author, and also as something that is not always attained, so that it can be employed both as a working hypothesis for interpreting works (which, like all such hypotheses, may later have to be modified or discarded), and as one of the criteria for judging them. From this it follows that they all treat unity in relative rather than absolute terms, since literary works—or their authors, if one suspects that those recent obituaries have been somewhat exaggerated—will be more or less successful in achieving this goal. Few people would maintain, for instance, that the Clown in *Othello* makes a significant contribution to the play (in fact, he is usually dropped in performances), so we would have to acknowledge that his presence detracts from its unity.[8] But this does not mean that the play is disunified or that the concept of unity cannot be fruitfully applied to it, because unity is not an all-or-nothing proposition, as the cultural materialists seem to think. Indeed, it is possible to make use of this concept (in any of the versions just discussed) to interpret and to judge literary works without believing that it has ever been achieved completely, or ever will be.

It is certainly true that many New Critics asserted that many plays possess the "highest possible unity" that integrates "every word of the text," and so on. But while such claims might be justified in dealing with short lyric poems (which is where the New Critical enterprise began), when applied to works of much greater magnitude and complexity they clearly overstate the case, and so render the conception of unity itself vulnerable to the sort of attack we are examining. Aristotle also seems to be guilty of this kind of hyperbole when he says that the plot of an epic should be "whole and complete in itself . . . like a single living organism" (1973, 23.1459ª19–21), for it is most unlikely that something "made" by art could actually attain the degree of unity found in something "grown" by nature. But the idea of organic unity is still applicable in the realm of art; like the idea of happiness in his *Nicomachean Ethics*, it is presumably to be regarded by authors as a "target to aim at" (1975, 1.2.1094ª25), and therefore by critics as a criterion for judging their relative success.

This conception of artistic unity as an intended goal of authors—not the only such goal, of course—seems to be confirmed by actual experience. There is good evidence, for instance, that Renaissance dramatists thought of their plays as unified wholes, because they objected to "unauthorized" additions to or deletions from them. Thus Shakespeare has Hamlet insist that clowns should "speak no more than is set down for them, for there be of them that will themselves laugh to set on some quantity of barren spectators to laugh too, though in the mean time some necessary question of the play is then to be consider'd" (3.2.39–43). And a number of dramatic quartos and folios contain statements by the author or publisher complaining that the plays were cut in performance and assuring the reader that they have now been printed in their "perfect" or "original" form.[9] We have much more evidence, of course, that most modern authors feel the same way about the unity of their creations. Moreover, if audiences then were anything like us, they assumed that the play they were witnessing was meant to provide a complete, unified experience. That is why we try to get to the theater before the opening curtain and return to our seats when the intermission is over—we do not want to "miss anything."[10] We also read the printed text of a play (or novel) with the same expectation, which Renaissance readers presumably shared; and if some pages are missing, we demand another copy that contains the "whole" work. And after seeing or reading a play, even those of us who are not practicing critics will object if we feel that it "didn't hang together," or that an episode in it was "irrelevant," or that some important matter was "left dangling." It would appear, therefore, that the conception of artistic unity was not invented by the New Critics or by Coleridge or even by Aristotle; it seems rather to be the normal assumption that underlies both the producing and the consuming of most literary works in our culture.

We might ask then why the cultural materialists have not taken these facts into account in their attack on artistic unity. The answer seems clear enough: what they are actually talking about, as several of those quotations indicate, is not this formalist kind of unity at all but another kind that is *ideological*, in the Marxist sense.[11] This may seem similar to the thematic unity of the New Criticism, but it is really quite different, because it is not propositional and is not intentional, for ideology in this sense is a construct of society that the author need not even be conscious of, which is one of the justifications given for The Death of the Author. In that respect, the cultural materialists' approach is much closer to another historical mode of interpretation, preceding the New Criticism, that was based on the idea of a cultural Zeitgeist. In the memory of people yet living, including myself, the plays of the Renaissance were regarded as sites of a fundamental conflict between two Zeitgeists called classicism and romanticism, which were also ideologies in this sense (although we did not use the word then). And since that conflict, like those sponsored by the cultural materialists, was supposed to be incapable of resolution, all the plays in which it was fought out were always disunified. Thus students were required to seek—and to find—traces of romanticism in plays that seemed to be wholly classical and vice versa (much like the projects recommended in some of the passages quoted earlier, which tell us to "search for underlying contradictions and conflicts" in an apparently unified text, to "fractur[e] the unified surface of the text to let the multiplicity of its social voices be heard," and so on).

The New Criticism changed all that by positing an authorial artistic intention that could integrate, more or less successfully, these romantic and classical adversaries, or any others. It could also integrate the kinds of conflicting ideologies favored in cultural materialism. In *King Lear*, to take an obvious example, we find an opposition between the organic or "feudal" view of nature and society espoused by Lear (1.4.275–89), Gloucester (1.2.103–14), and Albany (4.2.29–36), and the atomistic or "capitalist" view espoused by Edmund (1.2.1–22); but formalist critics could argue that this opposition was deliberately set up by Shakespeare as part of an overall unified design, and so could the prepoststructuralist Marxists, who were also intentionalists.[12] The cultural materialists, however, having killed off the author and hence the possibility of such a design, only see the opposition, which then becomes proof of the play's disunity. And any other conflict of this sort can be treated by them in a similar fashion, because what they are really asking for is not ideological *unity* but ideological *uniformity*—or, putting it another way, without the concept of an authorial design, the only possible meaning of ideological unity would be uniformity. And since no play shows such a uniformity, which would require the elimination of all dramatic conflict, each one turns out to be "disunified."[13] But the kind of unity that these critics are denying in the work is not the kind that anyone has ever affirmed.

Although this may explain how the cultural materialists are able to demonstrate the disunity of each work they deal with, it does not account for their assertions, found in many of the initial quotations, that this disunity is a necessary condition of all literary works, nor does it answer the question still hanging over us concerning the ground for their assertions that in all literary works this disunity is real while the unity is only apparent. For such assertions depend, not on inductions from individual works, but on deductive reasoning from universal laws. Here we encounter another fissure or contradiction in the cultural materialist approach itself, because these critics (again in company with most other poststructuralists) reject the belief in "universal truths" or "eternal verities," which they regularly include in their catalogs of formalist/humanist fallacies. It is surprising, therefore, to find that in their essays terms such as "all," "always" (or "always already"), "inevitably," and "never" appear with a very high frequency—much higher than in any formalist criticism I have seen. Apparently they themselves have a pipeline to some verities that sound pretty eternal, so that their real objection to the formalists must be that they subscribe to the wrong ones. One of the most eternal of these is that all societies—except a truly socialist society, of course—are fissured by "irreconcilable contradictions" (this is treated as a single linguistic unit, like "damnyankee" in the Old South).[14] From this it follows that the ideologies that are produced by and produce these societies must always be fissured by those contradictions, and therefore that those contradictions must always fissure the literary works that are produced by and produce those ideologies. What we have here, then, is the familiar Marxist dyad of the "base" and the "superstructure," the former embodying the real cause and the latter its less real effects. That is why these critics know in advance that all literary works will actually be disunified, even though they may appear to be unified. (They do not have to face the question of whether the literary products of a truly socialist society are also disunified, since apparently no such society has ever existed.) Thus this aspect of their treatment of artistic unity most closely resembles that of the Freudians, who also operate deductively from a universal law of causation that bypasses the artistic intentions of the author, although here the basic cause is located not in the author's society but in the author's psyche: since all psyches—except those of therapized Freudian critics, of course—are fissured by deep conflicts, these conflicts must always fissure the literary works produced by those psyches, no matter how unified the works may appear (in fact, as in the Marxist version, the apparent or surface meaning of the work will often attempt to conceal the real conflicts underlying it).[15] But we would have to maintain, again, that the kind of unity that is disproved in either of these two deductive systems is quite different from the unity treated in formalist criticism.

What conclusions, then, can we draw about this question of artistic unity? If the question is whether unity is really a characteristic of all literary works, then the answer must clearly be negative. No one, not even the most hopelessly irredeemable formalist/humanist, has ever claimed this, despite what the cultural materialists say. If the question is whether any particular literary work is really unified, the answer must be that there is no answer, since this depends on how one looks at it. Instead of trying to discuss what the work "really" is, I would like to resurrect the very useful little word *qua*, which signifies this crucial role of perspective. If we adopt the formalist perspective and look at a literary work *qua* artistic product—that is, as something consciously designed by an author to evoke a coherent and pleasurable experience in an audience—then it will turn out to be more or less effectively unified, as we found, and the concept of unity can therefore be applied both as a working hypothesis in interpreting it and as a criterion in judging it. The cultural materialists, however, along with most other poststructuralists, claim that this formalist perspective itself is no longer tenable because the work of Barthes, Foucault, Lacan, Althusser, and Derrida has invalidated the "humanist" assumptions (of a unified and autonomous author as the origin of meaning, etc.) on which it rests.[16] And this claim is now often accepted, which explains why there is a widespread impression that the concept of artistic unity is out-of-date, as I noted at the beginning, and why those humanist assumptions have become fallacies. But we have seen that most audiences in our culture (and apparently in the Renaissance) did expect a play to be unified, because they viewed it as a product designed to create a coherent effect that gave them pleasure; that is why they paid for their theater admission (or for the play-text) in the first place. (I refer to lay audiences—to people, that is, who will not write about or teach or take a test on the work they are seeing or reading.) And it is the formalist approach that can account for their expectation and their pleasure,[17] since it proceeds from the same basic perspective that underlies the experience of these audiences, so we must conclude that its conception of an artistic work, and therefore of artistic unity, cannot be invalidated by the attack we are examining or by any other, regardless of the latest advances in "theory." It will continue to be valid, although it may slip in and out of fashion in the academy.

It is essential to add, however, that this is not the only valid way of looking at literary works and hence at the concept of unity. For the work itself cannot tell us how we should regard it, and that is why we need the term *qua*. Any literary work, in addition to being a product designed by an author for an audience, is also necessarily a product of its society and of the psyche of its author, and therefore can be viewed from either of these perspectives. From this it follows that what might loosely be called the historical and the psychological approaches—which include, but are by no means limited to, Marxism and Freudianism—also have, and will continue to have, their own validity, although they too may slip in and out of fashion. And from their perspectives, it was shown, the concept of unity takes on meanings very different from the formalist concept, so that their answer to the question of whether any given literary work is unified could always be negative. But that answer does not really contradict the one given previously, since it results from another way of looking at the object.

This also applies to many of the other alleged formalist/humanist fallacies we have encountered in the course of this interrogation. Is the author or what is now termed the "subject" really unified and autonomous? The answer again is that it depends on our perspective, which is also true of the unity of "living organisms" that Aristotle refers to. *Qua* atomic structures, humans have neither unity nor autonomy; we are simply a concourse of particles with no clear boundaries, since these particles are continually entering and leaving us. But *qua* biological structures, we possess a high degree of unity and autonomy; when I get up in the morning, I do not leave parts of my body in the bed, nor do parts of the bed come along with me. And in the realm of literature we would say that, *qua* the formalist approach that views a literary work as the conscious product of an author, this author can be relatively unified and autonomous, while *qua* these other approaches he or she may never be unified or autonomous or even relevant, which is what The Death of the Author proclaims. Thus, this *qua* gives us the basis for critical pluralism, the recognition of an irreducible plurality of valid critical approaches, which enables us to live together and talk to each other because we can understand and respect our different perspectives. To adapt the immortal words with which Touchstone ends his speech on quarreling, "Your *qua* is the only peacemaker; much virtue in *qua*."

The trouble with this solution to the problem is that the cultural materialists also reject critical pluralism, which to them is another formalist/humanist fallacy. Many of their essays include at least one passing swipe at pluralism, where it is often bracketed by ironic scare quotes and preceded by some adjective like "naive" or "urbane" (an interesting pairing) or "liberal" or "benign," which are all bad words in their vocabulary.[18] The reason they are against it is that, unlike Touchstone, they are not seeking peace but victory. They do not want cultural materialism to be regarded as one among several valid approaches to literature; they want it to be the only valid approach, as can be seen in Belsey's references to it, in the passages quoted earlier, as "scientific criticism" (1980, 128, 138), meaning that all other approaches are unscientific, and in the final chapter of Eagleton's *Literary*

Theory (1983), which argues for that claim. And they see pluralism as a devious strategy to domesticate or neutralize their approach without really confronting it, like the "co-opting" and "repressive tolerance" we heard about in the sixties. What they demand instead is that non-Marxist critics engage them in a "struggle" or "contest for meaning" in the interpretation of literary works, a contest that they expect to win.[19]

Unfortunately, however, the cultural materialists never explain how they will win it. Unless they intend to force us into submission (poetics comes out of the barrel of a gun?), they will have to persuade us. But how can they persuade us that their interpretation of any work is superior to ours, when they insist that objective knowledge of the work is an illusion, and that all interpretations of it are "productions" determined by the interpreter's own political beliefs? For this would mean that they cannot appeal to any neutral or agreed-upon evidence within the work in a "contest" with non-Marxists, and consequently it is difficult to see how non-Marxists could ever be persuaded by a Marxist interpretation. There would not even be any reason for them to read it through, once they realized that its only claim to attention (and to superiority) was based upon its relationship, not to the work being interpreted, but to a set of political beliefs that they did not agree with. Presumably they would first have to be converted to Marxism, on political rather than aesthetic grounds, which is what Eagleton seems to be saying when he asserts that the disagreement between two readings generated by different critical approaches is really "a distinction between different forms of politics. . . . There is no way of settling the question of which politics is preferable in literary critical terms. You simply have to argue about politics" (1983, 209).[20]

The same kind of question also arises in feminist criticism, and here I can speak from personal experience, since a *PMLA* Forum letter signed by twenty-four people, reprinted in chapter 1, objected to my criticism of some feminist readings of Shakespearean tragedy because, among other things, I "fail[ed] to understand the serious concerns about inequality and injustice that have engendered feminist analyses of literature." What they were saying, in other words, is that my negative judgment of those feminist readings showed that I did not accept the feminist political agenda. I replied that I did accept it and considered myself a feminist (it should be clear by now that I do not consider myself a Marxist), but that this had no effect on my judgment of the readings, because I did not believe that a just political cause could justify interpretive errors in literary criticism. But suppose I did not accept the feminist political agenda—would that disqualify me from judging feminist readings of literature? Are we to say that only feminists can criticize feminist readings, and only Marxists can criticize Marxist readings? If so, it would follow that only liberal humanists can criticize liberal humanist readings, which would put some feminist and Marxist critics out of business.

I think this points to the most basic problem posed by the role of political beliefs in criticism: the problem of whether it is possible to reach a correct judgment, or even a correct understanding, of interpretations of literature without sharing the political beliefs of the interpreters. If it is not possible, then we are in the dilemma I just described, where each critical approach would be confined to its own hermeneutically sealed-off discursive space, and practitioners of different approaches would not be able to discourse with each other about the interpretation of a text or even about critical theory, and could only discuss the political validity of their respective beliefs, which is what Eagleton concludes ("You simply have to argue about politics"). I think there is a way out of this dilemma, however, that has already been indicated—namely, by rejecting the cultural materialists' rejection of objectivism and pluralism. If we believe, as I do, that one can attain objective knowledge of a literary text, it will then be possible to judge another critic's interpretation of the text even though his or her approach differs from ours; for instance, we can fault the interpretation for distorting the text (which was the main thrust of my critique of those feminist readings of Shakespearean tragedy). And if we believe, as I do, that there are a number of valid critical approaches, it will then be possible to judge interpretations produced by another approach in its own terms; for instance, we can fault the interpretation for being inconsistent with the postulates of that approach (which was the main thrust of my critique of the cultural materialists in this essay). Moreover, the belief in these two "fallacies" enables not only negative judgments of interpretations derived from other approaches but also positive ones, since such judgments also depend on objectivism and pluralism. We can, for instance, praise the interpretation of a text based on an approach different from our own because through it we have learned something significant about the text that we were not aware of before. I think most of us have had this experience, but it is only possible, again, when we believe that something is objectively "there" in the text to be learned, and that our own approach is not the only valid method of gaining access to it. If I am wrong, however, if objectivism and pluralism really are fallacious, and interpretations and judgments of interpretations really are determined by one's political beliefs, then it would follow that our professional journals and conferences should stop discussing literary texts or critical theories and should concentrate instead on debates about politics—about the relative merits, for example, of "bourgeois democracy" versus true socialism. Then, when enough people have been converted to the one right political creed, critical pluralism can be suppressed in favor of monism, which is the only alternative I can think of, and all of us, whether we want to or not, will have to join the attack on artistic unity.

11
Silence Is Consent, or Curse Ye Meroz!

> These books do not pretend to political neutrality. This ... involves a claim that criticism which pretends to neutrality is in fact effacing its political orientation and that such a manoeuvre is normally complicit with the dominant ideology.
> —Alan Sinfield, "Literary Theory and the 'Crisis' in English Studies"

> Neutrality in this case, is all one with opposition. *Curse ye Meroz, curse the Inhabitants thereof, because they come not forth to helpe,* silence is not always consent, but when we ought to speak it is.
> —Samuel Fawcet (1641)

BY NOW WE ARE ALL FAMILIAR WITH THE ARGUMENT INVOKED IN MY FIRST epigraph, since we have been hearing many versions of it over the past fifteen years from many British and American proponents of the new "oppositional" approaches to literary criticism. Later in the same essay (1983, 45) Sinfield also quotes with approval Terry Eagleton's assertion that conventional literary criticism "reveals its often unconscious complicity with [ideology], betraying its elitism, sexism or individualism in the very 'aesthetic' or 'unpolitical' language it finds natural to use of the literary text," and that "it has helped, wittingly or not, to sustain and reinforce [the] assumptions" of our "political system" (1983, 196). Criticism that is "assuming and proclaiming its 'descriptiveness,' its 'disinterestedness,' its ideological innocence," says Peter Widdowson, serves "to reproduce and naturalise bourgeois ideology as 'literary value'" (1982a, 3). Jean Howard's view of "the inevitably political nature" of literary criticism is presented as a rhetorical question: "Self-effacement, neutrality, disinterestedness—these are the characteristics privileged in the Academy, but are claims to possess them more than a disingenuous way of obscuring how one's own criticism is non-objective, interested and political?" (1986a, 43). Malcolm Evans insists that in literary criticism "'disinterestedness' is always, at best, an ideological flag of convenience," and that the supposedly disinterested New Criticism has a "concealed political agenda" that "sustains . . . characteristic bourgeois concern[s]" (1986, 100, 262–63); and Lynda Boose refers to "the overtly apolitical, though inherently (if blandly) conservative, practice of 'New Criticism'" (1987, 709). For Terence Hawkes, "traditional criticism pretend[s] to be politically neutral" (1995, 16); for Jonathan Dollimore, "traditional literary criticism" is "a politically conservative way of doing criticism" that is "spuriously impartial" (1993, xii–xiii); for David Margolies, "traditional character-imagery-plot [analysis] is reactionary" and "helps preserve the status quo" (1988, 52); and for Frank Lentricchia, "interpretation according to traditional humanism," with its "'disinterested' ways of reading," really "is not . . . apolitical; in the strict sense it is politically conservative" and "shores up things as they are" (1983, 10–11).

There are many more versions. We are told by Catherine Belsey that "traditional Anglo-American critical practice . . . becomes the accomplice" of "the dominant ideology" (1980, 109), by Donald Morton that it "has an ideological investment in the status quo" (1996, 472), by Antony Easthope that it is "complicit" with "bourgeois ideology" (1982, 147–48), and by Francis Barker and Peter Hulme that this ostensibly nonpolitical kind of criticism, when applied to *The Tempest*, has "often been complicit, whether consciously or not, with a colonialist ideology" (1985, 204). An older critic's praise of Shakespeare's plays as "profoundly moving, or spiritually restoring, or simply strangely enjoyable," according to John Drakakis, "subscribes tacitly to a teleological conception of Art not too far removed from the advice proffered by the Arts Minister . . . [that] 'You should accept the political and economic climate in which we now live'" (1995, 289); and the older criticism of these plays, according to Kiernan Ryan, is "reinforcing the beliefs upon which our patriarchal, class-divided culture depends" and "the illusions underpinning the status quo" (1995, 2). Gayle Greene says that "it seems rather late in the day to have to point out that all critical positions are ideological" and that interpretations "are determined by political ideology," including those from "approaches which are more traditional" and "pass as 'neutral' and objective" (1991, 23–24). And Daniel Boyarin, in his Forum letter reprinted in chapter 2, refuses to believe critics who "pretend that they are serving no interests," because it "should be by now commonplace . . . [that] they serve only the continued dominance of a particular gender, class, and culture" and are engaged in "a cynical attempt to enlist [others] as unwitting (and perhaps unwilling) allies in the reactionary protection of the privilege of that very gender, class, and culture."

This argument, moreover, has become the standard reply to any protests against the focus on politics in the new oppositional approaches. And since these protests almost always come from proponents of the older historical or formalist approaches, the reply typically takes the form of *tu quoque*, asserting that this older criticism, even though—or rather, precisely because—it does not discuss politics or take a political position, is really just as political but is on the other (conservative/reactionary) side, since it supports what Sinfield in the epigraph calls "the dominant ideology" or, as he later puts it, "the maintenance of the status quo" that this ideology legitimates (1983, 40). This is a very powerful argument, and I believe it has played an important part in the current polarization of our discipline, since it seems to eliminate the possibility of any discursive space outside the two warring poles, a point I will return to later. Indeed, it has been repeated so often that many people assume it is now an established truth, as can be seen in the exasperated complaints, published in 1991, by Boyarin that it "should be by now commonplace" and by Greene that "it seems rather late in the day to have to point [it] out" (after pointing it out she adds, "I find it astonishing that this needs repeating"). But since many of the critics who keep repeating this argument also keep telling the rest of us that the doctrines we regard as established, commonplace, and obvious are the very ones that should be "put in question," it seems only fair to subject their own argument to such an interrogation to see if it holds up. In this test I will draw most of my examples from interpretations of Shakespeare, but I think it should apply to the interpretation of any literature of the past. I want to emphasize, however, that it does not apply to all critics practicing the new oppositional approaches, who are a very diverse lot; I am concerned here only with those who use this argument, which is not integral to any approach—in fact, we will see that some oppositional critics reject aspects of it.

This argument really makes two distinct claims that are often conflated (as they seem to be in several of the statements just quoted) but should be examined separately. One claim is that supporting the dominant ideology and the status quo is just as political as opposing them, which is certainly true, although we may not realize it because in relatively stable societies such as ours this support requires no special effort or even thought. Moreover, those who are satisfied with the status quo tend to regard it as normal, just, or even natural, and therefore view its opponents as professional troublemakers with a sinister political agenda, which accounts for the "outside agitator" trope. I can still remember when the strikes accompanying the CIO organizing drive in the 1930s were blamed on these agitators, as were the activities of the Civil Rights movement in the 1960s. In both cases the people in power assumed that "their" workers or blacks were just as happy with existing social arrangements as they themselves were, and so must have been subverted by external political agents. (The same rationalization is now employed to support their own Marxist status quo by the people in power in China—Xiao Cai tells us that they blamed the 1989 student demonstrations in Tienanmen Square on the influence of "foreign reactionary forces" [1990, 8, 11], and Patrick Tyler reports that when tens of thousands of peasants rioted in Guizhou Province in 1994 to protest against their living conditions, "Communist Party officials blamed a handful of agitators who went from village to village to whip up anti-Government sentiment" [1995, A1].) We have to recognize that support of the status quo and its ideology is itself political, even when we are not conscious of it, and so we should be grateful to these new oppositional approaches for helping to raise our consciousness about such a basic fact of life.

Problems arise, however, when we turn to the second claim of this argument: that critics who do not discuss politics or take a political position in their treatment of literary texts are supporting the dominant ideology and the status quo. This too may seem persuasive, since it draws upon a very ancient and widely held belief embodied in the proverb "silence is (or gives or means) consent," and in such phrases as "unspoken agreement," "tacit consent," or "it goes without saying," and we can think of many instances in life and in literature where someone's silence is correctly interpreted in that way. In the closing scene of *As You Like It*, to take a simple example, when Duke Senior proposes that all his fellow exiles in Arden return to court with him, Jaques says he will remain in the forest (5.4.180–85), but the others are silent, which we take to mean that they agree to return. In fact, we are even surer of their consent here than in a similar situation in real life (those of us, that is, who have not abandoned the useful concept of authorial intention), since we can assume that Shakespeare counted on the audience interpreting their silence as consent, and so would have had anyone else who did not consent speak out like Jaques, whereas in the real-life situation some nonconsenters might have other reasons for keeping quiet.

It is also true, however, that in most situations, real or fictional, we never think of interpreting a person's silence as consent to anything, because there is nothing at issue that could be consented to.[1] There are even situations in which silence has a negative meaning. During the chanting of slogans at a political rally, a person's silence would probably mean dissent, and if the slogans were conservative, that silence would then be a tacit rejection of the chanters' acceptance of the status quo. This kind of tacit rejection of the surrounding community is also found in literature—in Hamlet's silence at the beginning of his first scene, for instance, or Iago's silence at the end of his last scene. And critics who were silent about the politics of literary works would be rejecting the dominant ideology if they practiced in the USSR during the reign of Zhdanov, who mandated the judgment of literature on political grounds. The significance of silence can also vary with the constituency: when opposition to the Vietnam War was widespread in colleges but not among the general public, the silence of some students on this subject might mean that they agreed with the prevailing view on campus, where this opposition "went without saying," and disagreed with the prevailing national view (although it could also mean that they did not subscribe to the campus orthodoxy but were unwilling to speak out); and when students are silent in class, no experienced teacher assumes that they all agree with the views she is propounding, since she knows that some may be opposed to them but afraid to challenge the person in power, or may be indifferent, or may not understand them. It seems evident, therefore, that the idea of silence meaning consent is not a general truth but only applies in certain specific contexts, which is how it is treated in our common law (American Law Institute 1981, sec. 69).

We must then see if this idea applies in the context defined by the argument we are interrogating, in which someone discusses a literary work without mentioning its politics or taking a political stand. It could hardly apply to an essay like Alice Walker's analysis of the printing of the quarto and folio texts of *Othello* (1953, 138–61); she never refers to the politics of the play and does not even note that the compositors of both texts were white working-class males, yet I do not think even the most oppositional of the new oppositional critics would claim that this silence reveals her attitude toward the status quo, because they would assume—and assume that she assumed—that such matters were not relevant to her bibliographical project. This is an extreme case, of course, but let us turn to an essay at the other extreme, Carol Sicherman's study of *Coriolanus*, where the project is clearly interpretive and the play clearly involves politics. One might have thought it was impossible to interpret this play without addressing its treatment of the conflict between patricians and plebeians or of the conceptions of masculinity and femininity, but that would be to underestimate the ingenuity developed by New Critical thematists in their final days when they were desperately searching for ever new central themes to lick the older ones.[2] Sicherman finds that the play is "conduct[ing] an extended exploration of the often precarious correspondence of words and meanings" (1972, 190), and then constructs a new close reading in terms of this "central problem" or "theme" that ignores the class and gender issues that seem so central to us today. Here, surely, we have a prime example of the kind of silence about politics that is supposed to indicate literary critics' support of the status quo or, in the terminology of several of the passages quoted at the beginning, their "complicity" with it.

There is a problem, however, because we must now determine *which* status quo these nonpolitical readings are supposed to be supporting or to be complicit with. Most of the people who employ this argument do not seem troubled about that question, even though in this case and others like it we have three different worlds, each with its own status quo: the world portrayed in the play (here republican Rome), the author's world (early modern England), and the world of postmodern America where the reading was produced. Presumably their argument refers to the third alternative, for they could scarcely claim that a critic today supports the social arrangements of Coriolanus's world or Shakespeare's, which are no longer available options. But how can they infer a critic's attitude toward the status quo of our own society from this silence about the politics of two earlier societies? Their most common strategy, as far as I can tell, is to treat the aspect of Shakespeare's society (and of the society presented in his play) that concerns them as if it has remained basically the same down to the present, often by translating it into an abstract social or political issue that seems to float free of history. This is curious, because these oppositional critics regularly condemn the formalists for viewing human problems (like Sicherman's "precarious correspondence of words and meanings") as transhistorical and transcultural, and regularly swear allegiance to the principles of historical and cultural specificity—indeed, they are capable of producing, in other situations, detailed accounts of the differences between Renaissance and modern society, and even between Elizabethan and Jacobean society. But the nature of this argument about silence may lead us to suspect that a number of them are prepared to rise above their historical principles for the sake of their oppositional politics.[3]

That suspicion is confirmed by some of the critics themselves, for while their assimilation of the world of Shakespeare (and of his plays) to our own is often tacitly assumed without comment, they can sometimes be quite explicit about it. Margot Heinemann finds that the "causes of disaster" in *King Lear* lie in "the horror of a society divided between extremes of rich and poor" that Lear indicts in his speech on "houseless poverty" (3.4.26–36) and that "the indictment is still, for us, very direct and near the bone," which she proves by citing statistics on the number of homeless people in England in 1990 (1991, 78), as if the social etiology and significance (and, she implies, the cure) of homelessness were the same in Lear's society and Shakespeare's and ours. Kiernan Ryan says that the "causes" of Lear's tragedy "are housed" in "the injustices of a stratified society" that was "class-divided . . . then as now," which has an "urgent bearing . . . on our own predicament" (1995, 98, 102–4), without noting that the class divisions are now very different and thus create a very different "predicament." John Turner locates the cause of this tragedy in "the injustices of the system" of feudalism depicted in the play and then asserts that these same "injustices" operate in the societies of Jacobean and modern England (1988, 109, 111, 117–18), which certainly are not feudal. In her study of *Troilus and Cressida* Gayle Greene takes the opposite tack to reach the same political goal—instead of extending feudalism forward she extends capitalism backward by explaining that the play has "relevance to the present" because "Cressida's fate is that of woman in capitalism," which "reduce[s] people to objects of appetite and trade" (1981/2, 39–40), but she fails to explain how the play could have shown this before the advent of capitalism, or what capitalism could have reduced women from (from the good old days of serfdom and *jus primae noctis?*). "That we are dealing with live issues" in *Macbeth*, Alan Sinfield maintains, "is shown by the almost uncanny resemblances between the Gunpowder Plot [of 1605] and the bombing in 1984 by the Irish Republican Army of the Brighton hotel where leading members of the British government were staying, and in the comparable questions about state and other violence that they raise" (1992, 106), although one of the states "we are dealing with" is an aristocratic oligarchy and the other a bourgeois democracy. For Catherine Belsey, the problem of "the legitimate limit of state violence" raised in *Henry V* "is an issue which modern societies in the free West have still not satisfactorily resolved" (1990, 455), which is not surprising, since she defines this "issue" at such an abstract level that it is unresolvable. And Graham Holderness claims that *The Taming of the Shrew*, in its treatment of "Katherina's plight," is "capable of delivering . . . an urgent address to immediate and inescapable political realities" (1991, 177), which are not identified, but the implication is that women today are in the same "plight" as Katherina, so that we confront the same "political realities."

Some other oppositional critics assimilate Shakespeare's world to ours in terms of ideologies rather than social issues. Jonathan Dollimore tells us that *King Lear* presents and questions the values of "essentialist humanism" that we still suffer from today (1993, 191–95). According to Linda Charnes's reading of *Antony and Cleopatra*, the "liberal humanist" mystification of "transcendent love," which is largely responsible for the difficulties of the titular characters, is still with us (in our Harlequin novels, among other things) and is responsible for many of the difficulties in contemporary gender relations (1992, 6, 11–12). We learn from Lisa Jardine that the "cultural construction of female guilt" in *Hamlet* "is still current" now (1991, 139), and from Lynda Boose that "the ideology of the . . . family" and "family roles" that we find in Shakespeare "was still firmly in place some four hundred years later" (1987, 711). Marion Wynne-Davies begins her essay on the rape of Lavinia in *Titus Andronicus* by asserting that "the issue of rape appears to be founded upon certain [male] premises about women's sexuality which have remained unchanged for five centuries," quoting the judge's summing up of a 1986 rape trial as evidence (1991, 129), and she concludes that the play makes us "question the values of a society which allows such a violation to occur" (148; I cannot tell if this refers to Lavinia's society or Shakespeare's or ours, but that does not matter, since it is supposed to be true of all three). Even when we are not given such explicit statements merging the social problems or attitudes of the Renaissance with those of today, however, it seems clear that the argument being tested here claims that an interpreter's silence about the politics of Shakespeare's plays really supports the status quo or dominant ideology of our own society—in Lentricchia's words, it "shores up things as they are."

A number of oppositional critics, including several quoted earlier, assert that formalist readings like Sicherman's support our status quo not only by their silence about politics but also by their use of various prepoststructuralist concepts that belong to the "bourgeois ideology" (a.k.a. "liberal humanism") that underwrites this status quo: the concepts of literature as a separate category of written works, of essential or inherent qualities in literature and life, of autonomous subjects and literary characters, of authorial intention, objective meaning, and so on. Some of them even try to divide critical approaches into two political camps, with the old formalism, which employs these concepts, on the Right and their own poststructuralism, which rejects them, on the Left—thus Toril Moi calls formalism an "inherently reactionary theory" (1983, 10).[4] But this simplistic scheme simply will not work. Marx and Engels themselves, no friends of the status quo, assumed many of these concepts in their comments on literature,[5] as did most of the Marxist critics until recently, as well as most of the early feminist critics. Some people on the Left have in fact protested that the political significance of these concepts is not inherent in them (which a card-carrying poststructuralist like Moi should know) but depends on how they are used—see, for example, Lisa Jardine (1986) and Stephen Foley (1991, 242) on the role of women and working-class men in the institutionalization of literary studies, Gerald Graff (1989, 174) and Diana Fuss (1989, xi–xii) on "anti-essentialist essentialism," and Terry Eagleton (1994, 6) on "the bugbear of the 'autonomous subject,'" which he associates with vulgar Marxism. And many oppositional critics who attack these concepts are happy to invoke them in dealing with texts on their side; thus Malcolm Evans deploys the full poststructuralist arsenal against Shakespeare's plays and the older criticism of them throughout most of his book, but at the end when he takes up the radical authors Gerrard Winstanley and Abiezer Coppe, he becomes an old-fashioned intentionalist (1986, 259–63), as do virtually all the new Marxists when they discuss Bertolt Brecht (Dollimore says that "it wouldn't make sense" to treat him otherwise [1993, 277]). Nor does the history of modern criticism bear out their scheme. There was a thriving group of Marxist formalists in the USSR before they were eliminated by Marxist socialist realists under Zhdanov, who are now scorned by Marxist cultural materialists because realism is supposed to be bourgeois. The formalist New Critics in their heyday covered most of the political spectrum, and Frederick Crews demonstrates that there is no necessary theoretical or practical connection between poststructuralism and radical politics (1995, 53–56). It seems, then, that this unsuccessful attempt to equate critical approaches with political positions does not really add anything to the basic argument that a critic's silence about politics means support of our status quo and its ideology.

We can now press on in our interrogation of this argument by asking *which aspects* of our status quo or its ideology are supported by the silence of these nonpolitical readings of Shakespeare. For the oppositional critics who use the argument never tire of reminding us that the dominant ideology of our society, or any other, is not a seamless web but an uneasy mixture of diverse and even contradictory components; and it should be just as evident that the status quo in our society, or any other, is not a monolithic, homogeneous entity but an evolving collocation of various institutions, relationships, and practices that are often in conflict. The argument, however, does not have to cope with such complexities, because it seems to focus on only one aspect of our status quo and ideology. Sinfield does not explain what it is in the statement quoted as my epigraph, although we can infer that it must be a very bad aspect, since support of or even neutrality toward it appears to be culpable (this is also implied by his term "complicit," which connotes guilt), but it is revealed in the foreword to *Political Shakespeare*, written by him and Dollimore, in a passage that begins with the same language:

> Cultural materialism does not pretend to political neutrality. . . . On the contrary, it registers its commitment to the transformation of a social order which exploits people on grounds of race, gender and class. (Dollimore and Sinfield 1994a, viii)

Apparently, then, criticism that pretends to political neutrality (they say this applies to "much established literary criticism") does not oppose this exploitation and so is, in the words of the epigraph, "normally complicit" with it.

This accusation is confirmed by the people quoted earlier who specify (without Sinfield's "normally") what it is that nonpolitical criticism is supporting: for Boyarin it is the same "dominance of a particular gender, class, and culture"; for Ryan, patriarchy and class division; for Barker and Hulme, colonialism; and for Eagleton, "elitism, sexism or individualism" and the "assumptions" of our "political system"—a system that he defines earlier as one "in which considerable private wealth remains concentrated in the hands of a tiny minority, while the human services of education, health, culture and recreation for the great majority are torn to shreds" (1983, 196). These statements assume that critics who are silent about politics are always and only supporting the most deplorable aspects of our society, and this also seems to be what the other people I quoted have in mind, even though they do not specify it. They never accuse nonpolitical critics of complicity with freedom of speech or the writ of habeas corpus, which are parts of our status quo, or with the egalitarian strain in our dominant ideology, nor are such critics permitted to split their votes by supporting the better aspects of our status quo and ideology and opposing the worse ones (the typical liberal position), since the argument apparently does not recognize the existence of any better aspects. This selective blindness is conspicuous in Eagleton's wholly negative definition, just quoted, of the "political system" these nonpolitical critics are sustaining, which is not allowed any redeeming features. (It must have had some recently, however, for those "human services" could not be "torn to shreds" by the Thatcher administration unless they had been put in place by previous administrations. Would he then argue that a critic writing during the pre-Thatcher era who was silent about politics was complicit with the establishment of these services? A question not to be asked.) The same selectivity can be seen in the passages cited earlier that assimilate elements of Shakespeare's society to our own, since these are always bad: extremes of poverty and wealth, homelessness, class division, the reduction of women to objects of appetite and trade, state violence, the subjugation of "shrews," the construction of female guilt, the toleration of rape, and the ideology of essentialist or liberal humanism that supposedly legitimates such things. Apparently no good aspects of Renaissance society (if there were any) persisted down to the present for critics who are silent about the politics of Shakespeare's plays to support or to be complicit with.

We should also note that all these bad aspects of the Renaissance world and ours turn out to be injustices that are regarded by the people employing this argument as modes of "oppression" or "exploitation," usually based on class or gender. Moreover, many of their statements seem to treat these various modes of oppression as components or consequences of a single, transhistorical, all-powerful, all-pervasive, and utterly evil system, which is what their oppositional criticism opposes. For the Marxists, this is the system of class oppression—or, more simply, "capitalism"—which they tend to essentialize and demonize as the ultimate cause of all the injustices in early, middle, late, and postmodern society. Of course, they recognize that it takes different shapes in different periods, which they can distinguish quite effectively when they are being historically specific, but behind these many shapes they usually see one devil, and the devil has no history. He is, according to Hamlet, a malevolent trickster who "hath power / T'assume a pleasing shape" to "abuse" us (2.2.599–603), and capitalism is, according to Peter Widdowson, a "huge confidence trick being played upon us," with an "infinitely protean dynamic" enabling it to "adapt and change" to "exploit" us (1988, 4); but it is still the same old devil.

Some feminist critics are also Marxists and therefore believe that class oppression is responsible for gender oppression and all other injustices.[6] But some others find the ultimate cause of human problems, past and present, in a single, omnipotent, omnipresent, and wholly evil "sex/gender system"— or, more simply, "patriarchy"—that is, again, often essentialized and demonized. Like the Marxists, they can recognize that it "takes a different form" in different periods, as Marianne Novy acknowledges (1984, 4), and they too have given us effective accounts of these historical distinctions, yet behind the different forms they tend to see the same basic "patriarchy," the oppression of men by women, which is not defined historically because it is supposed to govern all history.⁷ For both these groups, then, the question raised in this section about which aspects of our status quo are supported by nonpolitical criticism would be pointless, since they assume that there is only one significant aspect, the oppressive system based on class or gender (these two modes of oppression can be combined under the ideology of "humanism," which very conveniently is supposed to legitimate both capitalism and patriarchy and is invoked for this purpose in some of the passages quoted earlier). That is what concerns them in the status quo of our society and also what concerns them in the society and literature of the Renaissance. Although not all practitioners of the new approaches believe that this oppressive system is basically the same in both societies,⁸ many of them do believe it, and this will explain how their argument can connect a modern critic's silence about the politics of Shakespearean drama to support of our present status quo, since the critic's failure to oppose this oppression in Shakespeare's world (or in the world of his plays) is equivalent to "complicity" with the same oppression today.

We must now address the next question raised by our interrogation of that argument: in determining the meaning of a critic's silence about the role of this oppression in the work being interpreted, what significance is attached to his or her *intentions or motives* for that silence? The passage taken from Sinfield for my epigraph begs this question, or rather stacks the deck, in its use of the terms "pretends," "effacing," and "manoeuvre," which indicate conscious intention and even deception, and this also applies to the terms "disingenuous," "obscuring," "flag of convenience," "concealed," "pretends," "spuriously," "accomplice," "pass as," and "cynical" in the initial quotations from Howard, Evans, Hawkes, Dollimore, Belsey, Greene, and Boyarin. If critics deliberately choose to be silent about this oppression in order to conceal their support of our status quo, then of course their silence must mean support of our status quo—that is a tautology. A number of these passages seem to be saying, or at least implying, that this is always the case, but surely that cannot be true. Many nonpolitical critics, especially those practicing before the theoretical revolution of the 1980s raised our consciousness, probably did not make a conscious decision to avoid politics in their readings of literature or to use those readings to support the status quo, which some of them may have opposed (or, as I suggested earlier, they may have opposed certain aspects of it and supported others).

Moreover, when we read their readings we usually are not in a position to know or even to infer what their motive was, and yet this argument requires us to judge them. That is the problem.

We can get some help in dealing with this problem of intention by returning to the two essays discussed earlier: Walker's analysis of the printing of the texts of *Othello* and Sicherman's New Critical reading of *Coriolanus*. I said that I did not think even the most oppositional of the new oppositional critics would maintain that Walker's silence about politics reveals her attitude toward the status quo, because she must have assumed that such matters were irrelevant to her bibliographical project. Why then could not formalist critics like Sicherman enter the same plea by deposing that they did not believe gender or class oppression was relevant to their thematic project, which focused on a quite different topic, and that they did not wish to support our status quo or at least its oppressive parts? Of course, I cannot tell how everyone using this argument would respond to such a plea, but the answer of the argument, as it is usually deployed, seems to be that innocence is no excuse, that the silence of critics about this oppression makes them guilty of abetting it, regardless of their motives for being silent or their feelings about the oppression.[9] Their motives and feelings apparently do not matter, since the argument assumes the old Marxist distinction between "subjective" intention and "objective" effect. We do not hear much about it today, probably because the new poststructuralist Marxists are not supposed to believe in objectivism, and perhaps also because they are embarrassed by the way this distinction was wielded by Marxist regimes to prove that people who "subjectively" defined themselves as liberals or social democrats or even communists of the wrong sect were "objectively" reactionary counterrevolutionary fascists who had to be liquidated.[10] But it is implicit in this argument that critics' silence about oppression has the effect of complicity with it, even though they may not realize this and may not want to be complicit. The more generous of those quoted earlier (the ones who do not insist that these silent critics are just pretending to be neutral) refer to this as "unwitting" or "unconscious" complicity, but it is still complicity.

There is, however, a striking inconsistency in the way this argument is typically deployed, because most of the people who deploy it ask us to judge formalist criticism that is silent about politics in terms of its alleged conservative/reactionary effect, regardless of the critic's intentions, but ask us to judge their own oppositional criticism in terms of their declared intention—namely, to produce an oppositional effect. Moreover, we have some reason to wonder how concerned they really are about the conservative effect of this nonpolitical criticism, since they merely assert it without producing any evidence. Undoubtedly, a critical essay, like all other forms of human activity, has *some* political effect, but it is usually very small in the world outside the academy,[11] and it cannot be ascertained by looking at the essay itself, because, like the politics of those supposedly "bourgeois" concepts discussed earlier, it is not inherent but always depends on the specific situation. One can imagine situations in which even Sicherman's essay on the "precarious correspondence of words and meanings" in *Coriolanus* might have an oppositional political effect—for instance, if it were employed in the emancipatory struggle against the horrors of humanist logocentrism. The argument we are testing does not allow for such nuances, however, nor does it allow these nonpolitical critics to plead benefit of constituency by pointing out that their readings are written not for the general public but for a small group of colleagues, most of whom, one can assume, regard opposition to oppression as something that "goes without saying" and do not need any more lessons on the subject. This plea, like the plea of innocence we just considered, would presumably be dismissed as irrelevant, since the argument still requires all critics to perform their own oppositionality to oppression in every essay they write in order to avoid the charge of complicity with it, which could explain the continual repetition of the same unmaskings of the same oppression for the same audiences of the already converted that inflects so much of the new political criticism.

The new political critics, furthermore, do not seem to be very concerned about the political effects of their own criticism outside the academy, for while they regularly announce that it is intended to promote opposition to the status quo, they do not tell us why they believe—or expect us to believe—that it really does this. Some of them also try to assert this effect by calling their criticism "activist" and "transformative," as well as "oppositional," but again they fail to show that it produces any extramural activating or transforming (they even fail to reveal what specific action or transformation it is supposed to be producing). As John McGowan remarks, they "blithely claim political and material consequences for [their] theorizing that they never try to justify" (1993, 453), because they seem to assume that their intention not only determines the meaning of their criticism (despite the poststructuralist anti-intentionalist creed that most of them profess), but also determines its effect, independent of the circumstances. Therefore they do not have to confront the question of what the effect of this "activist" criticism actually is in any particular situation, or to consider the possibility that in some situations it could have an effect very different from the one they claim for it—it might, for example, serve those who write it and those who read it as a displacement of or surrogate for real political activity. Wendell Harris observes that this kind of criticism "allows the critic to avoid wrestling with the difficulties of existing social, political, or economic problems" and "shifts energy from combatting the actual ills of the existing economic/political system" (1996, 224). But that is not relevant to the argument we are examining here.

☙

Since this argument, in condemning critics who are silent about the politics of the works they interpret, does not and cannot ascertain the meaning of this silence from the critics' *intentions* or from the actual *effect* of their criticism, we must therefore return to the *context*, which we saw earlier will necessarily determine the meaning of any silence. This then raises the final question of our interrogation: how does the argument deal with the crucial problem of context? The issue can be clarified by a comparison with another argument against silence, which finally brings me to my second epigraph, taken from a Puritan sermon delivered during the crisis that led to the English Civil War (the text is Judges 5:23, in which Deborah and Barak celebrate the victory over the Canaanites and curse those who did not join the battle).[12] It may look like the argument we are testing, but there is a very significant difference. Samuel Fawcet bases his case on the intense conflict that was dividing the nation into two warring sides and so provides the specific context for his assertion that "we ought to speake" now, since any one who is silent about it, like the Merozites who sat out an analogous conflict, is giving "consent" to the other (Royalist) side, although he acknowledges that in other situations this proverb would not apply, as I too maintain. But the oppositional critics who use this argument cannot claim they are operating in a comparable specific and extraordinary context that is bringing us to the brink of civil war and could therefore justify their contention that those who do not take a political stand are giving aid and comfort to the enemy.

I have never seen any of these critics deal explicitly with this contextual problem, but the assumption that seems to underlie their argument—or would have to for it to be valid—is that there is always only one universal context, the aforementioned class/gender oppression, which, we have seen, is supposed to be an all-encompassing evil system dominating societies of the past and the present. From that assumption it logically follows that critics who do not oppose this oppression in interpreting the literature of an earlier society are supporting it in the status quo of our own society, and that it is the only aspect of our status quo they can support, and that they cannot split their votes by supporting some aspects of our status quo but not others. In the argument we are testing, this universal context of oppression is what takes the place of Fawcet's specific context of crisis and thus obliges us to speak against it in our criticism, so that critics who produce interpretations that, for whatever reason, do not oppose this oppression are complicit with it and should themselves be opposed. Only if we buy this totalized view of the world can we claim that a critic's silence about politics must mean support of the present status quo and therefore must be political.

It should come as no surprise to learn that I do not buy this view. I do not believe, for reasons I already indicated, that the status quo of our society is a single, monolithic system that we must be either wholly for or wholly against, and while it certainly contains unjust and oppressive elements, I do not believe it is entirely evil. I suspect that the people who use this argument do not really believe it either, because their demand that critics must voice an opposition to our oppressive status quo acknowledges that the right to oppose our status quo is itself an element of our status quo—a nonoppressive element, clearly, and one they do not oppose. And in their everyday lives, when not writing "activist" criticism, they are not always acting against the status quo, certainly not against all aspects of it. Indeed, I doubt if it is possible to be wholly against our status quo or wholly for it.[13] But if we reject this totalizing view, it does not logically follow that a critic's silence about politics *cannot* mean support of our status quo. Of course it can mean this, and sometimes it does, but it can also mean other things, depending on the specific context and the critic's intention. Therefore the argument we are interrogating, like the proverb it draws upon, is true in some instances but is not a general truth.

I do not want to close without mentioning another common argument that seems similar to this one and is sometimes combined with it. It also concerns the silence of the older critics, but a silence about theory rather than politics, and also frequently takes the form of a *tu quoque* rejoinder, in which the older critics' objections to the explicit—and often extensive—theorizing in the newer approaches are answered by the assertion that their own criticism is also based on a theory, even though they may not be conscious of it. I agree with this argument because, unlike the political one, it does not depend on any particular context or on anyone's intentions; it is a general truth that every critical approach assumes a theory of literature. I also believe that a wider acceptance of this argument would have a beneficial effect on our discipline, since it would lead those who are now "against theory" to examine and explain the theoretical foundations of their own approaches and therefore would empower them to enter into a productive dialogue with adherents of the newer approaches, instead of grumbling in the corridors. As Jean Howard points out, critics who are not "self-conscious about [their] theoretical position" and do not "examine it in the light of competing theories" will "fall back on the defense of common sense: i.e., the position that [their] critical practice depends on assumptions so self-evident that their truth is not in question" (1986b, 135). This argument should also, incidentally, end the present monopolization of the term "theory" by these newer approaches.

Moreover, since critical theories, as we found earlier, do not neatly line up on two opposing sides, this argument should work against the polarization of our discipline that I noted at the outset, whereas the argument that we tested, and flunked, contributes to the polarizing (and is also in part a result of this polarizing, which operates as a self-confirming vicious circle that feeds on itself). It forces critics, not to articulate their own positions in a dialogue with colleagues, but to choose between two hostile camps, even if they do not want to, in a Manichaean war of good against evil, and closes down dialogue by constructing a world where there is no other alternative, no neutral or intermediate ground, since "the only real question," as Michael Sprinker insists, is "Which side are you on?" (1991, 116). It also closes down any inquiry, because the basic principle of polarization is that all those who are not with us are against us, and so even the attempt to test the argument is relegated to the evil enemy camp (which I suppose will be the fate of this essay). Still worse, it has a tendency to infect those using it with self-righteousness by giving them the illusion that the criticism they write is helping to bring about a "transformation" that will eliminate the very real injustices of our society, and it is designed to make the rest of us feel guilty for writing other kinds of criticism, which may be the postmodern secular equivalent of the biblical curse upon Meroz.

12
The Politicized Language of Literary Criticism

Everyone recognizes that the language employed in most of the newer approaches to literary criticism is highly politicized (although the people employing it would claim that they have only un-depoliticized the older critical language); but no one, as far as I know, has discussed this phenomenon on the microsemantic level of the words themselves. I would like to rectify this omission, therefore, by examining the political implications of certain words, or rather combinations of words that I will call terms (i.e., *termes*, somewhere between *langue* and *parole*), selected because they are so frequently encountered in recent criticism. Before beginning this examination, however, I should explain that these terms are political in two senses: they are used by critics not only to make a political point but also, as Herbert Lindenberger notes, to identify themselves politically:

> When we read criticism nowadays, we are on the lookout ... for the signals emitted by the critic's terminology and prose style. We often note these signals even before attending to the arguments advanced ... for these signals tell us in short order what "sides" authors are on—the politics to which they are committed. (1990, 398–99)

This function is certainly not limited to literary criticism, for it is also found in many other areas of human activity; indeed, most social, political, and occupational groups have a special terminology of this sort to identify and bond insiders and distinguish them from outsiders. Thus these terms resemble the military Identify-Friend-or-Foe code (acronymized as IFF) that Lindenberger's reference to "signals emitted" may allude to—a radioed password that enables the receiver to identify the sender as a friend on the same side, and hence to identify anyone who fails to send it as a foe on the other side. Similarly, critics who emit these terms announce their allegiance to the side of the newer "oppositional" approaches and can assume that critics who do not emit them are on the enemy side, associated with the old formalist approach and its "bourgeois-ideology" of "liberal-humanism." Obviously the formalist/humanists also used many terms of this kind in their heyday, and have recently developed some new ones to signal their opposition to the new oppositional approaches—terms such as "jargon" (their code word for the newer critics' code) and "aesthetic standards" and, of course, "political correctness." While I believe that these terms also require scrutiny, I have not attempted to discuss them here, except for a few brief comments,[1] because we rarely find them in current literary criticism, although we have been inundated with them in the attacks on current literary criticism by the popular press.

I should also explain that there are two major differences between the newer critics' terms that I will examine and the military IFF code. The military signal changes daily so that the foe cannot learn and use it, while these terms change a little more slowly—not to prevent their "co-optation" by the formalist foe but to identify a "cutting-edge" vanguard that other friends on the same side must catch up with. And much more important, the IFF signal has no meaning beyond the identification, whereas these terms, as deployed in recent criticism, also convey or imply some specific political concepts. But because the terms have become part of their code, both senders and receivers tend to accept these concepts without question, which is why I think they should be examined. I want to emphasize, however, that my remarks will not apply to all the newer critics or to all the newer approaches, which include several different groups that disagree on many things, although they agree on opposing the old formalism. I will begin with terms generally limited to the Marxists (or cultural materialists) and some feminist critics associated with them, and then proceed to those also widely used in most of the other recent approaches.

1. Late-Capitalism. This term is employed by many Marxists to designate the present stage of capitalism and means that this is its final stage, to be followed shortly by its demise. As far as I can tell, the currency of the term itself in recent criticism stems from Ernest Mandel's *Der Spätkapitalismus* (1972, translated 1978), but the prediction it conveys has been with us since the publication in 1848 of *The Communist Manifesto*, which concludes by confidently asserting that Germany "is on the eve of a bourgeois revolution that . . . will be but the prelude to an immediately following proletarian revolution" (Marx and Engels 1959, 40–41). Similar predictions have been repeated with equal confidence at every opportunity since then. In 1917 Lenin published *Imperialism, the Highest Stage of Capitalism*, in which he demonstrates the "decay of capitalism" in its current stage ("highest" must mean that it will be going downhill from then on, and so is like "late") and says we are on "the eve of the proletarian social revolution . . . on a world-wide scale" (1940, 10);[2] and when a revised edition was published in 1940 the editors added "new data" to redemonstrate this "decay." We have also been informed that various wars and depressions marked the death of capitalism, that fascism was its final gasp,[3] and so on. The new Marxist critics preserve this mantic tradition with their term **Late-Capitalism**, which is often accompanied by the same metaphor of "decay," since many of them construct capitalism as a biological organism nearing the end of its life cycle. Margot Heinemann, for example, describes the present era as "capitalism in decay" shortly before naming it "late capitalism" (1994, 228–29), and Fredric Jameson refers to it as the "ultimate transformation of late monopoly capitalism . . . known as the *société de consommation*," which then turns out to be, in the vernacular, "the already decaying future of consumer society" (1977, 208, 211). His "ultimate," of course, makes the "late" even later.

Only a few years after publishing these words, however, Jameson announced to a startled world that "the Marxist 'science of society,' far from being a matter of prediction or making claims about historical inevitability, is exclusively a mode of understanding the past" (1983, 290), which was clearly not the view of Marx, Engels, or Lenin, as we just saw, or of all their followers who for all those years thought that the materialist "science of society" gave them the key to the future. It is easy to understand Jameson's disclaimer after the failure of every Marxist prediction (rather like an athletic coach, at the end of a disastrous season, explaining that he was not trying to win games); but it is not so easy to believe that he himself believes it, for near the end of this same essay he speaks of "late capitalism" (300), which seems to be a Marxist slip,[4] and in the following year he published an essay with "Late Capitalism" in its title (1984), which he used again as the title of a book (1990). Apparently the crystal ball was not turned in after all. And his colleagues, oblivious of this episode, have gone right on predicting the imminent demise of **Late-Capitalism.**

The situation reminds me of newspaper stories appearing from time to time about various sects that have calculated on the basis of biblical prophecy that the world will end on a certain day and assemble to await the event, which of course does not occur. A study of these sects by some sociologists (Festinger, Riecken, and Schachter 1956) found that the failure of the world to end does not weaken their members' faith in prophecy; they decide instead that their calculations were wrong and must be revised. And the repeated failure of **Late-Capitalism** to die on schedule does not lead Marxists to **Put-In-Question** their "science" of dialectical materialism that predicts this death, since they find other explanations for it, typically by blaming either the workers or the capitalists for being too materialistic. Michael Bristol, taking the first option, laments that the working-class movement "renounce[d] . . . a socialist alternative and confines its activities to struggling for a greater share in the North American standard of living" (1987, 221);[5] and Peter Widdowson takes the second, complaining of "the huge confidence trick being played upon us" in which the "protean dynamic of capitalism—ultimately cynical and without principle because its sole logic is profit—will continue to adapt and change, so thwarting any socialist opposition, which is, ironically, trammelled and limited by its defining principles and values" (1988, 4). Capitalists thus have an unfair advantage, since they greedily adapt to new circumstances, while socialists are too honorable to do this (which can also explain why the socialist economies have apparently lost the competition with capitalism and why their defeat is really a moral victory). These excuses, then, enable Marxists to deal with the stubborn survival of our system while continuing to predict its imminent death in the term **Late-Capitalism**.[6] Indeed, their use of the term seems to increase as the likelihood of its fulfillment decreases, suggesting that it may be invested with magical powers—with the hope (unarticulated) that it not only predicts but also hastens this death, so that if they intone it frequently and fervently enough the walls of capitalism will come tumbling down.

2. Unresolvable/Irreconcilable-Contradictions. This is also a Marxist term that gives us the reason that **Late-Capitalism** is late: it is dying of an acute case of "contradictions," and since they are "unresolvable" its death is inevitable. The claim has been repeated so often that we tend to overlook the political assumptions implicit in the term itself, and so it will be useful to unpack them by examining the two words that compose it. The word "contradiction" denotes a logical relationship: we say that a proposition contradicts another proposition, and by extension we can say that a fact contradicts a proposition. But what does it mean to say that two facts or factors of a social system contradict each other? This would only make sense if we assume that society could be organized according to some logical plan so that all its components will work together perfectly, for then the existence of any problem would prove that there is an illogical "contradiction" in the system. That is what Marxists do assume in their model of a communist utopia, which will by definition have no "contradictions."[7] But if we do not make this assumption, we will not find "contradictions" in society. When the workers in a factory go on strike, for example, this results not from a contradiction in the system but from a *conflict* between two groups within it, and conflicts between groups will occur in all conceivable societies short of utopia.

The adjective in this term, "unresolvable" or "irreconcilable" (Dollimore, we saw, has "intolerable"), is obviously making a prediction, and one that, despite Jameson's disclaimer, appears to be integral to the Marxist "science of society." Unlike the prediction embedded in **Late-Capitalism**, however, this one is correct, but not in the meaning assumed by Marxists. Their meaning follows directly from their model of a logical society, which requires that any "contradiction" must be "resolved" and eliminated, since if it is not this proves that the society is illogical and therefore doomed. But, again, if we do not accept their model, then their conclusion does not follow; the "contradictions" become conflicts, which are inevitable in any society, and there is no need to find a permanent "resolution" for them as long as the society is able to live with them. That is what our society does with its conflicts, through a series of continually shifting compromises and trade-offs between the groups involved. Many of these conflicts, such as those between capital and labor, actually are "unresolvable," as the Marxists assert, but then capitalism, unlike communism, does not promise final solutions, which always turn out to be illusions and often grim disasters. (Of course, some conflicts have disappeared over the years as a result of technological or other changes, or have been transformed into different conflicts.)

The impossibility of "resolving" these conflicts does not seriously threaten us, because our "bourgeois-democracy" has developed some very effective mechanisms for negotiating them and adapting to them,[8] which is just what Widdowson is complaining about. He calls this process "cynical and without principle" because it operates through self-interest (although this is the self-interest not only of the capitalists, as he assumes, but of each of the parties in each conflict) and does not permanently solve all our social problems, in the Marxist sense; but it explains why **Late-Capitalism** is still doing pretty well, despite those **Unresolvable-Contradictions**, while many Marxist regimes, which never acknowledged such "contradictions" and theoretically could not have any (which may be why they did not develop adequate mechanisms for dealing with them), have recently come tumbling down, even without the help of formalist critics intoning the term "Late-Socialism."

3. Race-Gender-Class. Jonathan Dollimore notes that "in some quarters" this "inseparable triad" is "articulated as one word" (1990b, 491), which is an understatement, since this term is now used in almost all quarters of the newer criticism (unlike the preceding two, which are usually limited to Marxists),[9] and almost always in the same way to designate the bases on which people are oppressed. Since we are so accustomed to the term and so opposed to this oppression, we may never think about the political implications of the triad, which I want to consider. In the first place, we should note that the three categories combined in it are not really of the same order. Susan Stewart calls them "the hierarchical categories of intrinsicality—race, gender, class" (1989, 13); but while all three are hierarchical, they are not all intrinsic. Although the significance of race and gender in any culture is socially constructed, they both have an intrinsic biological ground, but class does not (unlike caste distinctions in preindustrial societies that are determined by birth), which is why it is much easier to change one's class than one's race or gender. Partly for this reason, racial and sexual prejudices usually run much deeper than class prejudices and cut across class lines. Indeed, while some people in our society clearly are oppressed because of racism or sexism, it is not clear how they are oppressed simply because of classism.[10] (I am not denying, of course, that poor people suffer here in many ways, but this is not a result of their membership in the working class.) It appears, then, that the triadic formula elevates class to a status it does not deserve.

We should also note that, even if the category of race is extended to include ethnicity, the triadic formula still has some notable omissions and so seems to discriminate against many forms of discrimination, as can be seen by comparing it to the codes of conduct recently enacted by many of our colleges, which prohibit discrimination based on gender, race, and ethnicity (or national origin), and usually add age, disability, religion, and sexual orientation (Brown 1991, 4). It is interesting that none of them mentions class; apparently "worker" or "son-of-a-worker" are not terms of abuse on campus.[11] It is also interesting that neither the triadic term nor the campus codes include what in some parts of the world is one of the most pervasive and frightful forms of oppression—that based on the victim's political beliefs. The codes presumably omit it because it is not a serious problem in our colleges, but how are we to explain its absence from the term favored by "oppositional" critics who specialize in "political-awareness"?[12] Could it be that they do not oppose jailing or killing people for their political beliefs as long as the jailers and killers have the right beliefs and the victims have the wrong ones? I think it is more likely that they omit this category because **The-West** obviously has a much better record here than Marxist and Third World regimes (though I would argue that this is also true of most of the other categories). But the most important reason, we are about to see, is that it does not fit the model of oppression they have in mind.

The third point to note about this term is its implication that the three categories of oppression are really aspects of one overarching oppressive system, an implication that answers to, and is reinforced by, the powerful need felt by some people to believe that there is a single cause of all injustice and therefore a single cure, which we already encountered in Widdowson's fantasy of a "huge confidence trick" (1988, 4). While this term is used by many non-Marxist critics, it is Marxism that provides the clearest and simplest satisfaction of that need in its theory of the "base" and "superstructure," wherein the oppressive "exploitation" of the working class is the cause of all other oppressions,[13] which thus also become forms of "exploitation" that will disappear when—and only when—the primary form is eliminated. (This can be seen in Dollimore and Sinfield's declaration of their "commitment to the transformation of a social order which exploits people on grounds of race, gender and class" [1994a, viii], which implies that there is one agency that "exploits" the three groups and that they will all be liberated by one act of **Transforming-Society**.) Thus the Marxists have produced a unified field theory of oppression that promises us the final solution to all injustice. This could explain why the other categories of oppression are not in the triadic formula, since it is more difficult to define them as forms of "exploitation," especially the oppression of political dissidents (those in Marxist labor camps cannot be "exploited" because no capitalist profits from them). It also explains why class, even though it is of a different order, has been elevated into this formula, since it turns out to be the category that is, in Orwellian terms, more equal than the other two.

The simplicity and promise of this theory can be very tempting, and some feminist critics have bought it, asserting that the "root" of sexism "is economic" because it is "inherent" in the "exploitative . . . structures of capitalism," and that it therefore cannot be altered "without fundamentally changing the material circumstances" of our economic system, and that "late 'multinational' capitalism" is responsible for "the oppression and exploitation of women all over the globe" (Greene 1981/2, 41–42; Moi 1983, 10; McLuskie 1994, 90; Cotter 1995, 119). (Some other feminists just reverse this scheme so that sexism produces capitalism [al-Hibri 1981, 179], which makes as much or as little sense.) Some critics also claim that racism is caused by capitalism and will be cured by socialism. But the evidence against these theories is overwhelming. Both sexism and racism existed long before capitalism and flourish under socialism. The pronouncements from Marxist regimes that they do not have any gender or racial problems (which is supposed to explain why they do not permit any movements promoting the interests of women or minorities) are belied by some dismal facts, such as the plight of women in Romania and the flight of Jews from the USSR. But to disprove the Marxist theory it is not necessary to prove that all capitalist countries have better gender and racial relations than all socialist countries, since it is also significant that striking differences in these relations exist within the capitalist world and within the socialist world. The status of women is higher in Sweden than in Switzerland, and higher in Cuba than in the Democratic People's Republic of Korea. It is harder to make comparisons in the area of race, because the racial or ethnic mix, unlike the gender mix, is unique in each country, but clearly the treatment of minorities varies greatly in different capitalist countries, as it does in different socialist countries. This of course does not prove that there is no connection between sexism or racism and the economic system, for all aspects of a society are interrelated; but it does prove, as many feminist and minority critics realize, that they are very complex phenomena affected by many different social factors (which also applies to the other kinds of oppression noted earlier) and hence that there is no single cause or single cure of the problems of **Race-Gender-Class.**

4. **Natural-Essential-Eternal-God-given-Universal-Unchanging-Inevitable.** In this term, unlike the others, the constituent words are not all required for its meaning; in fact, they rarely all appear together like this but usually travel in combinations of two or three. It also differs from the preceding terms because, while it is only used by the newer critics (here including virtually all their approaches), it is never applied to them but always to the formalist/humanists, who are said to believe that various things, such as our economic system, the family, morality, and aesthetic values, are **Natural-Essential-Eternal-Etc.** (which is now generally known as "essentialism," equivalent to Stewart's "intrinsicality"), whereas the newer critics realize they are "socially-constructed." The term thus functions as a kind of negative or reverse IFF code: when critics accuse others of this belief, they identify themselves as friends and the others as foes. The charge is sometimes true, because some people (more in the past than today) do believe that some of these things have some of these qualities. One major problem with current applications of this term, however, is that they often fail to make these necessary distinctions among the believers, or the things, or especially the qualities, which are treated as more or less interchangeable. Thus in Jean Howard's essay, which is typical in this respect, "the essentialist ideology that sees identity as God-given and unchanging," and "the idea that women are universally prone to deception," and the belief that the "prerogatives" of the ruling class are "natural" and "inevitable" (1987b, 168, 174–76) are grouped together without any discrimination and are attributed, again without discrimination, to the dominant Elizabethan culture and to modern "humanist criticism," which imposes these ideas on

Elizabethan drama or is "complicit" with them (174, 176). But the various "essentialist" qualities combined in this term do not form a single package, and certainly not one that can be foisted on "humanist criticism." People who accept the theory of evolution, for example, among whom are many "liberal-humanists," do not think that what is **Natural** is **Unchanging**; those who are "secular-humanists" (a right-wing code word that again includes many "liberal-humanists")[14] do not think anything is **God-given**; and many "liberal-humanists" (including me) think that some human relationships have a **Natural** basis but develop differently in each society and so are not **Universal** or **Inevitable**.

The accusation conveyed through this term, as it is used by many of the newer critics, not only ignores these important qualifications and distinctions but is often simply untrue. This is obvious in the new Marxists' endlessly repeated assertion that "liberal-humanists" regard our capitalist class system and the "bourgeois-ideology" that legitimates it as "eternally or naturally given," "inevitable," "immutable," "fixed," "universal," "unchangeable," and so on.[15] I have a fairly extensive acquaintance with "liberal-humanists," but I have yet to encounter a single one who believes any of these things. Surely every schoolgirl and boy knows that capitalism only emerged a few centuries ago, that it does not operate in the same way in each society, and that it is continually developing in new directions, so it could not possibly be **Natural**, **Eternal**, **Universal**, **Unchanging**, or **Inevitable**. The Marxists want to believe that we believe it is, since that would explain why we have not tried to overthrow it (this is presumably what Widdowson means by that "huge confidence trick being played upon us") and why it must inevitably be overthrown when we realize that it is not inevitable. Unfortunately for them, however, the success of capitalism does not depend on these "essentialist" beliefs about economic class that no one believes. But this is not true of race and gender, the other two categories in the triadic formula, since many people still think that the current arrangements in these areas are natural, which is one reason that racist and sexist prejudices usually are much deeper than class prejudices, as I noted earlier. In these two areas the campaign against "essentialism" has a real case and deserves our full support, since it can make a very important contribution to literary studies as well as to the political struggle to improve our society.

Another, more general problem is also connected with this term, because the critics often apply it, even when they have a real case, in a way that overstates the role of social construction and understates the role of nature. A glaring example can be found in Richard Rorty's well-known pronouncement that "there is nothing to people except what has been socialized into them" (1989, 177), where the error becomes obvious as soon as we ask what the "them" is that this socializing goes into. Since it cannot be an empty space, there must be something to people beyond "what has been socialized into them." The fact is that we all come equipped with brains and nervous and glandular systems that are the products of thousands of years of evolution and are already programmed to act and react in certain ways (to remember the past, to generalize, to feel emotions, etc.), without which it would be impossible to have anything "socialized into" us; and it seems likely that this natural equipment affects (or at least sets limits to) our socialization. We do not know much about this process yet, but the little we know suggests that many aspects of human behavior may involve complicated interactions between natural potentialities and social actualizations. The newer critics' campaign against "essentialism," like their campaign against **Race-Gender-Class** oppression, tends to oversimplify and polarize these very complex phenomena.

The most serious problem in the current use of this term, however, is its definition as a negative IFF code, for this assumes that all "essentialist" concepts always serve the wrong (i.e., reactionary) side and so are inherently evil. But that attributes an essential quality to such concepts, which is why Gerald Graff calls it "anti-essentialist essentialism" (1989, 174). Since they have often been used to legitimate oppression, as I noted in connection with racism and sexism, it is easy to find examples to build this case against them, but it is just as easy to find examples on the other side. Most progressive movements *opposing* oppression—movements that the newer critics support—invoke the "essentialist" values of liberty, equality, or justice; indeed, without those values we could not know what oppression is or why it should be opposed. Some of the newest critics seem to realize this—Diana Fuss, for example, makes this point in *Essentially Speaking* (1989). The discovery, however, has not yet trickled down to members of the old critical vanguard, who have instead invented a stopgap doctrine called "strategic essentialism" (Heath 1978, 99; Spivak 1987, 205), which allows them to condemn "essentialist" concepts and use them anyway whenever it suits their purpose. One might have thought that this inconsistency (or hypocrisy?) would lead them to **Put-In-Question** their condemnation of "essentialism," but we are about to learn why it does not.

5. Put/Call/Place-In(to)-Question. This term names a very good thing that the newer critics continually do and the older formalist/humanists never do, according to the newer critics, which is why the newer critics must continually do it for and to them. I could not find any statements by these critics that explain the meaning of the term, since they seem to take this for granted, but they do provide some explanations of "critiquing," which is closely related to it (other related operations are "demystifying" and "denaturalizing"). Susan Stewart's essay (1989), an impassioned defense of "critiquing," gives us what has become its standard meaning: it is an all-out attack on targeted concepts that employs various strategies to destroy those concepts, such as showing that they are not **Natural-Essential-Eternal-Etc.**, or that they serve class "interests" (which always seem to be those of the ruling class), or that they conceal "contradictions" (which, we saw, are supposed to be inherent in our class society). She clearly regards this as an unqualifiedly good activity and apparently as the most—if not the only—important "work" a critic can undertake, since she implies that it is coextensive with "theorizing" and thus with **Making-Knowledge** (which she calls "creating new objects of knowledge" [12]); and her argument for it is devoted largely to arguing against any limitations that might be imposed upon it. Yet her own view of "critiquing" imposes two crucial but unstated limitations: she assumes it is limited to attacks on the concepts of the enemy, the bourgeois/humanist establishment, since it is "oppositional" (13), and she assumes it is limited to successful attacks that defeat those concepts. Presumably her own concepts, including that of "critiquing" itself, will not be "critiqued," and when "critiquing" wages war on an enemy concept, it will always be that concept and not the "critiquing" that has to cry uncle.

This idea of "critiquing" also applies to the term we are examining here, which can be seen as another way of stating it. For these critics, to **Put-In-Question** some concept is, again, to attack it with the intention of destroying it, and the term is used with the same two unstated limitations noted in "critiquing": it must work against a concept of the enemy (the same enemy, of course) and it must work successfully. It does not seem to occur to the newer critics who **Put-In-Question** the concepts of "liberal-humanism" that this operation could also be performed on some of their own concepts (such as their condemnation of all "essentialism"), or that some of the enemy's concepts could survive the operation—that a rigorous interrogation of "bourgeois-democracy," for instance, might conclude that, with all its problems, it is still preferable to any available alternative. That does not happen in their discourse, because when they **Put-In-Question** a concept, it is not given a chance to defend itself by answering the question or by asking its own questions back at the questioner (like the one about available alternatives). As they deploy the term, to put a concept *in* question really means to declare it *out* of the question.

There is a significant difference, however, between "critiquing" and **Putting-In-Question**. Critics who claim to be "critiquing" a concept feel obliged to assemble some arguments against it (as Stewart explains), since a "critique" is supposed to be "work"—in fact, we saw that it is supposed to be **Making-Knowledge**. But those who **Put-In-Question** a concept usually feel no such obligation; for them it seems to be enough simply to invoke the term. My general impression is that the term is most commonly used in the past tense (and often in the passive voice) to refer to a job (i.e., "work") that has already been done by others and so need not be repeated. Frequently we are given the names of the persons who did it—and they are always very Big Names—as if that settled the matter once and for all. Thus Catherine Belsey begins her influential book introducing and recommending the new approaches by asserting that the "work" of Barthes, Lacan, Althusser, and Derrida "has put in question" or "questioned" the humanist conceptions of an author and a text, which apparently is all that is required to make these conceptions "untenable" (1980, 2–3; yet this does not prevent her from treating Barthes, Lacan, Althusser, and Derrida as authors who are responsible for their texts). But sometimes we do not even get this information; we are only told that a concept has been **Put-In-Question** and are expected to conclude that it therefore can no longer be employed—at least not by anyone who does not want to be on the wrong side. For the term has become a double IFF signal: it itself is a positive code word that identifies friends of the new "oppositional" approaches, and at the same time it also inscribes any concept that it is applied to as a negative code word identifying their formalist/humanist foes. In this respect, then, it serves much the same function as the next term to be examined.

    6. Quotation-Marks. Some people may object that these are not words, but only because they have not yet learned that writing precedes speech. In fact, we have the words **Quote** and **Unquote** for these marks, and in the good old days when they enclosed actual quotations, a lecturer would begin the quoted passage by saying **Quote** and end it with **Unquote**, which did not cause any problems. But now they usually enclose a single word or phrase, and it sounds awkward to say "our **Quote** democracy **Unquote**," especially if this must be repeated many times in a paper. Some speakers therefore combine them into **Quote-Unquote**, but then they have to decide whether to say this before or after the word in question, neither of which is satisfactory. A more common solution is to adopt sign language by raising both hands with one or two fingers extended and executing a short wagging motion while vocalizing the word to be bracketed.[16] I have heard—or rather seen—lectures where this was done so often that I wondered why the speaker did not simply stipulate at the outset that the entire paper is in quotes, but of course that would not work, because this quoting is highly selective and the selecting usually is highly political. There is a book waiting to be written that could be called *The Politics of Quotation Marks*.

    It is important to understand that the words enclosed by these marks (or waggings) are not actual quotations; they are not taken from a specified text or ascribed to a specific author, since the marks do not really refer to these words but to the concepts that they name. These are nonquoting **Quotation-Marks**, which obviously must have some other purpose, and that purpose obviously is to cast doubt on the concept in question, to place it "under-erasure." But there are several reasons that we have so many of them sprinkling the pages of the newer criticism. Sometimes critics insert them simply to cover their flank (the left one, of course); the marks say, in effect, "Although I am using this concept, I am not so naive or out-of-touch as to be unaware that its status is now problematic." Edward Pechter makes the interesting suggestion that they may also record the critics' own uncertain or shifting position with respect to the concept (1991, 175). But clearly the most common reason for these marks is to indicate, not the critics' uncertainty about the problematic status of the concept, but their certainty that it no longer has any legitimate status at all. The marks, that is, are "oppositional," as are the critics responsible for their recent proliferation, who use them as a weapon to attack and destroy the concept they bracket, because the marks say to the reader, "Some people are so naive or out-of-touch that they still believe in this, but I know better and you better know better."[17] And since the concept attacked by these marks always seems to be one dear to formalist/humanist criticism, they have the same basic function as the term **Put-In-Question**, which means that they too emit a double IFF signal: they are a positive code identifying a friend while the word they enclose becomes a negative code that identifies a foe, or, putting it another way, these marks convert an enemy code word into a friendly one. Of course, they are even easier for the critic to employ than **Putting-In-Question** and also easier for the reader, who can register their meaning on a subliminal level and so carry away the impression that the concept must be illegitimate without having to exercise any thought about it.

The **Quotation-Marks** also resemble **Putting-In-Question** in another respect, namely, that the critics who wield this weapon against the enemy's concepts do not seem to realize that it can just as readily be turned against their own. We might take this sentence as an example:

> A major intervention of the new oppositional critics is aimed at demystifying the concept of "literature" as a category of "intrinsically valuable" works by insisting on its historical contingency.

I think we would all immediately recognize that this is a statement by one of the new oppositional critics; but let us try what these critics like to call a "repunctuation" of the text:

> A major "intervention" of the new "oppositional" critics is aimed at "demystifying" the concept of literature as a category of intrinsically valuable works by insisting on its "historical contingency."

It has now become a statement by an unregenerate formalist/humanist, even though its literal meaning is unchanged, which shows how easy it is to let these little marks do your arguing for you. The alert reader will have noticed that I occasionally succumb to the temptation myself in this essay by deploying them to oppose some of the terms of the new "oppositional" critics, including the terms they themselves deploy to label the old "liberal-humanist" criticism to which they are "oppositional." (In fact, my use of boldface type and even of hyphens also serves this purpose, since it too seems to **Put-In-Question** the new terminology.)

It would appear, then, that placing a word or phrase in **Quotation-Marks** aims at the same general effect as inserting "so-called" before it, although that is less common in current critical discourse, perhaps because it is considered less subtle. I remember a story from the 1960s in which a northern reporter arrived at the airport of a southern city to cover a civil-rights demonstration and asked the white taxi driver to take him to the headquarters of the local NAACP, only to receive a blank stare. Then he hit on the bright idea of asking to go to "the so-called headquarters of the so-called NAACP," whereupon he was driven directly to his destination. Presumably he could also have achieved this result by wagging his fingers at the right times—that is, if the driver had attended scholarly conferences—since the meaning is the same. But in some recent essays we find both of these tactics used in combinations, such as "our so-called 'democracy,'" that look to me like semiotic overkill, although it may only be overdetermination.[18] One could, of course, turn the tables on this phrase simply by repunctuating it to read "our 'so-called' democracy," a countertactic that in effect so-calls so-called, since the **Quotation-Marks** exorcise the exorcising power of "so-called" (a power the taxi driver must have felt) and at the same time mock the people who resort to it.

There are many other terms of this kind that I cannot examine here because of space limitations, but I will mention a few that I would recommend as subjects for further research.

7. Making/Producing-Knowledge. This is the term favored by many of the newer critics to describe the "work" that they do. It is meant to strike a blow against "empiricism" (which they associate with "humanism") by rejecting the naive idea that knowledge is simply out there waiting to be discovered, and foregrounding the role played in every discovery by the conceptual input of the discoverer. But their use of this term often goes to the opposite extreme by ignoring any input from empirical data, so that the whole operation is reduced to the maker's "theorizing."[19] Moreover, if **Making-Knowledge** is cut off from empirical data, it is also cut off from empirical verification, which raises the issue of how we know whether what is "made" is really "knowledge." These critics do not discuss this, although they are exploiting the implication that "knowledge" is true (otherwise they could say they are "making-theories" or "making-assertions"). They clearly believe that *they* are **Making-Knowledge**, but we need some research to find out if they extend this privilege to their opponents: were the formalists **Making-Knowledge** with their "close-readings" that were placed **Above-Ideology**, or am I **Making-Knowledge** in this essay that **Puts-In-Question** the term **Making-Knowledge**?

8. **Transforming-Society.** This term is favored by several groups of the newer critics to describe their goal. It is often combined with the **Race-Gender-Class** term, as we saw in Dollimore and Sinfield's "commitment to the transformation of a social order which exploits people on grounds of race, gender and class" (1994a, viii). Messer-Davidow is also committed to "transform a society that is stratified by gender, race, and class" (1988, 54), and Eagleton to "the transformation of a society divided by class and gender" (1983, 210; the omission of race is unexplained). Sometimes that is not mentioned but is presumably understood, as in Lentricchia's assertion that, since "our society is mainly unreasonable,"[20] we should "get involved in the process of transforming it" (1983, 2), or in Jameson's call for "a radical and systematic transformation . . . of our social relations" (1983, 302). If this code word has any specific political content, however, it must be a closely guarded secret. Critics who use it obviously want to suggest a very basic change, or else they would speak of "improving" or "reforming" society, but they never reveal what kind of change it is or how it can be promoted by writing literary criticism. The aim of research here would be to learn whether they are silent about this because they do not want the rest of us to know or because they do not know themselves.

9. **Above/Beyond-Ideology** (or **Transcend-Ideology**). This term is always used by the newer critics in a negative mode, since it is attributed to the formalists, who are said to believe that their approach and the authors and texts they apply it to are **Above-Ideology**, which requires the newer critics to demonstrate that they are wrong. As his title indicates, this is the main point of Kavanagh's essay, which concludes that "Shakespeare is, as

he always was, in ideology" (1985, 165). These demonstrations cannot fail, because they usually define "ideology" in the Althusserian sense as a "system of beliefs and assumptions, unconscious, unexamined, invisible," as Greene puts it, that is "the very condition of our experience of the world" (1991, 23).[21] In this sense, all humans and all human activities must by definition be "in ideology," which becomes a tautology. But a research project is obviously required to explain how the newer critics can know that others are "in ideology," since this would mean that they themselves are conscious of, and able to see and examine, this "unconscious, unexamined, invisible" system, and so must be **Above-Ideology**.[22]

10. The-West. This is one of the most fascinating of these terms. As used by many of the newer critics, it refers not to a geographic area but to a hypostatized and demonized entity that is supposed to be responsible for all the evil in the world. They often construct **The-West** as that overarching system of **Race-Gender-Class** oppression referred to earlier—as a vast white, male, capitalist, colonialist, phallocentric conspiracy (Widdowson's "huge confidence trick" once more) against all the victimized Others everywhere (including those in the geographic West). But it is also employed by many right-wingers (usually in the form of **Western-Values or The-Western-Heritage**) as a hypostatized and apotheosized entity that is the source of everything good in the world that must be protected from the assault of a vast conspiracy of Marxists, feminists, deconstructionists, and so on, and so it has become an IFF signal for both sides.[23] Research here might investigate the maneuvers adopted by both sides to evade or explain away the awkward fact that our major "oppositional" movements, including Marxism, feminism, and deconstruction, all emerged from **The-West**.

Another related research project I would recommend is a study of how these terms originate and catch on, which could tell us a great deal about the present state of our discipline. Only a short time ago, to take a minor example, I had never encountered the term "subaltern-studies," and if I had, I would have assumed that it referred to the junior commissioned ranks in the Royal Army. I first heard it in a committee meeting and had to ask what it meant, but in a few months I was seeing and hearing it everywhere. The speed of this dissemination is not itself so surprising, since it involves a small number of people who are in constant communication with each other and have a constant need to keep up with the newest IFF signals; but who invents these terms or decides which ones should pass into the code?

Unless this is done in secret (by an underground cell conspiring in a smoke-free room of some British polytechnic?), it should not be difficult to track down. And while we are at it, I would suggest some similar research on other political signals now circulating within and about our discipline, such as the right-wing-coded message that our new Marxist critics were student activists in the 1960s who lay low until they got tenure and then "came out," or the left-wing-coded message that our New Historicist critics were student activists in the 1960s who lost the faith while getting tenure and "sold out." I suspect that both messages are wrong, but no one has bothered to check them. We have recently seen some impressive studies of the early days of our discipline (such as Graff 1987), which must have required a very substantial investment of time and energy, yet we are still waiting for someone to undertake these much easier research projects on our present situation.

I have one final point to make about the terms examined here: none of them is specifically concerned with literary criticism, as that practice was formerly understood. In fact, the alert reader will have noticed that not a single literary work is mentioned by any of the people I quote in this essay, even though almost every one of them is a certified literary critic. This avoidance of references to literature was obviously intentional on my part (or would have been, if "intentionality" had not recently been **Put-In-Question** and in **Quotation-Marks**), but it was not at all difficult, since one can traverse substantial tracts of recent so-called "literary criticism" without encountering even the title of a literary work.[24] It should not be surprising, then, that these terms, which I said at the outset are among the most frequently used in this criticism, are not about literature in the traditional sense. Nor should it be surprising that they are all explicitly or implicitly about politics, for a major complaint of the old formalists is that the newer critics subordinate literature to politics because they are "ideological," which has become a right-wing code word for the enemy. Of course, the newer critics would reply, in terms of their own IFF code, that this complaint identifies those who voice it as reactionary-liberal-humanist apologists for **Late-Capitalism** and **Race-Gender-Class** oppression and **The-West**, who still believe that so-called **Quote** literature **Unquote** is a **Natural-Essential-Eternal-God-given-Universal-Etc.** entity that is **Above-Ideology**, whereas these newer critics are **Making-Knowledge** by **Putting-in-Question** this approach and showing that its attempt to separate literature from politics is itself a concealed political move designed to paper over **Unresolvable-Contradictions** and to prevent us from **Transforming-Society**. That is why they can claim that they have not politicized but only un-depoliticized the language of literary criticism.

13
The Current Polarization of Literary Studies

THE INCREASING POLARIZATION OF LITERARY STUDIES OVER THE PAST DECADE HAS created a situation that is unique in the history of our discipline. This of course is not the first time that we have been polarized. There was another major conflict some fifty years ago between the old historical scholars and what were then called the New Critics, but it differed from the present conflict in two very important respects. Although it obviously involved departmental politics, this had no direct connection to politics outside the academy. The New Critics were radical insurgents within their departments, but some of the early ones were politically conservative, and later the movement covered virtually the entire political spectrum. In the present conflict, however, the two sides are clearly connected to external politics, which is why they are usually called the Left and the Right. I am not happy with these labels, because they contribute to the polarization by conflating a number of different critical approaches at the two political poles, as I will point out later, but I am going to use them, since I cannot think of better ones.

The second important difference, which is a result of this political connection, involves the power situation. In the earlier conflict that situation was perfectly clear—the old historicists had the power and were gradually losing it to the New Critics. But in the present conflict a major argument centers on the question of who has the power. Each side sees itself as the underdog oppressed by the other side, which really has all the power, even though it claims that it is the oppressed underdog. I think that both sides are sincere about this,[1] and that they are both correct, depending on how we contextualize the conflict. In the context of the national political scene, the Left is correct: the right-wing critics have the big money behind them, which is used to finance several institutes and journals; they have the support of the national administration; and they have most of the public press on their side in the attack on "political correctness." (I should explain that I will not be mentioning "political correctness" here, except to mention that I will not mention it.) The Right is also still dominant in much of the academic hinterland, which is not a geographic designation. But if we shift the context to the prestigious academic heartland, the Right is correct, for the left-wing critics have the power, as anyone can see from the programs of recent Modern Language Association conventions and other important conferences, or the publisher's ads, or the contents of our leading journals.

Moreover, the Left sometimes tries to use this power to repress those who disagree with them. I was the target of such an attempt because of my *PMLA* essay "Feminist Thematics," which criticized some feminist readings of Shakespearean tragedy. *PMLA* had for several years been printing a steady stream of feminist essays; mine was the first and only one that criticized any aspect of this approach, but one was too much for some feminist critics. They sent off a protest to the *PMLA* Forum (reprinted in chapter 1) asserting that my essay should not have been published and that I should not have a successful academic career. (I want to make it clear at the outset that, although I will be drawing some of my examples of leftist tendencies from attacks on me like this one, which I think are more reliable evidence than the kind of anecdotes treasured by Dinesh D'Souza, I am not presenting myself as a suffering victim; my career has not suffered from these attacks—if anything, it has benefited, though that clearly was not the attackers' intention.) Even more revealing than this Forum protest was the fan mail I received from junior faculty members who praised my courage and said that on their campuses they were afraid to voice any objections to the feminist or other new approaches.[2] It had not occurred to me that I was being brave; it takes more courage for me to visit the dentist than it did to write that essay, but then I am not in the vulnerable position of my untenured correspondents. I believe they were accurately stating their perception of the situation in which they find themselves, and their perception is what matters. As the American Civil Liberties Union has often pointed out, the most insidious effect of repression is found, not in actual censorship, but in the atmosphere of intimidation that chills freedom of speech through self-censorship. The intimidators count on this: William Buckley used to defend McCarthy's work because it narrowed the range of public debate—that is, it frightened the commies and comsymps and shut them up; and from the Left, Michael Sprinker attacked my own work because it gives "regressive and hateful ideologues in the academy" the "license to say publicly what they might otherwise have kept to themselves" (1991, 115–16). They both want those who disagree with them to feel that they must keep quiet, which is how self-censorship operates. There have also been a few actual cases of censorship by the Left on campuses where teachers or students tried to silence people whose views they disliked—cases that are exploited by the Right and by the press, which usually ignores other cases, well documented by the American Association of University Professors, in which conservative administrations tried to silence or fire radicals and "troublemakers."

The efforts of some leftists to exercise their power in this way in the campus context may be caused by, and may in their own minds be justified by, their sense of powerlessness in the larger context, and their sense that their critics on campus are complicit with the powerful Right outside the academy. Thus two other reactions to my essay "Feminist Thematics" oppose the publication of critiques of feminist criticism because the women's movement has come under attack in a "backlash"; since they feel oppressed on the national scene, they want to suppress any criticism on the local scene (Greene 1991, 26–29; Woodbridge 1991, 290–92). But this mode of reasoning is itself a result of the political polarization of our discipline, and I would now like to look at some of its major tendencies. I must emphasize that they are only tendencies—they do not all apply to all polarizers. And what I have to say about them will not be very new; many of my points have been stated in the past, but I think they need to be stated again.

Polarization is the division of a field into two warring sides, into *us* and *them*, where each side is convinced that *we* are completely right and good and *they* are completely wrong and evil. Thus both sides demonize their opponents: some rightists do this literally, since they believe that Satan lurks behind the Left, while leftists are less literal but equally irrational in demonizing the Right. For each side treats the other as an infinitely expansible discursive space into which it can dump everything it loves to hate. The Right sees *them* as communist, atheist, feminist, homosexual subversives who promote multiculturalism, abortion, pornography, witchcraft, fluoridation, evolution, relativism, gun control, canon-bashing, flag-burning, welfare-bumming, humanism, free love, free hypodermic needles, and free-floating signifiers. And the Left sees *them* as fascist, sexist, racist, homophobic reactionaries who promote imperialism, colonialism, Eurocentrism, phallocentrism, witch-hunts, fundamentalism, foundationalism, essentialism, individualism, intentionalism, empiricism, idealism, formalism, and humanism.[3] Of course, these are caricatures of the two sides, caricature being what happens when each side demonizes *them* on the other side. And the caricatures attribute contradictory ideas to *them*, such as the promotion of feminism *and* pornography, or of empiricism *and* idealism.[4] That kind of contradiction is typical of demonizing and of the related phenomenon of racist or sexist scapegoating, in which black men are said to be feckless children *and* savage beasts, Jews are plutocrats *and* reds, women are frigid, castrative teases *and* nymphomaniacs, and so forth. One might have thought that highly educated academics would be immune to the appeal of scapegoating, but while they usually avoid it in matters of race or gender, some of them indulge in a political version that is just as mindless and vicious.

Because of the dynamics of polarization, both sides are defined, by themselves and by their enemies, at the opposite extremes of the political spectrum—at the far Right and far Left. And each side treats anyone who is not at its extreme position as belonging to the opposite extreme, according to the basic principle of polarizing that all those who are not with us are against us and so must be with *them*. Political rightists regard all those to their left as "left-liberals," which is often hyphenated as a single word and conflated with "radicals" (Kelner 1992, 37–38; Kramer 1991, 228–29), while the religious Right lumps them all together as "secular-humanists." And leftists regard all those to their right as "liberal-humanists," which they often conflate with "reactionaries" (Holderness 1992, 43; Moi 1983, 11). (There is an eerie resemblance between "secular-humanism" and "liberal-humanism"; the former is a pseudoreligion invented by the far Right to serve as its demonic enemy, while the latter is a pseudoideology invented by the far Left for the same purpose.) For both extremes homogenize as well as demonize the enemy and try to erase any intermediate positions. They also try to erase any differences among these intermediate positions: Marxists called our two major parties "Tweedledum and Tweedledee," and George Wallace insisted that "there's not a dime's worth of difference between them."

In this strategy, therefore, the far Right and far Left are tacit allies: each one depends on the other to justify its own existence, since each one presents itself as the sole alternative to the other. Thus in the 1930s the Communists claimed to be our only defense against Fascism, and Fascists claimed to be our only defense against Communism. Each extreme wanted to force upon us a choice of *either* Fascism *or* Communism, so they had a common interest in destroying any middle ground that could be a third alternative, a position from which we could answer: *neither* Fascism *nor* Communism. Fascism and Communism no longer pose real threats to us, though they survive as terms of abuse (for name-calling is another tendency of polarization); but the idea that we must choose between the far Right or far Left is still promoted by both extremes, since they both benefit from this polarizing. That is why they attack humanism, which we saw is on both of their hit lists,[5] and especially liberalism, which as "the L-word" is a favorite target of the Right and as "bourgeois-liberalism" is a favorite target of the Left.[6] When they are not shooting at liberalism, they are denying its existence: rightists often insist that liberals are really crypto-communists or fellow travelers, while Frank Lentricchia, speaking from the Left, dismisses them as "nervous conservatives" whose position is "mainly an illusion" (1983, 1–2). This view is also assumed in Margot FitzGerald's response (reprinted in chapter 2) to my "Bardicide" essay, in which she says that my criticism of Marxism associates me with red-baiters and the House Un-American Activities Committee; if I am against the far Left, that is, I must be for the far Right, since she has simply "disappeared" the liberals, who support neither Marxism nor McCarthyism and were victimized by both.

Another major tendency of this polarization is the engendering of conspiracy theories, which are part of the mechanism by which each side demonizes the other as the embodiment of everything it hates or fears. The Right constructs a vast conspiracy of subversives whose goal is to destroy our moral fiber, the family, the American Way of Life, and Western values, while the Left makes the West the demon of its theory of a vast conspiracy of reactionaries whose goal is to subjugate and exploit all the oppressed Others in the world. (Note that "the West" figures prominently in each theory, not as a geographic area, but as a hypostatized and homogenized entity that for the Right is the source of everything good and for the Left is the source of everything evil.)[7] The assumption underlying these conspiracy theories is that nothing is ever unplanned, so anything bad that happens anywhere in the world must be planned by *them*. I have heard a John Bircher maintain that a communist cell dominating our government caused inflation, and the same explanation was given for our "losing" China to Mao; and I have heard Marxists maintain that international capitalism deliberately created the troubles in Ulster and famines in Africa and our current recession, which is designed to keep the workers quiet and provide an excuse for firing radical teachers. Each side also has a conspiracy theory blaming the other for the Kennedy assassination.

Thus the leftist paranoid vision of a monolithic and malefic international capitalism serves the same function as the rightist vision of international communism or the Nazi vision of international Jewry. Indeed, these conspiracy theories of the far Right and far Left sound like *The Protocols of the Elders of Zion,* with just a change in the identity of the demons. They also yield the same satisfaction as the *Protocols* to a certain kind of mind by producing a simple division of humanity into villainous victimizers and virtuous victims, and locating a single cause of all our problems in those villains, and thus promising a single cure for all of them when the villains are extirpated in a final solution that will usher in utopia. This is a very powerful fantasy, and it is almost impossible to convince anyone caught up in it that there is no conspiracy, and hence no single cause or single cure of all our problems. These theories are impervious to argument, because any evidence you present to disprove the existence of a conspiracy is explained away as part of the conspiracy to conceal the conspiracy and so becomes proof of its existence.

Although the polarization I am discussing is basically political, it is insatiable and tries to colonize all fields of knowledge. It has not had much success with the scientists, who show little interest in dividing along these lines; we do not have right- and left-wing chemists, reactionary and radical physiologists, and so on. But it has been very successful in colonizing the humanities, and the rest of my essay will focus on the results in literary criticism. The basic polarizing tactic here is to line up the various *critical* approaches at the two *political* extremes. According to the far Right, all the new approaches, especially those associated with poststructuralism and the historicizing of literature, are creatures of the far Left and serve its political agenda, while the far Left claims that the old approaches, especially formalism or what was called the New Criticism, serve the politics of the far Right, and many leftists argue that the formalists' silence about the politics of literary works really means consent to or complicity with the rightist ideology, whether they are conscious of it or not.

The facts clearly show, however, that there is no necessary connection between critical approaches and political positions. The historicizing of literature is not new and need not be leftist; in fact, many of the old historicists who preceded the New Critics were political conservatives. Moreover, poststructuralists now cover most of the political spectrum, and this was also true of the New Critical formalists, as I said at the outset. And while a critic's silence about the politics of a literary work *may* indicate consent to or complicity with conservative ideology, it may also mean other things, depending on the context and the critic's motives.[8] These critical approaches have of course been put to various political uses by various groups at various times, but the approaches themselves have no inherent politics.

I now turn to some of the specific disputes about criticism that have recently been generated or exacerbated by this polarization. Many of them follow a common pattern in which the far Right and the far Left take extreme all-or-nothing positions that are clearly wrong, while the truth lies somewhere between them. I am embarrassed that I will have to make this point repeatedly, which seems to be belaboring the obvious; but it obviously is not obvious to a lot of critics today, so I will just forge ahead.

One of the most prominent of these disputes is about the canon, much publicized by the press, which delights in puns on canon wars. Here the polarized camps have taken diametrically opposite positions—the far Right defends the canon as a sacred repository of Western values, while the far Left attacks it as a sinister instrument of Western oppression. They are both wrong and for the same reason, since in order to wage this canon war, both sides must treat the canon as the embodiment of a single set of political and cultural values, which simply is not true. This point becomes evident if we stop treating the canon as a reified abstraction and think of the particular texts that compose it, for no one would maintain that the works of Homer, Dante, and Joyce, for example, endorse the same values, although they are all central to the Western canon. In order to get around this inconvenient fact, both sides in the dispute must homogenize the canon—just as we saw them doing to the idea of "the West" that the canon is supposed to represent—by ignoring many of its diverse and conflicting voices, including some pretty subversive voices. As Morris Dickstein observes, "[E]ach [side] needs the other to confirm its caricature of a monolithic canon freighted with a particular set of values that one camp upholds and the other condemns" (1991, A19). So in this conflict, as in the larger political arena, the far Right and far Left are tacit allies.

These canon wars often center on Shakespeare, which is my own field of specialization, and I am well aware that he has become the subject of a lot of pious cant by the Right. Whenever I hear politicians calling for the defense of Shakespeare from the barbarians on the Left, I want to ask them when they last saw or read one of his plays. The pious worshipers even have a shrine, the theater at Stratford-upon-Avon, visited each summer by masses of pilgrims—for many the visit is part of their packaged tour, and they do not seem to know or care what play they are seeing as long as they go through the ritual. Bernard Beckerman used to tell a story about the time he was seated in that theater next to a woman and her young son: the play was a comedy, and at one point the boy laughed, whereupon his mother turned to him and whispered, "Don't laugh; it's Shakespeare!" Leftists regularly attack this Bardolatry, but they are just as obsessed with the Bard; indeed, their flood of what they call "interventions" against him has actually enhanced his iconic status, and their approach to his plays is usually as grim and prim as the rightists'. Kathleen McLuskie, for example, warns us not to feel sympathy for King Lear, since doing so endorses the play's patriarchal ideology (1994, 100). In other words, Don't cry, it's Shakespeare! In this conflict neither the Right nor the Left can get emotionally involved in or enjoy his plays, which would be a distraction and would prevent them from constructing him as the symbolic saint or demon who provides the site of their conflict.

Moreover, this conflict requires both the far Right and far Left to assume that the canon is not only the embodiment of a single set of values but is also a single, unchanging list of great works. Again they are both wrong. We do not have a single canon but several different and overlapping ones—the pedagogical canon that is taught in schools, the critical canon that we discuss in our publications, the cultural canon that educated people are supposed to know, and more specialized canons for more specific groups or purposes.[9] And all these canons are constantly changing as works are added or dropped, or move from the center to the periphery or the reverse. Nor are they limited to great works of art. I remember taking a course in early American literature in which we read, among other things, William Byrd's *The History of the Dividing Line* and Philip Freneau's poem "On Mr. Paine's *Rights of Man,*" which could not by the wildest stretch of hyperbole be called great art, although they are in many of the college anthologies and therefore are part of the pedagogical canon. They are included for their historical rather than their aesthetic value and also, quite frankly, because this period did not produce enough great works to fill a semester course.

The canon, then, is not a sacred, immutable list of works chosen solely on the basis of sacred, immutable standards of merit, as the Right maintains. But the fact that the Right is wrong does not mean that the Left is right in attacking the canon as an arbitrary list that is chosen solely on political grounds and therefore should be abolished. That is all-or-nothing-ism. The canon is obviously based on some standards of merit, even though these change through time and are often mixed with other considerations. In fact, leftists acknowledge the existence of these standards when they claim that the works of women or minorities are *unfairly* excluded from the canon, since the very idea of fairness implies an impartial standard. Moreover, they argue for the inclusion, not of just any works from these neglected groups, but of specific works that they insist are at least as worthy as those already in the canon. And the authors in these neglected groups also clearly need the canon, for if it were abolished they would have no standards on which to be judged and no goal for their aspirations.

Closely related to this war over the canon is the dispute about the universality of the canonized works. Here again the polarized sides take diametrically opposite positions: rightists insist that great literature completely transcends the particularities of its time and place and can be universally understood and appreciated, while leftists insist that it is completely bound to its own historically specific culture and that anyone who thinks otherwise is guilty of essentializing human nature. (I should explain that to leftists essentialism is a crime only slightly less heinous than fascism.) And again both sides are wrong. No work of art, no matter how great it may be, is really universal in the sense that it can be understood and appreciated by all people in all times and places. Those who think that Shakespeare is universal in this sense should read the hilarious report of the anthropologist Laura Bohannan (1967), who was doing fieldwork with the Tiv tribe in West Africa and decided one day to prove that *Hamlet* is universally intelligible by recounting its plot to the tribal elders. She soon discovers that they do not comprehend crucial aspects of the plot that seem obvious to her or that they reinterpret them in terms of their own culture, with some very strange results. They cannot see why Hamlet is distressed by his mother's remarriage, since, as they explain to her, a widow must remarry as soon as possible in order to have a man to tend the family farm. They do not understand why he is concerned about what will happen if he kills Claudius at prayer, for they have no conception of an afterlife. But they are shocked that he would even consider killing Claudius, because, they tell her, no man may attack his senior relatives—he should appeal to his father's agemates, who could take revenge, but he cannot. The climax of her problems comes with Ophelia's drowning. They insist that only witches can make people drown, since water itself cannot hurt anyone, and that the witch here must be Laertes. One elder even figures out Laertes' motive: he needs money to pay his gambling debts in Paris and drowned Ophelia so he could sell her body to a medicine man for making charms. And when she gets to the fight between Hamlet and Laertes in Ophelia's grave, this elder seizes on it as a confirmation of his new close reading: Hamlet, he says, wants to prevent Laertes from selling Ophelia's body because the chief's son must not let another man grow too rich and powerful. At this point she gave up her attempt to prove that *Hamlet* is universally intelligible.

However, this demonstration that the play is not completely universal, as the Right maintains, does not demonstrate that it is completely bound to its time and place, as the Left maintains. For *we* can still comprehend it, and the explanation of this depends, not on assumptions about essential human nature, but on the fact that our culture, unlike that of the Tiv people, descended directly from the culture of early modern England. There have obviously been changes—we do not have absolute monarchs or believe in ghosts, for instance—but we can still understand these things, sometimes with a little historical reconstruction. More important, we understand how to respond to the plot and therefore can get emotionally engaged in it, since our feelings about human relationships are still relatively close to those that Shakespeare must have counted on in his audience. Laura Bohannan proves this point in the process of proving that the play is not universal, because her surprise at the failure of the tribal elders to understand things that seemed so obvious shows that Shakespeare still speaks to her, as he clearly does to those leftist critics mentioned earlier who attack his plays and warn us not to feel sympathy for his heroes. That warning makes sense only if they themselves can understand and respond to the plays, and so it contradicts their claim that the plays are completely bound to a specific time and place. I believe that this conclusion applies to all literary works of the past; they are not universal, but they can often transcend their particular cultural moment, depending on the distance between that culture and the reader's, and also upon the work itself: for example, I think that Shakespeare's tragedies are more accessible to us than those of John Fletcher, which seem more closely tied to specific cultural codes of his time. Therefore, in this dispute about the universality of literature the all-or-nothing stances of the far Right and the far Left are both wrong.

This is also true of the current dispute over the role of the author. Here once more the polarized sides take opposite extreme positions: rightists tend to regard authors as solitary geniuses who freely express their insights about life, which therefore constitute the meaning of their texts; but Catherine Belsey, speaking from the Left, asserts that, because of the work of Barthes, Lacan, Althusser, Derrida, and others, this conception of an autonomous author as the source of meaning has been "put in question" (1980, 2–3), which of course means it has been put *out* of the question, resulting in what is now called "The Death of the Author." This dispute has an obvious bearing on literary criticism, especially on intentionalist interpretation, but it reflects a more general and more overtly political conflict about the nature of the individual agent or subject. The far Right insists that the subject is completely unified, autonomous, and free, while the far Left rejects this idea as a mystification produced by bourgeois "humanist" ideology and insists instead that the subject is "interpellated" into, and hence is determined by, this ideology and riven by its contradictions.

On the question of the unity of the subject, both of these extreme views are wrong. Our consciousness is not wholly unified; we all harbor conflicting impulses and contradictory ideas. But that does not mean that we are without any unity, because all normal people have powerful integrative mechanisms that enable them to think and to act in a more or less coherent manner—if they cannot, they are put away in institutions. And even though our consciousness obviously changes through time, we feel that the person we are today is in a crucial sense unified with the person we remember being many years ago. We also feel this way about other people. In the recent controversy about Paul de Man, all the controverters, including a number of critics who in theory deny the unity of the subject, assumed that the author of those articles written in occupied Belgium and the Yale professor, although differing in many respects, were basically the same person. If they did not assume that, there would have been no controversy. Therefore the unity of the subject is not an all-or-nothing proposition.

This also applies to the subject's autonomy or freedom. The rightist idea of absolute autonomy and freedom is an illusion, because we all operate under many external and internal constraints. But it does not follow that we are not free, as the leftists maintain. In fact, to maintain this position they must assume the right-wing absolutist definition, and then argue that anything falling short it, such as "bourgeois democracy," is not real freedom.[10] But human freedom, like human unity, is not all-or-nothing, since it is always limited. At this moment I am free to make several choices— I can choose, for instance, to shut down my computer and watch TV. I choose not to, but my choices are limited by constraints that I cannot choose: I cannot choose to walk through a wall or to write in Urdu, since I do not know it. And this is true of all free choices, which are always made within unchosen conditions. That is what freedom means. If it were possible to choose all the conditions under which we choose, we would not be free— we would be paralyzed. But it is not possible, as Marx explains in his famous statement that "men make their own history, but they do not make it just as they please; they do not make it under circumstances chosen by themselves" (1959, 320), which is just what I am arguing. The new poststructuralist Marxists forget Marx's first clause—"men make their own history"— when they deny any freedom or autonomy to the subject, which would also deny Marx's and their own political agenda. There is no point in calling on workers of the world to unite if those workers are not agents who have enough autonomy and freedom to choose whether or not to heed this call.

The application of this dispute to literary criticism turns on the role of the author, who is of course a subject. If my argument about the subject is correct, then we must reject both the rightist view of authors as solitary geniuses who are completely free to express any meaning they like in their texts, and the leftist view of them as completely inscribed by the dominant ideology and therefore irrelevant to the meaning of their texts. Obviously Shakespeare and his fellow dramatists were not completely free—they were constrained by the censorship and theatrical conventions and the intellectual horizons of their day. But within these constraints they must have had a considerable degree of freedom, or else their plays would all be the same. The fact that their plays are not the same proves the relevance of authorial intention and refutes the leftist argument that the author did not have sufficient autonomy or freedom to be a source of meaning. Leftists often advance a second argument against intentionalist interpretation by claiming that we cannot recover the author's intention. But we all do this many times every day, whenever we are at the receiving end of a verbal message: from the words coming at us we try to infer the sender's intended meaning, and we are usually successful, which is why communication is possible.

Moreover, leftist critics never apply these two arguments against intentionalist interpretation to their own writing. As M. H. Abrams points out (1995, 34–36), they believe that when *they* are authors, they have enough autonomy and unity to be the source of meaning of their words and that their meaning can easily be recovered by readers, for they get angry when this does not happen and complain that they have been misinterpreted. But if their case against intentionalism is correct, then their interpretation of their own words would be no more valid than anyone else's interpretation of them, and there would be no such thing as misinterpretation. Their complaints, therefore, demonstrate that they do not really believe their anti-intentionalist argument. This is generally true of leftists who voice these theoretical objections to intentionalism; their own practice shows that literature can be interpreted in terms of authorial intention. But this does not mean that literature *must* be interpreted in this way, that it is the only valid approach, as some rightists assert. For the literary text cannot tell us how we should look at it, so it follows that there will be several other valid interpretive approaches. That, in fact, is a possible basis of critical pluralism, although there are other bases as well, because if one is really a pluralist, one should be pluralistic about one's pluralisms. I believe that this critical pluralism works against the polarization I have been describing and is the best antidote for it, but that would require a separate argument.[11]

I believe it would also be possible to show that in some of the other current disputes on critical issues the same polarizing dynamic pushes the two opposing sides into extreme and untenable positions. Even the division into two opposing sides is itself, of course, a result of this dynamic. Although I have examined these disputes in terms of political polarization, it would be naive to assume that this is the only factor involved. There is also a generational polarization; much of the heat in recent attacks on the new approaches is fueled by geriatric rage and expresses a nostalgic yearning for the Good Old Days and a fear of innovation, which is the disease of age. And the heated attacks on the old approaches often reflect the junior faculty's resentment of the senior faculty and refusal to admit that they have any redeeming qualities, which is the disease of youth. But even though these psychological factors contribute to it, as they did to the earlier conflict between historical scholars and New Critics, the present polarization of our discipline is fought out primarily in political terms and therefore is much more ferocious, since what is supposed to be at stake is the future, not merely of literary criticism, but of humanity itself.

This political formulation of the issues at stake is also responsible for another tendency of polarization that I noted at the outset—the attempts by the far Right and far Left to silence any opposition. In fact, each extreme regularly accuses the other of McCarthyism,[12] and for once they are both right. Although there are honorable exceptions, this intolerance is the general rule, since we saw that if you disagree with a polarizer you are not merely wrong but evil; you are the enemy, one of *them*, and hence must be prevented from corrupting the true believers. The milder form of this tendency is found in the tactics adopted by both extremes to ignore, dismiss, or even ostracize those who differ from them. Leftists complain, correctly, of these tactics on the Right, but they can be just as guilty: Michael Sprinker, for example, advises the people on his side not to answer adverse criticism (1991, 127), and Ivo Kamps reports that some feminist critics refused to contribute to his anthology, which included an essay of mine, because they did not want "to lend credence to Levin's arguments by engaging them" (1991a, 11). The result is an increasing isolation of the two extremes; each one now inhabits its own sealed-off discursive space where partisans only talk to and listen to each other. We even have journals that only publish essays by one side and are only read by adherents of that side, so the authors are preaching to the already converted, which means that they never have to defend their views, and that their readers never have to encounter any opposing views.

There are some rightists and leftists, moreover, who would like to go beyond ignoring the enemy's opinions and actually want to suppress them. This urge is not surprising, since neither extreme really believes in political pluralism, wherein the competition of different views is encouraged on the assumption that no one has a monopoly on the truth. Both the far Right and the far Left think that they have such a monopoly and therefore they oppose pluralism, even though they are its beneficiaries, because they see it as a trick by the enemy to co-opt or contain them.[13] Consequently, neither extreme supports the necessary conditions for pluralism—freedom of speech and the press and academic freedom—except, of course, for itself. Thus they both attack liberal organizations such as the American Civil Liberties Union for defending these freedoms for their enemies; rightists see it as a communist front, and leftists claim that it is complicit with sexism or racism. Elements of the far Right and far Left have even ganged up on it because of its stand against censoring pornography.[14]

This has also been the fate of *PMLA,* because, unlike the partisan journals I just mentioned, it does not side with either camp and remains open to all approaches. I have heard people insist that it has been taken over by the Left, and I know some who resigned from the MLA for this reason; but when it published Edward Pechter's critique (1987) of the New Historicism, Michael Cohen said that "it was hardly a surprise to find a reactionary article in that journal" (1988, 38), and Michael Sprinker dismissed it as belonging to *them* on the Right: "Let them have *PMLA,* if they want it" (1991, 127). It was also attacked by the critics I cited at the outset who protested against my essay "Feminist Thematics." One of them insisted that the publication of this essay by *PMLA* was "political," since it is part of the backlash against feminism (Greene 1991, 26–29—presumably she thinks the appearance of many feminist essays in this journal was *not* political); and another compared its publication to "yelling 'fire' in a crowded theater" (Woodbridge 1991, 292), which conjures up a vision of hundreds of literary scholars gathering in one room to read their copies of *PMLA* and then all stampeding for the door when they come to my essay. People who drag in that crowded theater analogy almost always want to justify the suppression of some idea they dislike. Few academics today will come right out for censorship; they usually have a special excuse of this kind— they say that they are in favor of free speech, but it is the wrong time or the wrong place or the wrong something else. But underlying this attack on those who publish anything from the enemy camp is an all-or-nothing stance that is an extension of what I called the basic principle of polarization: not only are all those who are not with us against us, but also all those who are not completely *against them* must be completely *for them.* Neutrality or impartiality, like the intermediate political positions discussed earlier, are out of the question in the world constructed by the far Right and far Left as a Manichaean total war of Good against Evil. In such a world, as Sprinker insists, "the only real question . . . is: Which side are you on?" (1991, 116).

The "Statement of Principles" of the newly formed Teachers for a Democratic Culture (TDC) asserts that many rightists in the National Association of Scholars (NAS) present current critical debates "not as a legitimate conflict in which reasonable disagreement is possible, but as a simple choice between civilization and barbarism" (Graff and Jay 1991, 1). That is true, but it fails to note that many leftists also deny the legitimacy of these debates by presenting them as simple choices, not between civilization and barbarism (which are the rightist code words for Good and Evil), but between the oppressed and their oppressors (which are the leftist code words). Unless it recognizes and opposes this tendency on the Left as well as the

Right, TDC is in danger of becoming a mirror image of NAS and will only increase our polarization instead of promoting a real dialogue that would benefit everyone. For even though I have been criticizing the far Right and the far Left, I do not want to leave the impression that I believe they are completely wrong about everything, which is most unlikely. There probably are useful things they could teach the rest of us (and even each other), as well as things they could learn from us (and from each other), yet this cannot happen until they begin to treat those who differ from them, not as the evil enemy, but as intelligent and well-meaning, though mistaken, colleagues who share some of their concerns. This certainly would not mean the end of disagreements in our discipline, which is neither possible nor desirable; but it would mean that the arguments advanced in these disagreements could be viewed, not as weapons in a war that are to be judged in terms of which side they are on, but as contributions to a dialogue to be judged in terms of their evidence and their logic, which I assume is what the TDC statement means by "reasonable disagreement." My hope is that the two polarized extremes will abandon their war and join this dialogue, and so my final message to them is not Mercutio's curse, "A plague o' both your houses," but the biblical benediction that I am adapting as a plea: Peace unto both your houses.

Notes

Introduction

1. Some of them oppose answering my arguments—see Kamps 1991a, 11, and Sprinker's advice to "stop wasting our time" by responding (1991, 127), which he ignored by writing this response.

2. One reason for selecting these particular responses is that they come from practitioners of the three major approaches that I deal with in this collection—the one in chapter 1 is from feminists, the two in chapter 2 are from Marxists, and the one in chapter 3 is from a New Historicist. I do not claim, however, that they are representative of these approaches.

3. An even sillier example of this tactic appears in a response by Neilson and Meyerson, not included in this collection, which claims that because I oppose Marxism I believe that "we live in the best of all possible worlds" (1998, 284, 286).

4. Several reviews of the book objected that because of this practice it was impossible for readers to check the correctness of my quotations or my interpretation of them, which is one reason that I abandoned it in these later essays.

5. I discuss this tendency in "Interdisciplinarity." In several essays omitted from this collection (1996, 1998a, 1998c, 1998d, 2001) I address some of this criticism that is devoted entirely to the politics of our day and does not even pretend to be about literature.

6. There are important differences, as well as similarities, between the old and the new historical criticism, which I discuss in "Historicizing," but they are not relevant here.

7. One explanation of this failure is that some of these critics do not proceed a posteriori from the effects to induce the cause, but begin with an a priori conception of what the cause must be.

8. These two qualifications are necessary because many of the old New Critics, who were also formalists, made the mistake of claiming that they were explicating the work "in itself" (simply "the words on the page," as they said) and that it expressed "universal truths."

9. I assemble some of this evidence in "Unthinkable Thoughts."

10. These are the first four of the six parts of tragedy listed in *Poetics* vi; the remaining two, song and spectacle, apply only to performances.

11. For a good example of this, see Maclean 1952.

12. Fuller 2000/1 lists fifty-four of these summer festivals in the United States and Canada.

13. Another approach to Shakespeare that is very well suited to undergraduate instruction is performance criticism, which I do not discuss in these essays. As far as I can

tell, most performance critics are intentionalists and mimeticists; certainly most directors and actors try to formulate and to convey a coherent conception of the overall meaning of the play they are producing and of the motivation of its characters.

14. Compare Coyle's complaint that reading Shakespeare "through the lens of character . . . offers the modern reader nothing" (1996, 9).

15. My "Reply to Michael Bristol and Gayle Greene" (1991), which is not included in this collection, ends with a more extended appreciation of feminist criticism. I should add here that, although I reject Freudianism and Marxism as pseudosciences, this certainly does not mean that I think Freud and Marx were always wrong. They were both brilliant men who opened up some promising paths for investigating the behavior of individuals and societies.

16. In "Interdisciplinarity" I suggest some reasons that may help to account for the continued appeal of Marxism and Freudianism in literary criticism.

CHAPTER 1. FEMINIST THEMATICS

This essay was published in *PMLA* 103 (1988): 125–38, and the Forum letter and reply in *PMLA* 104 (1989): 77–79.

1. For an account of the first phase see Neely 1981/2, 6–7, and for some examples, see Garner 1976 on Desdemona, Fitz 1977 on Cleopatra, and Smith 1980 on Gertrude; this phase is also a major concern of Dash 1981.

2. See, for example, Neely 1981/2, 4–9; Bamber 1982, chap. 1; Jardine 1983, 1–6; McLuskie 1994, 88–92; and the reviews of French's book in Erickson 1981/2 and Greene 1983.

3. Probably the two most important studies excluded for this reason are Bamber 1982 and Belsey 1985b.

4. See, for example, Neely 1985, 107–8, and French 1981, 241.

5. Similarly, both Dash (1981) and Greene (1995) argue that the sufferings of Othello and Desdemona are caused by the conventional sex roles imposed on them by society (see their statements of the theme quoted above). This is also Dreher's thesis, although she only deals with Desdemona, whose "tragic fate stems from slavish conformity . . . to the traditional norm for feminine behavior," showing that "Shakespeare repudiates" this norm defined by "patriarchal expectations" (1986, 93, 76, 92).

6. A number of the critics comment on this; see especially the witty account of the fates of Portia, Beatrice, and Rosalind in Park 1980.

7. Note the language of patriarchy: "What, goodman boy? . . . you'll be the man? . . . You are a saucy boy" (1.5.77–83). Kahn never deals with this episode and only refers to it once indirectly (1981, 95).

8. Erickson quotes this response in a note but says it "is too slender a thread" to exonerate Macduff from "the general pattern of distorted masculinity," shown in "his excessive violence in decapitating Macbeth" (1985a, 192). Kimbrough, however, regards it as "one of those great Shakespearean moments" because it points to "androgyny," which is Shakespeare's solution (and Kimbrough's) to the thematic "war between gender concepts" (1983, 176, 178). But he never mentions Macduff's decapitation of Macbeth, which is not very androgynous.

9. Like Berger (1982) and Neely (1985), Leverenz works very hard to score points against all the men. He tells us that Hamlet Senior's "peacetime behavior seems to have

been primarily sleeping on the job" (because of the Ghost's reference to naps) and that the former king was "more like Claudius than the Ghost can dare admit"; that when Laertes says to Ophelia, "Do not sleep, / But let me hear from you" (1.3.3–4), he means that "the body's natural desire to sleep must yield to the role of always-attentive sister"; and that even the grave diggers are "mini-Claudiuses" (1980, 117–18, 122).

10. It would take quite a bit of stretching, for instance, to connect the killing of Lady Macduff, which is Macbeth's only "violence against women," with any feeling he has about "vulnerability in relation to women."

11. Compare Greene's comment on this play: "In the comedies and romances, and in *Antony and Cleopatra*, women make themselves heard, but part of what is tragic about the tragic world here is that they do not. . . . [Emilia] is a woman capable of challenging male prerogatives and assumptions, who might be able to bring about a comic resolution" (1995, 59). Leverenz (1980), whose essay inspired Wilt (1981/2), avoids her difficulty with Ophelia by inventing a woman within Hamlet whom he should listen to but does not, so that his tragedy exemplifies the same thematic lesson.

12. See the comments of Camillo in 1.2, Antigonus and the unnamed lord in 2.1, and Dion and Cleomenes in 3.1. (Antigonus's view has changed in 3.3 because of his misinterpreted dream.)

13. In her survey, Neely criticizes the tendency of some feminists "to employ what might be called reverse sexism, attacking and stereotyping male characters" (1981/2, 4; see also 7).

14. Novy is unusual in acknowledging some embarrassment about this: "There is so much sympathy with Lear at the end that it seems cold to turn from feeling with him to any further analysis of the play in terms of sex-role behavior, but it is worth noting that part of the effect of the play is to impress on us the suffering created by these behavior patterns [imposed by patriarchy] and then to show us how inadequate they are" (1984, 162). She, Dash (1981), and Kimbrough (1983) can pity the hero because their themes, we saw, do not require an attack on him. But for McLuskie, who is not in this group (see note 20), any pity for Lear is a temptation that feminists must *resist*, since it "endorses" the play's "patriarchal" ideology (1994, 100, 102).

15. According to Erickson, for example, in their last scenes Othello exhibits a "powerful need for self-deception," Lear a "continuing self-evasion," and Malcolm's thanes an "escapist belief in an entirely masculine social order"; and Hamlet's "disturbed attitude toward female sexuality is neither squarely faced nor transformed and resolved." Antony is the honorable exception, because he finally "rejects the definition of masculinity" entailed in his soldier identity (1985a, 100, 115, 122, 78, 140).

16. See Novy 1984, 200–201; French 1981, 77; and Erickson 1985a, 116, 171–72. Similarly, some of the older thematists viewed Shakespeare's development as a continuous exploration of the one central theme that they found in all his plays.

17. The only apparent exception I noted is Gohlke, who begins by stating that she is "abandon[ing] a strictly intentionalist position"; yet she later says the tragedies "may be viewed as one vast commentary" on male attitudes, which they "examine" with "acute attention" (1980, 150, 161, 163). One of the few discussions of the problem among this group of critics is in Erickson 1985b; he argues that we must distinguish our attitude toward the treatment of gender in a play from Shakespeare's (as he does in 1985a, 36–37, 169–70, 182), but he does not address the prior question of how we know this treatment of gender is Shakespeare's subject.

18. For some examples, see Kahn on *The Taming of the Shrew* (1981, 114–17), Riefer on *Measure for Measure* (1984, 167–69), and Leininger on *The Tempest* (1980, 291–92).

19. Perhaps Wheeler might claim that Shakespeare deliberately misled his audience in order to test or educate them. This was a common rationale of the older ironic readings (see Levin 1979, 138–42), which reappears in Berger 1982 and Snow 1980.

20. This is the line taken by Jardine 1983, Belsey 1985b, McLuskie 1994, and a few other feminist critics, most of them British and associated with cultural materialism. They are not thematic (which is why I have excluded them) and so avoid some of the problems discussed here.

21. See Bamber's perceptive discussion of this point (1982, 14–16). Hamlet does not begin the play in this "normal" state, because of Gertrude's remarriage, but before that he was courting Ophelia. The only real exception is Timon, but he is seldom cited by these critics, perhaps because his misanthropy is so much stronger than his misogyny.

22. Dickes's "Desdemona: An Innocent Victim?" appeared in *American Imago* (1970); but we do not need to read it to find the answer to his titular question, for in the articles of that journal no one is ever innocent, except the authors of the articles. (The same issue includes "Desdemona's Guilt" by Stephen Reid.) French, like Snow, claims that Desdemona is "shown as near-ideal" since she "has no sexual guilt," is "whole," and so on (1981, 216–17).

Chapter 2. Bardicide

This essay was published in *PMLA* 105 (1990): 491–504, and the Forum letters and replies in *PMLA* 106 (1991): 314–16, 1172–74.

1. Many other terms are treated in this way, since a favorite strategy of these discourses is refutation by quotation marks, which I discuss in "Politicized Language." In Kavanagh 1985 these marks enclose not only "Shakespeare" but also "author," "create," "literature," "consciousness," "free," "real," "truth," etc.; and in Barker and Hulme 1985 they enclose "intentionality," "sources," "fact," "universal," and "works of art." See also note 11.

2. The cultural materialists could be called neo-Marxists, since they too are revisionist; but we will see that this revision (at least as it affects their readings) is much closer to the original, orthodox doctrine than is that of the neo-Freudians. Since I recently encountered some misunderstanding on this score, I want to make it clear that I am *not* trying to deal with any of these approaches as a whole; I am only concerned with the specific set of practices exemplified by the readings discussed here. I therefore exclude all readings within these approaches that adopt a "strong" intentionalist position.

3. Marxists also find fantasies in Shakespeare, which are also always bad but are political rather than sexual—Dollimore and Sinfield say that *Henry V* presents "the fantasy of establishing ideological unity" (1985, 225), and Dollimore calls the ending of *Measure for Measure* a "reactionary fantasy" (1994b, 84).

4. I discuss some feminist readings of this type in "Feminist Thematics."

5. This is Dollimore's point when he complains that "surprisingly critics have generally taken [the rulers of Vienna] at their word" that the real problem is sexual license (1994b, 72). Evans has it both ways: he claims that "the Shakespearean text" usually "displaces [Renaissance] social contradictions" and that formalist/humanist critics "attempt to displace" these "fundamental historical contradictions" in interpreting the plays (1986, 233, 244–45).

6. Howard 1986a, 30; Belsey 1980, 109. The same charge is made in Eagleton 1983, 81; Barker and Hulme 1985, 196–97; and Evans 1986, 249, 254.

7. The "vision" consists of one sentence of Bianca's (4.1.159–61). Murray feels no need to explain who did the concealing or why, although he makes no use of either the Marxist or the neo-Freudian rationale for concealment, which shows how automated the locution has become.

8. Dollimore is the only one to express any reservations about this practice: "Yet there is a limit to which the text can be said to incorporate those aspects of its historical moment of which it never speaks" (1994b, 85).

9. The titles of Orgel's essay, "Prospero's Wife" (1988), and of Kahn's, "The Absent Mother in *King Lear*" (1986), indicate the significance attached to these exclusions.

10. This passage is a good illustration of the locutions referred to in Erickson's remark quoted at the outset. Never before in the history of criticism have we owed so much activity to so few active verbs. We are not told who is supposed to be doing all this localizing, demonizing, displacing, projecting, hypostatizing, and reinterpreting, but presumably the play itself is responsible, since it makes the offer of ("allows") the scapegoating.

11. The second passage paraphrases Fredric Jameson, who applies this formula to all narratives and puts "solutions" in quotation marks (1981, 79). Brown similarly asserts the imaginariness of the resolution of *The Tempest* by adding these quotes whenever he mentions the play's "ending" or "close" (1994, 67–68).

12. Freud does not envision a final solution of our conflicts, but we saw that these critics are not orthodox Freudians. Cook is the only one who explicitly raises "the question of what might be an adequate 'feminine' alternative" to the play's masculine ethos (1995, 92), but she never answers it.

13. McLuskie is exceptional for her extensive and perceptive discussion of pleasure, but she comes to the same conclusion. She admits the "tragic power" of *King Lear* to engage our sympathy and thus to provide "aesthetic satisfaction" and acknowledges it is "a difficult pleasure to deny," yet she says we should deny it since it "endorses [the play's] ideological position" (1994, 98–100).

14. My favorite example comes (in two senses) from Snow, who claims that when Othello says, "Strumpet, I come" (5.1.33), "the language suggests that Desdemona is a 'strumpet' not so much because of her imagined infidelity as because of her sexual allure and the power it has to make him 'come'" (1980, 391).

15. To demonstrate the formulaic character of these statements I have confined the identification of their authors and of the plays to this note. They are (1) Howard on *Much Ado* (1987b, 172, 164), (2) Cook on *Much Ado* (1995, 100), (3) Belsey's summary of Pierre Macherey on the "classic realist text" (1980, 109), (4) Kavanagh on *King Lear* (1985, 159), (5) Newman on *The Taming of the Shrew* (1987b, 144), (6) Montrose on *A Midsummer Night's Dream* (1988, 44), (7) McLuskie on *King Lear* (1994, 106), (8) Dollimore and Sinfield on *Henry V* (1985, 211), and (9) Brown on *The Tempest* (1994, 66–67). Compare Belsey's conclusion that in the comedies, "even while it reaffirms patriarchy, . . . female transvestism challenges it precisely by unsettling the categories which legitimate it" (1985a, 180) and Howard's that, because of this transvestism, these "comedies reveal the constructed nature of gender definitions and distinctions even as they return women, at play's end, to their . . . places within the dominant patriarchal order" (1988, 436).

16. For other attempts to explain this, see Belsey 1980, 107, Brown 1994, 58; Evans 1986, 254; and Dollimore and Sinfield 1985, 215; and compare Brown's report that "recent important work on pastoral and amatory sonnet sequences has shown how such a rhetoric of love, charity and romance is always already involved in . . . power relations" (1994, 60).

17. See the passages quoted in "Artistic Unity", from Belsey 1980, Dollimore 1993,

Eagleton 1983, Barker and Hulme 1985, and Howard 1986a and 1987b on how these contradictions are "smoothed out" or "smoothed over," and so on, and how they "in reality" constitute the text.

18. The fact that there is no mother in either play is irrelevant: Kahn argues that "the absence of the mother points to her hidden presence" (1986, 36), and Sundelson uncovers one in Shylock, who "is more than just a castrating, punitive father; he is also a devouring mother" (1983, 87). We also saw that Orgel 1988, Adelman 1987, and Montrose 1988 find absent mothers in *The Tempest, Macbeth,* and *A Midsummer Night's Dream,* respectively, and I cite many more examples in "Interdisciplinarity."

19. See also Evans 1986, 263–64; Barker and Hulme 1985, 205; and Dollimore 1993, 271. (*Commitment* is now a code word for the politics of these critics; when Eagleton, on the dust jacket of Evans's book [1986], praises it for being "eloquently committed," he does not need to explain what it is committed *to*, since everyone inhabiting the discourse knows what this means. Another code word is *activist*, which seems to require no action beyond the writing of "activist criticism.") Non-Marxist feminists do not end their readings in this way, but they, of course, are actively committed to concrete political goals and have already achieved some significant results.

20. I discuss this ironic approach in Levin 1979, chap. 3.

21. See Dollimore 1994b, 72, 73, 76, 83, and Brown 1994, 58, 59, 60, 61, 64, 66, 67, to take just two of these essays, and also Howard's distinctions between the "surface" meaning and the "more subversive" meaning of the comic endings (1986a, 34) and between the "*apparent* threat" and the "real threat" to patriarchy in *Twelfth Night* (1988, 432).

22. See Brown 1994, 69; McLuskie 1994, 95; and Barker and Hulme 1985, 193, 205.

Chapter 3. Unthinkable Thoughts

This essay, along with Jonathan Goldberg's "Making Sense" and my reply to it, were published in *New Literary History* 21 (1990): 433–47, 457–62, 465–70, copyright © by the University of Virginia, and are reprinted by permission of the Johns Hopkins University Press.

1. There is a detailed comparison of the old and the new historical criticism in "Historicizing."

2. I list some of them in Levin 1979, 239, and join their attack in chap. 4.

3. There is a notable exception in Greenblatt's essay on *Othello* (1980, 248–50, 303–5), where his claim that excessive sexual pleasure in marriage was regarded as "sinful" is based on an old-fashioned parade of authorities, including St. Ambrose, St. Augustine, St. Jerome, Nicolaus of Ausimo, Jacobus Ungarelli, Juan Luis Vives, John Calvin, Samuel Hieron, Alexander Niccoles, William Perkins, John Rogers, and William Whately, with no evidence of how people at the time actually felt about it. We have good reason to believe that many of them had a much more positive view of marital sex; it is affirmed, for instance, in Juliet's epithalamium (3.2.1–31), although an older ideas-of-the-time critic, using the same kind of evidence and reasoning as Greenblatt, argues that Elizabethan audiences would have condemned her for this speech because she looks forward to the consummation of her marriage (Seward 1973, 130–32).

4. An early statement of this view appears in Barthes 1964, 125; see also R. Williams 1977, 46–47 (quoted in Kavanagh 1985, 147), and Belsey 1980, 126.

5. Shepherd also claims that "Elizabethan culture had no conception of 'homosexu-

ality' as a positive form of sexuality in its own right" (1986, 199), and Goldberg says there was "no recognition of homosexuality *per se*" (1991, 75).

6. Barker adds a qualification to "unthinkable": "Or at least no more conceivable than the absurd proposition that the arm could take the place of the spleen" (1984, 32).

7. I discuss this tactic in Levin 1979, 125–36.

8. Not all of them. Belsey sees that "the recognition of reality in fiction is primarily a matter of familiarity with the conventions used to depict a recognizable world" (1985b, 87), but this does not prevent her from using the conventions of the morality play to determine the medieval conception of selfhood (18); see also her statements under **Discovery No. 5.**

9. I supply the documentation for the following responses and assemble many more of the same kind in Levin 1980, 11–21. The spelling and punctuation of all quotations have been modernized.

10. Compare Shepherd's assertion that Hieronimo's "emotional speeches . . . present problems for the audience" because they "are highly patterned, noticeably rhetorical or remorselessly alliterative. . . . So even at the moments when the audience may look to be sharing the fullness of the unjustly treated father's emotion . . . there is the distancing effect" (1986, 167).

11. "But the art which employs words either in bare prose or in metres . . . happens up to the present day to have no name" (Aristotle 1973, 1.1447^{b}7–9). He is speaking of what is now the narrower sense of literature as fiction or "imaginative writing," but the point is the same. For a brief history of the concept of literature, see Wellek 1982, 3–18. In "(Re)thinking" I address the argument that we cannot think of something unless we have a word for it.

12. For examples of this reaction, see Jonson 1925–52, 9.13. The Shakespeare First Folio (published after his death) bears the more modest title, *Mr. William Shakespeares Comedies, Histories, & Tragedies*, but they are referred to as "works" in the epistle to the readers, Leonard Digges's commendatory poem, and the heading of the page listing the actors.

13. It reminds me of the two newborn infants placed in adjacent cribs in a hospital nursery: one turns to the other and says, "I'm a little boy, what are you?"; the second answers, "I don't know, how can you tell?"; whereupon the first lifts his coverlet, points downward, and explains, "Look, blue booties!"

14. If anyone really needs evidence of this, it can be found in *The Winter's Tale*, 2.2; *Henry VIII*, 5.1; and Middleton's *A Chaste Maid in Cheapside*, 2.2.

15. For evidence that some religious authorities of the time "regarded sodomy as the ultimate and most pervasive sexual perversion," and even "encourag[ed] prostitution to combat sodomy," see Hughes 1985, 165, 175–76.

16. Dollimore recognizes this when it suits his purpose. He insists that "the development in th[e] drama of character representation . . . is evidence less of Renaissance individualism than of an emergent realism" (1993, 175–76), because he wants individualism to be created later under bourgeois auspices; but elsewhere, as we saw, he uses changes in the mode of representing character as evidence for changes in the concept of the self. Fineman avoids this error by refusing to claim any direct connection between Shakespeare's "invention" of subjectivity in the sonnets and contemporary conceptions of the individual (1986, 46–47). For some less cautious attempts to locate (in various eras) the invention or discovery of our idea of selfhood, see Bloom 1998, Frondizi 1953, Gusdorf 1948, Hanning 1977, Izenberg 1992, Lyons 1978, Mascuch 1996, Morris 1987, Oppenheimer 1989, Snell 1953, Taylor 1989, Tripet 1967, and Van den Berg 1961.

17. The second historicist error he identifies is "the fallacy of the homogeneous past," which we found in these new historical critics as well as the old ones. He notes that these two fallacies often travel together, "since those who understand the sameness of individuals within a period do not very often perceive sameness among individuals across different periods" (Hirsch 1976, 38, 40).

18. Greenblatt acknowledges that another possible explanation of why this "unthinkable" modern concept of selfhood did not emerge at the trial might be "a self-evidence so deep and assured that the postulates quite literally go without saying" (1986a, 215). He never explains how it could have been articulated at the trial, or how it would figure in an equivalent case today.

19. He also claims that the discoveries "threaten" me, a tactic I discuss in "It's a Panic," appended to chapter 5.

20. Some of my remarks explicitly contradict his charge that I deny all change and difference: I said that Renaissance thought was "heterogeneous," that "attitudes toward gender have certainly changed," that "there obviously have been major changes in the representation of character," and that we have ideas that really "were unthinkable to people of the Renaissance."

21. He also gives me two ulterior motives that are meant to undercut my case against this discovery—that I was "offended" by the review where he announces it from the "very first sentence," and that I called it idiosyncratic because he "writes about sodomy." But I was not at all offended by his first sentence, which I agree with. And the link to sodomy is in his own head; I said the discovery "may be idiosyncratic" because he is the only one I could find who believes it, whereas all the others are affirmed by several critics.

22. Later this turns into the assertion that "for Downes, the best woman is a boy," which is quite a leap even for Goldberg.

23. In "Politicized Language" I discuss an extreme statement of this position in Rorty 1989.

Chapter 4. (Re)Thinking Unthinkable Thoughts

This essay was published in *New Literary History* 28 (1997): 525–37, copyright © by the University of Virginia, and is reprinted by permission of the Johns Hopkins University Press.

1. The performances of *Othello* are listed in Schneider 1979, 771–72.

2. Eagleton also claims that "for the theorists of antiquity, no . . . distinction between the ethical and the political was imaginable" (1994, 2); but Aristotle certainly imagines it in the *Ethics* and the *Politics*, and we find a sharp separation of ethics from politics—even a renunciation of public life—in some early Epicureans and Cynics.

3. I discuss this tendency in "Negative Evidence."

4. His qualified version is still not true; we have many medieval accounts, historical and fictional, of people rising from low stations and falling from high ones, which is what the Wheel of Fortune was all about. See also the definition of tragedy in Chaucer's "The Monk's Tale."

5. She also says that "all the other characters view as unthinkable" the marriage of Othello and Desdemona (Newman 1987a, 144), where she must mean "impossible," because they could not "view" it without thinking about it (even that is wrong—Cassio not only thought it was possible but abetted it [3.3.94–100]). This applies as well to Fish's

remark that "Milton would have found such a statement [about art] inconceivable" (1995, 31–32).

6. See Dollimore 1993, 271; and Belsey 1980, 3 and 1992, 37. Dutton suggests that the critics I cite merely "overstated their cases," since "the issue might not be what was unthinkable so much as what ideas carried most weight at the time" (1992, 224); but that is not their claim, and many of the ideas that they claim were "unthinkable" apparently *did* carry most weight at the time.

7. The phrase comes from Nietzsche and is used as the title of a book by Jameson (1972).

8. See Jackson 1991, chap. 6; Vickers 1993, chap. 1; and Tallis 1995.

9. Bennett and Kavanagh cite Williams's account (1977, 46–47) of when "literature" took on its current meaning, but they both ignore his statement that before then the word "poetry" was used.

10. De Grazia and Stallybrass point out this problem (1993, 263), but I may be more sensitive to it since I was once burned by an antedating (1983, 72), although it did not involve any unthinkable thoughts.

11. Some critics claim that "sodomy" covered more activities, although they disagree on which ones: Greenblatt says the Renaissance defined it in opposition to "the law of nature" that "bound sexual pleasure to procreation, and all sexual practices that did not further this end were sinful and hence prohibited" (1986b, 6), while Quilligan says "any sexual act that did not conduce to the lawful continuation of dynasty . . . would have been considered sodomy; the dividing line was not between 'natural' and 'unnatural' activity but between that which was dynastically significant and that which was not" (1993, 26). They never explain why nonprocreative or dynastically nonsignificant heterosexual relations are not mentioned in the sodomy laws.

12. I quote from Mager 1994, 142. There is an even sharper separation of male homosexuality from bestiality in Lev. 20:13, 15–16, and earlier in 18:22–23. Frantzen notes that in the Middle English poem *Cleanness* we find a "narrowing of the definition of sodomy to male homosexual anal intercourse" (1996, 451).

13. Some of these critics can admit this when they need to: Dollimore says "the Renaissance possessed a sophisticated concept of ideology if not the word" (1993, 18).

14. Pinker demolishes it in 1994, 55–67. See also Hill 1990, 97–98, where he refutes Pocock's claim that "men cannot do what they have no means of saying they have done" (1972/3, 122).

15. I quote from Belsey 1980, 5.

16. Although many of these critics are not Marxists, this belief seems to be related to the distinction made by older Marxists between "science" (where they were) and "ideology" (where everyone else was). Psychoanalysts are supposed to derive their special power from a laying on of hands—the "training analysis"—that descends from Freud, who analyzed and anointed himself.

17. Barker 1984, 15, 68; Evans 1986, 252–54; Holderness 1985, 22–23, 38; Howard 1987a, 323, 363. In "Bashing" I treated this as the only cause, which I now see was wrong.

18. They credit the discovery to Goldberg (see the quotation above in my discussion of epistemes), but it is also announced by other critics I cite in "Unthinkable Thoughts."

19. Some older historical critics had a similar stake in exaggerating the difference between Renaissance and modern attitudes toward revenge, love, filial obedience, and so on.

20. I discuss this term in "Politicized Language."

Chapter 5. Bashing the Bourgeois Subject

This essay and "It's a Panic" were published in *Textual Practice* 3 (1989): 76–86 and 4 (1990): 101–2, respectively, and are reprinted by permission of Taylor and Francis, Ltd. The web site address of the journal is http://www.tandf.co.uk. In "It's a Panic" I am replying to Belsey 1989, which is her response to "Bashing the Bourgeois Subject."

1. See the section on Discovery No. 5 in "Unthinkable Thoughts." I should explain that in the following discussion of the BHS I use the masculine pronoun, since the bashers themselves insist that it is conceived by and as a man (see especially the quotation from Moi below), although they never tell us how women conceive of themselves under BHSdom.

2. This is King Henry's advice to Hal (both presumably pre-BHSes) in *2 Henry IV*, 4.5.213–14.

3. See Barker 1984, 16, 68; Belsey 1992, 39, 44; Evans 1986, 83, 253; Holderness 1985, 22–23.

4. Goldberg's main target is Bamber's book (1982). Greenblatt, similarly, criticizes Brown's book (1986) for failing to "historicize" the idea of lesbianism, which he claims did not exist in the Renaissance (1986b, 6).

5. Erickson makes a similar point about the New Historicists' use of the terms "unhistorical" and "ahistorical" in controversies, but he suggests that Greenblatt's "invocation of the name 'historicism'" to "rule sexuality out of bounds" in criticizing Brown "covers an unacknowledged political move" (1987, 331). I cannot tell what it is, unless antagonizing feminist critics (which Goldberg also does in his essay) is political; but this may be another difference between the New Historicists and the cultural materialists, who often try to co-opt feminism.

6. See Stephenson 1986 and, for a more sophisticated version, Lerner 1986.

7. See Evans 1986, 252, and Belsey 1985b, 223, where she rejects "the construction of lost Utopias" and what she calls "its counterpart, the Whig interpretation of history" as "the affirmation of progress." These two views of history seem to be opposites, but she brackets them together as "characteristic of liberal humanism" since both are non-Marxist, which is another example of the Marxist difficulty in counting past two.

8. Compare Lentricchia's call for "a redemptive project" that would "make us whole again" (1983, 151).

9. This is Brecht's view, which he agrees with.

10. In her book's final chapter, titled "Changing the Present," she says, "The history of the subject in the sixteenth and seventeenth centuries indicates . . . radical discontinuities. On this reading the past affirms the possibility (the inevitability?) of change" (Belsey 1985b, 223).

11. See the quotations from Freud 1975 and Jones 1954 in "Negative Evidence."

12. The new Marxists invoke the unconscious when it serves their purpose, as in Jameson 1981.

Chapter 6. Son of Bashing

This essay was published in *Textual Practice* 6 (1992): 264–70, and is reprinted by permission of Taylor and Francis, Ltd.

1. I considered calling it the "child" or "daughter" of the "Bashing" essay but settled

on "son" to foreground the BHS's notorious proclivity for phallocentrism, patriarchy, and primogeniture.

2. He is quoting in part from Sharp 1980, 109.

3. See the statements cited in "Bashing" and also those in the section on "Politicizing Theory" in "Interdisciplinarity."

4. Delany, a prepoststructuralist Marxist, discusses this point (1995, 21–22).

5. See Belsey 1980, 7, 14, 19, 20, 26, 28, 32; Dollimore 1993, 259; Evans 1986, 34, 246; Kavanagh 1985, 163, 234; and Goldberg's response in chapter 3.

6. I discuss this tendency, with more examples, in "Silence is Consent" and "Polarization."

7. He acknowledges that "teaching Shakespeare's plays and writing books about them is unlikely" to achieve this, "but it is a point for intervention" (Sinfield 1994b, 178).

8. I discuss these terms in "Politicized Language."

9. The standard move of the new Marxists for explaining this away is to claim that these countries are not really socialist—see my reply to FitzGerald in chapter 2.

Chapter 7. Negative Evidence

This essay was published in *Studies in Philology* 92 (1995): 383–410, copyright © by the University of North Carolina Press, and is reprinted by permission of the publisher.

1. This is my free translation of the Latin in *Novum Organum*. He also cites this remark in *The Advancement of Learning* (Bacon 1915, 132–33). See the similar remark in Cicero (1956, 3.37.89), attributed to Diagoras of Melos, called the Atheist. Diogenes Laertius gives it to Diogenes the Cynic, but adds that some credit Diagoras (1958, 6.2.59).

2. See the critiques of these studies in Oliphant 1929, Fogel 1959, and Schoenbaum 1966. Today computerized attribution studies use much more sophisticated techniques and attempt to compare the stylistic habits of all possible authors.

3. See the parody of this approach in Maxwell 1930; he proves that Falstaff is Robert Greene.

4. For anti-Stratfordians the same function is served by the real author's need to conceal his identity, so any negative evidence (i.e., evidence that "Shake-speare" wrote the plays, or that their candidate did not) is explained as a result of the conspiracy required for concealment, and thus becomes positive evidence of the need for it.

5. Wickham, moreover, finds that *King Lear* is not about either of Winstanley's two topicalities but about King James's attempt to unify England and Scotland.

6. I published a few such discoveries in my youth, but see my critique in Levin 1998b.

7. I discuss this approach in Levin 1979, chap. 2.

8. This point is developed, with several examples, in "Historicizing."

9. A few years earlier Goldberg said that "no plays were written for court performance" and that "we know too little about the status of Shakespeare's texts to be able to determine that the one we have [in this case, *Measure for Measure*] is a court revision" (1983a, 231–32).

10. See also the hedged identifications quoted in "Historicizing" from Orgel's reading of *The Tempest* (1988), Wynne-Davies's reading of *Titus Andronicus* (1991), Erickson's reading of *Hamlet* (1991), and Greenblatt's reading of *King Lear* (1988a).

270   NOTES TO CHAPTER SEVEN

11. They include Armado, Gratiano, Touchstone, Orsino, and Sir Toby Belch; Lorenzo and Fenton marry down socially but up financially.

12. Many old topicalists start with similar assumptions: Winstanley says that Renaissance audiences expected plays to be about some current issue, which is why they were interested in them (1922, 3, 9, 18, 25—she does not ask why modern audiences would be interested in them); and Wickham claims that the "privileged status" of Shakespeare's company as the King's Men required them to produce "commissioned work" for and about the king (1973, 34–35).

13. The status of their canonical texts can be seen in Bristol's defense of his position on the ground that he "return[ed] to . . . the Marxist classics" (1991, 43). No biologist today would think of returning to the classic texts of Darwin to defend her position on evolution.

14. These sects are also usually named for their founders: Marxism has produced Stalinists, Trotskyites (who resplit into Shachtmanites and Cannonites), Maoists, DeLeonites (my old home), etc., and Freudians became Adlerians, Jungians, Horneyites, Rankians, and Reichians.

15. See also Jones's assertion that "the prevailing aversion from psychological [i.e., Freudian] analysis" of literature is "one more illustration of the constant resistance that man displays against any danger he may be in of apprehending his inner nature" (1954, 15), and Sprinker's that people who criticize Marxist analysis of literature feel "threatened and scared by us" (1991, 127). I discuss this tactic in "It's a Panic," appended to chapter 5. Marxists also dismiss adverse criticism by labeling it McCarthyism, red-baiting, or Cold Warism—see Hirschkop and Shepherd 1994, 116; Sprinker 1991, 125; and FitzGerald's Forum letter in chapter 2.

16. See Grünbaum 1984, 127–28, 209–14; Crews 1986, 81–86; and the devastating feminist critique in Weisstein 1970, 209–12.

17. See the quotation from Marmor 1962 in "Interdisciplinarity."

18. I cite the readings that produce all these mother figures in "Interdisciplinarity."

19. Orthodox Freudians were too inhibited (and sexist) to cross this gender boundary, which is a pity, because with the new freedom Jones could have gone on to prove that Laertes is also Hamlet's mother, daughter, and sister.

20. Freudians make small-scale predictions about their therapy—namely, that it will be therapeutic; but the results are not available for public inspection and they have shown no interest in making them available.

21. See the section on "Late-Capitalism" in "Politicized Language."

22. See Lewis 1995 and FitzGerald's Forum letter in chapter 2. It is analogous to the tactic used by some people who claim that religion makes people moral: when the negative evidence of churchgoing criminals is pointed out to them, their answer is that such people were not really religious.

23. Brown explains that he rejects Freudianism as "ahistorical, Europocentric and sexist," but says that "a materialist criticism deprived of such concepts as displacement and condensation would be seriously impoverished" (1994, 71).

24. I discuss both these readings in "Bardicide."

25. Oliphant observes that if Golding, one of these obsessed attributionists, proceeds with his method of parallel-hunting, "he will discover that fully ninety per cent of the plays of the last two decades of the sixteenth century are from the pen of Robert Wilson" (1929, 13). One of the parallel passages cited by Golding in his campaign for Wilson is "I thank you, sir," which I used earlier as an absurd example of this method.

26. From the day of his "conversion," Sprinker says, "I've never stopped being a

Marxist, nor has it ever occurred to me, all the surprising events in world communism over the past few years notwithstanding, that I ought to" (1991, 119–20). Of course, it must have occurred to him or he could not say that it never occurred to him. What he means, apparently, is that he never seriously considered reconsidering his faith in Marxism, despite all the negative evidence piling up against it in the extramural world. He seems to be proud of this.

27. Some readers may object that I am confusing empiricist with empirical, but that seems to be a distinction between naive empiricism, which assumes the facts are simply out there, and a more sophisticated empiricism which recognizes it is not that simple. It is the attackers who confuse the two by rejecting all appeals to empirical evidence as empiricism—see, for example, the quotation from Macherey 1978 in "Interdisciplinarity." I discuss the term "Making-Knowledge" in "Politicized Language."

28. The political effectiveness of these critics, as well as their intolerance of dissent, have recently been questioned in Cain 1993 and Ohmann 1992/3.

29. My prediction was partly fulfilled before this essay was published. A reader for a journal to which I submitted it earlier complained, as one reason for rejecting it, that it "reveals an attitude of expecting that pornography does *not* cause violence."

CHAPTER 8. INTERDISCIPLINARITY

This essay was published in *After Poststructuralism: Interdisciplinarity and Literary Theory*, ed. Nancy Easterlin and Barbara Riebling (Evanston, Ill.: Northwestern University Press, 1993), 13–43, and is reprinted by permission of the Northwestern University Press.

1. For a discussion of some other attempts at interdisciplinarity during the period dominated by the New Criticism, see Graff 1987, chap. 13.

2. The earliest citation of *interdisciplinarity* in the *OED* is dated 1937, but Frank 1988, which I highly recommend, records its appearance in 1926.

3. For Stewart, "Doing theory and doing interdisciplinary work are inseparable projects" (1989, 11), and for Dollimore, "One of the most important achievements of 'theory' in English studies has been the making possible a truly interdisciplinary approach" (1994a, 2).

4. The same argument is presented in Kahn 1985 and Kahn 1986, but in 1985, 79 she also cites some clinical evidence from Horney 1967 as support (see note 13 below). Although I refer to these theories collectively as a single feminist revisionist or neo-Freudian theory, I do not deny (nor does Kahn) their differences; I am less interested in the theories themselves than in how these critics use them. And while I call this revision "feminist," I realize that many feminist critics never employ it.

5. Kennard adds that "in borrowing Zinker's ideas, I do not imply that other theories might not work as well" (1986, 67), but a scientific theory is supposed to preclude some competing theories (see the discussion of falsifiability below).

6. Chodorow is a sociologist and psychoanalyst, and Dinnerstein a psychologist; Rich, of course, is primarily a poet and critic.

7. Some feminists also improve on Lacan (see Belsey 1986, 60–61, and Moi 1983, 6), which is understandable since his theory seems even more phallocentric than Freud's; what is hard to understand is why any feminist would want to use it.

8. Thus Dollimore, after explaining the nature of class oppression, adds that "it did not, and still does not, have to be so" (1994a, 15), and Chodorow says her theory "asks how

we might change things" (1978, 4). She now disavows her search in that book for a single cause and single cure of gender oppression (1989, 5–6, 15), but the literary critics have not yet caught up with her.

9. Of course, Cleopatra and Hermione really are mothers and Bertram really has one in the cast, but these relationships do not fit the theory.

10. Stallybrass increases his interdisciplinarity by also using Bakhtin's theory of the "grotesque body," after improving it to include all women's bodies (1986, 126), which makes the theory more useful for inserting "woman" into class conflict.

11. Snow, using the neo-Freudian mode of this same logic, says Iago "is really only the name and local habitation" of society's misogyny (1980, 386), which is the real villain of the play.

12. See my discussion of this point in "Negative Evidence."

13. This could also explain Horney's report that her men patients reveal an envy of pregnancy (1967, 60), which Kahn cites to confirm the neo-Freudian theory she endorses (1985, 79), but she ignores the clinical evidence supplied by Horney's women patients that does not fit this theory.

14. I point out in "Politicized Language" that Jameson now denies that Marxism is predictive (1983, 290).

15. In one amusing twist, Chodorow now reports that she is "criticized by Lacanian psychoanalytic feminists . . . for being empiricist" (1989, 18).

16. I examine this argument in "Silence Is Consent."

17. See Barker 1984, 48; Bristol 1991, 40; Eagleton 1983, 50, 198–99; and Evans 1986, 98, 198, 245, 263.

18. See Dollimore 1994a, 11–13 and 1993, 271; Evans 1986, 167, 253–54, 264; Gohlke 1980, 170; Goldberg 1985, 118; Greene 1981/2, 41; Howard 1987a, 323; and Sinfield 1994d, 131–32. A feminist version of the debate turns on the question of whether a theory that seems to promote their cause really "reinscribes" gender categories, and a Marxist version on the question of whether an apparently "subversive" theory is really implicated in the hegemonic "containment" strategy as part of that vast conspiracy (which includes the pluralism that tolerates the theory).

19. I discuss this Edenic rhetoric in "Bashing." Howard also politicizes historical inquiry by insisting that it is always a "history-for" some interest and that we must ask "what interests get advanced by it" (1987a, 323). Nor would she accept the answer that it advanced the interests of the discipline, which seeks to learn about the past; she wants to know what *political* interests are advanced (see also 363; and Barker 1984, 15, 68; Evans 1986, 83, 253).

20. See Belsey 1986, 57–58, and the quotation above from Brown 1994, 71.

21. One result is that most of the best students there went into science because, as an emigrant physicist explains, it was "not ideological. . . . This was one of the few fields where they could be more or less free" (Kolata 1990, C14). Cai reports the same tendency among the best students in communist China (1990, 12).

22. I discuss this point in "Negative Evidence."

23. Hence most of the "central themes" once in vogue also feature a hypostatized conflict of mighty opposites like appearance versus reality, wit versus witchcraft, eros versus agape, and so on.

24. I suggest some tests of this sort in 1979, 199–207, but they are limited to the formalist/intentionalist approach.

25. In one version Winnett distinguishes masculine from feminine narrative on the

basis of biological differences between the sexes. She explains that some women enjoy masculine narratives because they were "taught to read in drag" (1990, 516), but that could not explain why some men enjoy feminine narratives.

26. Bristol says that my work, Stanley Cavell's, and Stephen Greenblatt's reflect "very deep rifts" in our society, portending its demise (1990, 209–11). For many years Marxists have seized on any conflicts to predict the impending collapse of "late capitalism" from its "irreconcilable contradictions," as I point out in "Politicized Language."

27. See Moi 1983, 10; Greene 1980, 137 and 1981/2, 41–42.

28. Freudian critics who have undergone analysis sometimes claim that this guarantees they will not project their own problems onto the text, but this is a circular argument that assumes the validity of Freudian theory and Freudian therapy.

29. For critiques of post-Saussureanism see Jackson 1991, Vickers 1993, and Tallis 1995.

30. Compare this to Howard's concept of "history-for" (see note 19 above). In "Artistic Unity" I cite more contradictions of this kind from the new Marxists.

31. See Barker 1984, 18, 21; Belsey 1980, 89, 94, 125; Dollimore 1993, 35, 63–68, 153, 226, 246; Eagleton 1983, 136, 170, 187, 191; and Evans 1986, 140, 210.

32. There is even a contradiction in his formulation, which I discuss in "Politicized Language."

33. This point is also made in Butler 1989, 231–33.

34. Similar contradictions are generated by the question of whether it is politically more advantageous for homosexuals to claim that their sexuality is innate or acquired—see Kennard 1986, 64–65, and compare the terms "sexual preference" and "sexual orientation" (now preferred) in the passages quoted in "Politicized Language" from Modern Language Association 1992 and Fitterman 1992. Some of the disputes cited in note 18 above also involve the nature-nurture problem.

35. This of course will only work when essays are refereed, but a glance at my bibliography will show that many are now written on invitation for anthologies and so presumably escape peer review. I do not regard that as a healthy trend, even though this essay is part of it.

36. They might begin with Macfarlane's review (1979) of Stone's book on the family (1977). For examples of critics' uncritical acceptance of this book see Callaghan 1989, 114; Dollimore 1994a, 5; Erickson 1985a, x; Freedman 1989, 255; Gossett 1988, 113; Greenblatt 1980, 42; Hays 1980, 83; Jardine 1983, 80–81, 89; Kahn 1981, 14–16; and Stimpson 1980, 62.

37. I cannot do justice here to the new interdisciplinary programs in women's studies, cultural studies, and so on, because they are so varied. In general, I welcome programs that give students a good grounding in two or three disciplines but question the value of those that simply assemble (or cross-list) a collection of unrelated courses from various disciplines.

38. On this important point see Ellis 1990, 8, and Mueller 1989, 29–30.

39. The most intelligent review of this book that I have seen is by Nussbaum (1987).

Chapter 9. Historicizing

This essay was published in *REAL: Yearbook of Research in English and American Literature* 11 (1995): 425–48, and is reprinted by permission of Gunter Narr Verlag.

1. I use the more cumbersome term *historicizers* to avoid confusion with the New Historicists. The new historicizers include the New Historicists as well as the other schools just mentioned.

2. The same points are made in Howard's summary of the differences between the two historicisms (1986a, 24–25); see also Lerner's more skeptical account (1993, 274–77).

3. It is sometimes very explicit, as in Montrose's reference to the "realities of domination" in Elizabethan society (1986a, 317) and Orgel's to the "realities of contemporary kingship" (1988, 224). These historical "realities" are really real.

4. See the discussion of Discovery No. 3 in "Unthinkable Thoughts."

5. This includes nonverbal artifacts and even natural objects (such as skeletons) from the past, which historians treat as texts that must be interpreted.

6. See Levin 1979, chap. 4, for examples of these approaches in the old historical criticism.

7. I cite a number of examples in "Negative Evidence."

8. But see the quotations in "Negative Evidence" from Crewe's reading of *A Midsummer Night's Dream* (1987) and Patterson's reading of *King Lear* (1989).

9. Anti-Stratfordians use these alleged allusions to the aristocracy to prove that "the Shakespeare plays" must have been written by an aristocrat.

10. As topical readings become more generalized they can also merge into this approach—see Erickson's reference to "the general context of cultural tension in the 1590s" quoted above.

11. The particular passion dealt with in *Lear* is wrath, which gives us yet another historical explanation of the blinding of Gloucester: its purpose is to exhibit "the destruction caused by the passion" of wrath in Cornwall (Campbell 1930, 202).

12. This assertion is contested in Barroll 1991, chap. 2, and Yachnin 1991.

13. See Jameson's scandalously overtheorized move to occlude this problem by arguing that the historical context is "not some common-sense external reality" but is produced by the literary text, which "brings into being that very situation to which it is also, at one and the same time, a reaction" (1981, 81–82). It is not clear what "historicizing" could mean in this scheme, which sounds like the rationale for an ahistorical formalist criticism.

14. This comparison is complicated by the fact that McLuskie is a poststructuralist Marxist feminist and condemns readings like Novy's not only for "co-opting" Shakespeare but also for adopting a prepoststructuralist "mimetic" approach that she associates with "liberal feminism," which of course is bad (1994, 90).

15. Dollimore makes a similar point (1994a, 13). This problem of judging the "radicalism" of criticism even descends to the occasionalist approach: Williams opposes the claim that *A Midsummer Night's Dream* was written for a noble wedding because it serves "the politics of the scholarly right" (1990, 44), but Kavanagh uses it in his Marxist reading of the play (1985, 234).

16. Ryan says that *Lear* presents a "compelling dramatisation" of the evils of class division that "leaves us no choice" but socialism, yet he complains that other critics fail to notice this (1995, 98–99, 103), which looks like a paradox. I suspect that his compelling lesson will only be noticed by Marxists who already know it and so do not need it.

17. I examine this argument in "Silence Is Consent."

18. See the quotations in "Silence Is Consent" from Dollimore 1993, Heinemann 1991, Ryan 1995, and Turner 1988 on *Lear*, Greene 1981/2 on *Troilus and Cressida*, Sinfield 1992 on *Macbeth*, Belsey 1990 on *Henry V*, Holderness 1991 on *The Taming of the Shrew*, Charnes 1992 on *Antony and Cleopatra*, Jardine 1991 on *Hamlet*, and Wynne-Davies 1991 on *Titus Andronicus*. Lerner discusses this strategy, with more examples, and points out that

a "double standard" is operating: "Parallels with the present, if drawn by . . . political conservatives, . . . must be exposed as unhistorical, but if drawn by radicals are . . . legitimate" (1993, 280–81).

19. Heinemann denies that Lear's tragedy is caused by his actions since "the causes of disaster lie deeper than that" in "the horror of a society divided between extremes of rich and poor" (1991, 78), and Ryan says the causes of the tragedy "are housed beyond the conscious culpability of individuals, and should be sought in the iniquitous arrangements" of society (1995, 103).

20. Many of these Marxists condemn the old historicists and New Critics for being essentialist, as I noted, but apparently it all depends on whose ox is being essentialized.

21. See Cotter 1995, 119–21; Greene 1981/2, 41–42; McLuskie 1994, 90; and Moi 1983, 10.

22. Sometimes history is grafted onto this theory. Kahn's essay on *Lear* tries to relate its "maternal subtext" to the Jacobean reinforcement of patriarchy and the practice of wet-nursing (1986, 38, 41), but her earlier version of this essay (1982) arrives at the same interpretation of the play without enlisting any historical context. This is an example of the use of history as what Greenblatt calls "a convenient anecdotal ornament upon a theoretical structure" that is itself nonhistorical (1990, 151), and it testifies to the present power of Jameson's command.

23. Some come pretty close—see the statements of Roberts 1991, Boose 1987, and Wynne-Davies 1991 quoted in "Silence Is Consent."

24. Howard also comments on this (1986a, 15–16).

25. She associates this older enterprise with F. R. Leavis, but it is similar to the view of "the Elizabethan World Picture" held by many old historicists. Moisan notes that the new conception of a strife-torn Renaissance now "run[s] the risk of acquiring the aura of unimpeachable orthodoxy previously accorded the Great Chain of Being" (1994, 482).

Chapter 10. Artistic Unity

This essay was published in *Ideological Approaches to Shakespeare: The Practice of Theory*, ed. Robert P. Merrix and Nicholas Ransom (Lewiston, N.Y.: Edwin Mellen, 1992), 39–56, and *Beyond Poststructuralism: The Speculations of Theory and the Experience of Reading*, ed. Wendell V. Harris (University Park: Pennsylvania State University Press, 1996), 138–55, and is reprinted by permission of The Edwin Mellen Press and The Pennsylvania State University.

1. I discuss this in "Bardicide."

2. He is of course referring to the definition of criticism formulated by that archhumanist, Matthew Arnold.

3. Contrast the passage quoted earlier from the same book, where she says that this "scientific" approach "recognizes in the text" its inconsistencies (Belsey 1980, 128).

4. See, for example, the adverse criticism of Poe's "Ulalume," Kilmer's "Trees," and Lanier's "My Springs" in Brooks and Warren 1938, 358–62, 387–91, and 442–45.

5. Many others make the same point—see the quotations from Belsey 1980, Evans 1986, Howard 1987b, and Dollimore 1994b in the section "The text is silent" in "Bardicide," and also Macherey 1978, 85, 155, and Holderness 1985, 159.

6. See Levin 1979, chap. 2.

7. When they do recognize it, they usually subordinate it to the more important thematic unity—see, for example, Heilman 1956, 2–16.

8. We will not be surprised to learn there is a thematic reading that claims the Clown's scenes are "integral parts of the structure" of *Othello* because they "serve an important function in the overall thematic scheme" (Watts 1968, 349).

9. I collect a number of these statements in Levin 1986, 550–53.

10. We behave in a similar way if we are only seeing a collection of unrelated skits, since we still want to "get our money's worth"; but we are usually much more concerned if we are seeing a single work, when we might miss what Hamlet calls "some necessary question of the play."

11. I discuss the Marxist use of this term and Althusser's modification of it in "(Re)thinking" and "Politicized Language." There is a very useful and much fuller analysis of it in Bristol 1991.

12. For a good example of this older Marxist approach to *Lear*, see Delany 1995. Evans, in the new Marxist mode, finds that both world views are guilty of "essentialism" (another formalist/humanist fallacy) and are undercut by a third one embodied in the Fool, which is not intended and is not integrated into the play (1986, 224–32).

13. See Belsey's account of how materialist critics can exploit the fact that the plot of any fictional work "depends on impediments" and "obstacles to be overcome" and "on the establishment within the story of . . . norms and the repudiation of norms" (1992, 41–42); compare her remarks in 1985b, 9, 100, 111.

14. I try to explain this in "Politicized Language."

15. Cultural materialists of course can claim that Freudianism itself is part of bourgeois ideology and so is contradictory, while Freudians could easily discover that an unconscious Oedipal conflict is the real cause of cultural materialists' hostility to the bourgeoisie.

16. See, for example, Moi 1983, 4, and Belsey 1980, 3.

17. Cultural materialists have trouble with aesthetic pleasure and many simply ignore it. Belsey calls it "mysterious" (1985b, 10) and apparently never experienced it. Others admit its existence only to warn us against it, since it involves our empathetic engagement in the action and so makes us "complicit" with the play's ideology. Thus McLuskie asks us "to deny" it (1994, 98), and Heinemann, in explaining Brecht's opposition to "the politics of empathy," connects it to fascism (1994, 238).

18. See Drakakis 1985a, 17, 25 and 1993b, 407; Evans 1986, 98, 198, 245; Barker 1984, 48; Barker and Hulme 1985, 193; Holderness 1985, 160; Bristol 1990, 169; Eagleton 1983, 50, 198–99; and Rooney's book-length attack (1989). Eagleton thinks that pluralism combines parts of different approaches, but this is usually called eclecticism. Critics can be committed to a single approach and still be pluralists if they recognize other valid approaches, and an English department can be pluralistic even though each of its members practices only one approach.

19. Belsey 1992, 37, 39; Barker and Hulme 1985, 193, 205; Holderness 1985, 149; and McLuskie 1994, 95.

20. He is referring to the difference between a formalist and a feminist reading, but presumably this would also apply to a "contest of meaning" between a formalist and a Marxist.

Chapter 11. Silence Is Consent

This essay was published in *College English* 59 (1997): 171–90, and is reprinted by permission of the National Council of Teachers of English.

1. Locke said that anyone living in a country "give[s] his *tacit Consent*" to obey its

government (1967, 2.8.119), but I do not think many of the critics who use the argument we are testing would consent to this application of it—Belsey clearly does not (1985b, 120).

2. I discuss this tactic in Levin 1979, 28–41.

3. I must repeat that not all oppositional critics engage in this strategy; in fact some have objected to its abuses—see, for example, Dollimore 1993, xix–xx.

4. Compare Boose's statement, quoted at the outset, that the New Criticism is "inherently" conservative (1987, 709). Some people on the Right also attempt to divide critical approaches into two political sides, as I point out in "Polarization."

5. These comments are collected in Baxandall and Morawski 1973, Solomon 1973, and White 1992.

6. See Cotter 1995, 119–21; Greene 1981/2, 41–42; McLuskie 1994, 90; and Moi 1983, 10.

7. Roberts says that "the patriarchal system has shaped Western Culture for millennia" and "dominates all of Western written history" and is "still dominant in our culture" (1991, 16–17); see also the passage from Dworkin 1981 quoted in "Historicizing."

8. See, for instance, the forceful objections of Greenblatt to the ahistorical treatment of capitalism "as a unitary demonic principle" (1990, 151), and of Traub to the treatment of patriarchy "as a monolithic, transhistorical entity" (1995, 136).

9. Perhaps this is the "theory of negative culpability" referred to in the student paper that Gilbert and Gubar cite (1995, 83).

10. This kind of thinking still survives: Katz says that Gerald Graff is "a confirmed centrist" who is "actually reactionary" (1995, 303); Morton and Zavarzadeh argue that Graff and Gregory Jay, since they "criticize us," are "reactionary" and so belong—along with Stanley Fish, Richard Rorty, and Andrew Ross—to the same camp as Rush Limbaugh (1994, 32–33); and Morton, on his own, finds that Jonathan Arac and Jean Howard are "archconservative" (1996, 472). I too am called a "reactionary" by Boyarin (1991, 315) and Drakakis (1993a, 64).

11. See Fish 1995, 51–55, 96–101.

12. I am indebted to Thomas Kranidas for bringing this passage to my attention.

13. On this point see Bercovitch 1993, 21 and Rieff 1993, 63.

CHAPTER 12. POLITICIZED LANGUAGE

This essay was published in the *Centennial Review* 37 (1993): 281–304, and is reprinted by permission of the Michigan State University Press.

1. See the discussion below of **The-West** and notes 12, 14, and 23. (The terms I examine are in boldface type.)

2. An earlier version of the title has "latest" *(noveishii)* rather than "highest" *(vysshaia);* the prediction is in one of his prefaces dated 1920.

3. This was the party line in the 1930s but it survives today, even though fascism is gone and capitalism is not. In 1983 Eagleton could still say that "Fascism is a desperate, last-ditch attempt on the part of monopoly capitalism to abolish contradictions which have become intolerable" (66). He calls it "monopoly capitalism," which is not predictive, since that is taken care of by "last-ditch"; subsequently it becomes "late" (143, 199).

4. Elsewhere in this essay he characterizes the present stage of capitalism as "consumer" or "multinational" (Jameson 1983, 289) and "advanced" (295). In his "Reflections" I count five "late" capitalisms and one "advanced" in **Quotation-Marks** (1977, 212).

5. He also attributes this to "self-policing" within the working-class movement and "statutory repression," so the workers are not entirely to blame; presumably if these restraints were removed they would realize how much happier and richer they would be under that "socialist alternative."

6. Derrida objects to this term, not because of its predictive claim, but because it is so vague that Marxists can use it to evade explanation: when they confront something that "they cannot reduce . . . to [their] previous schemes" of classical capitalism, "they say, 'Well, that's late capitalism'" (1987, 254).

7. Their use of this term derives from Hegel's dialectic (even though many new Marxists disown "Hegelian Marxism"), but in Hegel the contradictions are between ideas that are partial realizations of an ultimate truth.

8. This was the hope of the authors of *The Federalist* (see especially No. 10), who assume there will always be conflicts between what they call "factions."

9. Jay refers to "the new shibboleth 'race-gender-class,' now invoked with numbing predictability" (1990, 30). (The word *shibboleth* itself is, I believe, the earliest recorded example of an IFF code.) He also argues, but on different grounds, that race does not have the same status as the other two categories.

10. This does not apply to most Marxist regimes, where former members of the bourgeoisie and even their children were persecuted as "class-enemies" (Rèv 1991, 3–7); in the Guangxi region during Mao's Cultural Revolution some were not only killed but also eaten (Binyan 1993, 4–5). And under many of these regimes the working class could not get into the best stores, which were reserved for the managerial class.

11. Note also the omission of class from the similar list in the Modern Language Association "Statement of Professional Ethics," which tells us not to "discriminate against others on any grounds, including race, ethnic origin, religious creed, age, gender, and sexual preference" (1992, 75), and in Fitterman's "dreams of a country where . . . the words, 'regardless of race, creed, gender, age, disability, and sexual orientation' are sacred words enshrined in our laws" (1992, 2).

12. "Political-awareness" is the left-wing's positive code word; the right-wing's negative code word for it is "political-correctness."

13. The Marxists' concept of "exploitation" derives from their "theory of surplus labor" that enables them to prove a priori that all workers in capitalist societies are always "exploited," no matter how much they are paid, because a profit is made on them, while no workers in socialist societies are ever "exploited," no matter how little they are paid, because no profit is made.

14. "Liberal-humanism" is the term of abuse (or negative IFF code) favored by the Left, including many of the newer critics, and "secular-humanism" is the equivalent term used by the Right. I examine the curious similarity of these terms in "Polarizing."

15. See Dollimore 1993, 9; Heinemann 1994, 239; Sinfield 1994b, 162, 165; Belsey 1985b, 7 and 1989, 88; Evans 1986, 35; Kavanagh 1985, 164; Sharp 1980, 109; Barker and Hulme 1985, 194; and my discussion of this argument in "Son of Bashing."

16. Since writing this, I learned that in the latest version of this signal only one hand is used. To be really cutting-edge, you rest an arm on the lectern while speaking, and when you come to the term in question you raise this arm languidly and flap the attached hand once, indicating that by now it should be boringly obvious that the term is *sous-rature*.

17. This is the primary meaning of the term "scare-quotes"—that they are meant to scare readers off the concept; but it could also mean that the writer is scared of the concept,

which would apply to the first two reasons above. I cite more examples of their use in "Bardicide" and "Bashing."

18. In totalitarian discourse this combination can become a tic: in a 1976 memorandum on the campaign against dissidents, Yuri Andropov (then head of the KGB, later of the USSR) uses it four times in four consecutive sentences, referring to "a so-called 'internal opposition,'" "the so-called 'movement for democratization,'" "the so-called 'Committee for the Protection of Human Rights,'" and "the so-called 'Russian Section' of Amnesty International." See also FitzGerald's Forum letter in chapter 2.

19. See Macherey 1978, 5, and my discussion of this point in "Interdisciplinarity."

20. Note the assumption that society can and should be organized according to a "reasonable" plan, which was examined under **Unresolvable-Contradictions**.

21. Greene is quoting in part from Belsey 1980, 5, and insists it is the only correct definition.

22. I suspect that the explanation lies in the old Marxist distinction between "ideology" and "science"; many new Marxists claim to reject it, but they seem to believe that when they prove their opponents are "in ideology," they themselves have seen the truth about ideology and therefore must be "in science."

23. This also applies to a related signal, "The-Canon," which one side sees as the sacred repository of **Western-Values** and the other as a sinister instrument used by **The-West** to oppress its "nonelite" victims. I discuss this term in "Polarization."

24. A good example is Stewart's essay (1989), which never mentions any literature or literary criticism, although it appears in a journal that, the editor tells us, "can be read with interest and profit by many, if not all, MLA members."

CHAPTER 13. POLARIZATION

This essay was published in *The Emperor Redressed: Critiquing Critical Theory*, ed. Dwight Eddins (Tuscaloosa: University of Alabama Press, 1995), 62–80.

1. While this underdog feeling seems quite real, some polarizers can turn it on or off at will. In the first part of Sprinker's essay (1991), the people on his side "remain truly embattled minorities whose meager gains over the years now appear to stand under threat" from my side, and they only want "the playing field [to be] truly levelled" so they can "sit down at the negotiating table" (123); but in the second part, which is an exercise in Marxist triumphalism, they are already "winning" what he calls a "war" against my side (126), and after their imminent victory they will not negotiate but "seize the guns [of my side] and melt them all down for scrap" (128). In the first part my work "has been utterly pernicious in its effects" (116), but in the second it has "no visible effect" (128); in the first it is "incomprehensible" that I "could feel seriously threatened" by his side (123), but in the second my side feels "threatened and scared" by his (127).

2. I received no letters attacking my essay. Academics do not send hate mail, perhaps because it cannot be included in one's curriculum vitae. They prefer to publish it.

3. Thus a mailing sent out by a right-wing organization says that supporters of an equal rights amendment in Iowa are part of a "socialist, antifamily political movement that encourages women to leave their husbands, kill their children, practice witchcraft, destroy capitalism, and become lesbians" (Lewin 1992, 24); and Woodbridge says she would expect holders of my "reactionary views" about criticism "to align themselves with Right-to-

Lifers, fundamentalist religion, Back-to-Basics in education, toughness on welfare bums, maintaining America's military might, respect for the police, warfare on drugs, allegiance to the flag, and putting Father back at the head of the family" (1991, 292).

4. In "Son of Bashing" I cite several examples of the tendency of the new Marxists to attribute apparently opposing positions, including empiricism and idealism, to the same enemy.

5. Graff notes the "odd-bedfellow" situation in which "the two current groups who get most intensely worked up over the inherent evil of 'humanism' are poststructuralist philosophers and members of the Moral Majority" (1984, 497).

6. "Bourgeois-liberalism" is what the Chinese government says it was shooting at in Tiananmen Square. Liberalism is also attacked by some radical feminists as sexist: MacKinnon claims that it is "the current ruling ideology" of "male dominance" (1990, 13), and Lahey that it "depends on the continuing instrumentalization and exploitation of women" (1990, 199–200), and Kappeler that it is "profoundly masculinist" and consists of "gentlemen advocating liberty and license for gentlemen—liberties to which the rights and liberty of women have habitually and routinely been sacrificed" (1990, 176).

7. I discuss this treatment of "the West" in "Politicized Language."

8. I argue this point in "Silence Is Consent"; see also the demonstration in Crews 1995 that there is no necessary connection between poststructuralism and left-wing politics.

9. On this point see Fowler 1979 and Harris 1991.

10. Both Barker (1984, 47) and Belsey (1985b, 145) assert that bourgeois subjects are really less free than feudal subjects because they are "internally disciplined," which is a "new and more insidious" form of control. But feudal subjects also had internal restraints; no society or individual could survive without them.

11. See my discussion of this issue in "Artistic Unity," and the insightful analysis of different kinds of pluralism in Booth 1979.

12. Some leftists argue that only rightists can commit McCarthyism, since it implies political power—compare the claim that only whites can be racist.

13. For leftist attacks on pluralism, see Barker 1984, 48; Barker and Hulme 1985, 193; Bristol 1990, 169; Drakakis 1985a, 17, 25; Eagleton 1983, 50, 198–99; Evans 1986, 98, 198, 245; and Rooney 1989. Most critics on the Left now champion cultural or ethnic (rather than political or critical) pluralism and claim that the Right opposes it; but in the past many leftists opposed it as a rightist conspiracy to fragment proletarian solidarity, a view that survives in Bristol 1991, 40.

14. This is the position of several essays in the Leidholdt and Raymond anthology (1990).

Texts (Formerly Works) Cited

Abrams, M. H. 1991. *Doing things with texts: Essays in criticism and critical theory*. Edited by Michael Fischer. New York: Norton.

———. 1995. What is a humanistic criticism? In Eddins 1995, 13–44.

Adelman, Janet. 1985a. Male bonding in Shakespeare's comedies. In Erickson and Kahn 1985, 73–103.

———. 1985b. "This is and is not Cressid": The characterization of Cressida. In Garner, Kahane, and Sprengnether 1985, 119–41.

———. 1987. "Born of woman": Fantasies of maternal power in *Macbeth*. In *Cannibals, witches, and divorce: Estranging the Renaissance,* edited by Marjorie Garber, 90–121. Baltimore: Johns Hopkins University Press.

———. 1989. Bed tricks: On marriage as the end of comedy in *All's well that ends well* and *Measure for measure*. In Holland, Homan, and Paris 1989, 151–74.

———. 1997. Making defect perfection: Shakespeare and the one-sex model. In *Enacting gender on the English Renaissance stage*, edited by Viviana Comensoli and Anne Russell, 23–52. Urbana: University of Illinois Press.

Adelman, Janet, et al. 1989. Forum letter. *PMLA* 104:77–78.

Aers, David. 1992. A whisper in the ear of early modernists; or, Reflections on literary critics writing the "history of the subject." In *Culture and history, 1350–1600: Essays on English communities, identities, and writing*, edited by David Aers, 177–202. Detroit, Mich.: Wayne State University Press.

American Law Institute. 1981. *Restatement of the law: Contracts*. 2d ed. St. Paul, Minn.: American Law Institute.

Andropov, Yuri. 1992. Untitled memorandum dated 15 November 1976. Translated by Library of Congress. *New York Times*, 15 June, A11.

Aristotle. 1973. *Poetics*. Translated by W. Hamilton Fyfe. Loeb Classical Library. Cambridge: Harvard University Press.

———. 1975. *Nicomachean ethics*. Translated by H. Rackman. Loeb Classical Library. Cambridge: Harvard University Press.

Bacon, Francis. 1878. *Novum organum*. Edited by Thomas Fowler. Oxford: Clarendon.

———. 1915. *The advancement of learning*. Edited by G. W. Kitchin. London: Dent.

———. 1955. *Selected writings*. Edited by Hugh Dick. New York: Random House.

Bamber, Linda. 1982. *Comic women, tragic men: A study of gender and genre in Shakespeare.* Stanford, Calif.: Stanford University Press.

Barker, Deborah E., and Ivo Kamps, eds. 1995. *Shakespeare and gender: A history.* London: Verso.

Barker, Francis. 1984. *The tremulous private body: Essays on subjection.* London: Methuen.

Barker, Francis, and Peter Hulme. 1985. Nymphs and reapers heavily vanish: The discursive con-texts of *The tempest.* In Drakakis 1985b, 191–205.

Barker, Francis, et al., eds. 1991. *Uses of history: Marxism, postmodernism, and the Renaissance.* Manchester: Manchester University Press.

Barroll, Leeds. 1991. *Politics, plague, and Shakespeare's theater: The Stuart years.* Ithaca: Cornell University Press.

Barthes, Roland. 1964. *Essais critiques.* Paris: Editions du Seuil.

———. 1977. The death of the author. In *Image-music-text,* translated and edited by Stephen Heath, 142–48. London: Fontana. Originally published in French in 1968.

Battenhouse, Roy. 1969. *Shakespearean tragedy: Its art and its Christian premises.* Bloomington: Indiana University Press.

Battersby, James L. 1991. *Paradigms regained: Pluralism and the practice of criticism.* Philadelphia: University of Pennsylvania Press.

———. 1996. *Reason and the nature of texts.* Philadelphia: University of Pennsylvania Press.

Baxandall, Lee, and Stefan Morawski, eds. 1973. *Marx and Engels on literature and art: A selection of writings.* St. Louis, Mo.: Telos.

Belsey, Catherine. 1980. *Critical practice.* London: Methuen.

———. 1985a. Disrupting sexual difference: Meaning and gender in the comedies. In Drakakis 1985b, 166–90.

———. 1985b. *The subject of tragedy: Identity and difference in Renaissance drama.* London: Methuen.

———. 1986. The romantic construction of the unconscious. 1981. Reprinted in *Literature, politics and theory: Papers from the Essex conference, 1976–84,* edited by Francis Barker et al., 57–76. London: Methuen.

———. 1989. The subject in danger: A reply to Richard Levin. *Textual Practice* 3:87–90.

———. 1990. Richard Levin and in-different reading. *New Literary History* 21:449–56.

———. 1992. Literature, history, politics. 1983. Reprinted in Wilson and Dutton 1992, 33–44.

Bennett, Josephine Waters. 1966. *"Measure for measure" as royal entertainment.* New York: Columbia University Press.

Bennett, Tony. 1979. *Formalism and Marxism.* London: Methuen.

Bercovitch, Sacvan. 1993. *The rites of assent: Transformations in the symbolic construction of America.* New York: Routledge.

Berger, Harry. 1982. Text against performance in Shakespeare: The example of *Macbeth.* *Genre* 15:49–79.

Binyan, Liu. 1993. An unnatural disaster. *New York Review of Books,* 8 April, 3–6.

Bloom, Allan. 1987. *The closing of the American mind: How higher education has failed democracy and impoverished the souls of today's students.* New York: Simon & Schuster.

Bloom, Harold. 1998. *Shakespeare: The invention of the human.* New York: Riverhead.

Bohannan, Laura. 1967. Miching mallecho, that means witchcraft. In *Magic, witchcraft, and curing*, edited by John Middleton, 43–54. Austin: University of Texas Press.

Boose, Lynda E. 1987. The family in Shakespeare studies; or—Studies in the family of Shakespeareans; or—The politics of politics. *Renaissance Quarterly* 40:707–42.

Booth, Wayne C. 1979. *Critical understanding: The powers and limits of pluralism.* Chicago: University of Chicago Press.

Boyarin, Daniel. 1991. Forum letter. *PMLA* 106:314–15.

Bradley, A. C. 1904. *Shakespearean tragedy.* London: Macmillan.

Bradshaw, Graham. 1993. *Misrepresentations: Shakespeare and the materialists.* Ithaca: Cornell University Press.

Bray, Alan. 1988. *Homosexuality in Renaissance England.* 2d ed. London: Gay Men's Press. The first edition appeared in 1982.

Bristol, Michael D. 1987. Lenten butchery: Legitimation crisis in *Coriolanus*. In Howard and O'Connor 1987, 207–24.

———. 1990. *Shakespeare's America, America's Shakespeare.* London: Routledge.

———. 1991. Where does ideology hang out? In Kamps 1991b, 31–43.

Brooks, Cleanth. 1947. *The well wrought urn: Studies in the structure of poetry.* New York: Reynal & Hitchcock.

Brooks, Cleanth, and Robert Penn Warren. 1938. *Understanding poetry.* New York: Henry Holt.

Brown, Judith. 1986. *Immodest acts: The life of a lesbian nun in Renaissance Italy.* Oxford: Oxford University Press.

Brown, Paul. 1994. "This thing of darkness I acknowledge mine": *The tempest* and the discourse of colonialism. In Dollimore and Sinfield 1994b, 48–71.

Brown, Steve. 1991. The Brown U. expulsion. *Civil Liberties* 373:1, 4.

Butler, Christopher. 1989. The future of theory: Saving the reader. In *The future of literary theory*, edited by Ralph Cohen, 229–49. New York: Routledge.

Cai, Xiao. 1990. China: Outward conformity, inner despair. *Academe* 76:8–12.

Cain, William. 1993. The crisis of the literary left: Notes toward a renewal of humanism. In *After poststructuralism: Interdisciplinarity and literary theory*, edited by Nancy Easterlin and Barbara Riebling, 127–40. Evanston, Ill.: Northwestern University Press.

Callaghan, Dympna. 1989. *Woman and gender in Renaissance tragedy: A study of "King Lear," "Othello," "The Duchess of Malfi," and "The white devil."* New York: Harvester Wheatsheaf.

Campbell, Lily B. 1930. *Shakespeare's tragic heroes: Slaves of passion.* Cambridge: Cambridge University Press.

Charnes, Linda. 1992. What's love got to do with it? Reading the liberal humanist romance in Shakespeare's *Antony and Cleopatra. Textual Practice* 6:1–16.

———. 1994. *Notorious identity: Materializing the subject in Shakespeare.* Cambridge: Harvard University Press.

Chodorow, Nancy. 1978. *The reproduction of mothering: Psychoanalysis and the sociology of gender.* Berkeley: University of California Press.

———. 1989. *Feminism and psychoanalytic theory.* New Haven: Yale University Press.
Cicero, Marcus Tullius. 1956. *De natura deorum.* Translated by H. Rackham. Loeb Classical Library. Cambridge: Harvard University Press.
Cioffi, Frank. 1970. Freud and the idea of a pseudo-science. In *Explanation in the behavioural sciences,* edited by Robert Borger and Frank Cioffi, 471–99, 508–15. Cambridge: Cambridge University Press.
Cohen, Michael. 1988. New directions in Shakespeare criticism. *Shakespeare Newsletter* 38:38–39.
Cohen, Walter. 1987. Political criticism of Shakespeare. In Howard and O'Connor 1987, 18–46.
Cole, Susan G. 1990. A view from another country. In Leidholdt and Raymond 1990, 191–97.
Cook, Carol. 1995. "The sign and semblance of her honor": Reading gender difference in *Much ado about nothing.* 1986. Reprinted in Barker and Kamps 1995, 75–103.
Cotter, Jennifer M. 1995. On feminist pedagogy. *minnesota review* 41/42:118–28.
Coyle, Martin. 1996. Attacking the cult-historicists. *Renaissance Forum* 1, no. 1.
Crewe, Jonathan. 1987. *Hidden designs: The critical profession and Renaissance literature.* New York: Methuen.
———. 1995. In the field of dreams: Transvestism in *Twelfth night* and *The crying game. Representations* 50:101–21.
———, ed. 1992. *Reconfiguring the Renaissance: Essays in critical materialism.* Lewisburg, Pa.: Bucknell University Press.
Crews, Frederick. 1986. *Skeptical engagements.* Oxford: Oxford University Press.
———. 1995. The end of the poststructuralist era. In Eddins 1995, 45–61.
Darwin, Charles. 1958. *The autobiography of Charles Darwin and selected letters.* Edited by Francis Darwin. 1892. Reprint, New York: Dover.
Dash, Irene. 1981. *Wooing, wedding, and power: Women in Shakespeare's plays.* New York: Columbia University Press.
Davis, Natalie Zemon. 1988. On the lame. *American Historical Review* 93:572–603.
de Grazia, Margreta. 1988. The essential Shakespeare and the material book. *Textual Practice* 2:69–86.
de Grazia, Margreta, and Peter Stallybrass. 1993. The materiality of the Shakespearean text. *Shakespeare Quarterly* 44:255–83.
———. 1997. Love among the ruins: Response to Pechter. *Textual Practice* 11:69–79.
Delany, Paul. 1995. *King Lear* and the decline of feudalism. 1977. Reprinted in Kamps 1995, 20–38.
Derrida, Jacques. 1987. Some questions and responses. In *The linguistics of writing: Arguments between language and literature,* edited by Nigel Fabb et al., 252–64. New York: Methuen.
———. 1988. *Limited Inc.* Translated by Samuel Weber and Jeffrey Mehlman. Edited by Gerald Graff. Evanston, Ill.: Northwestern University Press.
Dickes, Robert. 1970. Desdemona: An innocent victim? *American Imago* 27:279–97.
Dickstein, Morris. 1991. The ever-changing literary past. *New York Times,* 26 October, A19.

Dinnerstein, Dorothy. 1976. *The mermaid and the minotaur: Sexual arrangements and human malaise.* New York: Harper & Row.

Diogenes Laertius. 1958. *Lives of eminent philosophers.* Translated by R. D. Hicks. 2 vols. Loeb Classical Library. Cambridge: Harvard University Press.

Dollimore, Jonathan. 1983. Politics, teaching, literature. *LTP: Journal of Literature Teaching Politics* 2:108–19.

———. 1990a. Critical developments: Cultural materialism, feminism and gender critique, and new historicism. In *Shakespeare: A bibliographical guide*, edited by Stanley Wells, 405–28. 2d ed. Oxford: Clarendon.

———. 1990b. Shakespeare, cultural materialism, feminism, and Marxist humanism. *New Literary History* 21:471–93.

———. 1993. *Radical tragedy: Religion, ideology, and power in the drama of Shakespeare and his contemporaries.* 2d ed. Durham, N.C.: Duke University Press. The first edition appeared in 1984.

———. 1994a. Introduction: Shakespeare, cultural materialism and the new historicism. In Dollimore and Sinfield 1994b, 2–17.

———. 1994b. Transgression and surveillance in *Measure for measure*. In Dollimore and Sinfield 1994b, 72–87.

Dollimore, Jonathan, and Alan Sinfield. 1985. History and ideology: The instance of *Henry V*. In Drakakis 1985b, 206–27.

———. 1994a. Foreword: Cultural materialism. In Dollimore and Sinfield 1994b, vii–viii.

———, eds. 1994b. *Political Shakespeare: Essays in cultural materialism.* 2d ed. Ithaca: Cornell University Press. The first edition appeared in 1985.

Donoghue, Denis. 1998. *The practice of reading.* New Haven: Yale University Press.

Drakakis, John. 1985a. Introduction. In Drakakis 1985b, 1–25.

———. 1993a. Terminator 2 1/2: Or messing with canons. *Textual Practice* 7:60–84.

———. 1993b. Untitled review. *Renaissance Quarterly* 46:406–9.

———. 1995. "Fashion it thus": *Julius Caesar* and the politics of theatrical representation. 1992. Reprinted in Kamps 1995, 280–91.

———, ed. 1985b. *Alternative Shakespeares.* London: Methuen.

Draper, John. 1937. The occasion of *King Lear. Studies in Philology* 34:176–85.

Dreher, Diana. 1986. *Domination and defiance: Fathers and daughters in Shakespeare.* Lexington: University Press of Kentucky.

Dusinberre, Juliet. 1975. *Shakespeare and the nature of women.* London: Macmillan.

Dutton, Richard. 1992. Postscript. In Wilson and Dutton 1992, 219–26.

Dworkin, Andrea. 1981. *Pornography: Men possessing women.* New York: Putnam.

Eagleton, Terry. 1983. *Literary theory: An introduction.* Oxford: Blackwell.

———. 1986. *William Shakespeare.* Oxford: Blackwell.

———. 1994. The right and the good: Postmodernism and the liberal state. *Textual Practice* 8:1–10.

Easterlin, Nancy. 2000. Psychoanalysis and "the discipline of love." *Philosophy and Literature* 24:261–79.

Easthope, Antony. 1982. Poetry and the politics of reading. In Widdowson 1982b, 136–49.

Ebert, Teresa L. 1996. *Ludic feminism and after: Postmodernism, desire, and labor in late capitalism.* Ann Arbor: University of Michigan Press.

Eddins, Dwight. 1995. *The emperor redressed: Critiquing critical theory.* Tuscaloosa: University of Alabama Press.

Eliot, T. S. 1932. *Selected essays, 1917–1932.* New York: Harcourt, Brace.

Ellis, John M. 1990. Radical literary theory. *London Review of Books,* 8 February, 7–8.

———. 1997. *Literature lost: Social agendas and the corruption of the humanities.* New Haven: Yale University Press.

Empson, William. 1951. *The structure of complex words.* London: Chatto & Windus.

Erickson, Peter. 1981/2. Untitled review. In Greene and Swift 1981/2, 189–201.

———. 1985a. *Patriarchal structures in Shakespeare's plays.* Berkeley: University of California Press.

———. 1985b. Shakespeare and the "author-function." In Erickson and Kahn 1985, 245–55.

———. 1986. Untitled review. *Shakespeare Quarterly* 37:251–55.

———. 1987. Rewriting the Renaissance, rewriting ourselves. *Shakespeare Quarterly* 38:327–37.

———. 1991. *Rewriting Shakespeare, rewriting ourselves.* Berkeley: University of California Press.

Erickson, Peter, and Coppélia Kahn, eds. 1985. *Shakespeare's "rough magic": Renaissance essays in honor of C. L. Barber.* Newark: University of Delaware Press.

Evans, Malcolm. 1986. *Signifying nothing: Truth's true contents in Shakespeare's text.* Brighton, U.K.: Harvester.

Fawcet, Samuel. 1641. *A seasonable sermon for these troublesome times preached to the right worshipful company of the haberdashers Novem[ber] 23, 1641 in the parish-church of St. Mary Stainings in London.* London.

Ferguson, Margaret, Maureen Quilligan, and Nancy Vickers, eds. 1986. *Rewriting the Renaissance: The discourses of sexual difference in early modern Europe.* Chicago: University of Chicago Press.

Festinger, Leon, Henry W. Riecken, and Stanley Schachter. 1956. *When Prophecy Fails.* Minneapolis: University of Minnesota Press.

Fineman, Joel. 1986. *Shakespeare's perjured eye: The invention of poetic subjectivity in the sonnets.* Berkeley: University of California Press.

Fish, Stanley. 1980. *Is there a text in this class? The authority of interpretive communities.* Cambridge: Harvard University Press.

———. 1989. Forum reply. *PMLA* 104:219–21.

———. 1995. *Professional correctness: Literary studies and political change.* Oxford: Clarendon.

Fitterman, Marilyn. 1992. Twenty-five years: Looking back—and ahead. *NOW-NYS Action Report* 7:2.

Fitz (Woodbridge), L. T. 1977. Egyptian queens and male reviewers: Sexist attitudes in *Antony and Cleopatra* criticism. *Shakespeare Quarterly* 28:297–316.

FitzGerald, Margot. 1991. Forum letter. *PMLA* 106:1172–73.

Fogel, Ephim. 1959. Salmons in both, or some caveats for canonical scholars. *Bulletin of the New York Public Library* 63:223–36, 292–308.

Foley, Stephen. 1991. Nostalgia and the "rise of English": Rhetorical questions. In Wayne 1991, 237–55.

Foucault, Michel. 1979. What is an author? Rev. version in *Textual strategies: Perspectives in post-structuralist criticism,* translated and edited by Josué Harari, 141–60. Ithaca: Cornell University Press.

Fowler, Alastair. 1979. Genre and the literary canon. *New Literary History* 11:97–119.

Frank, Roberta. 1988. "Interdisciplinary": The first half-century. In *Words: For Robert Burchfield's sixty-fifth birthday,* edited by E. G. Stanley and T. F. Hoad, 91–101. Wolfeboro, N.H.: D. S. Brewer.

Frantzen, Allen. 1996. The disclosure of sodomy in *Cleanness. PMLA* 111:451–64.

Freedman, Barbara. 1989. Misrecognizing Shakespeare. In Holland, Homan, and Paris, 1989, 244–60.

French, Marilyn. 1981. *Shakespeare's division of experience.* New York: Summit Books.

Freud, Sigmund. 1975. *The standard edition of the complete psychological works of Sigmund Freud.* Edited by James Strachey. 24 vols. London: Hogarth.

Frondizi, Risieri. 1953. *The nature of the self.* New Haven: Yale University Press.

Fuller, Tammyanne. 2000/1. Shakespeare summer festivals 2001. *Shakespeare Newsletter* 50:93, 100, 102, 118, 122.

Fuss, Diana. 1989. *Essentially speaking: Feminism, nature, and difference.* New York: Routledge.

Garner, Shirley Nelson. 1976. Shakespeare's Desdemona. *Shakespeare Studies* 9:233–52.

Garner, Shirley Nelson, Claire Kahane, and Madelon Sprengnether, eds. 1985. *The (m)other tongue: Essays in feminist psychoanalytic interpretation.* Ithaca: Cornell University Press.

Gilbert, Sandra M., and Susan Gubar. 1995. *Masterpiece theatre: An academic melodrama.* New Brunswick, N.J.: Rutgers University Press.

Goddard, Harold. 1951. *The meaning of Shakespeare.* Chicago: University of Chicago Press.

Gohlke (Sprengnether), Madelon. 1980. "I wooed thee with my sword": Shakespeare's tragic paradigms. In Lenz, Greene, and Neely 1980, 150–70.

———. 1981/2. "All that is spoke is marred": Language and consciousness in *Othello.* In Greene and Swift 1981/2, 157–76.

Goldberg, Jonathan. 1983a. *James I and the politics of literature: Jonson, Shakespeare, Donne, and their contemporaries.* Baltimore: Johns Hopkins University Press.

———. 1983b. Untitled review. *Shakespeare Studies* 16:343–48.

———. 1985. Shakespearean inscriptions: The voicing of power. In *Shakespeare and the question of theory,* edited by Patricia Parker and Geoffrey Hartman, 116–37. New York: Methuen.

———. 1986. Untitled review. *Modern Philology* 84:71–75.

———. 1987. Speculations: *Macbeth* and source. In Howard and O'Connor 1987, 242–64.

———. 1988. Hamlet's hand. *Shakespeare Quarterly* 39:307–21.

———. 1990a. Making sense. *New Literary History* 21:457–62.

———. 1990b. *Writing matter: From the hands of the English Renaissance.* Stanford, Calif.: Stanford University Press.

———. 1991. Sodomy and society: The case of Christopher Marlowe. 1984. Reprinted in *Staging the Renaissance: Reinterpretations of Elizabethan and Jacobean drama,* edited by David Scott Kastan and Peter Stallybrass, 75–82. New York: Routledge.

———, ed. 1994. *Queering the Renaissance.* Durham, N.C.: Duke University Press.

Goleman, Daniel. 1990. Fluid identities. *New York Times Book Review,* 21 January, 12.

Gossett, Suzanne. 1988. "Man-maid, begone!": Women in masques. *English Literary Renaissance* 18:96–113.

Grady, Hugh. 1991. *The modernist Shakespeare: Critical texts in a material world.* Oxford: Oxford University Press.

———. 1993. Containment, subversion—and postmodernism. *Textual Practice* 7:31–49.

Graff, Gerald. 1983. The pseudo-politics of interpretation. In *The politics of interpretation,* edited by W. J. T. Mitchell, 145–58. Chicago: University of Chicago Press.

———. 1984. Humanism and the hermeneutics of power: Reflections on the post-structuralist two-step and other dances. *Boundary* 2:495–505.

———. 1987. *Professing literature: An institutional history.* Chicago: University of Chicago Press.

———. 1989. Co-optation. In *The new historicism,* edited by H. Aram Veeser, 168–81. New York: Routledge.

Graff, Gerald, and Gregory Jay. 1991. *Teachers for a democratic culture: Statement of principles.* Evanston, Ill.: Northwestern University

Greenblatt, Stephen. 1980. *Renaissance self-fashioning: From More to Shakespeare.* Chicago: University of Chicago Press.

———. 1986a. Psychoanalysis and Renaissance culture. In Parker and Quint 1986, 210–24.

———. 1986b. Splenditello. *London Review of Books,* 19 June, 5–6.

———. 1988a. *Shakespearean negotiations: The circulation of social energy in Renaissance England.* Berkeley: University of California Press.

———. 1990. *Learning to curse: Essays in early modern culture.* New York: Routledge.

———, ed. 1988b. *Representing the English Renaissance.* Berkeley: University of California Press.

Greene, Gayle. 1980. Shakespeare's Cressida: "A kind of self." In Lenz, Greene, and Neely 1980, 133–49.

———. 1981/2. Feminist and Marxist criticism: An argument for alliances. In Greene and Swift 1981/2, 29–45.

———. 1983. Feminist criticism and Marilyn French: With such friends, who needs enemies? *Shakespeare Quarterly* 34:479–86.

———. 1991. The myth of neutrality, again? In Kamps 1991b, 23–29.

———. 1995. "This that you call love": Sexual and social tragedy in *Othello.* 1979. Reprinted in Barker and Kamps 1995, 47–62.

Greene, Gayle, and Carolyn Ruth Swift, eds. 1981/2. *Feminist criticism of Shakespeare.* Two special issues of *Women's Studies* 9:1–215.

Grünbaum, Adolf. 1984. *The foundations of psychoanalysis: A philosophical critique.* Berkeley: University of California Press.

Gusdorf, Georges. 1948. *La découverte de soi.* Paris: Presses Universitaires de France.

Hanning, Robert. 1977. *The individual in twelfth-century romance.* New Haven: Yale University Press.

Harbage, Alfred. 1962. *Love's labor's lost* and the early Shakespeare. *Philological Quarterly* 41:18–36.

Harris, Wendell V. 1991. Canonicity. *PMLA* 106:110–21.

———. 1996. Marxist literary theory and the advantages of irrelevance. *Sewanee Review* 54:209–28.

Hawkes, Terence. 1995. *William Shakespeare: "King Lear."* Plymouth, U.K.: Northcote.

Hays, Janice. 1980. Those "soft and delicate desires": *Much ado* and the distrust of women. In Lenz, Greene, and Neely 1980, 79–99.

Heath, Stephen. 1978. Difference. *Screen* 19:50–112.

Heilman, Robert B. 1956. *Magic in the web: Action and language in "Othello."* Lexington: University of Kentucky Press.

Heinemann, Margot. 1991. "Demystifying the mystery of state": *King Lear* and the world upside down. *Shakespeare Survey* 44:75–83.

———. 1994. How Brecht read Shakespeare. In Dollimore and Sinfield 1994b, 226–54.

al-Hibri, Azizah. 1981. Capitalism is an advanced stage of patriarchy: But Marxism is not feminism. In *Women and revolution: A discussion of the unhappy marriage of Marxism and feminism*, edited by Lydia Sargent, 166–93. Boston: South End Press.

Hill, Christopher. 1990. *A nation of change and novelty: Radical politics, religion, and literature in seventeenth-century England.* London: Routledge.

Hirsch, E. D. 1976. *The aims of interpretation.* Chicago: University of Chicago Press.

Hirschkop, Ken, and David Shepherd. 1994. Forum letter. *PMLA* 109:116.

Holderness, Graham. 1985. *Shakespeare's history.* Dublin: Gill & Macmillan.

———. 1991. Production, reproduction, performance: Marxism, history, theatre. In Barker et al. 1991, 153–78.

———. 1992. *Shakespeare recycled: The making of historical drama.* London: Harvester Wheatsheaf.

Holland, Norman, Sidney Homan, and Bernard Paris, eds. 1989. *Shakespeare's personality.* Berkeley: University of California Press.

Horney, Karen. 1967. *Feminine psychology.* Edited by Harold Kelman. New York: Norton.

Howard, Jean E. 1986a. The new historicism in Renaissance studies. *English Literary Renaissance* 16:13–43.

———. 1986b. Scholarship, theory, and more new readings: Shakespeare for the 1990s. In *Shakespeare studies today: The Horace Howard Furness memorial lectures*, edited by Georgianna Ziegler, 127–51. New York: AMS.

———. 1987a. Recent studies in Elizabethan and Jacobean drama. *Studies in English Literature* 27:321–79.

———. 1987b. Renaissance antitheatricality and the politics of gender and rank in *Much ado about nothing.* In Howard and O'Connor 1987, 163–87.

———. 1988. Crossdressing, the theatre, and gender struggle in early modern England. *Shakespeare Quarterly* 39:418–40.

———. 1997. Necessary irritations. Unpublished paper presented at the meeting of the Shakespeare Association of America, Washington, D.C.

Howard, Jean E., and Marion F. O'Connor, eds. 1987. *Shakespeare reproduced: The text in history and ideology.* New York: Methuen.

Hughes, Diane Owen. 1985. Earrings for circumcision: Distinction and purification in the Italian Renaissance city. In Trexler 1985, 155–77.

Hunter, Dianne. 1988. Doubling, mythic difference, and the scapegoating of female power in *Macbeth. Psychoanalytic Review* 75:129–52.

Izenberg, Gerald N. 1992. *Impossible individuality: Romanticism, revolution, and the origins of modern selfhood, 1787–1802.* Princeton: Princeton University Press.

Jackson, Leonard. 1991. *The poverty of structuralism: Literature and structuralist theory.* London: Longman.

———. 1994. *The dematerialisation of Karl Marx: Literature and Marxist theory.* London: Longman.

Jameson, Fredric. 1972. *The prison-house of language.* Princeton: Princeton University Press.

———. 1977. Reflections in conclusion. In *Aesthetics and politics,* by Ernst Bloch et al., translated and edited by Ronald Taylor, 196–213. London: NLB.

———. 1981. *The political unconscious: Narrative as a socially symbolic act.* Ithaca: Cornell University Press.

———. 1983. Science versus ideology. *Humanities in Society* 6:283–302.

———. 1984. Postmodernism, or the cultural logic of late capitalism. *new left review* 146:53–92.

———. 1990. *Postmodernism, or, the cultural logic of late capitalism.* Durham, N.C.: Duke University Press.

Jardine, Lisa. 1983. *Still harping on daughters: Women and drama in the age of Shakespeare.* Brighton, U.K.: Harvester.

———. 1986. "Girl talk" (for boys on the left), or marginalising feminist critical praxis. *Oxford Literary Review* 8:208–17.

———. 1991. "No offence i' th' world": *Hamlet* and unlawful marriage. In Barker et al. 1991, 123–39.

Jay, Martin. 1990. Force fields. *Salmagundi* 85/86:27–32.

Jones, Ernest. 1954. *Hamlet and Oedipus.* 1949. Reprint, Garden City, N.Y.: Doubleday.

Jonson, Ben. 1925–52. *Ben Jonson.* Edited by C. H. Herford and Percy and Evelyn Simpson. 11 vols. Oxford: Clarendon.

Kahn, Coppélia. 1981. *Man's estate: Masculine identity in Shakespeare.* Berkeley: University of California Press.

———. 1982. Excavating "those dim Minoan regions": Maternal subtexts in patriarchal literature. *Diacritics* 12:32–41.

———. 1985. The hand that rocks the cradle: Recent gender theories and their implications. In Garner, Kahane, and Sprengnether 1985, 72–88.

———. 1986. The absent mother in *King Lear.* In Ferguson, Quilligan, and Vickers 1986, 33–49.

———. 1987. "Magic of bounty": *Timon of Athens,* Jacobean patronage, and maternal power. *Shakespeare Quarterly* 38:34–57.

Kamm, Henry. 1995. Poland reawakens to its history as communism's mirror shatters. *New York Times,* 26 January, A1, A10.

Kamps, Ivo. 1991a. Introduction: Ideology and its discontents. In Kamps 1991b, 1–12.

———, ed. 1991b. *Shakespeare left and right.* New York: Routledge.

———, ed. 1995. *Materialist Shakespeare: A history.* London: Verso.

Kappeler, Susanne. 1990. Liberals, libertarianism, and the liberal arts establishment. In Leidholdt and Raymond 1990, 175–83.

Katz, Adam. 1995. In reply to Gerald Graff. In *Left margins: Cultural studies and composition pedagogy,* edited by Karen Fitts and Alan W. France, 303–11. Albany: State University of New York Press.

Kavanagh, James. 1985. Shakespeare in ideology. In Drakakis 1985b, 144–65.

Kelner, Robert. 1992. Criticism self-criticism. *Lingua Franca* 2:37–38.

Kennard, Jean. 1986. Ourself behind ourself: A theory for lesbian readers. In *Gender and reading: Essays on readers, texts, and contexts,* edited by Elizabeth Flynn and Patrocinio Schweickart, 63–80. Baltimore: Johns Hopkins University Press.

Kimbrough, Robert. 1983. Macbeth: The prisoner of gender. *Shakespeare Studies* 16:175–90.

Kolata, Gina. 1990. Soviet scientists flock to U.S., acting as tonic for colleges. *New York Times,* 8 May, A1, C14.

Kramer, Hilton. 1991. The impact of the media. *Partisan Review* 58:227–30. Special issue entitled *The changing culture of the university,* edited by Edith Kurzweil.

Lahey, Kathleen. 1990. Women and civil liberties. In Leidholdt and Raymond 1990, 198–207.

Leidholdt, Dorchen, and Janice Raymond, eds. 1990. *The sexual liberals and the attack on feminism.* New York: Pergamon.

Leinenger, Lorie Jerrell. 1980. The Miranda trap: Sexism and racism in Shakespeare's *Tempest.* In Lenz, Greene, and Neely 1980, 285–94.

Lenin, Vladimir Ilyich. 1940. *Imperialism, the highest stage of capitalism.* Edited by E. Varga and L. Mendelsohn. Rev. ed. New York: International. Originally published in Russian in 1917.

Lentricchia, Frank. 1983. *Criticism and social change.* Chicago: University of Chicago Press.

Lenz, Carolyn Ruth Swift, Gayle Greene, and Carol Thomas Neely, eds. 1980. *The woman's part: Feminist criticism of Shakespeare.* Urbana: University of Illinois Press.

Lerner, Gerda. 1986. *The creation of patriarchy.* New York: Oxford University Press.

Lerner, Laurence. 1993. Against historicism. *New Literary History* 24:273–92.

Leverenz, David. 1980. The woman in Hamlet: An interpersonal view. In *Representing Shakespeare: New psychoanalytic essays,* edited by Murray M. Schwartz and Coppélia Kahn, 110–28. Baltimore: Johns Hopkins University Press.

Levin, Richard. 1979. *New readings vs. old plays: Recent trends in the reinterpretation of English Renaissance drama.* Chicago: University of Chicago Press.

———. 1980. The relation of external evidence to the allegorical and thematic interpretation of Shakespeare. *Shakespeare Studies* 13:1–29.

———. 1983. The Indian/Iudean crux in *Othello*: An addendum. *Shakespeare Quarterly* 34:72.

———. 1986. Performance critics vs. close readers in the study of English Renaissance drama. *Modern Language Review* 81:545–59.

———. 1991. Reply to Michael Bristol and Gayle Greene. In Kamps 1991b, 47–60.
———. 1996. Marxist criticism and/or/versus a clearer sense of justice. *Renaissance Forum* 1, no. 2.
———. 1998a. "Activist politics" and the job crisis in the humanities. *minnesota review* 48/49:265–75.
———. 1998b. Another "source" for *The alchemist* and another look at source studies. *English Literary Renaissance* 28:210–30.
———. 1998c. Capitalism and the Marxist imaginary at Yale (and elsewhere). *Journal X* 3:39–49.
———. 1998d. The protocols of the elders of late capitalism (USA branch). *Centennial Review* 42:29–49.
———. 1999. The old and the new materializing of Shakespeare. *Shakespearean International Yearbook* 1:87–107.
———. 2001. Selective quotations and selective Marxisms: A response to Alan Sinfield and David Siar. *Early Modern Culture* 1, no. 2.
———, ed. 1960. *Tragedy: Plays, theory, and criticism.* New York: Harcourt, Brace.
Lewin, Tamar. 1992. Scary monsters. *New York Times Magazine,* 18 October, 24–26.
Lewis, Tom. 1995. "Political correctness": A class issue. In *PC wars: Politics and theory in the academy,* edited by Jeffrey Williams, 90–108. New York: Routledge.
Lindenberger, Herbert. 1990. Introduction. Ideology and innocence: On the politics of critical language. *PMLA* 105:398–408.
Locke, John. 1967. *Two treatises of government.* Edited by Peter Laslett. 2d ed. Cambridge: Cambridge University Press.
Longhurst, Derek. 1982. "Not for all time, but for an age": An approach to Shakespeare studies. In Widdowson 1982b, 150–63.
Lovejoy, Arthur O. 1936. *The great chain of being: A study of the history of an idea.* Cambridge: Harvard University Press.
Lyons, John O. 1978. *The invention of the self: The hinge of consciousness in the eighteenth century.* Carbondale: Southern Illinois University Press.
MacCary, W. Thomas. 1985. *Friends and lovers: The phenomenology of desire in Shakespearean comedy.* New York: Columbia University Press.
Macfarlane, Alan. 1979. Untitled review. *History and Theory* 18:103–26.
Macherey, Pierre. 1978. *A theory of literary production.* Translated by Geoffrey Wall. London: Routledge. Originally published in French in 1966.
Macherey, Pierre, and Etienne Balibar. 1981. Literature as an ideological form: Some Marxist propositions. Translated by James Kavanagh. *Praxis* 5: 43–58. Originally published in French in 1974.
MacKinnon, Catharine. 1990. Liberalism and the death of feminism. In Leidholdt and Raymond 1990, 3–13.
Maclean, Norman. 1952. Episode, scene, speech, and word: The madness of Lear. In *Critics and criticism ancient and modern,* edited by R. S. Crane, 595–615. Chicago: University of Chicago Press.
Mager, Donald N. 1994. John Bale and early Tudor sodomy discourse. In Goldberg 1994, 141–61.

Mandel, Ernest. 1978. *Late capitalism.* Translated by Joris De Bres. London: Verso. Originally published in German in 1972.

Marcus, Leah Sinanoglou. 1986. Shakespeare's comic heroines, Elizabeth I, and the political uses of androgyny. In *Women in the Middle Ages and the Renaissance: Literary and historical perspectives*, edited by Mary Beth Rose, 135–53. Syracuse, N.Y.: Syracuse University Press.

———. 1988. *Puzzling Shakespeare: Local reading and its discontents.* Berkeley: University of California Press.

Margolies, David. 1988. Teaching the handsaw to fly: Shakespeare as a hegemonic instrument. In *The Shakespeare myth*, edited by Graham Holderness, 42–53. Manchester: Manchester University Press.

———. 1992. *Monsters of the deep: Social dissolution in Shakespeare's tragedies.* Manchester: Manchester University Press.

Marmor, Judd. 1962. Psychoanalytic therapy as an educational process: Common denominators in the therapeutic approaches of different psychoanalytic "schools." In *Psychoanalytic education*, edited by Jules Masserman, 286–99. New York: Grune.

Marx, Karl, and Friedrich Engels. 1959. *Marx and Engels: Basic writings on politics and philosophy.* Edited by Lewis S. Feuer. Garden City, N.Y.: Doubleday.

Mascuch, Michael. 1996. *Origins of the individualist self: Autobiography and self-identity in England, 1591–1791.* Stanford, Calif.: Stanford University Press.

Maxwell, Baldwin. 1930. The original of Sir John Falstaff: Believe it or not. *Studies in Philology* 27:230–32.

McAlindon, Tom. 1995a. Cultural materialism and the ethics of reading. *Modern Language Review* 90:830–46.

———. 1995b. Testing the new historicism: "Invisible bullets" reconsidered. *Studies in Philology* 92:411–38.

McGowan, John. 1993. Thinking about violence: Feminism, cultural politics, and norms. *Centennial Review* 37:445–69.

McLuskie, Kathleen. 1994. The patriarchal bard: Feminist criticism and Shakespeare: *King Lear* and *Measure for measure.* In Dollimore and Sinfield 1994b, 88–108.

Messer-Davidow, Ellen. 1988. The right moves: Conservatism and higher education. In *Literature, language, and politics*, edited by Betty Jean Craige, 54–83. Athens: University of Georgia Press.

Middleton, Thomas. 1938. *Hengist, King of Kent; or the mayor of Queenborough.* Edited by R. C. Bald. New York: Scribner's.

Mill, John Stuart. 1884. *A system of logic, ratiocinative and inductive.* London: Longmans, Green.

Modern Language Association. 1992. Statement of professional ethics. *Profession 92,* 75–78.

Moi, Toril. 1983. Sexual/textual politics. In *The politics of theory: Proceedings of the Essex conference on the sociology of literature*, edited by Francis Barker et al., 1–14. Colchester: University of Essex.

———. 1985. *Sexual/textual politics: Feminist literary theory.* London: Methuen.

Moisan, Thomas. 1994. Untitled review. *Shakespeare Quarterly* 45:480–83.

Montaigne, Michel Eyquem de. 1962. *Essais.* Edited by Maurice Rat. Paris: Garnier.

Montrose, Louis Adrian. 1986a. The Elizabethan subject and the Spenserian text. In Parker and Quint 1986, 303–40.

———. 1986b. Renaissance literary studies and the subject of history. *English Literary Renaissance* 16:5–12.

———. 1988. "Shaping fantasies": Figurations of gender and power in Elizabethan culture. 1983. Reprinted in Greenblatt 1988b, 31–64.

———. 1995. "The place of a brother" in *As you like it*: Social process and comic form. 1981. Reprinted in Kamps 1995, 39–70.

Morris, Colin. 1987. *The discovery of the individual, 1050–1200.* Toronto: University of Toronto Press.

Morton, Donald. 1996. Forum letter. *PMLA* 111:472–73.

Morton, Donald, and Mas'ud Zavarzadeh. 1994. Yes, exactly! If you "criticize" us, you are a "reactionary": An open letter to Gregory Jay and Gerald Graff. *Democratic Culture* 3:31–33.

Mowat, Barbara. 1996. Constructing the author. In *Elizabethan theater: Essays in honor of S. Schoenbaum,* edited by R. B. Parker and S. P. Zitner, 93–110. Newark: University of Delaware Press.

Mueller, Martin. 1989. Yellow stripes and dead armadillos. *Profession 89,* 23–31.

Mullaney, Steven. 1980. Lying like truth: Riddle, representation, and treason in Renaissance England. *English Literary History* 47:32–47.

Murray, Timothy. 1985. *Othello*'s foul generic thoughts and methods. In Trexler 1985, 67–77.

Neely, Carol Thomas. 1981/2. Feminist modes of Shakespearean criticism: Compensatory, justificatory, transformational. In Greene and Swift 1981/2, 3–15.

———. 1985. *Broken nuptials in Shakespeare's plays.* New Haven: Yale University Press.

Neilson, Jim, and Gregory Meyerson. 1995/6. Public access limited. *minnesota review* 45/46:263–73.

———. 1998. Mr. Levin's world. *minnesota review* 48/49:277–86.

Nevo, Ruth. 1988. *Shakespeare's other language.* London: Methuen.

Newman, Karen. 1987a. "And wash the Ethiop white": Femininity and the monstrous in *Othello*. In Howard and O'Connor 1987, 143–62.

———. 1987b. Renaissance family politics and Shakespeare's *The taming of the shrew*. In *Renaissance Historicism,* edited by Arthur F. Kinney and Dan S. Collins, 131–45. Amherst: University of Massachusetts Press.

Novy, Marianne. 1984. *Love's argument: Gender relations in Shakespeare.* Chapel Hill: University of North Carolina Press.

———. 1989. Shakespeare and the bonds of brotherhood. In Holland, Homan, and Paris 1989, 103–15.

Nussbaum, Martha. 1987. Undemocratic vistas. *New York Review of Books,* 5 November, 20–26.

Ohmann, Richard. 1992/3. On "PC" and related matters. *minnesota review* 39:55–62.

Oliphant, E. H. C. 1929. How not to play the game of parallels. *Journal of English and Germanic Philology* 28:1–15.

Oppenheimer, Paul. 1989. *The birth of the modern mind: Self, consciousness, and the invention of the sonnet.* New York: Oxford University Press.

Orgel, Stephen. 1988. Prospero's wife. 1984. Reprinted in Greenblatt 1988b, 217–29.

———. 1989. Nobody's perfect: Or why did the English stage take boys for women? *South Atlantic Quarterly* 88:7–29.

———. 1995. Insolent women and manlike apparel. *Textual Practice* 9:5–25.

Park, Clara Claiborne. 1980. As we like it: How a girl can be smart and still popular. In Lenz, Greene, and Neely 1980, 100–16.

Parker, Patricia, and David Quint. 1986. *Literary theory/Renaissance texts.* Baltimore: Johns Hopkins University Press.

Patterson, Annabel. 1989. *Shakespeare and the popular voice.* Cambridge, Mass.: Blackwell.

Patterson, Lee. 1990. On the margin: Postmodernism, ironic history, and medieval studies. *Speculum* 65:87–108.

Pechter, Edward. 1987. The new historicism and its discontents: Politicizing Renaissance drama. *PMLA* 102:292–303.

———. 1991. In defense of jargon: Criticism as a social practice. *Textual Practice* 5:171–82.

———. 1997. Making love to our employment: Or, the immateriality of arguments about the materiality of the Shakespearean text. *Textual Practice* 11:51–67.

Pinker, Steven. 1994. *The language instinct.* New York: Morrow.

Plato. 1946. *The republic.* Translated by Paul Shorey. 2 vols. Loeb Classical Library. Cambridge: Harvard University Press.

Pocock, J. G. A. 1972/3. Virtue and commerce in the eighteenth century. *Journal of Interdisciplinary History* 3:119–34.

Prosser, Eleanor. 1971. *Hamlet and revenge.* 2d ed. Stanford, Calif.: Stanford University Press. The first edition appeared in 1967.

Putnam, Hilary. 1988. *Representation and reality.* Cambridge: MIT Press.

Quilligan, Maureen. 1993. Beggars, hangmen, actors, thieves. *New York Times Book Review,* 25 April, 26.

Rabkin, Norman. 1967. *Shakespeare and the common understanding.* New York: Free Press.

Reid, Stephen. 1970. Desdemona's guilt. *American Imago* 27:245–62.

Rèv, István. 1991. In mendacio veritas. *Representations* 35:1–20.

Rich, Adrienne. 1976. *Of woman born: Motherhood as experience and institution.* New York: Norton.

Richards, I. A. 1926. *Principles of literary criticism.* London: Kegan Paul, Trench, Trubner.

Rickert, Edith. 1923. Political propaganda and satire in *A midsummer night's dream. Modern Philology* 21:53–87, 133–54.

Riefer, Marcia. 1984. "Instruments of some more mightier member": The constriction of female power in *Measure for measure. Shakespeare Quarterly* 35:157–69.

Rieff, David. 1993. Multiculturalism's silent partner. *Harper's,* August, 62–72.

Robbins, Bruce, and Andrew Ross. 1996. Mystery science theater. *Lingua Franca* 6:54–57.

Roberts, Jeanne Addison. 1991. *The Shakespearean wild: Geography, genus, and gender.* Lincoln: University of Nebraska Press.

Rooney, Ellen. 1989. *Seductive reasoning: Pluralism as the problematic of contemporary literary theory.* Ithaca: Cornell University Press.

Rorty, Richard. 1989. *Contingency, irony, and solidarity.* Cambridge: Cambridge University Press.

Rosenbaum, Ron. 2000. The play's the thing, again. *New York Times Book Review,* 6 August, 12–13.

Ryan, Kiernan. 1995. *Shakespeare.* 2d ed. London: Prentice-Hall. The first edition appeared in 1989.

Schneider, Ben Ross. 1979. *Index to "The London stage, 1660–1800."* Carbondale: Southern Illinois University Press.

Schoenbaum, S. 1966. *Internal evidence and Elizabethan dramatic authorship: An essay in literary history and method.* Evanston, Ill.: Northwestern University Press.

Sedgwick, Eve Kasofsky. 1990. *Epistemology of the closet.* Berkeley: University of California Press.

Seward, James. 1973. *Tragic vision in "Romeo and Juliet."* Washington, D.C.: Consortium Press.

Shakespeare, William. 1997. *The Riverside Shakespeare.* Edited by G. Blakemore Evans et al. 2d ed. Boston: Houghton Mifflin.

Sharp, Rachel. 1980. *Knowledge, ideology, and the politics of schooling.* London: Routledge.

Shepherd, Simon. 1986. *Marlowe and the politics of Elizabethan theatre.* Brighton, U.K.: Harvester.

Sicherman, Carol M. 1972. *Coriolanus:* The failure of words. *ELH* 39:189–207.

Sinfield, Alan. 1983. Literary theory and the "crisis" in English studies. *Critical Quarterly* 25:35–47.

———. 1992. *Faultlines: Cultural materialism and the politics of dissident reading.* Berkeley: University of California Press.

———. 1994a. *Cultural politics—Queer reading.* London: Routledge.

———. 1994b. Give an account of Shakespeare and education. In Dollimore and Sinfield 1994b, 158–81.

———. 1994c. Heritage and the market, regulation and desublimation. In Dollimore and Sinfield 1994b, 255–80.

———. 1994d. Introduction: Reproductions, interventions. In Dollimore and Sinfield 1994b, 154–57.

Smith, Rebecca. 1980. A heart cleft in twain: The dilemma of Shakespeare's Gertrude. In Lenz, Greene, and Neely 1980, 194–210.

Snell, Bruno. 1953. *The discovery of the mind: The Greek origins of European thought.* Translated by T. G. Rosenmeyer. Cambridge: Harvard University Press.

Snow, Edward. 1980. Sexual anxiety and the male order of things in *Othello. English Literary Renaissance* 10:384–412.

Sokal, Alan D. 1996. Transgressing the boundaries: Toward a transformative hermeneutics of quantum gravity. *Social Text* 46/7:217–52.

Solomon, Maynard, ed. 1973. *Marxism and art: Essays classic and contemporary.* New York: Knopf.

Spivak, Gayatri Chakravorty. 1976. Translator's preface. In *Of grammatology,* by Jacques Derrida, ix–lxxxvii. Baltimore: Johns Hopkins University Press.

———. 1987. *In other worlds: Essays in cultural politics.* New York: Methuen.

Sprinker, Michael. 1991. Commentary: "You've got a lot of nerve." In Kamps 1991b, 115–28.

Stallybrass, Peter. 1983. Rethinking text and history. *LTP: Journal of Literature Teaching Politics* 2:96–107.

———. 1986. Patriarchal territories: The body enclosed. In Ferguson, Quilligan, and Vickers 1986, 123–43.

Stephenson, June. 1986. *Women's roots: Status and achievements in western civilization.* Napa, Calif.: Diemer, Smith.

Stewart, Susan. 1989. The interdiction. *Profession 89,* 10–14.

Stimpson, Catharine R. 1980. Shakespeare and the soil of rape. In Lenz, Greene, and Neely 1980, 56–64.

Stockholder, Kay. 1987. *Dream works: Lovers and families in Shakespeare's plays.* Toronto: University of Toronto Press.

Stone, Lawrence. 1977. *The family, sex, and marriage in England, 1500–1800.* New York: Harper & Row.

Sundelson, David. 1983. *Shakespeare's restorations of the father.* New Brunswick, N.J.: Rutgers University Press.

Tallis, Raymond. 1995. *Not Saussure: A critique of post-Saussurean literary theory.* 2d ed. New York: St. Martin's. The first edition appeared in 1988.

Taylor, Charles. 1989. *Sources of the self: The making of the modern identity.* Cambridge: Harvard University Press.

Tennenhouse, Leonard. 1986. *Power on display: The politics of Shakespeare's genres.* New York: Methuen.

Tillyard, E. M. W. 1943. *The Elizabethan world picture.* London: Chatto & Windus.

Traub, Valerie. 1989. Prince Hal's Falstaff: Positioning psychoanalysis and the female reproductive body. *Shakespeare Quarterly* 40:546–74.

———. 1994. The (in)significance of "lesbian" desire in early modern England. In Goldberg 1994, 62–83.

———. 1995. Jewels, statues, and corpses: Containment of female erotic power in Shakespeare's plays. 1988. Reprinted in Barker and Kamps 1995, 120–41.

Trexler, Richard C., ed. 1985. *Persons in groups: Social behavior as identity formation in Medieval and Renaissance Europe.* Binghamton, N.Y.: Medieval and Renaissance Texts and Studies.

Tripet, Arnaud. 1967. *Pétrarque ou la connaissance de soi.* Geneva: Droz.

Turner, John. 1988. The tragic romances of feudalism. In *Shakespeare: The play of history,* by Graham Holderness, Nick Potter, and John Turner, 85–154. Basingstoke, U.K.: Macmillan.

Tyler, Patrick E. 1995. Deng's economic drive leaves vast regions of China behind. *New York Times,* 27 December, A1, A6.

Van den Berg, J. H. 1961. *The changing nature of man: Introduction to a historical psychology (Metabletica).* Translated by H. F. Croes. New York: Norton.

Vickers, Brian. 1993. *Appropriating Shakespeare: Contemporary critical quarrels.* New Haven: Yale University Press.

Walker, Alice. 1953. *Textual problems of the First Folio.* Cambridge: Cambridge University Press.

Watts, Robert A. 1968. The comic scenes in *Othello. Shakespeare Quarterly* 19:349–54.

Wayne, Valerie, ed. 1991. *The matter of difference: Materialist feminist criticism of Shakespeare.* Ithaca: Cornell University Press.

Weisstein, Naomi. 1970. "Kinder, Kuche, Kirche" as scientific law: Psychology constructs the female. In *Sisterhood is powerful: An anthology of writings from the women's liberation movement,* edited by Robin Morgan, 205–20. New York: Random House.

Wellek, René. 1982. *The attack on literature and other essays.* Chapel Hill: University of North Carolina Press.

Wheeler, Richard. 1981. *Shakespeare's development and the problem comedies: Turn and counter-turn.* Berkeley: University of California Press.

———. 1985. "And my loud crying still": The *Sonnets, The merchant of Venice,* and *Othello.* In Erickson and Kahn 1985, 193–209.

White, R. S. 1992. Marx and Shakespeare. *Shakespeare Survey* 45:89–100.

Wickham, Glynne. 1973. From tragedy to tragi-comedy: *King Lear* as prologue. *Shakespeare Survey* 26:33–48.

Widdowson, Peter. 1982a. Introduction: The crisis in English studies. In Widdowson 1982b, 1–14.

———. 1988. Terrorism and literary studies. *Textual Practice* 2:1–21.

———, ed. 1982b. *Re-reading English.* London: Methuen.

Williams, Gary Jay. 1990. Politics in fairyland: The scholarship on *A midsummer night's dream* as a court wedding play. *Shakespeare Newsletter* 40:44.

Williams, Jeffrey. 1999. The new belletrism. *Style* 33:414–42.

Williams, Raymond. 1977. *Marxism and literature.* London: Oxford University Press.

Williamson, Marilyn. 1986. *The patriarchy of Shakespeare's comedies: The plays in history.* Detroit, Mich.: Wayne State University Press.

Wilson, Richard, and Richard Dutton, eds. 1992. *New historicism and Renaissance drama.* London: Longman.

Wilt, Judith. 1981/2. Comment on David Leverenz's "The woman in Hamlet." In Greene and Swift 1981/2, 93–97.

Winnett, Susan. 1990. Coming unstrung: Women, men, narrative, and principles of pleasure. *PMLA* 105:505–18.

Winstanley, Lilian. 1921. *"Hamlet" and the Scottish succession: Being an examination of the relations of the play of "Hamlet" to the Scottish succession and the Essex conspiracy.* Cambridge: Cambridge University Press.

———. 1922. *"Macbeth," "King Lear" and contemporary history: Being a study of the relations of the play of "Macbeth" to the personal history of James I, the Darnley murder and the St. Bartholomew massacre and also of "King Lear" as symbolic mythology.* Cambridge: Cambridge University Press.

———. 1924. *"Othello" as the tragedy of Italy: Showing that Shakespeare's Italian con-

temporaries interpreted the story of the Moor and the Lady of Venice as symbolizing the tragedy of their country in the grip of Spain. London: Fisher Unwin.

Woodbridge, Linda. 1991. Afterword: Poetics from the barrel of a gun? In Kamps 1991b, 285–98.

Wynne-Davies, Marion. 1991. "The swallowing womb": Consumed and consuming women in *Titus Andronicus*. In Wayne 1991, 129–51.

Yachnin, Paul. 1991. The powerless theater. *English Literary Renaissance* 21:49–74.

Index of Plays

Each title is followed by the date of the first production (usually an approximation) and the author, if it is not Shakespeare.

All's Well that Ends Well (1602), 146, 160, 272n. 9
Antony and Cleopatra (1607), 33, 37–38, 40, 45, 47, 64, 104, 146, 160, 217, 260n. 1, 261nn. 11 and 15, 272n. 9, 274n. 18
As You Like It (1599), 136, 146, 160, 179, 206, 213, 260n. 6, 270n. 11

Chaste Maid in Cheapside, A (1611), Middleton, 265n. 14
Comedy of Errors, The (1592), 136, 140, 160
Coriolanus (1608), 32, 38, 115, 159–60, 214–15, 222–23
Cymbeline (1609), 136, 146, 160

Doctor Faustus (1592), Marlowe, 64
Duchess of Malfi, The (1614), Webster, 45, 89

Epicoene; or The Silent Woman (1609), Jonson, 87
Four Elements, The (1517), Rastell, 64

Ghosts (1881), Ibsen, 45

Hamlet (1601), 30, 32–34, 37–38, 41, 47, 83, 87, 89, 134, 136, 145–46, 150, 184–87, 202, 214, 217, 220, 252, 260nn. 1 and 9, 261nn. 11 and 15, 262n. 21, 269n. 10, 270n. 19, 274 n. 18, 276n. 10
Heir, The (1620), May, 89
Hengist, King of Kent; or The Mayor of Queenborough (1618), Middleton, 87
1 Henry IV (1597), 87, 146, 160, 179, 269n. 3
2 Henry IV (1597), 116, 146, 160, 179, 268n. 2, 269n. 3
Henry V (1599), 40, 57–59, 62, 65–66, 68, 141, 216, 262n. 3, 263n. 15, 274n. 18
1 Henry VI (1592), 88
2 Henry VI (1591), 189
Henry VIII (1613), 88, 95, 265n. 14

Julius Caesar (1599), 13, 38

King and No King, A (1611), Beaumont and Fletcher, 88, 95
King Lear (1605), 17, 32–34, 37–38, 41, 47, 58–60, 62, 66, 68–69, 83, 89, 134, 140–41, 146, 149, 160, 179, 181–87, 189, 193, 203, 216–17, 250, 261nn. 14 and 15, 263nn. 9, 13, and 15, 269nn. 5 and 10, 274nn. 8, 11, 16, and 18, 275nn. 19 and 22, 276n. 12

Locrine (1591), anon., 87
Love's Labor's Lost (1595), 270n. 11

INDEX OF PLAYS

Macbeth (1606), 23, 30, 32, 34, 36–38, 41–42, 47–48, 58–62, 64, 134–35, 140–41, 146, 160, 184, 196, 216, 260n. 8, 261nn. 10 and 15, 264n. 18, 274n. 18

Maid's Tragedy, The (1610), Beaumont and Fletcher, 89

Mariam, the Fair Queen of Jewry (1604), Cary, 64

Masque of Queens, The (1609), Jonson, 87

Measure for Measure (1604), 40, 58–62, 136–38, 141, 149, 184, 261n. 18, 262nn. 3 and 5, 269n. 9

Merchant of Venice, The (1596), 58, 61–62, 64, 69, 75, 146, 160, 179, 260n. 6, 264n. 18, 270n. 11

Merry Wives of Windsor, The (1600), 18, 269n. 3, 270n. 11

Midsummer Night's Dream, A (1595), 58–60, 64–66, 96–98, 134–36, 140–41, 184, 263n. 15, 264n. 18, 274nn. 8 and 15

Much Ado about Nothing (1598), 57–65, 136, 179, 260n. 6, 263nn. 12 and 15

Oroonoko (1695), Southerne, 105

Othello (1604), 9, 17, 30, 32–34, 36–38, 41–43, 45–48, 58–63, 65, 83, 89, 105, 146–47, 149, 158, 160–61, 169, 201, 214, 222, 260nn. 1 and 5, 261nn. 11 and 15, 262n. 22, 263nn. 7, 10, and 14, 264n. 3, 266nn. 1 and 5, 272n. 11, 276n. 8

Pericles (1608), 136, 160

Philaster (1609), Beaumont and Fletcher, 89

Richard II (1595), 160

Romeo and Juliet (1595), 30, 32, 34–35, 39–40, 43, 83, 98–99, 258, 260n. 7, 264n. 3

Selimus (1592), anon., 87

Spanish Tragedy, The (1587), Kyd, 89, 265n. 10

Taming of the Shrew, The (1594), 62, 66, 75, 85, 91, 216, 261n. 18, 263n. 15, 274n. 18

Tempest, The (1611), 40, 46, 57–58, 60, 62–66, 68–69, 75, 136, 140, 146, 160, 185, 196, 211, 261n. 18, 263nn. 9, 11, and 15, 264n. 18, 269n. 10

Timon of Athens (1607), 32, 160, 262n. 21

Titus Andronicus (1594), 141–42, 185, 217, 269n. 10, 274n. 18

Troilus and Cressida (1602), 146, 160, 216, 274n. 18

Twelfth Night (1600), 160, 264n. 21, 270n. 11

Valentinian (1614), Fletcher, 89

Winter's Tale, The (1610), 39, 47, 136, 146, 160, 261n. 12, 265n. 14, 272n. 9

Beaumont and Fletcher First Folio (1647), 88–89
Jonson First Folio (1616), 90, 265n. 12
Shakespeare First Folio (1623), 90, 265n. 12
Shakespeare Second Folio (1632), 88

General Index

Abrams, M. H., 93n, 255
ACLU, 13, 245, 256
Adelman, Janet, 51, 59–61, 160, 264n. 18
Aers, David, 104
Althusser, Louis, 93n, 109–11, 148, 205, 238, 242, 253, 276n. 11
Andropov, Yuri, 279n. 18
anti-Stratfordians, 55, 269n. 4, 274n. 9
anxiety: attributed to opponents, 13–14, 49, 54, 95, 122–23, 144, 151, 175n, 266n. 19, 270n. 15, 279n. 1; attributed to texts, 64
a priori reasoning, 143, 147, 149, 162–64, 168–70, 192–94, 203–4, 259n. 7
Arac, Jonathan, 277n. 10
Aristotle, 10, 13, 19, 50, 53, 90, 94, 105, 152, 169, 200–202, 206, 259n. 10, 265n. 11, 266n. 2
Arnold, Margaret J., 51
Arnold, Matthew, 68, 275n. 2
Artaud, Antonin, 84
artistic unity, 59, 67, 238; attack on, 195–200; defense of, 200–204; kinds of, 200–204, 206
attribution studies, 133–34, 136, 149, 269n. 2, 270n. 25
author: death of, 55–57, 71, 77, 79, 196, 198, 201–3, 206, 253; unity of, 50, 53, 205–6, 238, 253–54. *See also* intentionalism

Bacon, Sir Francis, 90, 131–33, 135, 143, 151, 269n. 1
Bakhtin, Mikhail, 272n. 10

Balibar, Etienne, 197
Bamber, Linda, 51, 260nn. 2 and 3, 262 n. 21, 268n. 4
Barker, Francis, 57, 60, 62, 64–65, 68, 70, 84, 86, 107, 109, 114, 116–17, 119–20, 124, 170–72, 196, 199, 211, 219, 262nn. 1 and 6, 264nn. 19 and 22, 265n. 6, 267n. 17, 268n. 3, 272nn. 17 and 19, 273n. 31, 276nn. 18 and 19, 278n. 15, 280nn. 10 and 13
Barroll, Leeds, 274n. 12
Barthes, Roland, 55, 72, 79, 93n, 205, 238, 253, 264n. 4
Battenhouse, Roy, 70
Battersby, James L., 111
Beauvoir, Simone de, 171, 173
Beckerman, Bernard, 250
Behn, Aphra, 105
Belsey, Catherine, 51, 59–60, 64–66, 68–70, 72–73, 86, 93, 112, 114–17, 120–24, 127–28, 156, 158, 164–65, 170–71, 188–90, 193, 196–98, 206, 211, 216, 238, 253, 260n. 3, 262nn. 20 and 6, 263nn. 15 and 16, 264n. 4, 265n. 8, 267n. 6, 268nn. 3, 7, and 10, 269n. 5, 271n. 7, 272n. 20, 273n. 31, 275n. 3, 276nn. 13, 16, 17, 19, and 1, 278n. 15, 279n. 21, 280n. 10
Bennett, Josephine Waters, 136–37, 184, 187, 190
Bennett, Tony, 108, 125–26, 267n. 9
Bercovitch, Sacvan, 277n. 13
Berger, Harry, 30, 32, 36–37, 42, 47–48, 51, 58, 61–62, 70, 260n. 9, 262n. 19

Bible, 105, 210, 224, 229, 267n. 12
Bloom, Allan, 153, 176
Bohannan, Laura, 252–53
Boose, Lynda E., 51, 211, 217, 275n. 23, 277n. 4
Booth, Wayne C., 10, 76, 280n. 11
Boyarin, Daniel, 13–14, 73–77, 79, 81, 211–12, 219, 277n. 10
Bradley, A. C., 177
Bray, Alan, 108
Brecht, Bertolt, 59, 84, 172, 196, 218, 268n. 9, 276n. 17
Bristol, Michael D., 230, 260n. 15, 270 n. 13, 272n. 17, 273n. 26, 276nn. 11 and 18, 280n. 13
Brooks, Cleanth, 153, 275n. 4
Brown, Judith, 268nn. 4 and 5
Brown, Paul, 57–58, 63–66, 68–69, 140, 157–58, 263nn. 11, 15, and 16, 264 nn. 21 and 22, 270n. 23
Buckley, William, 245
Burke, Edmund, 119
Burton, Robert, 94–95
Butler, Christopher, 273n. 33

Cain, William, 271n. 28
Callaghan, Dympna, 273n. 36
Campbell, Lily Bess, 82, 153, 156, 161, 186–87, 274n. 4
Carlyle, Thomas, 119
Cavell, Stanley, 273n. 26
censorship, early modern, 135–37, 141, 144; postmodern, 245–46, 254, 256–57
Charnes, Linda, 104, 106, 117n, 217
Chaucer, Geoffrey, 266n. 4
Chodorow, Nancy, 47, 72, 145–46, 148–49, 154–55, 162, 166, 168, 271nn. 6 and 8, 272n. 15
Christ-figures, 160–61
Cioffi, Frank, 122, 143, 168
Cixous, Hélène, 115
Cleanness ("the *Pearl* poet"), 267n. 12
closure, 41–43, 50–51, 60–63, 67, 73–74, 76, 261n. 15, 263n. 11
Cohen, Michael, 257
Cole, Susan G., 132–33, 151
Coleridge, Samuel Taylor, 201–2

common sense, 75, 92, 94–99, 101, 226
Communist Manifesto (Karl Marx and Friedrich Engels), 119, 126–28, 148, 228
complicity of critics, 11, 19, 22, 60, 151, 155, 191, 211, 215, 219–20, 222–23, 225, 235, 246, 249
condition and cause, 33–34, 50, 183, 191
conspiracy theories, 164–65, 242, 248–49, 269n. 4, 272n. 18
contradictions: ideological, 59, 67, 159, 172, 204, 253; social, 67, 74, 193, 204, 230–31, 273n. 26; textual, 59, 67, 196–97, 200, 204, 263n. 17
Cook, Carol, 61–63, 65–66, 263nn. 12 and 15
Coppe, Abiezer, 218
Cotter, Jennifer M., 233, 275n. 21, 277n. 6
Coyle, Martin, 260n. 14
Crewe, Jonathan, 85, 91, 107, 140–42, 274n. 8
Crews, Frederick, 218, 270n. 16, 280n. 8
critiquing, 236–38
Crosman, Robert, 175n
cultural materialism. *See* Marxist criticism

Darwin, Charles, 131, 143, 151, 166, 270 n. 13
Dash, Irene, 30, 33, 40, 260nn. 1 and 5, 261n. 14
Davis, Natalie Zemon, 104
de Grazia, Margreta, 93n, 105, 112, 267 n. 10
Delany, Paul, 189–90, 269n. 4, 276n. 12
de Man, Paul, 253–54
demonizing, 116–17, 120–21, 128, 192, 220, 242, 246–48, 250, 263n. 10, 277n. 8
Derrida, Jacques, 93n, 175n, 205, 238, 253, 278n. 6
Dickes, Robert, 48, 172, 262n. 22
Dickstein, Morris, 250
Dinnerstein, Dorothy, 47, 154, 271n. 6
disconfirmability, 135, 139, 143, 147–48, 161, 167–69, 175
displacement, 58, 60–61, 67–69, 144, 148–49, 155, 157–58, 161, 262n. 5, 263 n. 10, 270n. 23

304 GENERAL INDEX

Dollimore, Jonathan, 57–62, 65–66, 68, 70, 85–86, 108–9, 114–15, 120, 124–25, 141, 149, 193–98, 211, 217–19, 231, 233, 241, 262 nn. 3 and 5, 263 nn. 8, 15, and 16, 264 nn. 19 and 21, 265 n. 16, 267 nn. 6 and 13, 269 n. 5, 271 nn. 3 and 8, 272 n. 18, 273 nn. 31 and 36, 274 n. 15, 277 n. 3, 278 n. 15
Downes, John, 89, 97–98, 101, 266 n. 22
Drakakis, John, 128, 211, 276 n. 18, 277 n. 10, 280 n. 13
Draper, John, 185, 187
Dreher, Diana, 260 n. 5
D'Souza, Dinesh, 245
Dusinberre, Juliet, 29
Dutton, Richard, 267 n. 6
Dworkin, Andrea, 192, 277 n. 7

Eagleton, Terry, 64, 70, 73, 75, 84, 105, 117 n, 121, 195–96, 206–8, 210, 218–19, 241, 262 n. 6, 264 n. 19, 266 n. 2, 272 n. 17, 273 n. 31, 276 nn. 18 and 20, 277 n. 3, 280 n. 13
Easterlin, Nancy, 102 n
Easthope, Antony, 115, 211
Edenism, 118–21, 128, 165, 176, 268 nn. 7 and 8, 272 n. 19
Eliot, T. S., 119
Elizabeth, Queen, 134, 136, 140–41, 179, 184–86
Ellis, John M., 273 n. 38
empirical, 94, 114, 117 n, 128, 150–51, 155, 162–66, 241, 246, 271 n. 27, 272 n. 15, 280 n. 4
Empson, William, 94
Erickson, Peter, 30, 32, 34, 39, 43, 46–48, 51, 55, 79, 146–47, 160, 185–86, 260 nn. 2 and 8, 261 nn. 15, 16, and 17, 263 n. 10, 268 n. 5, 269 n. 10, 273 n. 36, 274 n. 10
essentialism, 11, 115, 120, 124–25, 128, 192, 217–18, 220, 234–37, 246, 251, 275 n. 20, 276 n. 12
Essex, Robert Devereux, earl of, 134, 184–85, 187, 189
Evans, Malcolm, 59, 64, 68, 84, 124, 172, 196, 198, 211, 218, 262 nn. 5 and 6, 263 n. 16, 264 n. 19, 267 n. 17, 268 nn. 3 and 7, 269 n. 5, 272 nn. 17, 18, and 19, 273 n. 31, 276 nn. 12 and 18, 278 n. 15, 280 n. 13

fascism, 118, 165, 222, 229, 246–47, 251, 276 n. 17, 277 n. 3
Fawcet, Samuel, 210, 224–25
Federalist, The (James Madison et al.), 278 n. 8
feminism, 49, 54, 132–33, 154, 173, 207–8, 242, 246, 257, 272 n. 18; concept of patriarchy, 31–35, 56–57, 113, 155, 192, 220–21, 260 nn. 5 and 7, 261 n. 14, 263 n. 15, 277 nn. 7 and 8; Marxist version, 120, 170, 220, 233; political agenda, 188, 194, 264 n. 19. *See also* neo-Freudianism
feminist criticism, 15, 49–51, 56, 82, 104, 113–14, 124, 155, 177, 182–83, 207–8, 218, 259 n. 2, 260 n. 15; history of, 29, 49, 52, 260 n. 1; Marxist, 52–53, 56, 188–89, 192–93, 216, 228, 262 n. 20, 274 n. 14; thematic, 31–46, 57. *See also* neo-Freudian criticism
Fineman, Joel, 265 n. 16
Fish, Stanley, 94, 165, 175 n, 266 n. 5, 277 nn. 10 and 11
Fitz, L. T. *See* Woodbridge, Linda
FitzGerald, Margot, 11, 13–14, 77–81, 248, 269 n. 9, 270 nn. 15 and 22, 279 n. 18
Fletcher, John, 253
Fogel, Ephim, 269 n. 2
Foley, Stephen, 218
formalism, 10–11, 18–22, 56, 77, 82–83, 118, 152–53, 164–65, 195–97, 199–206, 215, 217–18, 222, 228, 234, 236, 241, 243, 246, 249, 272 n. 24, 274 n. 13, 276 nn. 12 and 20
Foucault, Michel, 55, 72, 77, 79, 110, 205
Fowler, Alastair, 280 n. 9
Frank, Roberta, 271 n. 2
Freedman, Barbara, 273 n. 36
French, Marilyn, 30, 32, 38–39, 41, 43, 260 nn. 2 and 4, 261 n. 16, 262 n. 22
Freud, Sigmund, 143–44, 148–49, 162, 260 n. 15, 263 n. 12, 267 n. 16
Freudian criticism, 24, 117–18, 145, 149–

50, 156, 161, 167–68, 171, 177, 204, 206

Freudianism, 12, 96, 103, 156–57, 166, 270n. 14, 271n. 7; causal scheme, 68–69, 122, 144, 150, 154, 162, 204; clinical evidence, 144–45, 155, 162–63, 167, 271n. 4, 272n.13; concept of female orgasms, 163; concept of oedipal conflict, 69, 145–46, 154, 276n. 15; concept of penis envy, 49, 122, 154–55, 157–58, 163; pseudo-science, 122, 143; therapy, 12, 267 n. 16, 273n. 28. *See also* displacement

Fuss, Diana, 218, 236

Garner, Shirley Nelson, 51, 260n. 1
Gibbons, Brian, 98–100
Gilbert, Sandra M., 277n. 9
Goddard, Harold, 70
Gohlke, Madelon, 30–32, 37–38, 43, 47, 51, 170, 261n. 17, 272n. 18
Goldberg, Jonathan, 13–14, 83, 85, 90, 92, 94–103, 108, 110, 114, 117, 141, 179, 188, 264n. 5, 267n. 18, 268nn. 4 and 5, 269nn. 5 and 9, 272n. 18
Gossett, Suzanne, 273n. 36
Grady, Hugh, 190–91
Graff, Gerald, 11, 165, 175n, 218, 236, 243, 257, 271n. 1, 277n. 10, 280n. 5
Great Gatsby, The (F. Scott Fitzgerald), 10, 12
Greenblatt, Stephen, 85, 91–92, 103, 114, 117–18, 179, 185, 264n. 3, 266n. 18, 267n. 11, 268nn. 4 and 5, 269nn. 3 and 10, 273nn. 26 and 36, 275n. 22, 277n. 8
Greene, Gayle, 29–30, 33–34, 36, 38–39, 44, 46, 51, 120, 171, 173, 211–12, 216, 233, 242, 246, 257, 260nn. 15, 2, and 5, 261n. 11, 272n. 18, 273n. 27, 275n. 21, 277n. 6, 279n. 21
Grünbaum, Adolf, 270n. 16
Gubar, Susan, 277n. 9

Harbage, Alfred, 137, 184
Harris, Wendell V., 223–24, 280n. 9
Hartman, Geoffrey, 175n

Hawkes, Terence, 112, 211
Hays, Janice, 273n. 36
Heath, Stephen, 236
Hegel, Georg Wilhelm Friedrich, 165, 278n. 7
Heilman, Robert B., 275n. 7
Heinemann, Margot, 125, 141, 216, 229, 275n. 19, 276n. 17, 278n. 15
al-Hibri, Azizah, 233
Hill, Christopher, 267n. 14
Hirsch, E. D., 44, 92, 266n. 17
Hirschkop, Ken, 270n. 15
historical criticism, 15–18, 82–83, 118, 133–41, 153, 177–94; concepts of historicity of texts and textuality of history, 178–83, 187–88, 191–93; use of political criteria, 183, 188–94. *See also* ideas-of-the-time criticism; occasionalism; topicalism
Holderness, Graham, 83, 196, 198, 216, 247, 267n. 17, 268n. 3, 275n. 5, 276nn. 18 and 19
homosexuality, 85, 91, 98, 101, 105–6, 108, 264n. 5, 265n. 15, 266n. 21, 267nn. 11 and 12, 268n. 4, 273n. 34
Horney, Karen, 271n. 4, 272n. 13
Howard, Jean E., 57–62, 64–68, 73, 159, 187, 196, 198, 210–11, 226, 234–35, 262n. 6, 263n. 15, 264n. 21, 267n. 17, 277n. 10
HUAC (House Un-American Activities Committee), 78, 80, 248
Hulme, Peter, 57, 60, 62, 64–65, 124, 196, 211, 219, 262nn. 1 and 6, 264nn. 19 and 22, 272nn. 18 and 19, 273n. 20, 274n. 2, 275n. 24, 276nn. 18 and 19, 278n. 15, 280n. 13
humanism, liberal, 12–13, 22, 114–15, 117–18, 120, 123–24, 127–29, 155–56, 174, 204–6, 208, 211, 217–23, 234–41, 246–48, 256, 268n. 7, 274 n. 14, 278n. 14, 280nn. 5 and 6; secular, 120–21, 235, 247, 278n. 14, 280n. 5
Hunter, Dianne, 51, 140–41, 184

idealism, 48, 94, 98–99, 102, 115, 125, 128, 246, 280n. 4

ideas-of-the-time criticism, 82–83, 86–87, 110, 182, 186–88, 193, 264n. 3
ideology, 49, 51, 53, 118; bourgeois, 124–26, 129, 155–56, 210–13, 217, 228, 235, 253, 276n. 15; Marxist concept of, 57, 109–11, 202–3, 241–42, 267 n. 16, 276n. 11, 279n. 22
illusion, dramatic, 83–84, 87–90, 95–96, 100–101, 265n. 10
intentionalism, 19–21, 44–46, 50–52, 55–57, 71, 87, 93n, 198, 201–3, 205, 213, 217–18, 222–25, 243, 246, 253–55, 259n. 13, 261n. 17, 262n. 2, 272 n. 24
Irigaray, Luce, 115
ironic approach, 40, 44, 70–72, 87, 197–98, 262n. 19, 264n. 20

Jackson, Leonard, 267n. 8, 273n. 29
James I, king of England (James VI of Scotland), 106–7, 134–38, 140–41, 179, 182, 184–85, 187, 269n. 5, 270 n. 12
Jameson, Fredric, 69, 119, 148, 161, 170, 173, 177–78, 192, 229, 231, 241, 263n. 11, 267n. 7, 268n. 12, 272n. 14, 274n. 13, 275n. 22, 277n. 4
Jardine, Lisa, 51, 218, 260n. 2, 261n. 20, 273n. 36
Jay, Gregory, 257, 277n. 10
Jay, Martin, 278n. 9
Jones, Ernest, 145–46, 150, 268n. 11, 270nn. 15 and 19
Jonson, Ben, 18, 87–88, 90, 100, 105, 265n. 12

Kahn, Coppélia, 30, 32, 35, 39, 51, 59–60, 69, 146, 154–61, 166, 260n. 7, 261 n. 18, 263n. 9, 264n. 18, 271n. 4, 272n. 13, 273n. 36, 275n. 22
Kamps, Ivo, 256, 259n. 1
Kappeler, Susanne, 280n. 6
Katz, Adam, 277n. 10
Kavanagh, James, 58, 62, 66, 68, 84–85, 90, 105, 107–8, 125, 128, 140, 241–42, 262n. 1, 263n. 15, 264n. 4, 267 n. 9, 269n. 5, 274n. 15, 278n. 15
Kelner, Robert, 247

Kennard, Jean, 154, 156–57, 161, 271n. 5, 273n. 34
Kilmer, Joyce, 275n. 4
Kimbrough, Robert, 30, 32, 40, 260n. 8, 261n. 14
Kott, Jan, 128
Kramer, Hilton, 247
Kristeva, Julia, 155–56, 158, 165, 169
Kynaston, Edward, 89, 97, 101

Lacan, Jacques, 93n, 102n, 170, 205, 238, 253, 271n. 7, 272n. 15
Lahey, Kathleen, 280n. 6
Lanier, Sidney, 275n. 4
Leavis, F. R., 275n. 25
Leinenger, Lorie Jerrell, 46, 261n. 18
Lenin, Vladimir Ilyich, 228–29, 277n. 2
Lentricchia, Frank, 158–59, 161, 192, 211, 217, 241, 248, 268n. 8
Lenz, Carolyn Ruth. See Swift, Carolyn Ruth
Lerner, Gerda, 268n. 6
Lerner, Laurence, 274nn. 2 and 18
Leventen, Carol, 51
Leverenz, David, 30, 32, 37, 41, 44, 156, 161, 260n. 9, 261n. 11
Lewis, Tom, 270n. 22
Limbaugh, Rush, 277n. 10
Lindenberger, Herbert, 73, 227
literature: canon of, 99, 101, 249–51, 279n. 23; concept of, 84–85, 90, 99, 101, 108, 180, 217, 239–40, 243, 265nn. 11 and 12, 267n. 9
Locke, John, 276n. 1
Longhurst, Derek, 83–84
Lovejoy, Arthur O., 110, 118, 275n. 25
Lysenko, Trofim, 53, 166

MacCary, W. Thomas, 160
Macfarlane, Alan, 273n. 36
Macherey, Pierre, 66, 162, 197, 263n. 15, 271n. 27, 275n. 5, 279n. 19
MacKinnon, Catharine, 280n. 6
Maclean, Norman, 259n. 11
Mandel, Ernest, 228
Marcus, Leah Sinanoglou, 141–42, 182–84
Margolies, David, 211
Marmor, Judd, 163, 270n. 17

Marx, Karl, 119, 126–28, 143, 151, 163, 217, 228–29, 254, 260 n. 15, 270 nn. 13 and 14
Marxism, 12, 163–64, 222, 242–43, 247, 270 n. 14; causal scheme, 67, 122, 126, 147–50, 162, 167–68, 193–94, 204, 233; counting past two, 118, 128–29, 268 n. 7; political agenda, 77, 79, 113, 188, 194, 241; predictions, 148, 163, 170, 228–31, 277 nn. 3 and 4; pseudo-science, 122, 143
Marxist criticism, 24, 57, 118, 148–50, 161, 182, 189–90, 195–200, 204–8, 259 n. 2, 268 n. 5, 269 n. 4, 276 n. 12; claim to be scientific, 123, 206; socialist realism, 76, 165, 218
Maxwell, Baldwin, 269 n. 3
McCarthy, Joseph, 106–7, 151, 245, 248, 256, 270 n. 15, 280 n. 12
McGowan, John, 223
McLuskie, Kathleen, 51, 57, 60, 65–66, 68, 189–90, 193, 198, 233, 250, 260 n. 2, 261 n. 14, 262 n. 20, 263 nn. 13 and 15, 264 n. 22, 274 n. 14, 275 n. 21, 276 nn. 17 and 19, 277 n. 6
Messer-Davidow, Ellen, 241
Meyerson, Gregory, 259 n. 3
Middleton, Thomas, 18, 89, 100
Mill, John Stuart, 16–17
Moi, Toril, 115, 150–51, 155–56, 158, 163, 165, 172, 197, 200, 217–18, 233, 247, 268 n. 1, 271 n. 7, 273 n. 27, 275 n. 21, 276 n. 16, 277 n. 6
Moisan, Thomas, 275 n. 25
Montaigne, Michel Eyquem de, 109
Montrose, Louis Adrian, 59–60, 64–66, 84–85, 115, 160, 178–80, 185–87, 193, 263 n. 15, 264 n. 18, 274 n. 3
More, Sir Thomas, 109
Morton, Donald, 11, 211, 277 n. 10
Mueller, Martin, 167–68, 173–74, 273 n. 38
Murray, Timothy, 59, 263 n. 7

National Association of Scholars (NAS), 257–58
Neely, Carol Thomas, 29, 36, 41, 43, 51, 260 nn. 1, 2, 4, and 9, 261 n. 13

Neilson, Jim, 259 n. 3
neo-Freudian criticism, 47–48, 57–63; concept of feminine subtext, 59, 69, 71–72, 155, 160, 172, 275 n. 22; concept of mother-figures, 69, 146–47, 159–61, 264 n. 18
neo-Freudianism, 47–49, 56, 145–47, 157–58, 167; causal scheme, 47, 69, 145, 154, 271 n. 8; clinical evidence, 146, 155, 271 n. 4, 272 n. 13; concept of masculinity, 47–49, 155, 169, 172, 272 n. 11; concept of penis envy, 157–58; concept of preoedipal stage, 47, 69, 145, 147, 154
Nevo, Ruth, 160
New Critics, 9, 23, 56, 70–72, 82, 87, 128, 133, 138, 140, 143, 153, 165, 167, 177–78, 190–91, 195–98, 201–3, 211, 215, 218, 222, 244, 249, 255, 259 n. 8, 275 n. 20. *See also* formalism
New Historicists, 15, 76–77, 114, 117–18, 124, 177, 183, 188, 190, 243, 257, 259 n. 2, 268 n. 5, 274 n. 1. *See also* historical criticism
Newman, Karen, 62, 66, 105–7, 263 n. 15, 266 n. 5
Nietzsche, Friedrich Wilhelm, 267 n. 7
Novy, Marianne, 31–33, 39–40, 51, 146–47, 160, 182–83, 187, 189–90, 220, 261 nn. 14 and 16
NOW (National Organization for Women), 13, 54
Nussbaum, Martha, 76, 273 n. 39

objective knowledge 150–51, 163, 222; of history, 112, 117, 121, 127, 171–72, 272 n. 19; of texts, 56, 66, 68, 171–72, 198–200, 207–8, 217
occasionalism, 136–38, 140–41, 182–87, 269 n. 9, 274 n. 15
Ohmann, Richard, 271 n. 28
Olin Foundation, 132
Oliphant, E. H. C., 269 n. 2, 270 n. 25
oppression, 11, 19, 22, 56, 77, 155, 164, 166, 170, 191–93, 219–25, 232, 236, 242, 257, 271 n. 8, 278 n. 10; context of, 224–25; Marxist model of, 233–34, 272 n. 10, 278 n. 13

Orgel, Stephen, 60, 106–7, 185, 263 n. 9, 264 n. 18, 269 n. 10, 274 n. 3

Park, Clara Claiborne, 260 n. 6
Patterson, Annabel, 141, 274 n. 8
Patterson, Lee, 104
Pechter, Edward, 70, 77, 93 n, 140, 178–79, 239, 257
Pinker, Steven, 109, 267 n. 14
Plato, 35, 50, 110–11, 152
pluralism, critical, 10–11, 15–16, 22, 24, 205–9, 255–56, 276 n. 18, 280 nn. 11 and 13; political, 77, 79–80, 164, 256, 276 n. 18
PMLA, 51, 53, 245, 257
Pocock, J. G. A., 267 n. 14
Poe, Edgar Allan, 275 n. 4
polarizing, 56, 76, 78, 80, 128–29, 151, 164, 176, 212, 217, 226, 236, 244–58, 277 n. 10
political correctness, 228, 245, 278 n. 12
politicizing criticism: alleged political connection, 12–13, 56, 76, 150–51, 164–68, 176, 207–8, 210–25, 227, 244, 249, 277 n. 4, 280 n. 8; alleged political effect, 13, 69–73, 75–79, 112–13, 118–22, 127–29, 151, 165, 190, 194, 222–24, 226, 241, 271 n. 28
post-Saussurean, 93 n, 107, 109, 156, 171–72, 273 n. 29
Prosser, Eleanor, 186–87

Quilligan, Maureen, 267 n. 11

Rabkin, Norman, 139, 153
Rich, Adrienne, 47, 154, 271 n. 6
Richards, I. A., 153
Rickert, Edith, 134–36, 141, 184, 187, 190
Riefer, Marcia, 261 n. 18
Rieff, David, 277 n. 13
Robbins, Bruce, 174 n
Roberts, Jeanne Addison, 275 n. 23, 277 n. 7
Rooney, Ellen, 276 n. 18, 280 n. 13
Rorty, Richard, 172, 235–36, 266 n. 23, 277 n. 10
Ross, Andrew, 174 n, 277 n. 10

Ryan, Kiernan, 149, 182–83, 187, 189–90, 211, 216, 219, 274 n. 16, 275 n. 19
Rymer, Thomas, 105

scare quotes, 55, 75, 206, 238–40, 262 n. 1, 263 n. 11, 278 n. 17, 279 n. 18
Schoenbaum, Samuel, 269 n. 2
science, 92, 96, 102–3, 109, 143, 155, 174 n; relation to ideology, 49, 51, 53, 249, 272 n. 21; relation to testing, 122–23, 145–48, 157, 163, 168, 271 n. 5. *See also* empirical
Seward, James, 264 n. 3
Shakespeare, John, 150, 185
Shakespeare, William, 15, 17–22, 29, 55–56, 84, 87, 90, 100, 105, 128, 137, 139–41, 153, 159–61, 177, 190, 212–13, 250, 253–54, 259 n. 13, 265 n. 12, 270 n. 12
Sharp, Rachel, 269 n. 2, 278 n. 15
Shepherd, David, 270 n. 15
Shepherd, Simon, 84, 87, 108, 141–42, 264 n. 5, 265 n. 10
Sicherman, Carol M., 214–15, 217, 222–23
Sidney, Sir Philip, 90, 152–53
Sinfield, Alan, 57–59, 62, 65–66, 68, 70, 110, 124, 128–29, 141, 190, 198, 210, 212, 216, 219, 221, 233, 241, 262 n. 3, 263 nn. 15 and 16, 269 n. 7, 272 n. 18, 278 n. 15
Smith, Rebecca, 51, 260 n. 1
Snow, Edward, 30, 32, 41, 47–48, 51, 60–63, 70, 146–47, 158, 160, 169, 172, 262 nn. 19 and 22, 263 n. 14, 272 n. 11
Sokal, Alan D., 174 n
"Song of Myself" (Walt Whitman), 171
source studies, 136–37, 269 n. 6
Spenser, Edmund, 141–42, 179, 187
Spivak, Gayatri Chakravorty, 236
Sprengnether, Madelon. *See* Gohlke, Madelon
Sprinker, Michael, 151, 175 n, 226, 245, 256–57, 259 n. 1, 270 nn. 15 and 26, 279 n. 1
Stallybrass, Peter, 58, 61–62, 65, 93 n, 105, 112, 147, 149, 161, 196, 263 n. 10, 267 n. 10, 272 n. 10

Stephenson, June, 268n. 6
Stewart, Susan, 232, 234, 237, 271n. 3, 279n. 24
Stimpson, Catharine R., 273n. 36
Stockholder, Kay, 160
Stone, Lawrence, 175, 273n. 36
subject: bourgeois, 86, 108, 114–18, 123–27, 155–56, 165, 218, 253–54; Marxist, 121, 148, 268n. 10; pre-bourgeois, 85–86, 91–93, 96, 102–3, 107, 114–15, 118, 265n. 16, 266nn. 18 and 4
Sullivan, Harry Stack, 156, 161
Sundelson, David, 58, 61–62, 64, 69, 160, 264n. 18
Swift, Carolyn Ruth, 29, 51

Tallis, Raymond, 267n. 8, 273n. 29
Teachers for a Democratic Culture (TDC), 257–58
Tennnenhouse, Leonard, 142, 182–83, 186
thematism, 31–46, 138–40, 142, 144, 149, 167, 169, 175, 197, 200, 202, 215, 222, 272n. 23, 275n. 7, 276n. 8
theorizing, 152, 154–59, 162–69, 225–26, 237, 240–41, 271n. 3; contradictions within, 52, 93, 101, 106, 111, 128–29, 140, 171–73, 188, 198–99, 230–31, 253–55, 273n. 34, 274n. 13, 275n. 3; contradictions with practice, 178–81, 188, 204, 215–16, 218, 222–23, 255, 274nn. 3 and 18
Thompson, Ann, 51
Tillyard, E. M. W., 82, 110, 118, 128, 186–87, 193
Tompkins, Jane, 175n
topicalism, 134–36, 141–44, 149, 182, 184–87, 270n. 12, 274nn. 9 and 10
Traub, Valerie, 106, 160, 277n. 8
Turner, John, 140, 216

universal laws, 67, 69, 73, 147, 149, 158–59, 173, 192–93, 204

Vickers, Brian, 267n. 8, 273n. 29

Walker, Alice, 214, 222
Wallace, George, 247
Warren, Robert Penn, 275n. 4
Watts, Robert A., 276n. 8
Wayne, Valerie, 51
Weisstein, Naomi, 270n. 16
Wellek, René, 265n. 11
Wheeler, Richard, 46, 51, 160, 262n. 19
Wickham, Glynne, 136, 141, 185, 187, 269n. 5, 270n. 12
Widdowson, Peter, 210, 220, 230–31, 233, 235, 242
Williams, Gary Jay, 274n. 15
Williams, Jeffrey, 23
Williams, Raymond, 264n. 4, 267n. 9
Williamson, Marilyn, 141–42, 179
Wilson, Robert, 133, 270n. 25
Wilt, Judith, 38, 44, 261n. 11
Winnett, Susan, 272n. 25
Winstanley, Gerrard, 218
Winstanley, Lilian, 134–36, 141, 184–85, 187, 269n. 5, 270n. 12
Woodbridge, Linda, 51, 246, 257, 260n. 1, 279n. 3
Wynne-Davies, Marion, 185, 217, 269 n. 10, 275n. 23

Yachnin, Paul, 274n. 12

Zavarzadeh, Mas'ud, 11, 277n. 10
Zeitgeist, 110, 203. *See also* ideas-of-the-time criticism
Zhdanov, Andrei, 214, 218
Zinker, Joseph, 110, 154, 156, 161, 271 n. 5